THE LETTERS OF
ANTHONY TROLLOPE

THE LETTERS OF
ANTHONY TROLLOPE

EDITED BY

BRADFORD ALLEN BOOTH

Associate Professor of English
University of California, Los Angeles

GEOFFREY CUMBERLEGE
OXFORD UNIVERSITY PRESS
LONDON   NEW YORK   TORONTO
1951

Oxford University Press, Amen House, London E.C. 4

GLASGOW NEW YORK TORONTO MELBOURNE WELLINGTON
BOMBAY CALCUTTA MADRAS CAPE TOWN

Geoffrey Cumberlege, Publisher to the University

PRINTED IN GREAT BRITAIN

To
MURIEL ROSE TROLLOPE
whose affection for the memory of
her grandfather has made possible
the publication of these letters
and to
MICHAEL SADLEIR
who has done more
than any other living man to revive
and to perpetuate in our time
the reputation of
Anthony Trollope

PREFACE

PROCEDURE

COLLECTING THE WORLD'S FINEST LIBRARY OF TROLLOPE MATERIALS was the lifetime avocation of the late Morris Longstreth Parrish of Philadelphia, Pennsylvania.[1] Several years before his death Mr. Parrish projected an edition of the nearly 300 autograph Trollope letters that he had assembled. He and his efficient librarian, Miss E. V. Miller, transcribed the letters, but before editing was begun Mr. Parrish was side-tracked into perfecting his remarkable Stevenson collection, and the Trollope letters languished. At his death in 1944 his superb library of Victorian fiction was bequeathed under the terms of his will to Princeton University, where in the new library of that institution it is housed in an exact replica of Mr. Parrish's own library at Dormy House, Pine Valley, New Jersey.

Through the kindness of Princeton's librarian, Dr. Julian Boyd, the Trollope collection was opened to me for study in the winter of 1945. Subsequently, permission to publish was granted, and photostatic transcripts of all the holograph material were procured. These are now deposited in the library of the University of California, Los Angeles. Mr. Parrish had not quite cornered all the extant Trollope letters, but he had made a brave beginning, coaxing out of the limbo of the forgotten letters lost in the obscurity of Trollope's long banishment from the ranks of distinguished novelists. Only two other sizable collections exist. Miss Muriel Rose Trollope, Anthony's granddaughter, graciously gave me access to the eighty-three letters, chiefly to her father, which remain in her possession; and Mrs. Reginald Smith, daughter of Trollope's friend and publisher George Smith, permitted me to have transcripts made of the fifty-five letters in her library.

Of the remaining letters, virtually all have been discovered by

[1] For a sympathetic account of Mr. Parrish as a collector, see *The Trollopian: a Journal of Victorian Fiction*, Number One (Summer 1945), pp. 5–10; for an account of his Trollope collection, see ibid., pp. 11–19.

personal application to libraries, booksellers, and private collectors. Some three hundred personal letters of inquiry were written, and an announcement of the proposed edition was widely carried by the public press. The results of this search, while by no means sensational, were at least satisfactory. Several hundred more items turned up than had at first been expected. Of the total of 932 letters finally assembled considerably more than 750 are unpublished, and among those published a majority have appeared only in fragmentary form. That anything like a definitive census has been achieved is scarcely to be expected. An editor is constantly embarrassed by the scores of anonymous autograph-hunters, who, having procured a signature, tip it in an album and then either forget it or guard it jealously. But though many single letters have assuredly escaped the editor's drag-net, it will be unfortunate if any large collection has not been tapped. I shall very much appreciate any information which readers may possess as to the disposition of material which has been overlooked.

ACKNOWLEDGEMENTS

THE TASK OF COLLECTION, TRANSCRIPTION, AND ANNOTATION HAS entailed time, money, and the patient helpfulness of scores of individuals and institutions. I have been extremely fortunate on all these counts, and it is a great pleasure to acknowledge material aid without which the project could not even have been undertaken.

In 1945 I received from the American Council of Learned Societies a grant-in-aid which enabled me to study the Parrish collection and to make a preliminary survey of materials available. In the two following years the Committee on Research of the University of California, Los Angeles, gave me generous grants for the purchase of photostats and microfilm and for stenographic assistance. For the academic year 1947–8 President Robert G. Sproul of the University of California not only granted me sabbatical leave, but supplemented my income with a University Fellowship that gave me the freedom of fifteen uninterrupted months of study. In the spring of 1947 through a grant-in-aid from the American Philosophical Society I was able to spend two months in England checking through reference materials not available in the United States. For this very generous treatment from many agencies I am deeply grateful.

But without the letters there would obviously have been no book, and I wish to express my keen sense of indebtedness to those private collectors who have unselfishly turned over their Trollope letters to me: Mr. Moncure Biddle, Dr. Silvain S. Brunschwig, the Hon. Mrs. James Cecil, Dr. R. W. Chapman, Mr. H. W. L. Dana, Mr. Alban Dobson, the Rev. G. F. C. Dobson, Mr. Maurice Fitzgerald, the Hon. Mrs. Maurice Fitzgerald, Lady Grant Duff, Miss J. Havell, Mrs. Arthur Helps, Dr. Eric Millar, Commander Edmund Monsell, Mr. Cyril A. Munro, Sir John Murray, Mrs. E. S. Ouvry, Mr. Carl Pforzheimer, Capt. F. L. Pleadwell, Professor Richard Purdy, Dr. Herman T. Radin, Mr. Michael Sadleir, Mr. Paul Schoedinger, Mr. J. H. Spencer, Mr. Robert H. Taylor, Mrs. Arthur Tilley, John W. Watling, and the late Carroll A. Wilson.

Permission to publish letters in their possession has also been granted to me by the officials of the following libraries and institutions: Bodleian Library, Oxford; Boston Public Library; Fitzwilliam Museum, Cambridge; General Post Office, London; Harvard College Library; Haverford College Library; Historical Society of Pennsylvania; Henry E. Huntington Library; John Rylands Library; Library of Congress; Massachusetts Historical Society; Pierpont Morgan Library; Myers & Co.; National Women's Service Library, Oxford; National Library of Scotland; New York Historical Society; Berg Collection, New York Public Library; Parrish Collection, Princeton University Library; Public Library of Sydney, New South Wales; University of Leeds; University of Rochester; Alderman Library, University of Virginia; Yale University.

Special courtesies in the way of answering importunate queries and procuring for me all manner of other aid and advice have left me heavily indebted to Lt.-Col. Baddeley, secretary of the Garrick Club; Mr. J. H. Blackwood; Professor Florence Brinkley of Duke University; Capt. John Broadbent of the Royal Literary Fund; Mr. Thomas Drury, Librarian of the General Post Office, London, and his assistant, Mr. G. W. P. Devenport; Dr. Frederick

Gwynn of Harvard University; Professor Gordon Haight of Yale University; Miss Julie Hudson, curator of the Rare Book Room, Princeton University; Mr. Ernest Maggs; Mr. Robert F. Metzdorf, formerly curator of the R. B. Adam Collection, University of Rochester; Sir John Murray; Professor William Nitze of the University of California, Los Angeles; Professor Charles G. Osgood of Princeton University; Professor Gordon Ray of the University of Illinois; Professor Hyder E. Rollins of Harvard University; Professor George Sherburn of Harvard University; Mr. Arthur Swann; Mr. Robert H. Taylor; Professor Chauncey B. Tinker of Yale University; Mr. N. R. Udall, secretary of the Athenaeum Club; Dr. Ernest H. Wilkins, former president of Oberlin College; the late Carroll A. Wilson; Dr. Louis B. Wright of the Huntington Library; and Miss Mabel Zahn of Charles Sessler Co. I owe a special acknowledge-ment to Mr. G. F. James of the Melbourne University Press, who gave me the benefit of his thorough and detailed studies in Trollope's Australian travels. It is a pleasure to make special mention of the unfailingly friendly attentions of the library staff of the University of California, Los Angeles, especially those of Mr. Robert Vosper and Mr. Neal Harlow of the Acquisitions Department, who worked tirelessly in my behalf. Throughout my labours I have been heartened by the enlightened enthusiasm of my colleague, Professor Hugh G. Dick, who sustained me in two very difficult years with his confidence and his sympathy. Special thanks, too, must go to my wife, who on occasions without number helped me to solve the riddles of Trollope's illegibilities. Dr. R. W. Chapman brought to the reading of my typescript his very considerable experience in the techniques of editing, and he has saved me from an embarrassing number of blunders.

My deepest obligations and my keenest pleasure I have tried to express in the dedication. Mr. Sadleir has placed his know-ledge of Trollope at my disposal, and I have drawn from his well deeply. Miss Trollope, without whose kindness none of these letters could be published, has not only followed the progress of the book with the sharpest attention, but has also contributed to it many details known only to the editor.

When I announced this project several years ago I said that

it must be something of a communal effort. If it has not been exactly that, at least many of whatever virtues the collection has are the result of suggestions from scholars and enthusiasts in all the English-speaking countries. Its imperfections are solely the result of lacunae in the editor's knowledge of Victorian biography and bibliography.

EDITORIAL METHOD

THERE SHOULD BE NO NECESSITY IN THESE DAYS TO EXPLAIN WHY Trollope's letters are printed exactly as he wrote them—with such imperfections as exist baldly obvious. Yet it was the considered judgement of the late George Saintsbury, one of the chief critics of the art of letter-writing, that it is an editor's duty 'invariably to exclude mere trivialities, faults of taste, slovenliness of expression, etc. . . .'. To make such emendations is to give a false account of a man and his personality. Uncritical and dishonest tampering with texts on the part of nineteenth-century editors has made it necessary to repeat much of their work and to revaluate the character of many prominent men of letters. I have attempted to transcribe the letters literally, leaving misspellings and grammatical errors uncorrected. When through carelessness, however, Trollope omitted words or wrote an otherwise unintelligible passage, I have indicated that the confusion is his and ventured to suggest the intended reading. I have in no instance altered the text. Letters which have previously been printed have been re-examined carefully if the manuscript is available.

Like most of his contemporaries Trollope did not make a virtue of consistency in minor matters of form. The salutation, for example, may be followed by a period, a comma, a dash, or no mark of punctuation. At the end of a sentence there may be a period, a hyphen, or a dash. Precision in these details Trollope obviously considered of small importance. What he intended is also often obscured by the carelessness of his hand. And he seems rarely to have reread his letters for errors. In many instances I have had to use my judgement in reproducing the punctuation.

His signature takes many forms: often 'Anthony' is a mere manual flourish. But to normalize idiosyncrasies and modernize curiosities would be to destroy something of his personality.

In the headnote following the letter number I have given the addressee's name either in full or in the form used by Trollope, except where Trollope uses the last name only and there may be some doubt about the identification. In such cases I have used the last name only and attempted more precise identification in a footnote. I had originally intended to precede the text with a List of Letters. In the interests of space, however, it has been found necessary to abandon this plan, which would have entailed some repetition. Each headnote thus contains the italicized proper name of the owner or depositary of the manuscript. If the letter has been printed, this fact is noted.

When persons identified are of sufficient note to be found in encyclopaedias and such obvious reference works as the *Dictionary of National Biography*, the *Dictionary of American Biography*, Frederic Boase's *Modern English Biography*, Burke's *Peerage* and *Landed Gentry*, and *Who's Who*, bibliographical citation is assumed to be unnecessary. References to more specialized source-books are given in full.

In the matter of annotations I have tried to be as full, but as brief, as possible. If British readers are amused by identification of obvious persons and places, they must remember that to Americans these things may not be familiar; and vice versa. If the reader knows Rugby, or Harrisburg, he may skip the note; if not, it is hoped that the identification may be helpful.

In the interests of simplicity I have attempted to reduce the cue-titles and symbols to a minimum. The following, however, proved to be indispensable:

Austin	Alfred Austin, 'Last Reminiscences of Anthony Trollope', *Temple Bar*, lxx (January 1884), 129–34.
Autobiography	Anthony Trollope, *An Autobiography* (1883), ed. Bradford A. Booth (Berkeley and Los Angeles: University of California Press, 1947).
Bradhurst	*A Century of Letters*, ed. Minna Evangeline Bradhurst, priv. ptd. (London, 1929).
Escott	T. H. S. Escott, *Anthony Trollope: His Public Services, Private Friends, and Literary Originals* (London: John Lane, 1913).

PREFACE

Memoir	Frances Eleanor Trollope, *A Memoir of Frances Trollope*, 2 vols. (London, 1895).
Parker	W. M. Parker, 'Anthony Trollope and "Maga" ', *Blackwood's Magazine*, Number 1551 (January 1945), 57–64.
Reid	T. Wemyss Reid, *The Life, Letters and Friendships of Richard Monckton Milnes, First Lord Houghton*, 2 vols. (New York, 1911).
Sadleir, Bibliography	Michael Sadleir, *Trollope: a Bibliography* (London: Constable, 1928).
Sadleir, Commentary	Michael Sadleir, *Trollope: a Commentary* (London: Constable, 1927).
Stebbins	Lucy Poate Stebbins and Richard Poate Stebbins, *The Trollopes: the Chronicle of a Writing Family* (New York: Columbia University Press, 1945).
Taylor	Robert H. Taylor, 'The Trollopes Write to Bentley', *The Trollopian*, iii (September 1948), 83–98; iii (December 1948), 201–14.
Trollopian	*The Trollopian: a Journal of Victorian Fiction*, Summer 1945 et seq.
What I Remember	Thomas Adolphus Trollope, *What I Remember* (New York, 1888).
* * *	The beginning and end of a letter which survives only as a fragment.
. . .	A gap in the text, the nature and extent of which is explained in a footnote.
[ ]	Matter supplied by the editor.
⟨ ⟩	Matter scored through.

B. A. B.

LOS ANGELES
January 1951

xiii

CONTENTS

INTRODUCTION

ANTHONY TROLLOPE'S SON, HENRY MERIVALE TROLLOPE, WRITING a prefatory note to his father's autobiography, remarked casually that his father 'has not given any of his own letters, nor was it his wish that any should be published'. This is surely a curious request, coming as it does from a man who had just sanctioned the publication of a rather candid self-portrait. It leads one to question whether Henry Trollope was actually quoting his father or merely recording an inference from the manuscript before him. In view of the fact that he showed no hesitation in turning over to Mr. Michael Sadleir all the family letters for the authorized biography, one inclines to the latter belief. Yet one or two persons known to possess Trollope letters to-day have chosen to withhold them from publication and have quoted Henry Trollope's statement in defence of their decision. It might be well, therefore, to accept the statement tentatively and examine such reasons as may have evoked Trollope's alleged proscription.

When a man of public importance interdicts the printing of his letters, it is generally safe to assume that at least one of three considerations is operative. He may feel that what he has written privately is too personal for the public eye, or too revealing, perhaps of his peccadilloes or his human failings. Publication would tarnish the silver of his character and embarrass the good name of his family. Or he may feel that he will himself escape censure, but that the reputation of other persons still living should be protected. Or he may feel that his letters are simply not of sufficient interest to warrant publication.

It is not difficult, I believe, to see how Trollope was thinking. No one who has studied his character could be persuaded for a moment that anything in his career called for concealment. He was as circumspect in his personal life as he was in his fiction. Of course, he was a man's man—bluff, hearty, occasionally choleric. Hunting, card-playing, and club-life were the passions of his mature years. But he had only a gentleman's acquaintance with Bacchus and his pards, and he did not, to use one of his favourite quotations, 'sport with Amaryllis in the shade'. He worked honestly, lived modestly, and did not covet his neighbour's wife. *He* had nothing to fear from the publication of his letters. What about his correspondents and other persons casually or importantly mentioned? If he does call this still-living publisher an 'old fox' and that editress 'unfit'—what of that? His notorious outspokenness was such that he would scarcely have hesitated to sanction the publication of such mild reflections on those with whom he differed as appear in the letters. It was hardly on the score of his *amour propre* or his solicitude for that of his acquaintances that he was reluctant. It was rather, I think, his fear that his letters were not good enough.

It was characteristic of Trollope to depreciate his talent. In his autobiography, in his letters, in his conversations with friends he never sought to equate himself with the more distinguished men of his age. For most of his life he was a busy postal official, wresting from reluctant days a few grudging hours for literature. To maintain his killing pace he budgeted the minutes of the hours. Correspondence contended with other insistencies for odd moments in a day that began at 5 a.m. He trained himself to write *currente calamo*, but there was still little time for revision. If he managed somehow or other in his novels to divert a not unintelligent audience, nobody had a right to expect that in his letters, too, he would stalk words and trap imaginative phrases. For the most part his letters are perforce strictly functional, often indeed perfunctory, without stylistic embroidery or rhetorical flourish. They are of a genre entirely different from Thackeray's, for example, and it is highly likely that Trollope was diffident about their appeal to general readers. It may perhaps be inevitable that a man who spent thirty-three years of his life in the Post Office should regard his own letters unsentimentally as merely serving the needs of essential communication. Thackeray could afford to make personal letters a part of his creative life, an entity in pure literature. Trollope, writing a utilitarian business letter to, say, John Blackwood, dispenses with many of the embellishments which make Thackeray's letters delightful. But his clean, simple objectivity is the characteristic quality of the best in applied literature.

English prose style may as readily be studied through letters as through any other prose form, for in their diversity they exhaust the potential of variety. Abstract, concrete; rhythmic, hobbling; sincere, artificial; dignified, comic; original, imitative; dull, vivid—all these and many other familiar qualities of style are to be found in letters. In all periods from Jacobean to contemporary, some writers have established a permanent reputation chiefly by their correspondence. These men, on whose work have been set up the criteria by which it is the custom to judge all letters, have not always provided the happiest models for our time. The effect upon other readers than the person addressed is often too obviously calculated; the shadow of the printer falls over the pages. The writer who addresses posterity rather than his correspondent is writing an essay, not a personal letter. Thus, much of the correspondence of the eighteenth century, sometimes called the Golden Age of Letter Writing, is pretentious and affected in content, precious and bombastic in style. There is still awe in the stateliness of Doctor Johnson's heavy tread, charm in the unexpected neatness of Thomas Gray's lighter step, naturalness in the intimate approach of Swift. But surely the sardonic trivialities of Lady Mary Wortley Montagu, the egoistic didacticism of Chesterfield, and the petty gossiping of much of Horace Walpole are subject to serious critical deflation. Even the 'divine chit-chat' of Cowper is tinged with pale femininity. In *The Bertrams*, Trollope, speaking of the art of letter-writing, advises the rejection of Walpole as a model in favour of Byron. Of course, there is much to be said for Byron's breezy, animated style; but the chasm between his mannerisms and Trollope's honest homeliness is too broad for leaping. Nobody, I think, will deny Trollope the sincerity which Byron so noticeably lacked. Latterly, we have been moving towards a barer, cleaner style and a more forthright masculinity as standards of excellence. Easy grace and unlaboured spontaneity have taken the place of studied elegance. Concern for values has largely taken the place of gossip. This is not to disparage the very real merits of eighteenth-century epistolary art. To do so would be to evince a serious lack of literary judgement. I mean merely to suggest that the 'art' bulks somewhat too large and that the content is often flaccid.

Trollope had an instinctive perception, in our day ratified by all critics, that a simple style is a good style. In everything he wrote he repudiated artificiality and complexity, emphasizing the virtues of sincerity and simplicity. But, above all, he worked for intelligibility, the *sine qua non* of good writing. In his *Autobiography* he put the matter succinctly:

> Any writer who has read even a little will know what is meant by the word intelligible. It is not sufficient that there be a meaning that may be hammered out of the sentence, but that the language should be so pellucid that the meaning should be rendered without an effort of the reader;—and not only some proportion of meaning, but the very sense, no more and no less, which the writer has intended to put into his words.[1]

This essential simplicity and intelligibility recently prompted Mr. Harold Nicolson to suggest to a group of Yugoslavs in London that Trollope's *Doctor Thorne* should be one of their first reading exercises in English literature.

As a corollary to intelligibility Trollope named harmoniousness. The writer

> must so train his ear that he shall be able to weigh the rhythm of every word as it falls from his pen. This, when it has been done for a time, even for a short time, will become so habitual to him that he will have appreciated the metrical duration of every syllable before it shall have dared show itself upon paper.[2]

Both of these qualities are characteristic of his letters. He knew what he wanted to say, and he had learned to say it in an uncomplicated and not unpleasing manner. Perhaps, realizing his limitations, he did not try to do more than this.

The letters which Trollope was so fond of inserting in his novels as to make them in some instances an integral part of the structure are often considered the best of their kind in English fiction. As the occasion demands, they are witty, or ponderous, or satiric, or frivolous, or gay. Clearly, Trollope put his very best into them. That he did not *always* put his literary best into his personal letters is perhaps unfortunate, but it assures the naturalness which we value in the type. He never tried to impress his correspondents with false dignity or false wit, with the far-sought allusion or the long-meditated quip. The letters

[1] *Autobiography*, ed. Bradford A. Booth (Berkeley and Los Angeles: University of California Press, 1947), p. 196.
[2] Ibid., pp. 197–8.

are business-like: firm, precise, pointed. If in their intense purposefulness they are different from those of his literary contemporaries, they are by no means without positive qualities of rare merit.

It is not to be expected, however, that Trollope's letters will push their way into anthologies and 'treasuries'. They are not in the first place sufficiently dramatic. Further, they lack Walpole's infinite variety and undeniable charm, though they are free of course from his petty spitefulness. They do not have the stylistic grace of Lamb's or Meredith's, the ready facility of Stevenson's, the fecund imagination of Thackeray's, the amiable idiosyncrasy of FitzGerald's. But that they will interest students of Victorian literature in general and admirers of Trollope in particular is the basic assumption of this book. They are not weighted with Gray's occasional petulance, Wordsworth's sense of moral responsibility, George Eliot's tension, or Dickens's egoism. And most of them have a biographical and critical relevance that makes them primary documents of the utmost importance for the full appreciation of Trollope's literary life and career. His relations with his publishers, with his literary contemporaries, with casual and with intimate friends are vividly re-created in a personal way. Trollope's correspondence is virtually a log-book of the busiest man of Victorian letters. There are materials for the analysis of character that the biographer will find instructive. There are commentaries on Trollope's own work and on that of his contemporaries that the critic will find penetrating.

Dr. Johnson once wrote (ironically) to his friend Mrs. Thrale:

In a man's letters, you know, Madam, his soul lies naked, his letters are only the mirror of his heart: Whatever passes within him is shown undisguised in its natural process: nothing is inverted, nothing distorted: you see systems in their elements: you discover actions in their motives.

Through his letters we do, indeed, come to see Trollope more clearly. But he was ever the shy, diffident Englishman, embarrassed by the man who wore his heart on his sleeve. If Trollope unlocked his soul to his correspondents, the less Trollope he. In his letters he addressed by their given name only members of his family. This formality does not proceed from an icy reserve, and it probably does not reflect, as some have charged, an instinctive fear or distrust of passions and emotions. It is chiefly a matter of Victorian social convention. In spite of the warning of the opening sentence some readers of the *Autobiography* have thought it curious that Rose Heseltine Trollope is mentioned only briefly. Yet nobody misunderstands the impersonality of *The Education of Henry Adams*. Trollope's reticence in private matters is most certainly not to be construed as the absence of feeling, and the publication of the family letters, where there is assuredly no lack of affection, should conclude such debate. It is particularly regrettable, however, that most of Trollope's letters to his mother have disappeared, for the relations between the two have been widely misinterpreted.[1] Such letters as remain, however, contain no slightest hint of the animus towards his mother which Trollope is supposed to have felt. If Tom Trollope took exception to Anthony's characterization of Frances Trollope in the *Autobiography*, it is more than likely that through a lifetime's intimacy with his mother Tom had lost the perspective to judge objectively. The novelist of character must train himself to observe men and women sympathetically but unemotionally. This Anthony Trollope had learned to do, even when the subject was his mother.

What Trollope inadvertently reveals of himself in his letters is not for the most part startlingly new, but while reinforcing well-grounded impressions it does serve to correct certain recent misconceptions of his character. If there is any novelty in the self-portrait it is in the softer lines, in the kindlier eyes, and in a less irritable expression than some of the biographical artists have given us. In the fine series of letters to Mary Holmes, for example, there is a sympathy and understanding that did not fail when the response was ungracious. The correspondence with John Blackwood illustrates the firm friendship that had its origin in mutual trust and respect. The letters to George Eliot show that in his open admiration for genius Trollope was without a shred of jealousy. That he had still in middle age a touch of gallantry is the inference from the well-known letters to Kate

---

[1] Frances Eleanor Trollope collected a good deal of this correspondence for her biography of her mother-in-law, and T. H. S. Escott, Trollope's first biographer, apparently had access to it. But it has since been lost.

Field. There is ample evidence that he did not suffer Mrs. Grundy gladly: the spirited defence of Lady Wood's *Sorrow on the Sea* and of his own 'Mrs. General Talboys', as well as the splendid letter on adultery in fiction of 10 March 1865. People have been told that Trollope was not a particularly charitable man. They will see from the note to Mrs. Alfred Austin of 30 January 1882 that charity was indeed against his principles— a wretched expedient in a sorry world; but they should observe that, like Emerson, he never could withhold the alms; that, as in the instance of Robert Bell, Shirley Brooks, Follett Synge, *et al.*, he was always one of the first to organize aid for an impoverished man of letters or his family. We see that Trollope could be righteously indignant with his publishers, as is clear from the letter to Chapman & Hall of 20 December 1865. People who have never read a chapter of his novels know that he bargained sharply with his manuscripts. They will be surprised to read the letter to Mr. Harding of 13 August 1880. What other popular author whose books had made thousands for his publishers ever voluntarily reimbursed them when one of his novels lost money? Occasionally the angry Trollope of tradition pounds the editorial table, as in the letter of 22 January 1870 in which he lectures a bogus polyhistor, or when he harpoons a critic who has wounded his pride, as in the scathing note to Miss Davies. But these excursions into bad temper are noticeable chiefly because they are set in a general atmosphere of easy composure and sweet reasonableness.

In spite of the amazing renascence of Anthony Trollope in the last two decades, the final word has by no means been spoken. Some years ago the present writer projected a critical study of Trollope's mind and art. In the summer of 1944, while materials were still being collected, the death of Morris L. Parrish made available, under circumstances which have been described in the preface, his magnificent collection. It was at once apparent that no further significant work on Trollope could be done until the letters were sifted and studied; for though they do not materially alter the established reading of Trollope's character, they add so many facts as to become a source-book for the future biographer and critic.

The editor of the personal letters of an important writer is usually faced with a troublesome decision. Should he for the information of the student and research scholar publish *all* the letters, or should he for the pleasure of the informed but non-technical reader select only those of special interest and discard the others? Occasionally, as in the instance of Professor Gordon N. Ray's recent monumental edition of Thackeray letters, it is clear that we should see every scrap of paper, routine social notes no less than the dramatic letters to Mrs. Brookfield. The fame of Thackeray justifies an all-embracing inclusiveness. But with Anthony Trollope the case is altered. No good purpose would be served by printing in full all the letters and notes that have been collected. Too many of them are concerned purely with minor details of business, the interest of which was personal and temporary. It is hoped that the compromise that has been adopted will prove satisfactory to both groups of readers. Only those letters are printed in full which add something to our knowledge of Trollope's character or career, or which by some happy expression merit inclusion as independent works of literary art. But every Trollope letter of which I have information is listed, not in an appendix but in its proper chronological place, and its substance is briefly noted.[1] If objection is raised that the continuity of the book as a narrative is broken, it can only be suggested that students, for whom the collection is primarily intended, will probably find the present arrangement more satisfactory.

Numerically, as against the collection of the letters of other Victorian novelists—such as Dickens, Thackeray, George Eliot, Stevenson, and Meredith, the present group of Trollope letters is definitely on the thin side. There are several reasons for this comparative paucity. First, Trollope's literary career began late. Dickens published *Pickwick Papers* at the age of 24, Thackeray the *Yellowplush Correspondence* at 26, George Eliot *Scenes of Clerical Life* at 38, Stevenson *Travels with a Donkey* at 28, Meredith *The Shaving of Shagpat* at 28. But Trollope published

---

[1] I have not thought it pertinent to reprint all of Trollope's open 'letters to the editor', using only those which seemed relevant to some developing situation in his life. I omit a letter on the 'Swiss Guards', *Athenæum*, No. 1835 (27 Dec. 1862), 848; and a series of four letters on 'The Luxemburg Route to Basle' in *The Times*, 24 Sept. 1874, p. 4; 28 Sept., p. 5; 27 Nov., p. 6; 10 Dec., p. 7.

The Warden at 40 and *Barchester Towers* at 42. His real fame came only with *Framley Parsonage* at 45. He knew nothing of society—social, intellectual, or literary—until 1861. As a result, he did not correspond during his early years with persons of established position. Furthermore, such was his obscurity that only a clairvoyant could have seen a reason to preserve his letters. Second, much of his correspondence was destroyed in the lean years that followed his death, even by those who should have known better. Third, unlike many of his contemporaries Trollope had few close friends outside London. There was not an insistent call on him to maintain a large social correspondence. And though he travelled frequently and widely, he was always so occupied with newspaper articles and the accumulation of material for books that he had little time for more than an occasional breathless note to his family. Thus Thackeray's letters number thousands, Trollope's only hundreds.

Fortunately, among those hundreds there are scores which make articulate the mind and heart of one of the finest of English novelists. We watch Trollope in moments of frustration, of exultation, of irritability, of serenity, of turmoil, and of peace. Through the most merciless lenses, the examination of letters written with no thought of publication, Trollope appears man-size, without distortion. Like his characters he is neither seraphic nor devilish, neither much wiser nor more foolish than the generality of educated Victorians. But with the great kindliness of spirit and the understanding compassion toward all men that grew out of his own early suffering, he peoples an imaginary county with men and women so sharply drawn with strokes of quiet humour and Horatian satire that his name has achieved a currency that would have amazed him. These letters will give us a fuller appreciation of his boundless activity, of his unaffected simplicity, and, perhaps, of his keen-eyed genius.

LIST OF ADDRESSEES

WITH LETTER NUMBERS

1 8 3 5

1. To RICHARD BENTLEY.[1] 24 May 1835.
Robert H. Taylor.[2] *Taylor*, p. 85.

In view of the general assumption that Trollope wrote nothing before *The Macdermots of Ballycloran* (1847) it is interesting that his earliest extant letter should refer to 'lucubrations of my own' at the age of nineteen.

My dear Sir

I called on you the other day at the request of the lady who is correcting the sheets of my mothers work—[3] The Printers send the sheets very irregularly; in fact for the last month I believe they have not sent any— Of course you are the only judge of the time when the book is to appear, but perhaps you may not be aware of the dilatoriness of the Printers.

I now ask to trouble you on my own less important score— Is it in your power to lend me any assistance in procuring the insertion of lucubrations of my own in any of the numerous periodical magazines &c which come out in such monthly swarms— I am not aware whether you are yourself the Proprietor of any such—[4] My object of course is that of turning my time to any account that I am able, and if you would put me into the way of doing so, & excuse the liberty I am taking you would much oblige

My dear Sir
Yours truly
ANTHONY TROLLOPE

Sunday 24 May 1835.

22—Northumberland S[t] [5]

[1] Richard Bentley (1794–1871) was a highly successful publisher of novels with whose firm Trollope was to have desultory connexion until the very year of his death.

[2] As explained in the preface, the italicized name in the headnote indicates the owner or depositary of the manuscript. Unless otherwise noted I have seen either the original or a photostatic transcript. The material following the owner's name indicates the place of previous publication. See the preface for the list of cue-titles.

[3] Probably *Paris and the Parisians in 1835.*

[4] *Bentley's Miscellany*, edited by Dickens, was not established until two years later.

[5] For an account of Trollope's life in Northumberland Street see his *Autobiography*, chap. iii, p. 45.

1 8 3 6

2. To THOMAS ADOLPHUS TROLLOPE.[1] January 1836. London. *Not traced. Memoir*, i. 248.

This letter and the many family letters that follow survive only in such fragments as were printed by Frances Eleanor Trollope.[2]

*   *   *

Mamma will, I feel confident, have a second thousand of the Paris.[3] No work of hers was ever abused so much—or sold so fast—or praised in the periodicals so little,—especially by her own party.

*   *   *

3. To THOMAS ADOLPHUS TROLLOPE. 12 February 1836. Hadley. *Not traced. Memoir*, i. 259.

My dear Tom,

It is all over! Poor Emily[4] breathed her last this morning. She died without any pain, and without a struggle. Her little strength had been gradually declining, and her breath left her without the slightest convulsion, or making any change in her features or face. Were it not for the ashy colour, I should think she was sleeping. I never saw anything more beautifully placid and composed. . . .[5] It is much better that it is now, than that her life should have been prolonged only to undergo the agonies which Henry[6] suffered. Cecilia[7] was at Pinner[8] when it happened, and she has not heard of it yet. I shall go for her to-morrow. You went to the same house to fetch her when Henry died.

*   *   *

[1] Thomas Adophus Trollope (1810–92), Anthony's elder brother: novelist, Tuscan historian, newspaper correspondent.

[2] Frances Eleanor Trollope (? 1834–1913), novelist, second wife of T. A. Trollope. The above excerpt is taken from her biography of her mother-in-law. The very considerable family materials which she collected for this work, including Anthony Trollope's letters to his mother over a period of some twenty-five years, have unfortunately disappeared.

[3] As Trollope predicted, a second thousand *was* sold.

[4] Emily Trollope (1818–36).

[5] The ellipses here and elsewhere *passim* are in the *Memoir*.

[6] Henry Trollope (1811–34).   [7] Cecilia Trollope (1816–49).

[8] At Pinner, near Harrow, lived Sir Francis and Lady Milman. Cecilia went to them when Emily's tuberculosis made it necessary for her to leave home.

1 8 3 7

4. To JOHN MURRAY.[1] 2 February 1837.
Sir John Murray.

My dear Sir

I believe my Brother saw you before he left Town on the subject of the 'Belgium'[2] and the account between yourself and my Mother, and that you either gave him or promised to give him a cheque for £25— My mother has mentioned the subject in a letter I received this morning, and as it [is] so much the quickest way of learning what has been done, I have ventured to write to you about it— Would you have the kindness to send me a line, I shall be writing to my Mother tomorrow, or next day, and excuse the trouble I am giving you—

Dear Sir
Yours very truly
ANTHONY TROLLOPE

Genl Post Office
2 Feb 1837

5. To RICHARD BENTLEY. 20 February.
Muriel Rose Trollope. Not seen.

General Post Office
20 Feb. 1837

My dear Sir,

I called this morning in the hope of seeing you on the subject of a message from my mother.

She has written to me saying that she has found her expenses so high, that she is pressed for money, and she wishes to know if you would object to advance her £100 as you have part of the MS of her Austrian book[3] in your hands, and as the rest is almost

---

[1] John Murray (1778–1843), publisher of the well-known series of guide-books as well as the *Quarterly Review* and miscellaneous works of *belles-lettres*. Correspondence with Mrs. Trollope preserved in the Murray files, which were kindly opened to me by Sir John Murray, indicates that she was interceding with Murray at this time to obtain literary employment for Anthony.

[2] *Belgium and Western Germany in 1833*, 2 vols. (London, 1834).

[3] *Vienna and the Austrians*, 2 vols. (London, 1838).

completed. It would [? be] a great accomodation to her—and would not make you incur any risk. If you would be kind enough to send me a line at your *earliest* convenience I would call on you any evening that you would name, and speak to you on the subject. I wish to settle it as soon as possible, as my mother writes pressingly on the subject.

Yours very truly,

ANTHONY TROLLOPE

6. To RICHARD BENTLEY. 16 September 1837. London.
   Robert H. Taylor. Taylor, pp. 85–6.

Trollope asks that Madame de Montalk be assured of sole rights to do the French translation of his mother's *Vienna and the Austrians* (1838) and that she be given the sheets as they are printed.

1 8 3 9

7–9. To A. DONNADIEU. 12 March 1839. 23 March 1839.
   [? 25 March 1839.] London. *Parrish Collection*.

Three notes, arranging to introduce his mother and to dine. Alexander Donnadieu was an officer under Bonaparte who came to England about 1829 and supported himself as a musician and a dealer in autographs.

1 8 4 7

10. To RICHARD BENTLEY. 16 October 1847.
    Robert H. Taylor. Taylor, p. 86.

The novel referred to in the following letters is *The Kellys and the O'Kellys* (1848).

Clonmel Cº Tipperary
16 October 1847

My dear Sir.

When in London in May last I spoke to you respecting a novel which I was then writing, and which I told you I would probably have finished in October. You said that if you publish it, you would like to do so in November.

It is now all but completed—and I would wish to know at what time you would wish to publish it, if you do publish it.

I will *not part with the MS on any other terms than that of pay-*

ment for it.[1] I mean, that I will not publish it myself—or have it published on half profits—or have the payment for it conditional on the sale. It is, & must be, much more the publishers interest to push a work when it is his own property.

If you wish it under these circumstances, I will send you the MS. But I should be glad to know at what time you would think of publishing it. I could immediately send the MS of the whole wanting about 60 pages— It may however be a month before I am able to complete it, as the opening of the Irish Railways take up all my time.

very faithfully yours

Richard Bentley Esq   ANTHONY TROLLOPE
  Publisher
  New Burlington Street

11. To RICHARD BENTLEY. 30 October 1847. Clonmel. *Robert H. Taylor. Taylor*, p. 87.

Through the agency of Mr. Milton—probably Trollope's cousin John Milton, later Sir John (1820–80)—Trollope submits the uncompleted manuscript of *The Kellys*.

12. To RICHARD BENTLEY. 21 November 1847. Tralee. *Parrish Collection*.

Trollope requests that his manuscript be sent to John Milton at the War Office.

1 8 4 8

13. To HENRY COLBURN.[2] 27 March 1848. *Parrish Collection*.

Killarney 27 March 1848

My dear Sir,

I have heard from my friend Mrs Merivale[3] that you have expressed yourself willing to publish my novel on the half

[1] Trollope found that he could not sell the manuscript of *The Kellys and the O'Kellys* on these terms. Colburn finally published it on the half-profits system. See Sadleir, *Bibliography*, p. 260; and see also letter No. 13, *infra*.

[2] Henry Colburn (?–1855), an active London publisher who was once a partner of Richard Bentley.

[3] It is impossible to say to which Mrs. Merivale Trollope refers. It may be to the widow of John Herman Merivale, or to the wife of one of his sons: Herman, Charles, and Trollope's lifelong friend John.

profit system—but have declined to make any offer of a price
for it. I dislike the half profit, as all writers do; but as I should
wish to have the novel published by you, I will accede to your
proposal. I shall be glad of course to have a draft of an agreement
signed by yourself, which I will copy and sign for you, if I
approve it. I must however stipulate that the proof sheets be sent
to myself for correction. I shall be glad to know when you
propose that the work shall appear.

It is now finished, and I will take an early opportunity of sending you the second portion of the 3rd volume.

Very faithfully yours
ANTHONY TROLLOPE

H Colburn Esq

14. To FRANCES TROLLOPE. Spring. Ireland.
Not traced. Memoir, ii. 123–4.

*   *   *

Everybody now magnifies the rows at a distance from him.
You write of tranquillity in Tuscany, where we expected to hear
of revolt, provisional governments, and military occupation.
And I get letters from England, asking me whether I am not
afraid to have my wife and children in this country, whereas all
I hear or see of Irish rows is in the columns of the *Times* newspaper. . . . Here in Ireland the meaning of the word Communism
—or even social revolution—is not understood. The people have
not the remotest notion of attempting to improve their worldly
condition by making the difference between the employer and
the employed less marked. Revolution here means a row. Some
like a row, having little or nothing to lose. These are revolu-
tionists, and call for pikes. Others are anti-revolutionists, having
something to lose and dreading a row. These condemn the pikes,
and demand more soldiers and police. There is no notion of anything beyond this;—no conception of any theory such as that of
Louis Blanc.[1] My own idea is that there is no ground to fear any

---

[1] Louis Blanc (1811–82), French socialist who advocated nationaliza-
tion of property by government through working men's associations. In
1847 he became a Leftist leader and played an important part in the
February Revolution of 1848.

general rising either in England or Ireland. I think there is too much intelligence in England for any large body of men to look for any sudden improvement; and not enough intelligence in Ireland for any body of men at all to conceive the possibility of social improvement.

* * *

1 8 4 9

15. To JOHN TILLEY.[1] 7 April 1849.
Mrs. Arthur Tilley.

Mallow. 7 April 1849

My dear John

I cannot say that I have been sorry to get your last letter—I have felt so certain since Cecilia's last relapse, that she could never recover, that I have almost wished that her sufferings should end. I know, that altho you have expected her death, it will still come to you as a great blow—but you are not the man to give way to sorrow— You will be absent from your office, I suppose, for a month or six weeks—bring mama over here—it will be infinitely better for you—for you both—than remaining alone in the house which must for a time be so sad a place to you. I greatly grieve that I cannot at once start so as to be with you on Tuesday—but I could not go without crippling myself with regard to money, in [a] way which not even that object would justify—and I am sure you would think me wrong to do so—it is a great comfort to me to have seen her so shortly before her death.

I will write to mama either tomorrow or on Monday.

God bless you my dear John—I sometimes feel that I led you into more sorrow than happiness in taking you to Hadley
Very affectionately yours
ANTHONY TROLLOPE

[1] Trollope had introduced his friend John Tilley (1813–98), later Sir John, a rising young Post Office official, to his sister Cecilia. They were married 11 Feb. 1839. Cecilia died 4 Apr. 1849.

16. To THOMAS ADOLPHUS TROLLOPE. Autumn.
Mallow, Ireland. *Not traced. Memoir*, ii. 175.

*　　*　　*

I cannot pretend to condole with you on Mrs Garrow's[1]
death, for it is impossible that it should be a subject of sorrow to
you. But of course Theodosia[2] must feel it. I am sorry to hear
that she required such a prescription as that of Dr. Latham.[3]
Where do you mean to go? It is well for you that some of the
continental republican bubbles have burst. This time last year
you would hardly have known where to pitch yourself. I suppose
you can now go to Florence for the winter, if you so please. I
hope at any rate that you will both be with us next summer.
Ireland is sloppy—the south especially so—but it is warm as it is
sloppy. We have hardly any snow or frost, and generally no
really cold weather until March.

*　　*　　*

1850

17. To FRANCES TROLLOPE. 29 January.
Not traced. Memoir, ii. 178.

Tipperary, January 29th, 1850.
Dearest Mother,

You will have been very much shocked to hear of your
brother's[4] death, for I am afraid the previous accounts which
you have received had not made you expect it—at least not so
suddenly. Till the last week I had no idea that he was in immediate danger. It appears that latterly he entirely wanted the
spirit and hope which might have given him strength to rally.
It seems that it was not the actual disease, but the consequent
weakness which caused his death; and that for some time previous

---

[1] Theodosia Abrams Fisher Garrow (1766–1849), mother of Tom
Trollope's first wife.
[2] Theodosia Garrow Trollope (1825–65).
[3] Dr. Latham advised leaving England for the south of France. Tom
Trollope discusses Mrs. Garrow in his *What I Remember* (New York, 1888),
pp. 380–1.
[4] Henry Milton (? 1784–16 Jan. 1850).

to it he was in a state almost of lethargy. His death will be a most severe blow for you and my aunt Mary;[1] for he was a most affectionate, fond brother.

*   *   *

18. To FRANCES TROLLOPE. Spring. Ireland.
Not traced. Memoir, ii. 179.

*   *   *

We are very sorry. But we have no right to complain. Indeed, the incurring the chance of losing her at any moment after we had become fond of her, was the only drawback to the pleasure of taking her. . . .[2]

My uncle's death has put a stop to my hand-book for the present. I am, however, not inclined to give it over. I mean to go to London and see Murray.[3] I shall be there and back within a week. I hope to go next Tuesday—*i.e.* this day week. Of course I shall be with Tilley. Tell Tom that I finished 'La Vendée' and sent it to Colburn.

*   *   *

19. To FRANCES TROLLOPE. May. Ireland.
Not traced. Memoir, ii. 203–4.

*   *   *

I am very glad you are suited with a house. I hope we may live to see it! At any rate I hope nothing will prevent our all meeting under the shadow of some huge, newly invented machine in the Exhibition of 1851. I mean to exhibit four 4 vol. novels—all failures!—which I look on as a great proof of industry at any rate. I want you and Tom to make out six lists each containing thirteen names, modern or ancient (Biblical characters excluded), of the following persons:—

  1. Great men;—*i.e.* men who have moved the world, not

[1] Mary Milton Clyde.
[2] The Trollopes had taken in a daughter of John Tilley and Cecilia Trollope Tilley. She returned to her father at his marriage to Mary Anne Partington, Cecilia's cousin.
[3] Murray declined the guide-book to Ireland. See *Autobiography*, chap. v, p. 73.

literary or scientific merely. 2. Great women. 3. Men of genius.
4. Great Captains. 5. Great Rebels. 6. Statesmen. Ask Theodosia to make a list also. I have got different people to do so,
and then I [?shall] see how they all tally together.

*   *   *

20. To THOMAS ADOLPHUS TROLLOPE. Summer.
Ireland. *Not traced. Memoir*, ii. 205.

Dear Tom,

I send the lists with the number of votes, including yours and
Theodosia's. You pay a poor compliment to women, by having
recourse to fiction to fill a female list. You have no man of genius
for the first four thousand years, and only one man who in-
fluenced the world; only one rebel, and one great woman.
Theodosia is equally fond of moderns. She admits no great man
or statesman before Christ, and only Eschylus as a man of
genius. I believe Metternich is the only living man mentioned
in the lists as I send them,—yes; Wellington. Tell Theodosia
I cannot allow Cathelineau[1] to be called a rebel, as he took up
arms for his king. We certainly should have had Masaniello,
John of Procida, and Huss. Only seven names have been *unani-
mously* voted: Shakespeare, Mahomet, Joan of Arc, Napoleon,
Richelieu, Pitt, and Wolsey;—all of them modern. And yet I
should be inclined to say that Caesar was the greatest man who
ever lived. So much for the lists.

I don't think there is any obstacle to our coming to Florence
in the summer—say May or June—of 1852. And there is nothing
on earth we should like better.

*   *   *

21. To FRANCES TROLLOPE. Summer. Ireland.
Not traced. Memoir, ii. 186.

*   *   *

God send we may all meet in 1851, when I mean to put three
or four works into the Exhibition. They will, at any rate, give
me as much encouragement as Colburn does!

[1] A leader of the Catholic and royalist insurrection against the revolu-
tionary government in La Vendée; hence Trollope's interest.

. . . . Strangely enough, until I got your letter, I had seen nothing of the case in the Dublin papers.[1] I shall not fail to send you all particulars of the trial,—if she is tried.

* * *

22. To THOMAS ADOLPHUS TROLLOPE. July–August. Ireland. *Not traced. Memoir*, ii. 213.

* * *

To be sure there are certain very palpable delights in being *expeditus*;—in living in other people's houses, being served by other people's servants, eating other men's roast and boiled, and having one's *gendarmerie* paid for by other men's taxes! But still there is a comfort, a solidity, a *nescio quid decori* [? *decoris*], in one's own arm-chair by one's own fireside, which after all I should not wish to want.

* * *

1 8 5 1

23. To THOMAS ADOLPHUS TROLLOPE. March. Ireland. *Not traced. Memoir*, ii. 215.

* * *

I grieve to find that you and Theodosia do not intend coming to London next summer. Your stay in Italy will, I presume, occasion my mother's. And there is our pleasant party broken up! I cannot tell you how I grieve at this. . . . *We* intend going to see the *furriners* in June. I think it will be great fun seeing such a crowd. As for the Exhibition[2] itself, I would not give a straw for it,—except the building itself, and my wife's piece of work which is in it.[3] I suppose you have nearly completed your decorations and improvements.[4] I hope I shall live to see them. I have just

---

[1] A clergyman's wife had been arraigned on a charge of murdering her husband under circumstances of peculiar atrocity.

[2] The Great Exhibition at the Crystal Palace in Hyde Park.

[3] She designed and embroidered a threefold screen which won a bronze prize.

[4] The Villino Trollope soon became the centre of the English colony in Florence.

finished an article on Charles Merivale's 'Rome', and sent it to
the Dublin University Mag. But I doubt their printing it.[1] It is
too late, and they don't know me.

* * *

24. TO FRANCES TROLLOPE. 7 May. Limerick.
Not traced. Memoir, ii. 218.

* * *

It is May by the calendar, but February by one's feelings as
affected by rain, winds, and cold air. The oldest inhabitant knows
nothing like it. . . . I regret more and more every day that Tom
is not to see the Exhibition. I am sure it is a thing a man ought to
see. John Tilley is enthusiastic, and knew all about it before it
was opened; corresponds with all the Secretaries and Commissioners, and has regularly made a study of it! I think he is
right. It is a great thing to get a new pleasure. . . . Will there
be no such thing as a cheap trip from Florence by which a man
could come to London and go back within a fortnight or so?
Touching the 'Papal Aggression,'[2] my opinion is that nothing
at all should have been done. I would have let the whole thing
sink by its own weight. . . . We set up *very much* the idea of going
to Italy in the summer of 1852. I hope we may live to do it. At
present we are all agog about going to London. Rose[3] is looking
up her silk dresses, and I am meditating a new hat!

* * *

25. TO THOMAS ADOLPHUS TROLLOPE? May.
Ireland. *Not traced. Memoir*, ii. 217.

* * *

My article on Charles Merivale's 'Rome' is in the May No. of
the Dublin University Magazine:—a periodical which, I presume,
has not a large sale in Florence! Charles Merivale sent me

[1] It *was* published: 'Merivale's History of the Romans', *Dublin University
Magazine*, xxxvii (May? 1851), pp. 611–24.
[2] The creation of a Roman Catholic hierarchy in England in 1850. The
new Roman Catholic dioceses did not conflict in name with the Anglican
dioceses. The so-called 'Aggression' was noisily resented at the time.
[3] Rose Heseltine Trollope (1821–1917).

word that it was the best review of the work which had appeared. Certainly it is by no means the most laudatory. I wrote it for the purpose of differing from him on a certain point.

*   *   *

26. To THOMAS ADOLPHUS TROLLOPE.
September. Exeter. *Not traced. Memoir*, ii. *223.*

*   *   *

If you cannot come to Mahomet, Mahomet shall go to you, but I should greatly prefer your coming here, as I have such very heavy work on hand. You would, moreover, see Rose and Harry[1] who are with me. I should much like you to see little Harry.

*   *   *

27. To G. H. CRESWELL.[2] 20 November. Guernsey.
General Post Office, London.

Trollope writes briefly on the subject of increased postal accommodation in the rural districts.

28. To G. H. CRESWELL. 21 November. Guernsey.
General Post Office, London.

In the following report Trollope suggests the erection of the now familiar pillar letter-boxes.[3]

Guernsey
21 November 1851

Sir,

There is at present no receiving office at St. Helier, and persons living in the distant parts of the town have to send nearly a mile to the principal office. I believe that a plan has obtained

[1] Henry Merivale Trollope (1846–1926).
[2] The earliest copy of the *List of Officers in the General Post Office* in which I have found Creswell's name, that for 1857, describes him (p. 7) as Surveyor for Western Ireland.
[3] In a recent biography (Lucy Poate Stebbins and Richard Poate Stebbins, *The Trollopes: the Chronicle of a Writing Family* [New York: Columbia University Press, 1946], p. 356) Trollope has been denied credit for this innovation. But the voluminous correspondence on the subject in the library of the General Post Office, London, refers to the plan again and again as 'Mr. Trollope's suggestion'.

in France of fitting up letter boxes, in posts fixed at the road side, and it may perhaps be thought advisable to try the operation of this system in St. Helier—postage stamps are sold in every street, and therefore all that is wanted is a safe receptacle for letters, which shall be cleared in the morning of the despatch of the London Mails, and at such other times as may be requisite. Iron posts suited for the purpose may be erected at the corners of streets in such situations as may be desirable, or probably it may be found to be more serviceable to fix iron letter boxes about five feet from the ground, wherever permanently built walls, fit for the purpose can be found, and I think that the public may safely be invited to use such boxes for depositing their letters.

Should the Postmaster General be willing to sanction this experiment, I would recommend the four sites which I have marked with red ink on the enclosed small map of the town, the site of the principal office being marked with a black cross. In this event no expense need be incurred for clearing the letters from the boxes, as this duty on post mornings would be performed by the person who brings in the rural receiving house bags, and at the other times by the town letter Carrier.

I can give no estimate of the cost of erecting such letter boxes as those proposed. It would probably be necessary to consult the town authorities before the different localities were absolutely fixed.

ANTHONY TROLLOPE

29. To G. H. CRESWELL. 21 November. Guernsey.
General Post Office, London.

Trollope writes a very long and detailed report on 'The revision of the rural posts in the island of Jersey'.

30. To FRANCES TROLLOPE. 1851.
Not traced. Memoir, ii. 218.

*　　*　　*

I have read—nay, I have bought!—Carlyle's '*Latter Day Pamphlets*,' and look on my eight shillings as very much thrown away. To me it appears that the grain of sense is so smothered up in a sack of the sheerest trash, that the former is valueless. He does not himself know what he wants. He has one idea— a hatred of spoken and acted falsehood; and on that he harps through the whole eight pamphlets. I look on him as a man who was always in danger of going mad in literature and who has now done so. I used to swear by some of his earlier works. But to my taste his writings have lost their pith and humour, while they have become stranger, and more uncouth, than ever.

*   *   *

1 8 5 2

31. To Thomas Adolphus Trollope. March.
Not traced. Memoir, ii. 231–2.

*   *   *

I am delighted not to find myself scolded for having changed our purposed plans. I trust, when 1853 does come, I may find myself repaid for my patience by the *greenth* of your lawn. A twelvemonth does not seem so long to wait now as it did ten years ago. It ought to seem longer, for as one has fewer months to come one should make more of them. But somehow, the months and years so jostle one another, that I seem to be living away at a perpetual gallop. I wish I could make the pace a little slower. . . . Whom should I meet in Exeter the other day but our old acquaintance S. J. I brought her to dine with us. She is not in the least changed. She still tells wonderful romances about herself and all the rest of the family; says ill-natured things about other people; laughs, talks, and eats, and makes herself sufficiently agreeable for a short time. I was glad to see her for the sake of old times. . . . She, S. J., has written three books; and if Mama were only in England, she, S. J., would get her, Mama, to *have them published for her*, as she, S. J., sadly wants to make some money! Perhaps you had better not tell Mama. It would make her so bitterly lament not being in England! I do hope to take six weeks next year,—about May, as you suggest,—and trust that nothing may again prevent our getting to Italy.

*   *   *

15

32. To FRANCES TROLLOPE. 28 September.
Haverfordwest.[1] *Not traced. Memoir*, ii. 241–2.

*　　*　　*

We have heard a rumour (some one told John Tilley in Kensington Gardens!) that Theodosia is about to make Tom a father.[2] If so, why has not Tom told us what we should have been so glad to learn from him? If it be true, I heartily wish Theodosia well through her trouble. . . . I have been expecting, dearest mother, to hear either from you or Tom these two months. I hope you have not both forgotten me!

We are now living, or staying for a while rather, in South Wales. Rose and the bairns are at a place on the sea-side called Llanstephan, where there is plenty of air and bathing. We shall stay in Carmarthen during November, and then go to Gloucester for the winter. Harry and Freddy[3] are quite well, and are very nice boys:—very different in disposition, but neither with anything that I could wish altered. . . . We are all here getting dreadfully sick of the Duke of Wellington. He is administered at all hours, and in every shape. The papers have no other subject, and people write, speak, and think, of nothing else. Oh, that he was well buried, and there an end![4] I have heard fifty anecdotes of him in the last five days,—all equally applicable to any one else.

I had a couple of civil letters from Sir John Trollope[5] recently, about using his interest for me at the G.P.O. And I believe he has done what he could do. But I ought not to want any private interest. The more I see the way in which the post-office work is done, the more aggrieved I feel at not receiving the promotion I have a right to expect. However, this does not really annoy me. I can't fancy any one being much happier than I am,—or having less in the world to complain of. It often strikes me how wonderfully well I have fallen on my feet. . . . My kindest love to Tom

---

[1] A small town in the south-west corner of Wales.
[2] Beatrice Trollope (1853–81) was born the following March.
[3] Frederick James Anthony Trollope (1847–1910).
[4] Wellington died 14 Sept. and was buried 18 Sept. 1852. This letter may have been written on 18 September and misdated in the *Memoir*.
[5] Sir John Trollope (1800–74), later (1868) Baron Kesteven, was a wealthy landowner and M.P. for Lincoln. He was a grandson of Thomas Middleton Trollope, who was a brother of Anthony's grandfather.

and Theodosia. I will write to him soon; and I hope he will do
the same to me.

*   *   *

33. To THOMAS ADOLPHUS TROLLOPE. 5 October.
Haverfordwest. *Not traced. Memoir*, ii. 242–3.

My dear Tom,

Though I wrote to my mother only last week, I must send a
line to acknowledge your letter. . . . I am glad you are to have a
child. One wants some one to exercise unlimited authority over,
as one gets old and cross. If one blows up one's servants too
much, they turn round, give warning, and repay one with interest. One's wife may be too much for one, and is not always a
safe recipient for one's wrath. But one's children can be blown
up to any amount without damage,—at any rate, for a considerable number of years. The pleasures of paternity have been
considerably abridged, since the good old Roman privilege of
slaying their offspring at pleasure, has been taken from fathers.
But the delights of flagellation, though less keen, are more
enduring. One can kill but once; but one may flog daily, and
always quote Scripture to prove that it is a duty. And then the
gratification of disinheriting a disobedient son, and sending him
adrift, with the determination that no calf shall be killed on his
return!

A daughter, I fear, does not offer so much innocent enjoyment.
But some fathers do manage to torment their daughters with a
great degree of very evident and enviable satisfaction. I have
none, and therefore have not turned my attention to that branch
of the subject.

You don't at all say when you expect to see your child, but
from Mama's letter to Rose I presume it will be early in the
Spring. I shall be very anxious to hear that Theo and her baby
are well and out of danger. Alas, alas, the Duke of Wellington
is dead, or of course you would have had him for a godfather.

Joking apart, I am heartily glad to hear the news, and assure
you that, to my thinking, nothing that could happen to you would
be so likely to add to your happiness as this.—(You know all
about the fox who lost his tail!).

*   *   *

34. To the EARL OF HARDWICKE.[1] 25 November.
British Museum.

Gloucester
25th Nov 1852.

My Lord

I understand that it is probable that your Lordship will soon have to appoint a new Superintendent of Mail Coaches, and I hope you will not consider that I am taking an undue liberty in soliciting the appointment.

I have been 18 years in the service, and I believe I may confidently refer your Lordship to any of the officers under whom I have served, and especially to Col Maberly,[2] as to my fitness for the situation.

Should your Lordship find it expedient to entrust to me the duties of the office in question, I will not fail to devote to them my best energies and attention.

I have the honor to be,

My Lord,
Your Lordship's most obedient Servant
ANTHONY TROLLOPE

The Right Honble
The Earl of Hardwicke

35. To T. TODD WALTON.[3] 27 November.
Parrish Collection.

Llandilo. 27 Nov. 1852

My dear Sir,

May I trouble you with a very troublesome commission. Mrs Trollope wishes to have the lumber which at present burdens you at Bristol, sent by luggage train to her present address. No 5 Paragon buildings Cheltenham—. I dont know how many

---

[1] Charles Philip Yorke, fourth Earl of Hardwicke (1799–1873), postmaster general in Lord Derby's ministry, 1852; admiral, 1863.
[2] William Leader Maberly (1798–1885), secretary of the General Post Office, 1836–54. It is not likely that Col. Maberly gave Trollope a good character, for reasons described in the *Autobiography*, chap. iii, pp. 38–40. At any rate, Trollope did not get the position.
[3] I have not been able to identify this correspondent with certainty, but he was probably the son of Thomas Todd Walton of Clifton, Gloucestershire, who died in 1857. Llandilo is a little town about twenty miles north of Swansea in Wales.

articles there are, but if you could have the address as above put on them, & the articles forwarded, she & I would be your debtors— There will necessarily be a large outlay in porters &c, but you are used to large advancements for official purposes, & if you will make this on my account, & let me know the tot of the whole, I pledge myself to reimburse you at any rate with as much punctuality as the money order office does.

There are I believe some maps—a case of maps— That had better be sent by post, addressed to me—'to be kept at the post office till Mr Trollope's arrival—'

You are not, I hope, my enemy—but if you were, & if I could not bring myself to wish you well in a charitable christian manner, but were excited by the Devil to wish you all evil, I could wish you nothing worse than a residence in South Wales for the rest of your life—

Pray give my compliments to Mrs Walton— I trust neither she, nor either of your boys have been washed away in the floods— Clifton tho has probably escaped— I have very frequently had to swim for it. The people here are mostly swimming at present—those at least who are not sinking—

Yours always very truly

T. T. Walton Esqr   ANTHONY TROLLOPE

1 8 5 3

3 6. To the General Post Office. 25 January.
General Post Office, London.

Trollope submits a long communication on the distribution and delivery of the mails on the island of Jersey.

1 8 5 4

37. To THOMAS ADOLPHUS TROLLOPE. 28 June.
Muriel Rose Trollope.

Coleraine[1] 28 June 1854

My dear Tom—

Tilley to whom I sent your last letter anent the routes begins

[1] A town on the Bann River, Co. Londonderry, Ireland.

his answer thus 'Tom is a tyrant—to hear is to obey'—to the
which I say ditto—specially as to obeying. Our route out shall
be—Paris, Geneva–Simplon–Como–Milan–Venice. Our route
home will be afterwards discussed—but we shall be found to be
babes in your hands. On one point only can you not have your
way—5 weeks—ie. 35 days must be our widest limit. Suppose
we leave London—night of 4th September could we not do the
proposed route—reach Venice 15 Sept—stay our full 12 days—
leave 27th & get home by 6th October? This would give us 9
days out—and 9 home—but if this would hurry both journeys too
much we could take 11 out & gallop back—though we long to
see something of the Tyrol—

We suggest going back Innsbruck–Munich–Frankford–
Cologne–Ostend which is one of your routes— Now when a
man leaves Kensington which train does he take to Geneva? I
presume Paris–Chalons– and—not Lyons I suppose—probably
Besancon—however tell us the quickest route from Paris to
Geneva.

From Geneva over the Simplon—queries[?]—What time by
Vet[1]—? & what time by diligence?[2] are there diligences? if Tilley
does not come would not a vet be very dear for two? & should
places be taken, if by diligence, beforehand—? & where should
one stop between Geneva & Milan—? In fact just give me a
concise Murray[3]—the bits we want— You know all about it of
course to the very houses at which every vehicle starts—

You will hear from my mother all about my Surveyorship[4]—
I trust my state of vassalage is over— So the Turks have come
out strong—and the Czar has gone back—not in the least because he is beaten, but merely to oblige his friend the Emperor
of Austria! If peace be made, without extracting some plumage
out of his tail, there will be a row in the house— Lord Aberdeen
undoubtedly would consent to such a peace, if he dared.[5]

---

[1] Vettura: a four-wheeled carriage used in Italy.
[2] Diligence: a public stage coach.
[3] Murray's handbooks for travellers.
[4] Trollope had been recommended to a Surveyorship. The appointment,
according to Post Office records, was made 11 Oct. 1854.
[5] George Hamilton Gordon, fourth Earl of Aberdeen (1784–1860),
became head of a strong coalition ministry shortly after the death of Peel
in 1850. But the diplomacy that drew England into the Crimean War
wrecked the ministry.

Give my kindest love to Theo— Rose would write, but she does not know I am writing— You say nothing of my lady Bimba—[1]

Ever yours,
A. T.

Our object will be to spend as much of our time in coming as we can near the Alps—but Rose stipulates that she must have one night to sleep in 4—
What is the time from Milan to Venice?

38. To FRANCES TROLLOPE. 28 June.
Muriel Rose Trollope.

Coleraine 28 June 1854

Dearest Mother—

I have received from London today, not my appointment as Surveyor—but what is tantamount to a direct promise of it— Urquharts[2] pension was settled—whereon Tilley asked Lord C[3] to appoint me at once. His answer was—'He must wait till July— I will then appoint Beaufort[4] & Trollope at the same time—' Now I don't at all understand this, except he chose from some cause that Beaufort shall be my senior—nor do I think that I shall get my appointment in July, as the vacancy to which Beaufort is to succeed will not then yet exist—but I do look on my appointment now as a certainty—and therefore I write at once to you to tell you— As to the income—it is not fixed—but I presume it will not be less than £600—and mine has been that for the last nine months— I think it will be about £650— This I mean in Ireland, which is worth £750 in England— Should I go to England I do not think it would exceed £700—if it came to that—at least not for some years—[5] Should I however get the chance of going to England I should take it.

[1] Bimba (Ital. 'baby'): Beatrice Trollope, who was about 15 months old at this time.
[2] Postal records show P. Urquhart to have been Surveyor for Dublin.
[3] Charles John Canning, Earl Canning (1812–62), postmaster general, 1853–5; governor-general of India, 1856–62.
[4] J. St. L. Beaufort, Surveyor for Birmingham.
[5] The *List of Officers in the General Post Office* for 1857 records (p. 7) Trollope's salary for that year as £700, top for his rank.

Now you know all about my official prospects— I do feel my-self certain of my district and I know you will rejoice with me— I would much sooner however have to communicate the fait accompli—, as we all know that there are slips.

I write to Tom about our route—but I still have this doubt— if Lord Canning wont fill up the district before September I may very probably not get away—& of course I must let you know early in August— His Lordship said July—but one can't bind Lords down to what they say always—

Then comes the important question of residence— Where shall we live? We both dislike the north—& the districts may all be changed—but this also we must discuss on a gondola. We wont buy our furniture at any rate till we have discussed with you the colour of the drawing room curtains—

Harry came home from Cork today—with such a Cork brogue —& such a pair of cheeks—& no shoes to his feet— They must both go to some school here in the North after midsummer— We are all now going to the sea side for a month. Fred is some-what delicate—he is so miserably thin—he is like a skeleton— but full of life & spirits—a horse threw him last week and trod on his hand—how he escaped is marvellous—but he only had one nail squeezed off—

Tilley's coming also is dubious—more so than mine, for I do believe we shall get away—but he can't or won't leave till all these changes are over—nor R. Hill[1] either—& then when the changes are complete, of course Hill, will have the first choice.

God bless you dearest mother
ever your own little boy
A. T.

On reading over my letter I find it to be most wretchedly dis-connected, and all but unintelligible—but I am writing at 3 AM— & I want to write at once—so pray try to make it out—

---

[1] Rowland Hill, later Sir Rowland (1795–1879), founder of the penny post and one of the great names in British postal history, was at this time secretary to the Post Office.

39. To T. TODD WALTON. 23 November.
Parrish Collection.

Strabane[1]   23 Nov. 1854.

My dear Sir

I am very much obliged for your kind note— Yes, I should prefer to be employed in England, but we cant get all we want— & failing that I should prefer the South to the North of Ireland, preferring on the whole papistical to presbyterian tendencies. I shall hope to leave this district some day, but till then shall endeavor to make myself contented.

Bristol is unfortunately not the thoroughfare from the North of Ireland to any place, unless it might be Pile[2] or Portishead[3]— but still I shall hope to see you and Mrs Walton again some day before we are too old to remember each other. When I do so I shall endeavor to come in summer, remembering the very pleasant febrifuge which you prescribed & supplied.

In the mean time, tho the North of Ireland is not the choicest permanent residence, it has some charms for the tourist—& should you take my advise & visit there, I beg to offer myself as your host & guide.

My present residence is Belfast, but I hope to be enabled to move to Dublin which is a nice city enough.

always faithfully yours
ANTH TROLLOPE

Do you find your troubles less, now that the Porter girl no longer deluges you with all the blood of all the Howards & such like other incapables?

[1] Strabane: a town near Londonderry in Northern Ireland.
[2] Pile: Pile March, Gloucestershire, near Bristol.
[3] Portishead: a watering-place on the estuary of the Severn near Bristol.

1 8 5 5

40. To WILLIAM LONGMAN.[1] 17 February. *Destroyed.*[2]

Dublin.   17 Feb. 1855

My dear Sir,

I should feel much obliged to you if you would tell me whether sale of *The Warden* has been so far satisfactory.[3] My object in asking you is this. When the book was written, I intended to write a second part for publication in the event of the first part taking and the tale was framed on this intention.[4] I have written about one third of the second part and if I should hear from you that the sale of the first part has hitherto been fairly successful I will make an effort to finish the second before I go abroad on 1st May.

Very faithfully yours,
ANTHONY TROLLOPE

41. To WILLIAM LONGMAN. 27 March. *Destroyed.*

Trollope forwards to Longman the manuscript of *The New Zealander*.[5]

42. To C. BRANUM. 15 October. Gwedore. *Parrish Collection.*

Trollope instructs Branum (a minor postal clerk not otherwise identifiable) to quit the Strabane and Sligo car, but hopes he will not entirely lose Branum's services. (Gwedore is a town east of Bunbeg, Co. Donegal, Ireland.)

[1] William Longman (1813–77) in 1839 became a partner in the well-known publishing house founded in 1724 by his great-uncle.
[2] Messrs. Longmans Green & Co., Ltd., inform me that their Trollope autographs were destroyed in the London fire of 29 Dec. 1940. Through the courtesy of Mr. Michael Sadleir I am able to print transcriptions which he made from the originals when he was writing his *Trollope: a Commentary*.
[3] *The Warden* had been published the previous month.
[4] The second part was, of course, *Barchester Towers*.
[5] The manuscript of this book, still unpublished, is in the possession of Trollope's granddaughter, Miss Muriel Rose Trollope.

1856

43. To the editor of *The Athenæum.*[1] 5 February.
Richard Purdy.

In a formal, third-person note Trollope submits an article on the third
number of *Little Dorrit*. The interesting implications of this article, which
was not published, have been discussed at length elsewhere.[2]

44. To WILLIAM LONGMAN. 20 December.
Destroyed. Sadleir, *Commentary*, p. 162.

Derry[3]
Dec. 20, 1856.

I am sorry that I am such a distance from you. Were I in
London we might more easily settle as to what you would wish
to have withdrawn from *Barchester Towers* and as to what I
would not object to withdraw.[4] I beg at any rate to assure you
that nothing would be more painful to me than to be considered
an indecent writer.

I shall have no objection to altering any scene open to objection
on this score but I do object to reducing the book to two volumes
—not because I am particularly wedded to three but from a
conviction that no book originally written in three can be judi-
ciously so reduced. . . . But I do not think that I can in utter
ignorance have committed a volume of indecencies. I do not now
remember what can be the sin of the special scene to which
you allude. Of course the woman is intended to [? appear][5] as
indifferent to all moralities and decent behaviour—but such
a character may I think be drawn without offence if her vice be
made not attractive.[6]

But I do not now write in my own defence. I propose to get
my friend Mr Tilley to call on you. You will find him a suffi-

[1] William Hepworth Dixon (1821–79).
[2] See Bradford A. Booth, 'Trollope and *Little Dorrit*', *The Trollopian: a
Journal of Victorian Fiction*, ii (Mar. 1948), 237–40.
[3] Derry: properly Londonderry, Northern Ireland.
[4] Longmans were at this moment perturbed about 'improprieties' in
fiction because their recent edition of *Roderick Random* had been attacked on
the ground of indecency.
[5] The original manuscript was damaged by fire, and the reading is conjectural.
[6] The reference is, of course, to the Signora Neroni.

ciently rigid censor. If you can explain to him to what you object
or can show him the passages marked they will either be altered
or else the MS. withdrawn. I do not think I should be disposed
to make other changes than those suggested on the score of
delicacy. Mʳ Tilley will however have carte blanche to act for
me in any way.

Very faithfully yours,
ANTHONY TROLLOPE

45. To JOHN [? MERIVALE].¹ 21 December.
Parrish Collection

There are few examples of Trollope's humour. That which follows is
particularly interesting because of the use made of it in *Brown, Jones and
Robinson*.²

Derry, 21. Decr 1856.

My dear John,

I am much ashamed of myself that I have not sooner given up
my time and attention to the affairs of the G— & G— But in
truth I was unwilling to turn to such a matter till I could do so
with a clear mind & full attention—& that time has not even yet
arrived. However I can wait no longer.

And first as to the great question of the motto—with which
I must confess I have bothered my brain not to sufficient purposes
— Brother Molesworth offers many which have in them a savor
of wit—but they hardly hit the point with full swing— One
may say that in any motto for a G— & G— Club, the goose
and glee must each be brought forward as bearing on each other
—and as little else as possible must be in it— It must refer also
to the goose as comestible (not sibillant—and here let me say
that the crest should be a couchant goose—impennatus et coctus
—plucked & roasted—& on a field lanceal—viz a dish—this
I look on as *very* material to the true spirit of the matter.) It
must refer, I say, to the goose as comestible—and to the glee

¹ John Lewis Merivale (1815–86), son of John Herman Merivale of
Barton Place, Devon, was Trollope's schoolfellow at Harrow and his life-
long friend. See *Autobiography*, pp. 46, 58, 82.
² Compare the Goose and Glee Club with the description of the Geese at
the 'Goose and Gridiron' in *Brown, Jones and Robinson*, chap. xviii. The
Goose and Glee Club of Silverbridge is mentioned in *The Last Chronicle of
Barset*, chap. xlii.

as following on, & in some sort consequential on, the goose— I utterly deprecate any allusion to Cann—as host—it would be unworthy of the club— The motto hardly admits of canting heraldry—which requires some special name—if for instance you chose to specify solely your great present V— P— you might have a pair of moleskin breeches for your crest—& Moles worth—(or value) for your motto— That I take it would be canting heraldry. What would suit the club best would be Macaronic heraldry— A motto that would run in English and Latin— Such for instance as the following (only it does *not* run in English)

Can't a tory bus answer—

(It might be "Can't a tory answer." The goose is for the singers— & so give an idea of politics beautifully misleading to the novices)

The motto should be so written—and to the un⟨in⟩itiated would so remain a mystery, but to those who had sat these full five years below the goose (respecting which proposed rule anon) it would, with many injunctions as to secrecy, be explained that the true motto was

'Cantatoribus anser'

The goose is for the singers.

I cannot however get over the 'bus'—
The following might suit—

   "Cantabit vacuus?"[1]

   (goose)

   "Hic hic Cantantibus answer"

'Can an empty man sing? Here—here is a reply to those who will sing' The goose being of course tipified in the 'answer'—

This however does not satisfy me— I must however remark that the caesura, and the intervening goose, will make the us in vaccuus, quite as long as you please.[2]

I think very little true reason has been adduced by brother Molesworth for admitting recitations— There is an almost Indian love of the scalping knife in his wish for bores that the throes of the bored might be the source of gratification to others— The milk of human kindness runs too freely in my veins to allow me to participate his views.

---

[1] Juvenal, *Satires*, x. 22: 'Cantabit vacuus coram latrone viator.'
[2] In Latin prosody -*us* is lengthened only if a consonant follows.

But my dear President let me above all things counsel you against what I cannot but regard as a most insidious proposition on the part of the V— P—. What forsooth! take to yourself powers to suspend the law in exceptional cases—!

Let me descend to a lower arena to show you to what this would lead.

The speaker of the H of Commons rules the debates of that section of Parliament. Members have a right to speak— What would be his position were he called on, mero motu—out of his own will & judgement, to suspend this law in exceptional cases— Fancy him forbidding a Spooner to speak, while he listened to Disreali [*sic*]— Would the house hold him?

No—if you once admit recitations—farewell then to all quiet harmony—farewell the genial song, the easy pipe, the hot tumbler— Men will not come from North & South, from distant London & remote mines of Cornwall to hear long stories tamely drawn out— Each 'mutus frater' (let me call your attention to the name) would be desirous of being honored by a recitation— Let such *be* fratres muti— Maintain the spirit of your club— Let it be the G. & G— Be true to your colors whatever you do— Nor can I more cordially agree with that proposed elimination from the Statutes of the rule De non mingendo in poculis peuteribus— Who would wish to see removed from the Cambridge code that law which forbids students to play at marbles in the high street? It is good to maintain these remembrances of olden days— Had not some one once sinned such a rule would not have existed— Can it be that the V. P. was the sinner, & thus wishes to expunge the record of his own disgrace?

I quite agree that no flunky should be admitted— No member should have a flunky within 5 miles at the time of sitting— I would suggest—"Ne famulus adeps liceat infra quinque millia passuum"—

I would also suggest that at table the goose should be in the middle—(or geese on both sides)— That new members should sit below the goose— That the 'Cantantes' should rise to higher seats after eating three geese—the 'Muti' after 5—

And now with much solemn reserve I would also propose one further statute— I fear the club is going from its holding, stranding from its moorings, becoming the plaything of radicals— I am terrified by that dreadful innovation of your V. P. respecting recitations— Even you cannot live forever— That you will preside for the next 40 years let no man doubt—but what if 41 years hence a recitating president should suggest that singing should be forbidden! How would your ghost lie in its grave at Barton! The rule I would propose is—Ne mutus frater sit praeses—

Yours ever
ANTHONY TROLLOPE

The V. P.s letters have been very welcome—but why Emma Nesseaus note about the brandy?[1]

1 8 5 7

46. To WILLIAM LONGMAN. 10 January.
Destroyed.[2] Sadleir, *Commentary*, pp. 162–3.

Dublin.
Jan. 10, 1857

My dear Sir,

I have just heard from M^r. Tilley that he has seen you respecting *Barchester Towers*, and I am led by what he says to fear that you do not think well enough of the MS. to publish it on terms to which I could agree. If this be so, it will be useless for me to give you further trouble by making arrangements as to any alterations.

It appears that you think £100 too high a sum to pay in advance for the book. It seems to me that if a three vol. novel be worth anything it must be worth that; and that it is vain for an author to publish such a work with any view to profit if he is to

---

[1] At the foot of the letter there are several notes in other hands, notably the following from W. H. M. (probably W. H. Molesworth, whom I have not been able to identify):
Dear Paul
Will you kindly give a perusal to this letter. You see the Presidents wishes respecting the motto— You may send it to Hugo, but he must send it back to me, as Trollope is the talented author of the "Warden" &c & when he becomes Ch Dickens or Thackreay [*sic*] this letter will be valuable
Yours fraternally W H M—
[2] Published in excerpt and discussed in Sadleir, *Commentary*, pp. 162–3. Longman acceded to Trollope's demands.

consider such a sum as this excessive. Indeed were it to be regarded as full payment of the work it would be wholly inadequate.

Of course there is no reason why you should pay so much or half so much if you do not judge the article to be worth so much of your money. But it is a reason why we should not deal. You allege very truly and with great kindness that a change of publisher will be prejudicial to my interests as an author. I feel that this is true. But I also feel that if a novel of mine in three vol. is not worth to a publisher £100 I have no interest to prejudice and that I cannot depreciate in value that which is already so valueless.

If therefore you are of opinion that you cannot afford to pay in advance so moderate a price as £100 I think it will be better for me to withdraw my MS. In such case I shall be very sorry to be deprived of the value of your name on my title-page. I think your form of agreement with your authors too vague as to the period of your interest in their work. Unless you buy a copyright surely a term could be put to your [? interest].[1] Otherwise the author is left without the power of republishing in an after time when your interest in the work shall have ceased.

A. T.

47. To WILLIAM LONGMAN. 18 January. Donnybrook.[2] *Destroyed.*

Trollope accepts Longman's terms and agrees reluctantly to give the publisher continued right of publication for an unspecified number of years.

48. To WILLIAM LONGMAN. 1 February. *Destroyed.* Sadleir, *Commentary*, pp. 163–4.

Donnybrook.
Feb. 1, 1857.

I now send your reader's list with my observations and I feel inclined to think that you will be contented with what I have

---

[1] Mr. Sadleir's copy of the letter, from which I print, omits one word at this point.

[2] A village south-east of Dublin.

done. I have complied completely with by far the greater number
of his suggestions and have done so in part with all but three.
I have de bon coeur changed all the passages marked as being too
warm. And I believe in every case have struck out the whole of
what was considered objectionable. I have complied with all
the objections to short passages whether I agreed or no in the
[? validity]¹ of the objections, being willing to give way wherever I could do so. In the longer passages marked as ineffective
I have with two exceptions either omitted or re-written them.
In these two cases objection is made to two whole chapters that
they are tedious. I will not praise myself by saying that they are
not so, but I must profess that I cannot make them less so. I am
sure you do not expect a perfect novel from me and must . . . .²
Were I to withdraw these chapters I must write others and I am
quite sure that such patch work would not be an improvement on
the original composition. . . .²

49. To WILLIAM LONGMAN. 3 March.
Destroyed. Sadleir, *Commentary*, p. 165.

March 3, 1857.

*   *   *

At page 93 by all means put out "foul breathing" and page 97
alter "fat stomach" to "deep chest", if the printing will now allow
it. But I should have thought the sheets had been taken off long
ago. I do not like a second title nor the one you name. I do not
wish the bishop male or female to be considered the chief character in the book. I was puzzled for a title but the one I took at last
is at least inoffensive and easy of pronunciation.

I write in a great hurry in boots and breeches, just as I am
going to hunt but I don't like to delay answering your very kind
letter. I am very thankful to Longmans for the interest they feel
in the book.

¹ A word is omitted in Mr. Sadleir's transcript, and the restoration is
conjectural.
² The copy of this letter is imperfect.

50. To G. C. CORNWALL, Secretary of the Post Office at Dublin. 18 April. *Yale University.*

Trollope took pride in his official reports (see *Autobiography*, chap. viii, pp. 114–15). They are naturally of rather narrow interest to-day, but I include the following as representative.

Trim[1]   April 18. 1857

Sir.

In returning these papers on the subject of a house to house delivery, I beg to say that I consider the subject one of so much difficulty that I hesitate to express a decided opinion as to its feasibility without more information than I possess.

A house to house delivery is I believe effected in France; but I imagine that the appetite for letters is, in the rural districts of France, less craving than with us; and that more time can be consumed in their distribution than could be possible in England as regards the bulk of letters. Presuming that a delivery were arranged which would effect a distribution of all rural letters at, say as an average hour, 10 am on every other morning, there can I think be little doubt that individual energy, would, as regards nine tenths of the correspondence, be brought to bear in such a way as to forestall the official delivery, and leave but a tithe to be counted as absolutely benefitted by the official arrangement.

This difficulty has already been felt in carrying out the existing rural posts. It has been vain to compute the revenue arising from a gentlemans letters, or those of a commercial establishment, unless, when they were to be delivered, either at the beginning of a walk or else by a man going out in a tolerably direct line. Such persons will not esteem it a boon to have their letters carried to them over a circuit.

In arranging a house to house delivery in England the letters found actually available towards affording the revenue required for the increased expense, will be pretty nearly confined to those for the poor and for farmers.

But I feel myself, with much hesitation, compelled to differ from the English Surveyors in the opinion expressed by them, through Mr Godby on the 12th ultimo, that it would be delusive to take as the basis for the proposition of a post correspondence

[1] Trim: a town about 25 miles north-west of Dublin.

which would not in effect be invariably, or perhaps not usually, delivered by that post. My impression is that such a correspondence may fairly be taken as giving the revenue required for the delivery, whether in fact it be officially delivered or not. For instance; if the Squire of a parish, A, get his letters by his own postboy, I think that the halfpenny each on his correspondence, which by the existing rate is applicable to the delivery of rural letters, may in each case be fairly applied to the delivery of those of his less opulent neighbors, farmers, B. C. and D. In such case we afford him a delivery if at any time he chose to avail himself of it. Had not this theory been already adopted to a considerable extent I imagine that the rural delivery now carried out would not have been so far extended as it has been.

Should a house to house delivery be decided on, and any sum per letter be fixed on as that applicable to the purpose,—say a sum not to exceed 1 per letter—I think it should be allowed to the Surveyor so to count *all* letters distributed beyond the free delivery of principal post towns, or of sub offices established in places which may fairly be termed towns. A limit should be fixed—all letters might be excluded when delivered to the number of, say 250 a week, by free delivery in the street—

Should it be found that under such a computation a house to house delivery could be effected under any post town, at a rate not (say 1) exceeding the amount allowed per letter for all the rural letters, I think that such proposed delivery should be regarded as satisfactory, altho' the letters actually carried out might cost 2 per letter.

It would probably be desirable in testing this to make some occasional subdivision of districts less in area than that now served by some of our post towns. The reduction of offices has made this very arbitrary. It would, perhaps, be absurd to take the pence derived from the letters of a gentleman living near Exeter[1] or Crediton,[2] and expend them on delivering the letters of farmers in the north of Cornwall. In such extreme cases however it would be easy to revert to the area of the reduced offices.

It would perhaps hardly be judicious to direct the establish-

---

[1] Exeter: the well-known cathedral city in central Devon.
[2] Crediton: a market town eight miles NW. of Exeter.

ment of a house to house delivery throughout the country irrespective of expense. When some sum has been decided on, it
may perhaps be expedient that the Surveyors should from time
to time report at what offices they consider that the house to
house delivery will under such a restriction be feasible. They
have it seems been requested, to report each as to two offices.
They will know with tolerable accuracy where facilities for such
a measure exist; and where there are great obstacles in the way.
The localities offering the facilities may pretty [? certainly] be
considered as having prior claims to those which offer only
obstacles. From my remembrance of the places I should say that
a house to house delivery might be easily effected under Stroud[1]
where there is an extensive rural post district, but that it could
hardly be done at any reasonable cost under Crediton where
there is also an extensive rural post district.

In this manner the house to house delivery could I think
gradually extend itself till it covered the kingdom. By the time
that the thinner populated districts were reached experience
would have been gained as to the best manner of overcoming the
difficulties of such deliveries, and various relaxations of the rule
would have probably crept in, both as to the occasional expenditure of a higher sum than that named, and an occasional delivery
less frequent than thrice a week.

My impression is that the house to house delivery should in
all cases be an addition to and engrafted on the present rural
post system, and that it can only be carried out by one means—
viz by allowances to Sub Postmasters for the work to be done.
The present rural posts may of course be extended; walks may
be lengthened or new walks established, but I doubt whether
anything could be done in this way towards the house to house
delivery now suggested. Anything so to be done would probably
be done irrespective of that measure.

The allowance to be made to the Sub Postmasters should not,
I think, be regulated so much by the distance from house to
house over which the persons employed might have to walk, as
by the probable time which would be expended daily in the
deliveries. It would of course be desirable that a three day
delivery should not all take place on the same three days— A Sub

[1] Stroud: a town 12 miles south of Gloucester.

Poster should be enabled to deliver—say to the right on Mondays, Wednesday, and Fridays, and to the left on the alternate days.

The arrangements made would be as it were a kind of contract; the Sub Poster would bind himself for the sum allowed to deliver free all letters left at his office for his district—those within a specified boundary on Mondays, Wednesdays and Fridays, and those within another specified boundary on the other days.

There would of course be much difficulty in the fast carrying out of such an arrangement. Not the least would be that of enforcing this contract or agreement— Letters for poor people would be left, not at their houses, but at houses more or less near to them. The poorer classes would however gradually learn their rights in this particular, and a fairly adequate performance of the duty might be ultimately looked for.

It will probably be remembered that the carrying out of such an arrangement thro' any district must be a work of time, and would add very much to a Surveyors labors— A house to house delivery for any district cannot, I imagine, be well suggested originally, or afterwards well carried out without any minute local knowledge.

I have presumed that in reporting on this subject I am not wished to allude in any special way to Ireland. A house to house delivery in Ireland would, I imagine, be more expensive than in England altho labor is less costly, the distances being so much greater over which single letters would have to be conveyed.

I am
Sir,
Your most obedient Servant
ANTHONY TROLLOPE

51. To WILLIAM LONGMAN. 24 April. Dublin.
Destroyed.

In the proof of the title-page of *Barchester Towers*, Trollope struck out 'Author of *The Warden*': 'I think an author should proclaim nothing of himself.' Longman protested, and on this date Trollope finally yields. He also acknowledges his £100 cheque and asks for copies of reviews to be sent him.

35

52. To WILLIAM LONGMAN. 15 July. Derry.
Destroyed.

Trollope asks whether or not Longman would be interested in *The Struggles of Brown, Jones and Robinson*. 'It will be intended as a hit at the present system of advertising but will of course be in the guise of a tale. Publishers' advertisements are not reflected on.'

53. To WILLIAM LONGMAN. 21 August.
Destroyed. Sadleir, *Commentary*, p. 172.

Dublin

21 Aug. 1857

*   *   *

I have finished a three vol. novel.[1] Though it is ready I do not want it to be published now or sooner than you approve. What I do want is to know on what terms you would be willing to publish it. While you were from town I got a letter from your firm not saying much about the sale of *Barchester Towers*, while your letter just received though it gives no bad news gives none that are good. From this I suppose I may imagine that you do not consider the sale satisfactory. If this be so to such a degree as to make your firm unwilling to deal with me on such terms as are usual for works of fiction of fair success, perhaps I may be giving you useless trouble by sending you my MS. I am strongly advised not to publish without getting a price that may be regarded as in some way remunerative. If therefore you think your firm will decline to purchase from me at some such price perhaps you will say so.

My project of a tale in one vol. still holds good but it is not written.[2]

*   *   *

54. To WILLIAM LONGMAN. 29 August.
Destroyed. Sadleir, *Commentary*, p. 172.

Dublin.

29 Aug. 1857

*   *   *

I certainly did mean you to understand by my last letter that I should want a better price for another novel. Indeed I may say

---

[1] *The Three Clerks.*   [2] *Brown, Jones and Robinson.*

at once that I would not under any circumstances take less than double what I received before, viz: two hundred pounds in advance and as you seem to think that your firm will not give more than £100 I fear it will hardly be worth while for you to have the MS. read.

I am sure you do not regard £100 as adequate payment for a 3 vol. novel. Of course an unsuccessful novel may be worth much less—worth indeed less than nothing. And it may very likely be that I cannot write a successful novel, but if I cannot obtain moderate success I will give over, and leave the business alone. I certainly will not willingly go on working at such a rate of pay.

* * *

55. To Richard Bentley. 10 October.
Estate of Carroll A. Wilson.

Florence 10 Octr. 1857

My dear Sir:—

I hope to be in London on this day week, the 17th Saturday— and to call on you with reference to the MS I left in your hands at about 12. The boats however along the coast have become irregular thro' bad weather so that it is possible I may not be able to reach London till Sunday morning. It would I presume be impossible for me to see you on that day—but I shall feel obliged if you will let me have a line addressed to the London Bridge Hotel, written on Saturday, should I not see you on that day:—so that I may get it there on the Sunday morning, & that you will send the MS to that address should you determine to decline it, so that I may also find that at the hotel on the Sunday morning—[1]

Very faithfully yours
Anthony Trollope

[1] For a discussion of Trollope's negotiations with Longman and Bentley over *The Three Clerks* see *Autobiography*, chap. vi, pp. 92–4 and Sadleir, *Commentary*, p. 173.

56. To WILLIAM LONGMAN. 18 October.
Destroyed. Sadleir, *Commentary*, p. 173.

Dublin.
18 Oct. 1857.

*   *   *

I promised to let you know what I did about the MS. of my
new novel. I disposed of it yesterday to Mr Bentley who acceded
to my own terms.[1] The sum I asked was indeed higher than that
I suggested to you. I know, however, that this will not break any
bones between you and me.

*   *   *

57. To RICHARD BENTLEY. 3 November. Dublin.
Robert H. Taylor. Taylor, p. 87.

Trollope acknowledges Bentley's note for £250, returns corrected proofs,
and declares that he did not sell the copyright of *Barchester Towers* to
Longmans.

58. To RICHARD BENTLEY. 21 November. Dublin.
Parrish Collection.

Trollope returns final proofs, and asks for six copies of the book and all
reviews.

1 8 5 8

59. To ROSE TROLLOPE. 31 January.
Muriel Rose Trollope.

Paris Sunday night
31 Jany 1858

Dearest Love,

Here I am, & here also is Tom—& . . .[2] —& that other
Italian fellow who used to be hanging about when they were
selling their pots & pans. They have got a whole heap of their
things here—& a great many more are coming—but the sale

---

[1] In a letter to Trollope dated 13 Oct. Bentley agreed to pay £250 for
the copyright.
[2] Proper name illegible.

will not be for three weeks. Tom is sanguine as to the result—
I fervently wish however that he were out of italy.

My mother it seems is very well—& their fear now is that she
should eat too much. It appears that the modicum of wine has
now become quite an affair of routine.

It seems that Tom will get nearly £3000 by Garrows death,[1]
and as this £3000 is all over & above what he expected, it ought
to relieve him from all his embarrassments—he has also had a
very good offer for his house—so good that were I he I should
certainly take it.

I have not got to work yet tho' I had meant to do so today—
It has been a nasty wet muddy day & I have been slopping about
with Tom & doing nothing—except smoking a cigar in order
to prepare myself for the Turkish nargileh of which I must of
course take a few whiffs—just to prove that I am in a Moham-
medan country—

I was with Judith today for an hour or so— She is just the
same as ever—vegetating up 5 pair of stairs—talking of politics
as if she understood all about them—

I had an awful passage from Dover to Calais, & was very
sick— I thought I was going to be [? thrown] to peices, & indeed even now I am hardly all right—in spite of having eaten a
very good dinner at the hotel des Princes—when we dined with
Judith— Tomorrow we talk of going to Chartres to look at the
painted glass—The next morning I believe I start for Marseilles.
I will if possible write again before I go.

God bless you my own dearest love—

Ever your own
A. T.

60. To R o s e T r o l l o p e. 2 February.
  Muriel Rose Trollope.

Paris 2, Feb. 1858

Dearest love.

Thanks for your nice letter which I got this morning. I have
hardly a minute now. The two latin words were 'toga virilis'[2]—

---

[1] Joseph Garrow (1789–1857), father of Theodosia Trollope.
[2] In the first edition of *Doctor Thorne* these words appear as 'toga virile'.
Frederic Harrison (*Early Victorian Literature* [London, 1895], p. 203)
uses this error as a horrible example of Trollope's slovenly habits! Either

I do not know of what chapters you want the headings—in vol 2—

Chap 7—Mr Moffat falls into trouble

     8—Sir Roger is unseated

     9—Retrospective—

     10—Louis Scatcherd.

     11—Sir Roger dies.

I now send you Chap 12—'War'— This I think will be good for 18 of your pages. You will of course let me know— The slips are long— I think I have made it intelligible how it goes— You must of course be careful about the reading, and also alter any words which seem to be too often repeated.

If Harry has subscribed 5/ to the library out of his own pocket of course you will repay him & charge me. All the other points in your letter will I think have been already explained— I will write a line if I can from Marseilles, I shall however be but a few hours there. Yesterday we went to Chartres, where you & I will go some day to see the painted glass— It is the finest in the world—& is magnificent.

I have not been idle to get so much done in Paris, with Tom by my side, & all the comparative provocations to sightseeing, even of Paris, around me. I have not been inside the Louvre— It is now one, and I have been writing all day— I must do 5 of my pages daily, or I cannot accomplish my task—

Do not be dismal if you can help it— I feel a little that way inclined, but hard work will I know keep it off.

God bless you dearest love— My best love to the boys—& love to Mary— I am glad Ella succeeds.

Ever dearest love

your own,

A. T.

Rose Trollope, who could not decipher her husband's handwriting, did not make the correction in the proof, or the printers were careless. It is possible that Trollope himself was responsible for the many excellent emendations in the second edition noted by Carroll A. Wilson in Sadleir, *Bibliography*. 'Addenda and Corrigenda' (1934), p. 2.

61. To EDMUND YATES.[1] 11 March.
Not traced. Yates and Sadleir.[2]

Alexandria[3]
11 March 1858.

My dear Yates,

It is a matter of great regret to me that I should miss you. But were I to stay now I should lose my only opportunity of going to Jerusalem. I had hoped to have got there and back before you came out, but it has been impossible for me to start till to-day. I shall probably still see you on the 22nd. At Cairo see (above all) the newly-opened catacombs of Sakkara—by taking a horse and mounted guide you may see that and the Pyramids of Ghizeh in one day. Hear the howling dervishes of Cairo at one on Friday. They howl but once a week. Go to the citadel of Cairo, and mosque of Sultan Hassan. See, also, the tombs of the Caliphs. Heliopolis is a humbug, so also is the petrified forest. At Alexandria see the new Greek church they have just excavated. Go to the Oriental Hotel at Alexandria, and Shepherd's at Cairo.

Yours ever,
ANTHONY TROLLOPE

62. To RICHARD BENTLEY. 28 April. Cadiz.[4]
Robert H. Taylor. Taylor, p. 87.

On 25 January Bentley had written Trollope that he had miscalculated the sale of *The Three Clerks* and that he therefore could offer only £300 for *Doctor Thorne.* Trollope now replies that 'the day after I last saw you, I sold the MS of Dr Thorne to Mr Chapman'.[5]

63. To RICHARD BENTLEY. 12 August. Glasgow.
Parrish Collection.

Trollope returns *The Three Clerks,* having made many excisions for the cheap edition which appeared in January 1859.

[1] Edmund Yates (1831–94), novelist, founder of *The World,* and long Trollope's somewhat tempestuous colleague in the Post Office.
[2] Published in *Edmund Yates: His Recollections and Experiences,* 2 vols. (London, 1884), i. 113–14; and in Sadleir, *Commentary,* p. 189.
[3] Trollope was on a special mission to conclude a postal treaty with the Egyptian government.
[4] Cadiz: a port city in south-west Spain.
[5] From Chapman & Hall Trollope received £400. But over the years he confused the time lapse between seeing Bentley and Chapman. See *Autobiography,* chap. vi, p. 99.

64. To B. BLAKE.[1] 1 October.
   Parrish Collection.

                                    (Post Office)
                              Dublin   1 October 1858

My dear Blake

I was very glad to get your letter, and glad to hear that you were out, as it would break the monotony of your life at Edinbro.

Your own bond is certainly not yet executed as the papers have been delayed here. They desired Fitzgibbon[2] to get a magistrates certificate as to my sufficiency—and I would not let him do it—and so the paper has been to & fro. It was absurd asking for a magistrates certificate in my case as the men in the office know better as to my means than any magistrate can do—However, to prevent further delay I did get a magistrate—& the paper went in only today.

Do not lose any opportunity when you are at country offices of getting up the rural posts. Make a point of walking them all with the men whether you are employed to do so, or no. You will learn by doing so the system of rural posts, and it will soon be known that you have learnt it—and this will lead to your being employed as a Surveyors clerk, when there is need for such employment. You should do all you can to learn a Surveyors business when you are travelling. It will be sure to be useful to you.

Let me know when you have executed your own bond. I suppose there will be no further delay.

                              Yours very faithfully
                              ANTHONY TROLLOPE

I think the lad I have got, will do for a stationary clerk. His name is Irvine.[3] He comes from the Queens Dublin office.

----

[1] J. B. Blake, second-class postal clerk, Scotland.
[2] R. Fitzgibbon, Surveyor's Clerk, first class; Trollope's immediate inferior.
[3] J. Irvine, Stationary Clerk under Trollope and Fitzgibbon.

65. To E. Chapman.[1] 20 October. Dublin.
Parrish Collection.

Trollope asks for a copy of the current *National Review.* 'I see that I am handled in it—I must know whether for good or bad.'[2]

66. To B. Blake. 11 November. London.
Estate of Carroll A. Wilson.

Trollope is glad to find Blake still at Thwaites (a small town north-east of Bradford in Yorkshire), but advises him to go to the London office when he is approached on the subject of a transfer.

67. To E. Chapman. 2 December. St. Thomas, West Indies.[3] *Parrish Collection.*

Trollope forwards the manuscript of the first seven chapters of the third volume of *The Bertrams.* John Tilley will read proof.

68. To B. Blake. 25 December. Kingston, Jamaica.
Parrish Collection.

Kingston, Jamaica.
Decr 25, 1858.

My dear Blake,

I have been very happy to hear that you have been selected to go to Mr Warren's[4] district as acting Surveyors clerk in lieu [?] of Mr Hobson,[5] who takes charge of my district. If you succeed there, as I do not doubt you will, it will be a very great step for you, and coming so soon after your recent appointment it ought to put you in good spirits. A Surveyors clerkship is by far the nicest appointment which a young man can have in the post office service; and I know none so desirable in any other branch of the

---

[1] Edward Chapman (1804–80) in 1830 founded with William Hall a publishing house that soon became famous, issuing the books of Dickens, Carlyle, and the Brownings. Trollope's association with the firm was life-long.
[2] 'Mr. Trollope's Novels', the *National Review,* vii (Oct. 1858), 416–35. In a very keen twenty-page article the critic was highly complimentary, but counselled less and better work.
[3] Trollope had left London 16 Nov. on an official postal mission to the West Indies.
[4] J. Warren, Surveyor for the Northern District (Aberdeen), Scotland.
[5] R. Hobson, Surveyor's Clerk, first class.

Civil Service. Make yourself useful where you are now, and you will be sure of such an appointment permanently before long.

I am getting on with my work here, but it will I fear be very long before I get home. I am terribly bothered by the musquitoes. Let me have a line to say how you get on.

I hear that Mr R. R. Smith[1] who was in Central District in Ireland, goes to the South Scotland district, and that Mr Barnard[2] goes to his.

very faithfully yours
ANTH TROLLOPE

Let me have a line to say how you get on. Send it to the care of Mr Tilley.

You will have 15/ a day while travelling as a Surveyors clerk. Do not be too economical. You should always live at the hotels as a gentleman. It will pay best in the long run.

1 8 5 9

69. To E. CHAPMAN. 11 January. Kingston, Jamaica.
Parrish Collection.

Kingston   Jany. 11, 1859
Jamaica.

My dear Sir

I send you in two parcels, the two first vols of The Bertrams corrected—& the second portion of the 3 vol. up to page 260— of MS. There will be 35—or 40 more— which will give it ample length. You shall have them by the next mail. This will give it you by 16th February—as the copy has not come out to me, but will be corrected by Mr Tilley, this will give you ample time. The proof of what I now send will also be corrected by Mr Tilley.

And now, as I have always a prudent eye to the future, I shall be glad to know whether you will think well of a volume of travels on these parts— As I dont yet know how far a field I shall wander, I cannot say what will be comprised—Jamaica, Cuba—

---

[1] Surveyor for the Southern District (Edinburgh), Scotland.
[2] W. W. Barnard, Inspector of Mails.

British Guiana—Panama—& God knows what other latitudes or longitudes.

My idea is about 450 pages of the Dr Thorne size—i e so much matter—to be put into one goodly volume—in such shape as you may prefer; to come out before Xmas. MS—to be with you by 31 October— (most probably a good deal earlier.) Price £250 for three years.[1]

Whether this would suit you—or whether no—be kind enough to let me have an answer. Send it to Mr Tilley. I suppose the cheap edition of Dr Thorne is by this time in existence.

Ah—I wish Providence had made me a publisher.

Yours very truly
A N T H O N Y   T R O L L O P E

E Chapman Esqr

70. TO FRANCES TROLLOPE. 27 January. At sea.
Not traced. Memoir, ii. 283–4.

[Brig *Linwood*, January 27, 1859.]

Dearest Mother,

I must write you a line to tell you how I am going on in my travels, tho' my present position is not very favourable for doing so.

I finished my business in Jamaica last Monday, and then, by way of making a short cut across to Cuba, I got into this wretched sailing vessel. But we have been becalmed half the time since, and I shall lose more time than I shall gain. I believe that in these days a man should never be tempted to leave the steamboats.

I am now on my way to the Havana, and shall have to travel across Cuba to reach it. When I have done there, I go via St. Thomas to Demerara,—thence to Panama,—thence I hope to the States, where I have some idea that Rose may meet me.[2] In this way it will be 1860 before I can see you or Florence. But what could I do? When I had accepted the shorter journey which

---

[1] *The West Indies and the Spanish Main*, Anthony Trollope's first excursion into the family field of travel books, was published 1 Nov. 1859. Chapman & Hall agreed to Trollope's terms. See Sadleir, *Bibliography*, pp. 27, 267.

[2] She did not.

was first proposed, I could not well refuse it when it became longer, and the scheme larger.

I liked Jamaica very much, but did not like Kingston, the chief town, at all. I met with very great hospitality in the island, and found the country to be very, very lovely. I went over the whole island, and saw as much of it, I flatter myself, as any man ever did in the time. I think I shall save the Post Office £1300 a year by my journey there. I like to feel that the expense has not been for nothing.

Tom will be in England, I presume, when this reaches you, looking after the family literature. John Tilley says that he has done all that he can. His house is now quite full, and he *cannot* stow away any more Trollope books. This is since the cheap editions have set in upon him! . . . .

I found your novels advertised with quite new names,—one by that horrid blackguard R.[1] Should not this be stopped? And then there's 'The Days of the Regency, by Mrs Trollope,'[2] brought out by Thomas Hodgson in his Parlour Library. Surely you never wrote a 'Days of the Regency'? The worst is that it makes an appearance as tho' you were in league with the publishers in palming off old novels. . . .

Tom and I both come out in March,[3] and both under the same auspices, namely those of the Messrs. Chapman. . . . Do not be angry at the bad writing, for the ship tosses.

My best love to Theo and Bimba. I had hoped to have been with you all about the time you will get this letter.

Your own affectionate son,
ANTHONY TROLLOPE

71. To B. BLAKE. 10 July.
Parrish Collection.

Dublin 10 July, 1859.

My dear Blake.

I got home last Tuesday, & I go up to London next Tuesday. Your first letter telling me that you had got the place in the Sec's

---

[1] Possibly George Routledge, who had issued *The Ward of Thorpe Combe* in his 'Railway Library' as *The Ward.*

[2] A reissue (1857) of Mrs. Trollope's novel *Town and Country* (1848).

[3] Anthony Trollope's *The Bertrams* and T. A. Trollope's *A Decade of Italian Women.*

office has not reached me. One parcel of letters is travelling after me somewhere— Your subsequent letter of 3 June I received at New York.

I *am* sorry you have gone into the Secretary's office— I think you were somewhat impatient— It is true your salary was low, but you were receiving 15/- a day for every day—& therefore your position at the moment was not bad. You would probably have remained there for a considerable time, and would I think have got the permanent appointment.

However I do not at all find fault with you. As you did try it was well to get it, & the appointment is certainly an eligible one. I believe the salary rises by £10 per an. & that you can look forward to another, better class, above you.

Still, were I you, I would look forward to a Surveyors desk. Your chance is not shut up by your going into the Secretary's office, tho' it certainly is not so good as it would have been in the other position. Let me know if you would still wish for that change.

If I remember rightly you did not lose your leave of absence last year by my absence, but by the fact of your own promotion. When a man is changing from office to office in the process of furthering his own interests, as you are doing—and as young men should certainly strive to do—they must thereby lose the privilege of leave of absence. A man going fresh into an office cannot expect his leave as regularly as a man who has been sometime fixed. In a large office too the juniors must put up with the winter months.

If you write address
> G. P. O.
> London.

Ever very faithfully yours
ANTHONY TROLLOPE

72. TO ROSE TROLLOPE. 2 August.
Muriel Rose Trollope.

To ye ladie of Waltham House in ye Countie of Herts. These— Deareste Madame

Havinge withe infinite trouble & pain inspected & surveyed

and pokèd manie and diverse holes in ye aforesaid mansion, I have at ye laste hiréd and taken it for y^r moste excellente ladie-ship—to have and to hold from ye term of St Michaels mass next comynge. The whiche Waltham House is now the property of one Mistress Wilkins, who has let it to your lovynge lord & husband for 7—14—or 21 yeares, with manie and diverse clauses which shall hereafter as time may serve be explained to your excellente ladieship—

In ye mean time I am with all true love and affection your ladieships devoted servant and husband

ANTHONY TROLLOPE

The second daye of this monthe of Auguste in the yeare of our Lord 1859

73. TO RICHARD BENTLEY. 8 August.
Robert H. Taylor. Taylor, pp. 87–8.

Dublin. 8 Augt 1859.

My dear Sir.

Your letter of the 4th. Inst has followed me here.

When you were about to bring out your 5/– edition of *The Three Clerks*, I reduced the book by about 60 pages, and I fear I should find it impossible to put out 100 more. It gives more trouble to strike out pages, than to write new ones, as the whole sequence of a story, hangs page on page— There is an episode— a story of some 40 pages in the three vol edit., which I would put out if that would suit you— But even that w^d require some care as it is alluded to in different places.[1]

I should not at all object to your midwifery for a new book. But as long as Mr Chapman will give me what I ask him for my goods, of course I shall continue to sell them to him.

very faithfully yours

ANTHONY TROLLOPE

R Bentley Esq

[1] The reference is to negotiations for publication of the novel in the 'Bentley Standard Novels' series, for which it was either the second or third title issued. The publication date was Mar. 1860. See Sadleir, *Bibliography*, p. 23.

74. To FLETCHER HARPER? 1 September.
Moncure Biddle.

London.

1st September, 1859.

(Address,

General Post Office, London.

My dear Sir.

Thank you for your letter & the other for £40—which it covered. That sum has been paid to me by Mr Low.

I think of writing a series of tales, of which the two which I have sent you will be the two first—to be called when completed, 'Tales of all Countries' Each would refer to some different nation or people; and in each case to some country which I have visited. They would run to from 24 to 28 in number, & would average in length 10 of your monthly magazine pages.

My intention would be to republish them in two series, as they should be finished, certainly here in England, and I should hope in the States, with your assistance.

What I now want to know is whether it would suit you to publish one such tale monthly. If not brought out monthly, the project would run over too long a period. About 12 would make one volume for republication.

I have already given you stories about the States[1] and Belgium.[2] You should have a story of the Pyrenees[3] about the end of October if the project would suit you—& then the series regularly as fast as you would want them

Very faithfully yours

ANTHY TROLLOPE

Of course it would be understood that I should have the power of republication in England as soon [as] a series of 12 (say) had appeared in your Magazine.[4]

[1] 'The Courtship of Susan Bell', *Harper's New Monthly Magazine*, xxi (Aug. 1860), 366–78.

[2] 'Relics of General Chassé', *Harper's New Monthly Magazine*, xx (Feb. 1860), 363–70.

[3] This story did not appear in *Harper's*.

[4] The only other story published in *Harper's* was 'The O'Conors of Castle Conor', xx (May 1860), 797–806.

75. To F. Hill. 6 September.
General Post Office, London.

G. P. O. London.

6 September 1859

My dear Sir.

The papers referring to the projected changes in the routes of the West Indian packets have again been referred to me, together with the scheme as proposed by the Company[1] and the objections made by the Company to my scheme.

As I go out of town today I shall not see you; and it is probable that the matter will be settled before my return; I therefore think it well to say a few words to you on the matter which I can hardly put into an official report.

The Company, in objecting to the proposition for making Jamaica our headquarters, shew that they can not bring back the vessels to Southampton under my plan, so as to give an interval of even an entire day, whereas an interval of 3 days is required. But in shewing this they go on the presumption that the vessel which runs to Colon[2] must return on the return journey, i e the same vessel. But there is no necessity for this. *Such is not the case now.* The vessel which now goes down to Colon passes the up vessel on the St Thomas[3] side of Colon, between Carthagena[4] & Colon— And such should still be the case. The vessel from Jamaica to Colon should not return at once; but on the next trip.

Of course it is for the advantage of the Company to encrease the number of miles and diminish the number of vessels— But the interests of the Crown are exactly opposite to this. Providing there be two vessels from Jamaica to Colon & back, the Colon route need offer no impediment to our proposition.

It is absurd for the Company to allege that a first class ship cannot work from Colon to Jamaica or from Jamaica to St Thomas at above 9 miles. The former journey is a very fine one for ordinary work, being opposed by no wind— And as to the latter,

---

[1] Other correspondence on this subject in Post Office files indicates that the company was the Royal Mail Packet Co.

[2] Colon: city at the Atlantic end of the Panama Canal.

[3] St. Thomas: one of the Virgin Islands.

[4] Carthagena: a city on the Atlantic coast of Colombia.

tho it be in the teeth of the trade wind & therefore a difficult route for a small ship, it should offer no impediment to 10 miles an hour with a first class vessel.

The route to Cuba and the Mexican ports offers the only real difficulty. This difficulty will cease when we are able to land our mails on the southern side of the island;—say at Cien Fuegos; but I cannot recommend that this should be done till the railway between that port and the Havana be completed.

In the meantime one of three things should be done: Either the Company should work from Jamaica to Tampico[1] at a quicker pace than 9 miles—say 10— which would not be difficult on the route *to* Tampico; & thus save time—or else they should keep a small vessel to run from Tampico to Vera Cruz[2] & back, making Vera Cruz the end of their main line; or they should have two vessels in the Station, so that the same vessel which goes to Tampico need not return on the same trip.

I think that one of these three things should be done, till the necessity of running round to the Havana be prevented; and that the service to such a port as Tampico should not stand in the way of a change which would in other respects be so beneficial to British interests.

I have made some observations officially on the Company's objections; but you may probably see M[r] Clifton[3] on the matter before it is decided. I have thought it best to explain this to you privately. *Of course* the Company do not desire a diminution of mileage; but they do desire a diminution in the number of vessels employed, in comparison with the mileage—

But we desire a diminution of mileage—in order that the distances may be available elsewhere; and we feel that we have a right to demand a fair number of ships for the service, seeing the enormous amount of the Crown Subsidy.

I am very anxious that the point should be carried, as I am certain it would greatly benefit our own interests.

Very faithfully yours
ANTHONY TROLLOPE

F. Hill Esq

---

[1] Tampico: an important Mexican east coast seaport.
[2] Vera Cruz: Mexico's largest port; 200 miles south of Tampico.
[3] Probably an official of the Royal Mail Packet Co.

76. To W. M. Thackeray. 23 October.
Not traced.[1]

Donnybrook.

Dublin.

October 23 1859.

Dear Sir,

I do not know how far the staff of your new periodical[2] may be complete. Perhaps you will excuse my taking the liberty of offering to make one of the number if it be not so.

I will tell you exactly what would be my views, and you will as frankly tell me whether they would suit you.

I am writing a series of stories to be called—unless I change the name, Tales of all countries. I began them last summer with the view of publishing them first in Harpers magazine, & then of republishing them here. He has two of them already in his hands.

My idea is to publish one a month, & to republish the 12 in a single vol at the end of a year. They wd run in this way for two years. They would occupy, each, from 8 to 13 pages of a big-paged magazine—such as yours may probably be.

If it suited you to take one each alternate month, I would send one for each alternate month to Harpers. It does not suit him to have to take one monthly—or I would send them all to you, if you so wished.

If this idea would suit you, you would probably let me know your rate of pay. Harper gives me £20 for each story—or £2 a page for 10 pages. Of course I have the right of republication whenever it may suit me.

I have five of these stories now by me. Each refers to or is intended to be redolent of some different country—but they apply only to localities with which I am myself conversant.

You will I hope at any rate excuse my writing to you in this manner.

Yours faithfully

Anthony Trollope

As I have before me a letter from Harper respecting these stories which I must answer, perhaps you will let me have a reply as soon as may be convenient to you.

[1] My text for this letter is Trollope's own copy, now preserved with many of his business papers at the Bodleian Library, Oxford. The original has never turned up.   [2] The *Cornhill Magazine.*

77. W. M. THACKERAY to TROLLOPE. 28 October.
Autobiography, chap. viii, pp. 116–17.

So important to Trollope's future as a novelist was the following letter
from Thackeray that it might well be regarded as the turning-point of his
life.

36 Onslow Square, S. W.,
October 28th.

My dear Mr Trollope,—Smith & Elder have sent you their
proposals; and the business part done, let me come to the
pleasure, and say how very glad indeed I shall be to have you
as co-operator in our new magazine. And looking over the
annexed programme, you will see whether you can't help us
in many other ways besides tale-telling. Whatever a man knows
about life and its doings, that let us hear about. You must have
tossed a good deal about the world, and have countless sketches
in your memory and your portfolio. Please to think if you can
furbish up any of these besides a novel. When events occur, and
you have a good lively tale, bear us in mind. One of our chief
objects in this magazine is the getting out of novel spinning,
and back into the world. Don't understand me to disparage our
craft, especially *your* wares. I often say I am like the pastry-cook,
and don't care for tarts, but prefer bread and cheese; but the
public love the tarts (luckily for us), and we must bake and sell
them. There was quite an excitement in my family one evening
when Paterfamilias (who goes to sleep on a novel almost always
when he tries it after dinner) came up-stairs into the drawing-
room wide awake and calling for the second volume of *The Three
Clerks*. I hope the *Cornhill Magazine* will have as pleasant a story.
And the Chapmans, if they are the honest men I take them to be,
I've no doubt have told you with what sincere liking your works
have been read by yours very faithfully,

W. M. THACKERAY.

78. To GEORGE SMITH.[1] 25 November.
Mrs. Reginald Smith.

Maldon,[2] 25 Nov. 1859.
Address, G.P.O. London

My dear Sir,

I return the proof of the article—[3] I *have* cut out a page—[4] but it was as tho you asked for my hearts blood.

And the fault must have been your own in giving me too long a page as a sample— I had even the words counted, so that I might give you exactly what I had undertaken to give & no more. I should like to have the MS with the proof. A man is sometimes at a loss for his own meaning till he sees his own MS. It can all be sent by book post.

As I must send back these sheets—I hence attend the press; but I should like to have a revise *in duplicate*—so that I might keep one.

Yours very truly
ANTHONY TROLLOPE

G Smith Esq

Were I to lessen the number of paragraphs it would make it read heavy

79. To GEORGE SMITH. 25 December. Waltham Cross.
Not traced.[5] Sadleir's transcript.

Trollope questions Smith about a cheque which he thinks is drawn in excess of the amount due. He adds, 'I congratulate you warmly on your first number.'

[1] George Smith (1824–1901), proprietor of the Smith, Elder publishing house and of the *Cornhill Magazine*. He and Trollope were to become devoted friends. Among Smith's later achievements was the proprietorship and the planning of the *Dictionary of National Biography*.
[2] Maldon: a small river port ten miles east of Chelmsford in Essex. Trollope made frequent trips out of London in pursuit of his postal duties.
[3] The first number of *Framley Parsonage*, published in Jan. 1860.
[4] The manuscript of *Framley Parsonage* is in the library of Harrow School, but chaps. i–xviii are missing.
[5] Many of Trollope's letters to George Smith, apparently all of the large group owned by Smith's daughter Elizabeth (Mrs. Yates Thompson), have disappeared. Mr. Sadleir, from whose transcripts I print, saw them twenty years ago. But they have not been traced since Mrs. Thompson's death.

80. To W. M. THACKERAY. 28 December.
Parrish Collection.

Waltham Cross.
28 December
1859

My dear Sir,

Allow me to congratulate you on the first number of the magazine. Putting aside my own contribution, as to which I am of course bound to say nothing laudatory whatever I may think, I certainly do conceive that nothing equal to it of its kind was ever hitherto put forth—

The great aim in such a work should be, I think, to make it readable, an aim which has been so constantly lost sight of in a great portion of the pages of all magazines. In your first number there is nothing that is not readable,—with the single exception above mentioned;—and very little that is not thoroughly worth reading.

Very faithfully yours

W. M. Thackeray Esq   ANTHONY TROLLOPE

1 8 6 0

81. To GEORGE SMITH. 20 January. Waltham Cross.
Not traced. Sadleir, *Commentary*, p. 202.

*   *   *

I think the scene most suited to an illustration in part 3 of Framley Parsonage would be a little interview between Lord Boanerges and Miss Dunstable. The lord is teaching the lady the philosophy of soap bubbles, and the lady is quoting to the lord certain popular verses of a virtuous nature. The lord should be made very old, and the lady not very young. I am afraid the artist would have to take the description of the lady from another novel I wrote called Doctor Thorne.[1]

As this occurred to me I mention it, but I still leave the matter to your better judgement,—or to anyone else who may have a better judgement.

*   *   *

[1] Trollope refers to a scene in chap. viii, but Millais chose a scene from chap. xi ('Lord Lufton and Lucy Robarts'), and his illustration appeared in No. 4, not No. 3.

82. To GEORGE SMITH. 12 February. Cambridge.
    Not traced. Sadleir, *Commentary*, p. 203.

Trollope forwards additional manuscript of *Framley Parsonage* and adds,
'Should I live to see my story illustrated by Millais[1] nobody would be able
to hold me'.

83. To GEORGE SMITH. 3 March.
    Mrs. Reginald Smith.

My dear Sir.
    I have to thank you for your liberally premature payment—
but I had not anticipated that I should have drawn upon your
funds so much before the legal time.
    But I do feel that a few months sooner or later can be nothing
to the happy possessor of an established literary property such
as the Cornhill Mag. commanding a *fixed* sale of a
                        100,000 copies!!
                        Yours very truly
                        ANTHONY TROLLOPE
                        Waltham House
                        3 March 1860

84. To ? 21 March. Huntingdon.[2]
    Parrish Collection.

Trollope arranges with an unknown correspondent for an interview at
Waltham House.

85. To GEORGE SMITH. 2 April.
    Mrs. Reginald Smith. Sadleir, *Commentary*, p. 207.

                        Waltham, 2 April 1860.
My dear Sir.
    I send back the revises of Chapters 13, 14, 15, 16, 17, 18, &
the corrected sheets of Chapters 19, 20, 21, 22, 23, & 24.
    Look at page 18—& chapter 15, in the revise, & see what the

    [1] John Everett Millais, later Sir John (1829–96), the distinguished painter
and one of the original Pre-Raphaelites. He became one of Trollope's closest
friends and admirers.
    [2] Huntingdon: county town of Huntingdonshire, 58 miles north of
London.

printer has done for me by changing a word in one line instead of in the one below. Utterly destroyed the whole character of my own [? most] interesting personage. If he dont put the word back I shall resign.

Yours very truly
ANTY TROLLOPE[1]

86. To CATHERINE GOULD.[2] 13 April.
   Parrish Collection.

Waltham Cross.
April 13 1860.

My dear Catherine.

I have no more doubt than you have,—and probably in truth much less, that a man like Gould with good education & good intellect may make money by writing. I believe that the profession requires much less of what is extraordinary either in genius or knowledge than most outsiders presume to be necessary. But it requires that which all other professions require,—but which outsiders do not in general presume to be necessary in the profession of literature,—considerable training and much hard grinding industry— My belief of book writing is much the same as my belief as to shoemaking.[3] The man who will work the hardest at it, and will work with the most honest purpose, will work the best.

All trades are now uphill work, & require a man to suffer much disappointment, and this trade more almost than any other. I was at it for years & wrote ten volumes before I made a shilling—, I say all this, which is very much in the guise of a sermon, because I must endeavor to make you understand that a man or woman must learn the tricks of his trade before he can *make money* by writing.

As regards the Cornhill magazine, hitherto nothing has been published but articles from persons on the staff—i e bespoken

---

[1] The exact form of Trollope's signature is often highly dubious. Sometimes he clearly abbreviates his given name, but frequently after a few letters he trails off into illegible squiggles.

[2] Catherine Grant Gould (Mrs. Mitcombe Gould) was the daughter of Colonel Grant, a friend of the elder Trollopes at Julians. She was a favourite of Anthony's sisters.

[3] Cf. *Autobiography*, chap. vii, pp. 102–3.

articles from persons known as writers to the Editor or proprietor. If Gould likes to send up an article, I will ensure that it shall be read. That is all that I can do— I have myself nothing to do with any part but my own story— But I can secure so much for you, & will do so very willingly. The Manager of the magazine told me the other day that he had 2,000 articles lying by him from persons not on the staff—i e, outsiders. Of course it is not possible that a quarter of them should be read.

I have been very sorry to hear that Mrs Grant[1] suffered so much. I heard from Perry[2] that you were with her the other day, and I was very anxious to go down to Hillingdon:[3] but I was forced to go out of town, and you had gone before I returned. Peregrine seems to feel confident that it is only an affair of time & that she will recover in a month or two. Peregrine was to have been with me this week, but he could not leave Anna, he thought when she was weak. His boy Wessley is with my boys here.

I do hope that I may before long have an opportunity of seeing you & Gould here. I can safely say that there is no one I would sooner have under my own roof than yourself— I am 14 miles out of town on the Norwich line of railway. My house is Waltham house Waltham X.

My wife would send her love but she is not here at this moment.

always yours most sincerely
ANTHONY TROLLOPE

87. To H. WATKINS. 13 April. Waltham House.
Parrish Collection.

Trollope orders several photographs, saying, 'I think the portrait as it now stands will do very well. It looks uncommon feirce [*sic*], as that of a dog about to bite; but that I fear is the nature of the animal portrayed.' (Herbert Watkins is listed in the *Post Office London Directory*, 1860, as a photographic artist of Regent St.)

[1] Mrs. Gould's mother.
[2] Peregrine Birch, a clerk in the House of Lords, married another of Colonel Grant's daughters.
[3] Hillingdon: a town in Middlesex, west of London.

88. To GEORGE SMITH. 8 May. London.
Not traced. Sadleir, *Commentary*, pp. 207–8.

Garlant's [*sic*] Hotel,
Suffolk Street.

*   *   *

Touching the story for the C. M. wanted for six numbers, I think I could do one that would not be known as mine by intrinsic evidence. I have the story, that is to say the plot, but the scene is laid in Italy. In such case it would be indispensable that I should know at once, as I shall myself be going to Florence this month, if this Committee be brought to an end.[1] I fancy the Italian story would be less easily recognized than Jones, Brown & R.[2] My belief, however, is that these things always get wind [?]. If you really think of either let me know at once.[3]

*   *   *

89. To GEORGE SMITH. 10 May. London.
Mrs. Reginald Smith.

'When the mountain would not go to Mahomet, Mahomet went to the mountain. However in this case that horrid affair at the P.O. made Mahomet perform the greater part of the journey.' Trollope asks Smith to come down to Waltham for the week-end to meet Tom Trollope.

90. To GEORGE SMITH. 16 May. Waltham.
Mrs. Reginald Smith.

Trollope suggests the scene for Millais's second *Framley Parsonage* illustration: 'Was it not a lie?'

91. To GEORGE SMITH. 23 May.
Mrs. Reginald Smith.

My dear Mr Smith.

I can hardly tell you what my feeling is about the illustration to the June N° of F. parsonage. It would be much better to omit

[1] The Select Committee on Civil Service Appointments. See *Parliamentary Papers*, 1861, xix, No. 1664: 'Sixth Report of Her Majesty's Civil Service Commissioners.' Trollope's evidence is to be found on pp. 529, 530, 532.

[2] Smith unfortunately chose *Brown, Jones and Robinson*, one of Trollope's poorest stories, and the Italian novel was never written.

[3] I print from Mr. Sadleir's transcript.

it altogether if it be still possible,—tho I fear it is not—as the copies will have been sent out. The picture is simply ludicrous, & will be thought by most people to have been made so intentionally. It is such a burlesque on such a situation as might do for Punch, only that the execution is too bad to have passed muster for that publication.

I presume the fact to be that Mr Millais has not time to devote to these illustrations, & if so, will it not be better to give them up? In the present instance I certainly think that you & Mr Thackeray & I have ground for complaint.

very truly yours
ANTHY TROLLOPE

Waltham Cross
23 May 1860

Even the face does not at all tell the story, for she seems to be sleeping. I wish it could be omitted.[1]

92. To GEORGE SMITH. *6* June. Waltham.

Trollope instructs Smith's printer to leave his text unaltered, and makes a suggestion about first printing as a series of papers in the *Cornhill* a book on the East Indies which Trollope and Smith have been projecting.

93. To JOHN TILLEY. 13 June. General Post Office.

Trollope answers an official question as to whether promotion by seniority should be made general throughout the Civil Service or only in the lower classes.

June 13, 1860

I think that promotion by seniority should be the rule throughout the service, excepting always Staff appointments.

Under the head of Staff appointments I intend to include all the situations to which are attached special duties of superintendence, and they may usually be defined as positions to the holders of which some special name is attached,—such as chief clerk, superintendent, inspector, or the like.

---

[1] Millais's illustration, depicting Lucy Robarts's refusal of Lord Lufton at the end of chap. xvi, *is* very bad. Lucy, who has thrown herself on the bed, weeping, is wearing a dress with an enormous bustle and spreading flounces that makes her look very like a peacock. But see Trollope's praise of Millais in the *Autobiography* (chap. viii, pp. 125–6).

With these exceptions I think that all promotion should go by seniority, *and as a matter of right*, a certificate of general competence being only required.

I myself hold a very strong opinion that the good of the service would be best forwarded by such a rule and that the largest aggregate amount of good work would be thus secured. I presume however that it is not intended that I should argue the matter at length on the present occasion.

ANTHONY TROLLOPE

94. To GEORGE SMITH. 28 June. Waltham.
Not traced. Sadleir's transcript.

Trollope arranges to meet Smith at the Post Office.

95. To GEORGE SMITH. 3 July.
Mrs. Reginald Smith. Sadleir, *Commentary*, pp. 208–9.

Private.

G. P. O. 3 July, 1860

My dear Mr Smith.

C & H have accepted all my terms as to the serial.[1] I therefore am not in a position to accept your proposal on that head.

On the other two matters,—the India question and the short story for the Magazine I would accede to your propositions—if it would suit you to carry them out without the serial.[2] I.E. I would write the book on India, 2 vols, octavo say 400 pages in each volume, with three papers in the magazine for £3000—the book to come out in October 1861, and the papers in the magazine as soon as may be.

I would also give you the short story for the magazine—8 numbers 16 pages for each, to be inserted in any eight continuous months between October 1861 and October 1862—for £600—i e £75—a number.

I should certainly like to do the India book, but will not break my heart if the plan falls to the ground. Per se going to India is a bore,—but it would suit me professionally.

[1] *Orley Farm* was published by Chapman & Hall in twenty monthly parts, Mar. 1861–Oct. 1862.
[2] Apparently it did not suit, for both matters were dropped.

Even should you accede, the matter must still remain partly undecided till I hear whether or no I get the leave. I do not think I should have any difficulty.

I shall not be in town again till Friday. Shall I come to you then or you to me. I shall be here at 11.30 am, if that would suit you, or would be with you at 11 am in Cornhill. I will then have with me the 8 remaining numbers of the Framley P.—that is to say the whole *'womb of time.'*

Yours always
ANTHONY TROLLOPE

96. To GEORGE HENRY LEWES.[1] 9 July.
Mrs. E. S. Ouvry.

Waltham Cross
July 9, 1860

My dear Sir,

I have asked the Duke of Argyll[2] for a nomination for your son[3] to the situation of supplementary clerk in the Secretary's office of the G.P.O. This is by far the best position in which a lad can enter our office & the only one,—putting aside one or two positions which are exceptional—which I would recommend a friend to seek for a youth.

I should not, naturally, have mentioned this to you till I had received the Dukes answer,—were it not for this reason. There are now two existing vacancies, & he may give me a recommendation for one. It is no great favor as there are always 3 or 4 recommended, between whom there is a competitive examination. I tell you this now, as if you think well of the matter, it may be expedient that your son should employ himself with reference to it. The subjects of examination are Handwriting Dictation in English—which means spelling, ordinary arithmetic including the rule of three, & composition. A young man may volunteer

---

[1] George Henry Lewes (1817–78), the distinguished journalist, biographer of Goethe, and 'husband' of George Eliot. He was to become one of Trollope's closest friends.
[2] George Douglas Campbell (1823–1900), Chancellor of St. Andrews University, Lord Rector of Glasgow University, President of the Royal Society of Edinburgh, Postmaster-General, 1855–8 and 1860, Secretary of State for India, 1868–74.
[3] Charles Lee Lewes (1843–91).

on other things—but that which is essential is a fair knowledge
of figures, and a fair knowledge of English. The subject on which
most men break down is spelling.

Should the Duke give me the nomination I will explain to you
what is the nature of the situation. The office is the one in which
I entered the service.

You will I am sure understand that I am by no means certain
of the nomination, & that I only mention the circumstances to
you in the present stage, as the time may be of value.

                                        Yours very truly
G H Lewes Esq   ANTY TROLLOPE

97. To GEORGE HENRY LEWES. 20 July.
Mrs. E. S. Ouvry.

                                        Waltham
                                        July 20, 1860
My dear Mr. Lewes.

The tide in the affairs of our young man has so far come—
May it lead on to fortune!

You will see that the D of Argyll has given him the nomination for the Secretary's office. He will either have to compete
with 3 or 4 for one situation or with 6 or 7 for two.

When I asked for the nomination I did not wish to tell you, &
put his name down—G—at a shot. If, as the chances are, it be
not G, let me have a line saying what it is.

You shall either here [*sic*] from me or from Mr Barlow on
what day he should present himself at the G.P.O.

The danger to young men educated on the continent is in
spelling & in ordinary English idioms.

My belief is that if you took the 12 most popular authors in
England they would all be beaten.

For myself I should not dream of passing. I sd break down in
figures & spelling too, not to talk of handwriting.

I regard a situation in the Civil Service—if it be a decent
situation, as those in the Secretary's office G.P.O. are—to be
valuable in this respect. It neither necessitates nor tends to
create dishonesty, & leaves ample time for other work. The
church, if this pill can be swallowed, incapacitates a man for

most other work. And medicine requires all a man can possibly give. I know no basis for a literary career so good as an appointment in the C Service—always presuming the man who must live by the sweat of his brow.

Yours always

ANY TROLLOPE

98. To GEORGE SMITH. 21 July. Waltham.
   Not traced. Sadleir, *Commentary*, p. 209.

*   *   *

Many thanks for the Magazine. The Crawley family is very good,[1] and I will now consent to forget the flounced dress. I saw the *very pattern of that dress* some time after the picture came out.

There is a scene which would do well for an illustration. It is a meeting between Lady Lufton and the Duke of Omnium at the top of Miss Dunstable's staircase.[2] I cannot say the number or chapter as you have all the proofs. But I think it would come in at the second vol. If Mr Millais would look at it I think he would find that it would answer. If so I would send him the vol. of Dr Thorne in which there is a personal description of the Duke of O.

The R. Paper is not so severe as I thought it would be—[3] but it is better so.

*   *   *

99. To GEORGE HENRY LEWES. 23 July.
   Mrs. E. S. Ouvry.

Waltham Cross   July 23. 1860

My dear Lewes.

I have written to have the name altered from George to Charles.

I do not know exactly when the examination will take place,

---

[1] Millais's illustration in the August number of *Cornhill*.

[2] Millais accepted Trollope's suggestion, and the illustration appeared in the October number.

[3] Thackeray's Roundabout paper was 'On Screens in Dining-Rooms', *Cornhill Magazine*, ii (Aug. 1860), 252–6. It was a reply to an attack by Edmund Yates. The quarrel is described in Sadleir, *Commentary*, pp. 204–6.

but it will not be long [? after the] first. I will let you know as
soon as I can, or else your son shall hear from Mr Barlow.

Rejected candidates are not as a rule allowed to present themselves again, tho' there is no reason why a rejected candidate
should not have another nomination to that or any other office.
The reason why they cannot come forward again is this. If they
were allowed to do so; they would constantly present themselves,
& the patronage book of the Postmaster General would always
be encumbered with the same names. Indeed men would hold on
till they did get in, and the competitive system would become
dropped. I can explain this to you more fully when I see you.

Yours very faithfully
ANTHONY TROLLOPE

100. To ? 25 July.
Estate of Carroll A. Wilson.

Dear Sir.
Many thanks for the book you have sent me, which I have just
now received & will read.

As regards the negroes, I in writing of them have written of
them as free men; you in pleading for them, plead for them in
their condition as slaves. I am quite as eager for their freedom
as you can be, abhorring slavery on all accounts. But I have not
therefore felt myself debarred for [? from] describing in what
I believe to be true language the condition in which they now
exist in our West Indies.

Yours faithfully
ANTHONY TROLLOPE

Waltham House   July 25—1860

101. To GEORGE SMITH. 29 July.
Mrs. Reginald Smith. Sadleir, *Commentary,* p. 210.

My dear Mr Smith.
I will sign a dozen such receipts if your accountant wishes it—
altho I was told in London last week that a lady denies that I
wrote F. P. claiming to be the author herself. I don't know what
better compliment she could pay to the book.

I will send back Chaps 28–29–30—corrected tomorrow. I suppose I did correct 25–26–& 27, but I dont remember.

Yours always

ANTY TROLLOPE

I have a story, written within the last ten days, about the Holy Land— I suppose it would not be wanted by you for the magazine. It would run 30 pages & have to be divided in two,— or three if you preferred. But, as I said, I do not presume it would be wanted, & therefore ask the question almost idly.

The name is

The Banks of Jordan.[1]

If you see it or hear of it elsewhere dont mention it as being mine. Not that I have any idea of publishing it immediately.

Waltham

Sunday 29 July 1860

102. TO GEORGE SMITH. 1 August. Waltham.
Not traced. Sadleir's transcript.

Trollope submits the manuscript of 'The Banks of the Jordan'. 'If it should suit you, keep it, if not return it without scruple.' Smith rejected the story, and it subsequently appeared in the *London Review*, ii (5, 12, 19, Jan. 1861). It was later reprinted in *Tales of All Countries*, Second Series, under the title 'A Ride Across Palestine'. See letter No. 104, *infra*.

103. TO SAMPSON LOW.[2] 4 August. Cambridge.
Parrish Collection.

Trollope promises to call.

104. TO GEORGE SMITH. 9 August.
Mrs. Reginald Smith.

Smith had objected to the indelicacy of certain passages in *The Banks of the Jordan*. Trollope defends himself against Victorian taste, but the public reaction to the story (see letter 118, *infra*) when it was published elsewhere proved Smith a shrewd judge.

Ipswich.[3] 9. August. 1860.

My dear Mr Smith.

There shall be no rap on the knuckles. I do nothing in that line

[1] See letter No. 104, *infra*.
[2] Sampson Low (1797–1886) was a publisher among whose properties the valuable *English Catalogue, 1753–1882*, is most familiar.
[3] Ipswich: the county town of Suffolk, 75 miles north-east of London.

unless I am purposely rubbed against the hair. But you city publishers are so uncommonly delicate, whereas anything passes at the West End! I shall never forget a terrible & killing correspondence which I had with W. Longman because I would make a clergyman kiss a lady whom he proposed to marry— He, the clergyman I mean; not he W Longman. But in that instance William Longman's church principles were perhaps in stake.

The affair of the saddle, and that other affair of the leg— (I think I said leg—) could be arranged; but I fear the proposal won't suit in other respects. Did you ever buy your own meat? That cutting down of 30 pages to 20, is what you proposed to the butcher when you asked him to take off the bony bit at this end, & the skinny bit at the other. You must remember that the butcher told you that nature had produced the joint bone & skin as you saw it, & that it behoved him to sell what nature had thus produced. Besides one cannot shorten a story. Little passages are sure to hang on to what is taken out— Words occur which are unintelligible because of the withdrawal of other words, & the labor of rearrangement is worse than the original task.

And then, I can by no means part with the copyright. It is one of many stories written or to be written which will come out in subsequent shapes—I trust to my profit. I have, indeed, already arranged for the republication of one such volume.

As to the sum named, had you taken the story, leaving me the copyright and sent me 50 guineas, I should have been satisfied & said nothing— But I am doing better than that with the others. Much better than double that, including the republication & copyright.

As to the smoothness of skin, beard &. I had thought of that— but I should have declared my mystery at once, had I described those feminine appearances. Besides it behoved me not to make my man out to be too much of a fool in not having made the discovery himself.

Do not tell of me if you hear of my story in the 'Birmingham Halfpenny Cyclopedia' or the 'London Laborers Social Friend'.

You can return the MS at your leisure to Waltham Cross, which is my present address.

Yours always

ANTHONY TROLLOPE

105. To GEORGE HENRY LEWES. 9 August.
Mrs. E. S. Ouvry.

My dear Lewes.

I hear that C. L. Lewes was at the head of the Poll at that Civil Service examination, & I suppose I may congratulate him in being a Queens servant. I hope I shall soon shake hands with him over his desk at the Post Office.

Do not let him begin life with any ideas that his profession is inferior to others. Men may live as vegetables, or again as dead sticks, in the Civil Service. But so they may, & so many do, in the church & as lawyers. But in the Civil Service now a days, exertion will give a man a decent gentlemans income not late in life, if it be accompanied by intellects not below par. I do not know what more can be said of any profession except that in others there are great prizes. To compensate this the Civil Service allows a man, who has in him the capacity for getting prizes, to look for them elsewhere. A government clerk, who is not wedded to pleasure, may follow any pursuit without detriment to his public utility. One such man in our days edits the Edinbro, a great gun in his own way;[1] another has written the best poem of these days;[2] a third supplies all our theatres with their new plays;[3] and a fourth plies a small literary trade as a poor novelist.[4] We boast also of artists, philosophers, newspaper politicians, & what not.

Do not therefore let him think that six hours a day at the shop is to be the Be all & End all of his life.

Yours always
ANY TROLLOPE

Waltham
Augt 9, 1860

[1] Henry Reeve (1813–95) was a staff writer for *The Times* and editor of the *Edinburgh Review*, 1855–95.
[2] Matthew Arnold?
[3] Probably Tom Taylor.
[4] Trollope himself, of course.

106. To GEORGE HENRY LEWES. 14 August.
Mrs. E. S. Ouvry.

August 14
1860

My dear Lewes.

There are two men just appointed to the Secretarys office, your son being one. The man who first comes to duty stands senior. Let your son present himself at once to Mr Parkhurst[1]—at whose table I am now writing. If he then wants a few days leave of absence he can get it, but it may [? save] him one step in seniority.

I hear that he passed quite a first rate examination. He got the full numbers for general intelligence which is *very* unusual.

Very faithfully yours
ANTHONY TROLLOPE

107. To EDWARD CHAPMAN. 23 August.
John Rylands Library.

Waltham Augt 23—1860

My dear Chapman,

I send back N° 1—which you may not consider quite complete as far as I am concerned.[2] You shall not have such trouble with the others.

Can I take the 8 Commandment to Florence?[3] That is can you spare it till the end of October? Not that I think it worth carrying so far, but Tom may like to see it. It is —— to my way of thinking.

Yours always
ANY TROLLOPE

The boys are very much obliged to you, & declare they'll call on you again next holyday.

---

[1] According to Post Office records R. Parkhurst was Chief Clerk, Secretary's Office.

[2] Trollope probably refers to the proof of *Orley Farm*, though the first of the shilling parts did not appear until Mar. 1862.

[3] Charles Reade, *The Eighth Commandment* (London, 1860): a book on literary property and dramatic copyright.

108. To George Smith. 15 September.
Bradford A. Booth.

My dear Smith,

Many thanks for the copy of Millais' illustration which I like very much.[1] The scene makes a better picture than the ladies bustle—however I shall not mean to say a word more about that.

Thanks also for the spectacles. I will call & pay the first time I am in London. I go, I think, 22 Inst, could you let me have a copy of the Mag by that time? If so I can take it out with me.

I wrote to my brother saying that you were to have a second Italian article by 12 October, & you will have it without fail.[2] What about any beyond that? I do not mean for the next consecutive numbers, because that would be giving you too much of our Italian colony. —But as to other similar articles after a month or two? I should like to know whether you will think more desirable as my brother would probably write them for others; if you do not want them. I do not want an instant or decisive answer to this; but should be glad to let him know what are your or Thackerays ideas about it, as soon as you have an idea—or he.

Yours always
Any Trollope
Cambridge. Sept. 15—1860.

109. To George Smith. 22 September.
Mrs. Reginald Smith.

Waltham house
22 September 1860

My dear Smith,

Yesterday as I was sitting with my wife over the 'damp' number of the last,—rather next—Cornhill, a large parcel arrived from the railway. One attains by experience an intuitive perception whether or no a parcel is or is not agreeable; whether it should be opened on one's study table, or sent down to the butlers pantry. This parcel I myself opened at the moment, &

[1] For the tenth number of *Framley Parsonage* (*Cornhill*, Oct.).
[2] Published as 'Italy's Rival Liberators', *Cornhill Magazine*, ii (Nov. 1860), 591–6.

took from it fold after fold of packing paper—varying from the strongest brown to a delicate tissue of silver shade—till I reached,—a travelling bag.

'I never ordered it' said I angrily.

'It's a present,' said my wife.

'Gammon—It's a commission to take to Florence for some dandy and I'll be——'

For a moment I fancy she imagined it was intended for her, but we came at once on a brandy flask & a case of razors, and that illusion was dispelled.

'It's the lady who said she wrote your book intending to make you some amends,' she suggested.

And so we went on but never got near the truth.

No one is more accessible to a present than I am. I gloat over it like a child, and comfort myself in school hours by thinking how nice it will be to go back to it in play time. In that respect I have by no means outgrown my round jacket, & boy's appurtenances.

Whether or no I shall ever become a proficient in using all those toilet elegancies with which I now find myself supplied,—gold pins, silver soap-dishes, & cut glass, I cannot say. I feel a little like a hog in armour, but will do my best.

However let me thank you sincerely for your kind remembrance. I argue from your good nature that you are satisfied with all the work I have done for you, & that after all is better than any present. I also feel that I owe you some cadeau of worth, seeing that you have brought me in contact with readers to [be] counted by hundreds of thousands, instead of by hundreds.

Thanks also for the Deux Mondes.[1] I should not have seen it, but for your kindness. That number I am glad to have, but, as a rule, for dull, hard reading, with nothing in it, recommend me to the deux mondes.

I will tell my brother what you say. You may be sure of the six pages exactly. The first time I am in London I will call in to see the drawings on wood. I am now just starting for Italy.

Yours very faithfully
ANTHONY TROLLOPE

[1] Smith was calling Trollope's attention to E. D. Forgues, 'Romans de la vie anglaise: *The Bertrams* et *Castle Richmond*', *Revue des Deux Mondes,* xxiv (2ᵉ pér., 1860), 369–98.

110. To W. LITTLE.¹ 22 September.
Historical Society of Pennsylvania.

Waltham House
Waltham Cross.
22 Sept 1860

Sir,

I am not able to write a continuous story or romance for the London Review,² as my hands are full in respect to work of that description.

I am writing a set of stories of which the first series will be republished in May next, called,—or then to be called, 'Tales of all Countries'. I intend to complete a second series, eight in number, and if they would suit Dr Mackay³ I could make terms with him for bringing them out in his periodical from the beginning of next year.⁴ None of the second series have been as yet published or disposed of. Indeed one only is as yet written.

The stories would average in length 20 pages of the Cornhill Magazine; or at any rate should not be less than that. My price would be £50 for each story, the right of republishing being mine, after, say six months. My intention would be to republish them in May 1862.

I am
Sir
Your obedient Servant

W. Little Esq   ANTHONY TROLLOPE
'London Review' Office

111. To GEORGE SMITH. 1 October.
Mrs. Reginald Smith.

Florence   October 1, 1860

My dear Smith,

I—and the travelling bag—are here all safe. And *we*, with my brother are thinking of going to Naples, in about ten days. I need

---

¹ Manager of the *London Review*.

² The *London Review and Weekly Journal*, a new periodical the first number of which had appeared 7 July 1860.

³ Charles Mackay (1814–99), editor of the *London Review*, had previously edited the *Glasgow Argus* and the *Illustrated London News*.

⁴ The *London Review* purchased serial rights to eight stories at £20 each. But they published only three themselves, disposing of the others elsewhere.

hardly tell you that Naples is at the present moment the centre of all that is most interesting in Italy. I write to you now especially, to know whether you would like to have an article on the state of affairs at Naples—and between Garibaldi and Rome,—from my brother. It would be dated from Naples, and as he would have the means of knowing what is being done there from those who are really engaged in settling or endeavouring to settle the affairs of Italy I think he would give you an interesting paper. In this case I would bring it back with me in ample time for you to put it into type for your December number. i e, the number printed & published in November. You must answer me at once as we propose to start on 10th of this month. Address to Florence. As there would be but one article on Naples I would suggest that the length should exceed the six pages, as it would be very difficult to tell the story in that space—say 8—or if possible 10. But your orders in this respect should be obeyed. The other article on Tuscan politics will leave here on 6th of this month, & will be with you by or before the 12th

Yours always
ANTHONY TROLLOPE

112. To GEORGE SMITH. 27 October.
Mrs. Reginald Smith.

Florence
October 27, 1860.

My dear Smith.

Your letter of the 8th did not reach us,—i e me & my brother till our return from Rome. I had calculated that I might have got your reply before we started on the 12th, but it did not arrive till we had gone.

On reaching Rome we found that we could not get on to Naples without running more risk than the occasion warranted. There was between us & it a Scylla & Charybdis of Garibaldian & Neapolitan armies which made any such attempt very imprudent; and consequently we remained at Rome.

With reference to your proposed article my brother will write the ten pages for the December Number—to be ready, in your hands, by 12 November—*dated from Rome* & giving you the state of things as existing there; but *quite understanding* that you are not in any way bound to take it unless you please to do so.[1] That you will doubtless think the best thing he can now do. You will get this letter about 1 November, & could not receive it in time to say yes or no. If you do not wish the article on Rome, you can send it to me in England.

I shall be home about the 5th or 6th & will see you soon after that. I shall be glad to hear your opinion of the 'Temple Bar'.[2]

If you will kindly pay into Coutts' to the account of T. Adolphus Trollope what money is due to my brother, he will be much obliged.

very truly yours
ANTHONY TROLLOPE

After all it seems probable that Rome will become the capital of the united Italia.

113. To GEORGE SMITH. 6 November.
Mrs. Reginald Smith.

Waltham   6 Nov. 1860

My dear Smith.

The story shall be done, & shall be with you without fail by 11 am Tuesday 13th Instant—18 pages exact.[3] I say 18 that you may be able to make sure, & thinking that that number may be most suitable—being the mean of 16 & 20— If 20 (twenty) will suit you better, & if you will say so by return, you shall have 20 exact— If I don't hear again from you it will be 18—

It shall be among the most inward of my inward things—no one being privy to it but my wife—

Yours always
ANTHY TROLLOPE

Have no scruple in saying 20—if that amount will be most convenient—

I quite understand & agree to your terms as to the use of the copyright of the story—

---

[1] Published as 'The Pope's City and the Pope's Protectors', the *Cornhill Magazine*, ii (Dec. 1860), 719–28.

[2] The first number of *Temple Bar* had just been published.

[3] I do not find anything in the next few numbers that answers this description.

114. To GEORGE SMITH. 6 November. Waltham Cross.
Mrs. Reginald Smith.

At the request of Chapman, Trollope asks Smith if he has any objection
to the serialization of *Orley Farm* beginning 1 March rather than 1 May.
Smith had none.

115. To GEORGE SMITH. 10 November.
Not traced. Sadleir, *Commentary*, p. 213.

Waltham.   Nov. 10. 1860.

My dear Smith,

I shall be in London on Tuesday and will call to settle the
important question as to the young lady's copy of the A. Nights.[1]
Will you kindly send in to Milroy telling him not to pack the
box till I call.

Thanks for the letter about Miss Blagden's book.[2] I do not
suppose you will make a fortune by it;—nor, I suppose, will she.
Can you say when it will be published; and also can I tell her that
she may have the sum which the American publisher will give for
sheets? Do not forget that she wants to describe the novel as by

Ivory Beryl.

I have completed Mrs Talboys. My wife, criticising it, says
that it is ill-natured. I would propose you should call it

Mrs General Talboys.[3]

I hope and trust that there is not and never has been any real
General of that name. If so, we must alter it. I shall always call it
'Mrs Talboys at Rome'—but you will probably choose to sink
the Rome, as you have an article in the same number about the
eternal city.

116. To GEORGE SMITH. 13 November.
Mrs. Reginald Smith.

Piccadilly.   13. Nov. 1860.

My dear Smith.

I have just been with Mrs Stirling[4] who wishes to get from me

[1] See letter No. 117, *infra.*
[2] *Agnes Tremorne*, published 1861 without the pseudonym.
[3] See letter No. 118, *infra.*
[4] Probably Mrs. Fanny Stirling (1813–95), the actress. There is no
mention of a dramatic version of *Framley Parsonage* in Percy Allen, *The
Stage Life of Mrs. Stirling* (London: Unwin, 1922).

permission to dramatise some scenes out of Framley parsonage—
She wishes to have it brought out at Drury Lane before Xmas.
Have you any objection? The difficulty seems to be that they will
have to guess at the ending, but I do not think this could possibly
do the magazine any harm— Will you let me have a line. If you
write tomorrow address to Stafford. If on Thursday—to the
Secretary's office, G. P. O. to be forwarded. I have promised to
see her & give her an answer on Friday.

Yours very truly
ANTHY TROLLOPE

117. To KATE FIELD.[1] 15 November.
Boston Public Library. Sadleir, *Commentary*, pp. 213–14.

Waltham Cross.
November 15, 1860.

My dear Miss Field.

I have fulfilled my promise as far as the Arabian Nights[2] are
concerned, having seen a copy put into the box which is to take
out to Beatrice her saddle. I hope it will do you good mentally
and morally. (I saw yesterday over a little school this announcement put up—'In this establishment morals and mentals are
inculcated'; and if your education be not completed, I would
recommend you to try a term or two. The mentals may be unnecessary, but the morals might do you good.) Don't attempt
to read them—the A^n N^{ts}—through at a burst, but take them
slowly and with deliberation and you will find them salutary.

I am beginning to feel towards you & your whereabouts as did
your high-flown American correspondent. Undying art, Italian
skies, the warmth of southern, sunny love, the poetry of the
Arno and the cloud cleft [?] Appennines, are beginning again
to have all the charm which distance gives. I enjoy these delicacies

---

[1] Mary Katherine Keemle Field (1838–96) was an American journalist,
actress, author, lecturer, and singer. Trollope was to become devoted to her,
and, without mentioning her name, to refer to her very tenderly in his
autobiography (p. 262).

[2] 'Anthony Trollope is a very delightful companion. I see a great deal of
him. He has promised to send me a copy of the "Arabian Nights" (which I
have never read) in which he intends to write "Kate Field, from the Author",
and to write me a four-page letter on condition that I answer it.' Kate Field
to Mrs. Milton T. Sanford in Lilian Whiting, *Kate Field: a Record* (Boston,
1899), p. 123.

in England—when I am in Italy in the flesh, my mind runs chiefly on grapes, roast chestnuts, cigars, and lemonade. Nevertheless let me council [*sic*] you in earnest not to throw away time that is precious. If in some few years time you shall hear and read of precious things in Florence which then you do not know, you will not readily forgive yourself in that you did not learn to know them when the opportunity was at your hand.

Give my love to Miss Blagden. I shall write to her as soon as I can answer her letter. And tell[1] . . . triumph at Florence.

Remember me most kindly to Cleopatra—to whom, by the bye, I propose to send a very highly bred asp, warranted of unadulterated poison. Recommend her to that picture of Guido's with reference to the elegant use of the animal.[2] Tell her also and tell yourself that I shall be delighted to see you both here when homesickness takes you away from Florence. Not that it is homesickness with you in the least. . . .[1]

I do not in the least know your address—so send this to the care of my brother. Kate Field, near the Pitti might not reach you.

118. To W. M. THACKERAY. 15 November.
Parrish Collection. New York Times Book Review, July 13, 1941, p. 18.

Waltham Cross.
November 15. 1860

My dear Thackeray.

I trust you to believe me when I assure you that I feel no annoyance as against you at the rejection of my story.[3] An

---

[1] Four lines have been cut away from the manuscript at this point.

[2] Mr. James H. Breasted, Jr., Director of the Los Angeles County Museum, informed me that Trollope refers to the Turin *Death of Cleopatra* by Guido Reni.

[3] 'Mrs. General Talboys' was subsequently published in the *London Review* (ii [2 Feb. 1861], 129–33) and in the *Tales of all Countries*, Second Series. It proved to be too strong for the *London Review* also. Miss Muriel Trollope has a letter written to her grandfather on behalf of the *London Review* by Laurence Oliphant, who complains of Trollope's first two stories for that magazine (the first story was 'The Banks of the Jordan' [see letter No. 104, *supra*]), saying that readers were objecting to the 'low moral tone of the stories'.

impartial Editor must do his duty. Pure morals must be supplied, and the owner of the responsible name must be the Judge of the purity. A writer for a periodical makes himself subject to this judgement by undertaking such work; and a man who allows himself to be irritated because judgement goes against himself is an ass. So much I say, that I may not be set down by you as disgusted, or angry, or malevolent. But a few words I must say also in defence of my own muse.

I will not allow that I am indecent, and profess that squeamishness—in so far as it is squeamishness and not delicacy—should be disregarded by a writer. I of course look back for examples to justify myself in alluding to a man with illegitimate children, and to the existence of a woman not as pure as she should be. I think first of Effie Deans.[1] Then coming down to our second modern great gun— Observe how civil I am to you after the injury you have done me— I reflect upon the naughtinesses of Miss Beatrice,[2] all the more naughty in that they are told only by hints;—and also of the very wicked woman at Tunbridge Wells who was so surprised because young Warrington did not 'do as others use' with her—[3] I forget whether it was her daughter, or her niece or her protegee. Then there is that illegitimate brat in Jane Eyre with the whole story of her birth; and Hetty Sorrel[4] with almost the whole story of how the child was gotten. I could think of no pure English novelist, pure up to the Cornhill standard, except Dickens, but then I remembered Oliver Twist and blushed for what my mother and sisters read in that very fie-fie story.[5] I have mentioned our five greatest names & feel that I do not approach them in naughtiness any more than I do in genius.

But in such cases, you will say, the impurities rest on the heads of the individual authors,—and that you must especially guard the Cornhill. Well. But how have we stood there? History perhaps should be told even to the squeamish, and therefore the

[1] In Scott's *The Heart of Midlothian.*
[2] Beatrix Esmond, in Thackeray's *Henry Esmond.*
[3] See Thackeray's *The Virginians*, chap. xix. The quotation is from *Lycidas*, l. 67.
[4] In George Eliot's *Adam Bede.*
[5] Trollope probably refers to the relationship between Bill Sikes and his companion Nancy.

improprieties of the improper Georges must be endured. But how about the innuendoes as to the opera dancers which made the children of Terpsichore so mad thru the three Kingdoms?[1]

You speak of the squeamishness of 'our people.' Are you not magnanimous enough to feel that you write urbi et orbi;[2]—for the best & wisest of English readers; and not mainly for the weakest?

I of course look forward to bringing out my own story in a magazine of my own— It will be called 'The Marble Arch', and I trust to confound you by the popularity of Mrs Talboys.

Joking apart— I must declare that I disagree with your criticisms. But at the same time I assure you that I am quite satisfied that you have used your own judgement impartially & with thoroughly good intention.[3]

always yours
ANTHONY TROLLOPE

119. To GEORGE SMITH. 15 November. Lichfield.[4]
Not traced. Sadleir's transcript.

Trollope gives Smith full leave to negotiate with Mrs. Stirling and asks for the return of the manuscript of 'Mrs. Talboys'. 'I am sorry you put yourself to the expense of printing it. I need hardly say that you will owe me nothing.'

120. ANTHONY TROLLOPE from W. M. THACKERAY.
17 November. *Parrish Collection.*

Novr 17. 1860.
36 O. Square

My dear Trollope.

I am just out of bed after one of my attacks, w^h leave me very nervous and incapable of letter writing or almost reading for a day or two. So, as your letter[5] came, and upon a delicate subject too—I told one of the girls to read it.

---

[1] See Thackeray's *Lovel the Widower*, chap. i, and his 'Thorns in the Cushion' (*Works* [Biographical Edition], xii, 214–15).

[2] From the Pope's blessing.

[3] For Thackeray's reply see letter No. 120, *infra*.

[4] Lichfield: a town in Staffordshire ten miles north of Birmingham; famous as Dr. Johnson's birthplace.

[5] See letter No. 118, *supra*.

I give you her very words—I can't help it if they are not more respectful. She says after reading the letter 'He is an old dear and you should write him an affectionate letter.'

Then I had courage to have your letter read. I am another, am I? I always said so.

'The Marble Arch' is such a good name that I have a months mind to take it for my own story.

Always yours
W M T.

121. To GEORGE SMITH. 25 November.
Mrs. Reginald Smith.

Norwich.[1]   25, Nov. 1860.

My dear Smith,

Remember I have not corrected any further in F. P. I fear I must ask your people for a revise, which I have not had for the last few numbers, as I think I have [? seen] a little independent punctuation—no doubt better than my own,—but still not my own. I am not clear also that I have not come across a slight omission or two, which I could not verify not having the MS; and which I do not care to verify not being bellicose about trifles.

I congratulate you on two thoroughly good articles. That by Paterfamilias,[2] & 'behind the curtain.'[3] Is the latter by Tom Taylor?[4] What became of Hollingsheads paper about the publishers?[5]

Yours always
A. T.
Address Waltham

Ariadne[6] begins finely, but waxes sloppy & commonplace to-

---

[1] Norwich: the capital of Norfolk, 115 miles north-east of London.

[2] 'A Second Letter to the Editor of the "Cornhill Magazine" from Paterfamilias', the *Cornhill Magazine*, ii (Dec. 1860), 640–9. Through the kindness of Sir John Murray, the present proprietor of the *Cornhill Magazine*, I learn that the article was by Matthew James Higgins (1810–68), a journalist well known as 'Jacob Omnium'.

[3] Sir John Murray informs me that the article was by John Hollingshead.

[4] Tom Taylor (1817–80), popular dramatist, author of *The Ticket-of-Leave Man* and *Our American Cousin*.

[5] John Hollingshead (1827–1904), journalist and long-time manager of the Gaiety Theatre. The private records of the *Cornhill Magazine*, as they survive to-day, do not identify any such article by Hollingshead.

[6] 'Ariadne at Naxos', pp. 674–6. This poem (and also the illustration)

wards the end. Maria has watched for her lover with red eyes,
almost once too often. Who is the poet? & who the artist? The
latter has a fine idea of a frame, but why has he [? not] framed
to produce a face?

122. To T. TODD WALTON. 26 November.
Parrish Collection.

(Post Office)
Norwich.   26 November
1860

address Waltham Cross.

My dear Sir,

Do you know what is a tontine?[1] I do not. But I have an interest
in a tontine—whatever that is—established in Bristol heaven
knows how many years ago— I know nothing more about it than
that this interest is derived from a share in such undertaking
originally the property of the Revd Wm Milton[2] who then lived
at, or in the neighborhood of, Bristol—and that the life (still
living) which he put into the concern was that of his daughter,
then Mary Milton, now Mrs Clyde.[3] Have you, without giving
yourself any trouble, the means of learning whereabouts in
Bristol, or from whom, I could learn anything as to this tontine?
I believe it, or they, or he, or she, as the case may be, owns house
property in Bristol.

Hoping you will excuse my troubling you on such a matter I
am yours always[4]

ANTHONY TROLLOPE

T. T. Walton Esq
Bristol—

was by Joseph Noël Paton (1821–1901), later Sir Joseph, Queen Victoria's
limner for Scotland. A revised version is published in his *Poems by a Painter*
(London, 1861) as 'Ariadne: Four Sketches from the Antique'.

[1] According to the *Shorter Oxford English Dictionary* a tontine is 'a
financial scheme by which the subscribers to a loan or common fund receive
each an annuity during his life, which increases as their number is diminished
by death, till the last survivor enjoys the whole income'.

[2] William Milton (1743–1824), Anthony Trollope's maternal grandfather.

[3] Mary Milton Clyde's birth is established in Walton's answering note
to this letter as 1776. I have not been able to learn the date of her death.

[4] The following note is written by Walton on the last page: 'Mary

123. To GEORGE SMITH. 30 November.
Mrs. Reginald Smith.

Waltham.   Nov 30—1860.

My dear Smith,

I send the proof of N° 13— When do you illustrate again.
You have four to give to 13–14–15–& 16.

I make the amende honorable about the omitted passage or
passages. I thought that a certain line & a half was in N° 12, but
I have found it in N° 13— I always think a revise is well if it be
not troublesome. I have cut out five or six lines to bring in that
last bit of a page.

I have read Ariadne again. Your modest poet has got it in
him—or her, but s^d have chosen a less hackneyed subject—

Yours always
A. T.

124. To MARY CHRISTIE.[1] 9 December. Waltham.
Estate of Carroll A. Wilson.

Trollope tries to find a mutually satisfactory date for a visit.

Milton* 7 years old in 1 Augt. 1783 now at Exeter, and on Monday the
general meeting will take place when she will get about £30. 200 shares
on 190 Lives—now only 12 remain, and the Property will eventually be
divided among 5 survivors.'

Answered to above effect

T. T. W.   1860
3, Dec. 60   1783
              ——
               77

*widow of Capt: Clyde in Army'.
Commander Charles Clyde (d. 1853) was a Navy, not an Army man. See
W. R. O'Byrne, *Naval Biographical Dictionary* (London, 1849), i. 201–2;
and John Marshall, *Royal Naval Biography* (London, 1832), iii, Pt. 2,
p. 402.

[1] Mary Christie was apparently a sister of Catherine Grant Gould, and
her mother the widow of Colonel Grant, the friend of Frances Trollope.

125. To F R A N K I V E S S C U D A M O R E.[1] 18 December.
Parrish Collection.

(Post Office)

My dear Scudamore,

I have sent on your suggestion[2] to Tom Hughes.[3]

Your prospectus is very good—only ugly. Could you not make it out, giving the days, & names, & titles—? I suppose all your men can now give you their titles. And then they are fixed. Lewes, whom I saw last night at Mudies great flare up,[4] wants chalk and a diagram board. He is very hot about his board. I have promised— Have I done wrong? He wants to know about locale, hour, &c &c. Could you not write him a line,

15 Blandford Square.

Yours ever

A N T H O N Y T R O L L O P E

18 Decr 1860

126. To T H O M A S A D O L P H U S T R O L L O P E. ? 1860.
Not traced. What I Remember, pp. 394–5.

In the excerpt below Trollope is criticizing Elizabeth Barrett Browning's poem, *A Musical Instrument.*[5]

* * *

The lines are very beautiful, and the working out of the idea is delicious. But I am inclined to think that she is illustrating an allegory by a thought, rather than a thought by an allegory. The idea of the god destroying the reed in making the instrument has, I imagine, given her occasion to declare that in the sublimation of the poet the man is lost for the ordinary purposes of man's life. It has been thus instead of being the reverse; and I can hardly believe that she herself believes in the doctrine

[1] Frank Ives Scudamore (1823–84), the most brilliant of the mid-century post office executives. He served as assistant secretary and second secretary, positions which he won over Trollope's head.
[2] For a series of lectures to be delivered by men of letters before postal employees.
[3] Thomas Hughes (1822–86), novelist, biographer, educator; author of the famous *Tom Brown's School Days* (1857).
[4] On 17 Dec. a large new hall and a library were opened in the rear of the premises of Charles Edward Mudie (1818–90), the founder of the famous Mudie's Lending Library. See *The Times* for 18 Dec.
[5] Published in the *Cornhill Magazine,* ii (July 1860), 84–5.

which her fancy has led her to illustrate. A man that can be a poet
is so much the more a man in becoming such, and is the more
fitted for a man's best work. Nothing is destroyed, and in preparing the instrument for the touch of the musician the gods do
nothing for which they need weep. The idea, however, is beautiful, and it is beautifully worked. . . . In the third line of it [the
seventh stanza], she loses her antithesis. She must spoil her man,
as well as make a poet out of him—spoil him as the reed is
spoiled. Should we not read the lines thus:[1]

> Yet one half beast is the great god Pan
> Or he would not have laughed by the river.
> Making a poet he mars a man;
> The true gods sigh, etc.?

*   *   *

1 8 6 1

127. To GEORGE SMITH. 5 January.
Mrs. Reginald Smith.

Waltham Cross.   Jany 5, 1861

My dear Smith.

I have been very glad to get your letter. I should have been
unhappy to feel myself severed from the most popular periodical
publication of the day, & assure you that I will do the best I can
for you with B. J. & R.[2] I propose that you shall have the entire
MS. some time in July.

Always yours

G Smith Esq   ANTHONY TROLLOPE

[1] The original reads:

> Yet half a beast is the great god Pan
> To laugh, as he sits by the river,
> Making a poet out of a man.
> The true gods sigh for the cost and pain,—
> For the reed that grows nevermore again
> As a reed with the reeds in the river.

Dr. Chapman reminds me that these concluding lines are quoted with great
effect following Phineas Finn's trial. See *Phineas Redux*, chap. lxvii.

[2] It is not clear why Trollope thought he might lose his connexion with
the *Cornhill*. Perhaps his part in starting the Thackeray–Yates quarrel had
not been entirely forgiven, or perhaps Smith had taken offence at Trollope's
recent intimation that his text was being tampered with.

128. To GEORGE SMITH. 8 January.
Mrs. Reginald Smith.

Suffolk Street.   Wednesday night.
8 Jany 61
My dear Smith.

I have only just got your note. The Civil Service Gazette I think I may say did not report the lecture. The Morning Post, Daily News & Telegraph did. I send you the Telegraph as being the fullest.[1]

I shall probably call tomorrow between one & two, but you are always eating little plates of cold meat or pork pies at that time.

Yours always
ANTHONY TROLLOPE

129. To GEORGE SMITH. 26 January.
Mrs. Reginald Smith. Sadleir, *Commentary*, p. 215.

Waltham X.   26 Jany. 1861.
My dear Smith.

Thanks for your check for £26.5/. You w^d have been quite welcome to the article.[2] For such a subject the payment is more than liberal.

Indeed I consider it so high for—'padding' that I ought to make it known to the Saturday.[3]

Yours always
ANTY TROLLOPE

You have three! novels this time—which must be very depressing to the padding trade.

130. To ? 29 January.
Historical Society of Pennsylvania.

Trollope writes to an anonymous acquaintance to acknowledge the gift of a volume of poems.

[1] The lecture, the first of a series of five referred to in letter No. 125, *supra*, was delivered 4 Jan. 1861 at St. Martin's-Le-Grand. It received a full and enthusiastic report in the *Daily Telegraph*, 5 Jan. 1861, p. 3. An anonymous reply and clarification appeared in the same paper 24 Jan. 1861, p. 5.
[2] 'The Civil Service as a Profession', the *Cornhill Magazine*, iii (Mar. 1861), 214–28.
[3] The *Saturday Review* and the *Cornhill* continued for some years to live on rather unfriendly terms.

131. To MARY CHRISTIE. 16 February.
    Parrish Collection.

Waltham X, Feb. 16, 1861

My dear Mary,

I have received your note & one from Perry, and am very much distressed to hear what you tell me about your mother. And yet, if it be impossible that she should recover I do not know how one can wish that she should linger on in suffering. I do so wish I could have seen her again. Not that to her it could have been any pleasure, & to me, tho I delighted to see her & was always happy to see that the expression of her face & the tone of her voice was the same that it was in old days, yet it was very painful to feel that she would never be herself again. Of all friends that I have ever had out of my own family she has been the dearest.

I would send her my best & kindest love but that probably she may be too weak to be told of any one but those who are nearest to her. I am sure that she has known that I have loved her well.

It will be a great blank when she has gone. I shall have a line from some of you when the day does come. I wish I knew how I could be of service to you—

Dear Mary
Always yours affectionately
ANTHONY TROLLOPE

132. To GEORGE SMITH. 1 March. Waltham.
    Mrs. Reginald Smith.

Trollope thanks Smith for sending complimentary copies of the *Cornhill* to T. A. Trollope and John Tilley while his serial was in progress. 'I hope you will continue to send me one as I shall still consider myself on the staff.'

133. To ? 13 March. Chelmsford.
    Parrish Collection.

Trollope declines a dinner invitation at Ongar. He has been hunting: 'We had a wretched day of it today—ploughing about thro the mud & rain—all day in the woods—our great success was the digging out of one fox. The run was 10 minutes. The digging out 50—'

134. To GEORGE SMITH. 24 March. Waltham Cross.
Not traced. Sadleir's transcript.

Trollope asks for copies of the three-volume edition of *Framley Parsonage* for himself, Tilley, Merivale, and the Post Office Library. 'Now that you have two houses seeing you is out of the question. You are always just gone to the other place, or at any rate just going.'

135. To DOROTHEA SANKEY.[1] 24 March.
Donald F. Hyde.

In a Sotheby catalogue (1942) the following was called 'one of the most extraordinary letters ever offered for sale'. It provoked vigorous controversy in the press,[2] but every informed student considers it to be a Trollopian joke.

Waltham Cross
March 24, 1861[3]

My dearest Miss Dorothea Sankey

My affectionate & most excellent wife is as you are aware, still living—and I am proud to say her health is good. Nevertheless it is always well to take time by the forelock and be prepared for all events. Should anything happen to her, will you supply her place—as soon as the proper period of decent mourning is over.

Till then I am your devoted Servant
ANTHONY TROLLOPE

136. To GEORGE SMITH. 31 March. Waltham.
Mrs. Reginald Smith.

Trollope acknowledges his copies of *Framley Parsonage*. 'It is not your holydays that make you so difficult of access, but that double counting house —at each of which you spend 10 minutes ten times a day, living the best part of your life in cabs.'

[1] Clement Sankey Best-Gardner (*Memorials of the Family of Sankey*, 1207–1880 [priv. ptd., 1880]) lists Dorothea Sankey as the seventh child of Matthew Villiers Sankey of Coolmore, Co. Tipperary, Ireland. Since her father died in 1815, she was at least 45 years of age in 1861. She did not marry. Another Sankey whom the Trollopes knew well (see letter No. 885, *infra*) was her brother Jacob Hierom Sankey, who was married in 1844, as were the Trollopes.

[2] See the *New York Times*, 12 Aug. 1942, p. 17; 13 Aug. p. 18; 16 Aug. pp. 2, 9; 18 Aug. p. 20. See also Michael Sadleir, 'Trollope's Proposals', *Times Literary Supplement*, 10 Aug. 1946; Alban F. L. Bacon, 'Friend of Trollope's', *The Spectator*, clxxvii (6 Dec. 1946), 613, with discussion 13 Dec., p. 644 and 20 Dec., p. 676.

[3] As it appeared in the *New York Times* the letter is misdated 1851, the error being perpetuated in all subsequent accounts.

137. To Mrs. S. C. Hall.[1] 7 April.
Parrish Collection.

Waltham House
Waltham Cross.
7 April 1861

My dear Mrs. Hall.

I am much flattered by your kind offer to join your staff. As you say, my Cornhill tale has at last come to an end; but I have already begun another which is coming out monthly in a separate form. I have also two other engagements with publishers, and the three together would prevent my doing you justice, if I were to accede to your tempting proposal at present. The time may however come when, if you are of the same mind, I may join your establishment for a while.

very faithfully yours
ANTHONY TROLLOPE

138. To George Henry Lewes. 7 April.
Mrs. E. S. Ouvry.

Waltham Cross, April 7, 1861

My dear Lewes,

I must consider your letter as in some degree special, and give it a special answer.

You take me too closely au pied de la lettre as touching husbands & lovers. As to myself personally, I have daily to wonder at the continued run of domestic & worldly happiness which has been granted me;—to wonder at it as well as to be thankful for it. I do so, fearing that my day, also, of misery must come;—for we are told by so many teachers of all doctrines that pain of some sort is mans lot. But no pain or misery has as yet come to me since the day I married; & if any man should speak well of the married state, I should do so.

But I deny that I have done other. There is a sweet young blushing joy about the first acknowledged reciprocal love, which

[1] Anna Maria Hall, usually known as Mrs. S. C. Hall (1800–81), was a prolific writer of the pale sort and editor of the *St. James's Magazine*, to which reference is here made. Trollope subsequently (Sept. 1861) contributed to her periodical an essay on 'Our National Gallery'. See letter No. 141, *infra.*

is like the bouquet of the first glass of wine from the bottle—
It goes when it has been tasted. But for all that who will confuse
the momentary aroma with the lasting joys of the still flowing
bowl? May the Bowl still flow for both of us, and leave no touch
of headache.

When do you go Alpwards? & what do you do before that?
I shall be here from Sunday 14<u>th</u> to Friday (morning) 19<u>th</u> but
with no one in the house but wife & boys. Again from Monday
23<u>rd</u>, to Sunday 28<u>th</u> & then shall have friends—who will like to
meet you. Can you name a day for either period? Of course a man
who comes here sleeps here.

Yours always
ANTHONY TROLLOPE

139. To ? ANNA C. STEELE.[1] 10 May.
University of Virginia.

Suffolk Street May 10—1861

My dear Anna—

Yes; I understand it all, & have gone thro' it all myself.
But of the first book of mine that was published in a cheap form I
did cut out over 64 pages,—working very painfully in the doing
of it. Since that I have been careful so to reduce myself in the
first writing, that I have had nothing to cut out.

If it be impossible, or very disagreeable with you, you shall
not be asked; but before I see Chapman I think it well to write
to you & explain. The 32 pages—(he does not ask 64—) need
not be elided in one place, nor even in 30 places, but it may be
possible that by going thro' the work you might find passages
the omission of which would not do material damage.

Now on to Chapman & his reasons;—which are reasonable.
In the first place he sent word to you proposing to call upon you
but found you gone;—& therefore had no alternative but writing.

Of course in all cheap editions the margin of profit is comparatively small and depends upon a large sale. But if the expenses be much greater than that generally incurred, the small

---

[1] Anna Caroline Wood Steele (d. 1914), daughter of Trollope's friend
Lady Wood, was a minor novelist who published with Chapman & Hall.
The book referred to is probably her *Gardenhurst*.

margin of profit suffers much. Now the paper for an extra two sheets—viz 32 pages, and the extra setting up, of course costs money—and in a 5/ volume this cannot be remedied by closer printing, as it can in the 2- or 3 vol- edition. Again one of those volumes if too thick & fat loses in attractiveness of appearance, & all that tells on the sale. So much I say that you may know that your own interests as well as Chapmans would be served by your reducing the matter.

Of course to an author all these material considerations are vile bonds, repressing the divine afflatus— But the divine afflatus has to suffer, where pecuniary views force themselves forward. Remember that I & a dozen better than I am have to tuck ourselves into contracted limits every month.

However you shall not be compelled if it goes utterly against the grain with you. Think it over again & then let me have another line—to Waltham.

Yours always
ANTY TROLLOPE

At any rate you must not blame Chapman who spoke to me first. He is decidedly right to ask—for your interest as well as his own.

140. TO JOHN EVERETT MILLAIS. 1 June.
Parrish Collection.

My dear Millais.

It strikes me I said I would send you an order for my lecture—[1] and therefore do so— Do not consider that I suppose you to be bound to come. It will be a horrid bore;—tho perhaps not so bad as dining at the M House.[2]

Yours always
ANTHY TROLLOPE

Cambridge   June 1, 1861

I quite forget all your legitimate addresses.

----

[1] For some reason the lecture was not given. See letter No. 141, *infra*.
[2] Mansion House: the Lord Mayor's residence and the scene of many banquets.

141. To GEORGE SMITH. 11 June. Waltham.
Not traced.

'I send the lecture—unlectured— I have reduced it as much as I well can.'[1]

142. To GEORGE SMITH. 16 June. Waltham Cross.
Mrs. Reginald Smith.

Trollope refers to 'positive villainy' in the mix-up of spectacle cases after a party at Smith's. He adds: 'All right about the 3 articles—say 16 pages each. You wont put the name of course. I dont want to be tarred & feathered before my time.'[2]

143. To GEORGE SMITH. 26 June.
Not traced. Sadlier, *Commentary*, p. 216.

*   *   *

I should like to have a little chat with you about your proposition. There are two drawbacks to your offer. In the first place you want the copyright. And in the next place you will, I presume, wish to extend the publication over a considerable time.

Presuming the novel to be intended for the magazine—which would be the manner of publication I should prefer—it would extend over 20 months. The money stretched over that time, with an interdict against other writing of a similar class, would as you will see, not come to so much as it looks.

Therefore before I give a definite answer I should like to see a little more of your plans.

Of course you would not bring the novel out separately. It must either be for the magazine or as a separate serial. As the latter it would run over 16 months; but in that case could not commence till November or October 1862.

I could not of course give it you, binding myself down against

[1] The *Cornhill* records do not show any article by Trollope in the next few months. Smith apparently rejected it. Trollope then sent it to Mrs. Hall's *St. James's Magazine*, where it appeared in September as 'Our National Gallery'. The subject would, of course, account for Millais's interest. I quote from Mr. Sadleir's transcript.

[2] I do not find any such articles, and Sir John Murray tells me that the records of the *Cornhill*, though admittedly imperfect, do not show further contributions by Trollope in the following months.

other similar writing, till I knew something more as to your wishes as to time etc. . . . I shall probably be in town this day week, i.e. next Wednesday. Will it be city or west end on that day?

You will thus get your quid piecemeal. But I will have my quo in a lump when it is finished.[1]

*   *   *

144. TO GEORGE SMITH. 30 June. Waltham Cross. *Mrs. Reginald Smith.*

Trollope sends the manuscript of the first number of *Brown, Jones and Robinson* and invites Smith to Waltham House for a week-end.

145. TO MRS. S. C. HALL. 3 July. Waltham Cross. *Parrish Collection.*

Trollope sends Mrs. Hall his lecture: 'Our National Gallery.' 'I go away next month. Perhaps you will cause your Chancellor of the Exchequer to send me his check before I do so.'

146. TO GEORGE HENRY LEWES. 3 July. *Mrs. E. S. Ouvry.*

(Waltham House,
Waltham Cross.)
Wednesday July 3—1861.

My dear Lewes.

I cannot resist the triple temptation you offer me, & will be with you tomorrow at 5 PM, to dinner. I confess I should very much like to meet Carlyle, but imagine he is a man who does not like being entered in upon by everybody—Mihi cura non mediocris inest fontes ut adire remotos atq haurire queam vitae praecepta—,[2] on you however be the responsibility if in such a matter you do what you should not. I suppose I can get down from our station by train at 11.30 pm.

Yours always
ANTHONY TROLLOPE

[1] This letter describes negotiations for the publication of *The Small House at Allington*, which was serialized in the *Cornhill*, Sept. 1862–Apr. 1864.
[2] Horace, *Satires*, ii. 4. l. 94.

147. To JOHN TILLEY. 4 July.
  General Post Office, London.

For the Secretary

I agree altogether with Mr Good,[1] and think that the moveable indicator is not required in places for which these boxes are intended, and would be too complicated for the class of persons by whom they would be worked.

An attempt of such a kind, if a failure, places the Office in great difficulty, and I think that the cases of failure would be very numerous.[2]

ANTHONY TROLLOPE
July 4, 1861.

148. To GEORGE SMITH. 9 July.
  Mrs. Reginald Smith.

(Waltham House,
Waltham Cross.)
July 9, 1861

My dear Smith.

To save you trouble I have had your agreement copied, & have signed & now send the copy. If you wish to have it in your own writing I will sign another.

The agreement as drawn out is in accordance with what passed between us; but there are points I don't quite like. You have I believe a 2/6 set of novels. I trust it will not suit your views to put it into that, as your doing so would go far to prevent any after publication at a higher rate—

I find I have given uncommon short measure for the first number of B. J. & R—barely over 15 pages. I hate short measure as I do poison; but I hate inserting little bits to lengthen a chapter. Will it suit if I make some other number somewhat longer? If the exigencies of the magazine require 16 in the next number, I will do you another page. Let me know this at once.

Yours always
ANTHONY TROLLOPE

G Smith Esq

---

[1] J. P. Good, Surveyor, Gloucester district.
[2] Postal Min. No. E. 9,586/71.

149. To KATE FIELD. 9 August.
Boston Public Library. Sadleir, *Commentary*, p. 217.

My dear Kate.

The great distance, added to my bald head, may perhaps justify me in so writing to you. I thank you heartily for your letters, one of which I have already sent off in a note from myself begging that rooms may be kept for us in the Tremont House.[1]

Has not this battle been terrible?[2] The worst of it is, that by no event could a stronger presage of long bloodshed be given. Had the Southerners been thrashed it would have led to some compromise; but victory on the part of the Southerners can lead to none. It is very sad, and one cannot but feel that the beginning of the end has not yet come.

You were thinking of returning.[3] But as you say nothing about it, and as I hear nothing of it from others, I suppose your plans are altered. I can not but think that Florence is at present the better residence for you.

Remember me most kindly to Cleopatra—if the sacrifice be still incomplete.
                              Yours always most sincerely
                                ANTHONY TROLLOPE
                                Waltham Cross
                                Augt. 9, 1861

150. To HENRY T. TUCKERMAN.[4] 1 November.
    Not traced.[5]

*   *   *

We are alarmed at the idea of an Embargo. I hope it is only a maneuvre [*sic*] of the Administration. . . . No man can have ⟨a⟩ greater or better object than that of making Englishmen understand Americans & Americans English.

*   *   *

[1] On 24 Aug. Trollope left for the United States on an official postal mission. The Tremont House was a well-known hotel in Boston.

[2] The first battle of Bull Run, 21 July 1861.

[3] To the United States. The Fields were in Boston by October.

[4] Henry T. Tuckerman (1813–71), essayist, biographer, poet. In his *America and Her Commentators* (New York, 1864, pp. 232–44) Tuckerman reviews at length Trollope's *North America*. He praises the book in general, but censures Trollope's inadequacy of preparation.

[5] This excerpt was published in the Anderson Galleries Catalogue of the Edwin W. Coggeshall sale, 25–27 Apr. 1916, item 597.

151. To GEORGE SMITH. 3 November.
Mrs. Reginald Smith.

(Waltham House,
Waltham Cross.)
November 3—1861

My dear Smith.

Many many thanks for your thoughtful remembrance of a poor author's worldly wants.

I have not seen Mr Millais since I don't know what distant time, & have said nothing to him about those five illustrations. Is he not still in Scotland?

As regards the last three numbers Mrs Millais wrote to 'your' Mr Williams for the subjects—& I sent them thro Mr Williams, —while you were gambling at Homburgh— Guided by this I have supposed he has wished to have his subjects closely marked out—I will go on doing so—& w^d suggest that you s^d always send the paper to him. If he chooses to change the subject I shall not complain. I feel however that the author can select the subjects better than the artist—having all the feeling of the story at his fingers' end.

Yours always
A. T.

152. KATE FIELD. 5 November.
Boston Public Library. Sadleir, *Commentary*, p. 218.

New York   November 5, 1861

My dear Kate,

I am amused by the audacity of your letter. Ever since we have been here we have been abusing you for not keeping your word. You told us that we should find you in the neighbourhood of New York. That you would let us know your address there or thereabouts. And that we were to trust you to meet us—not at Boston, but New York. Now you turn upon us as tho' we were to blame.

However we will forgive you on condition that you remain at the address named till next Tuesday—this day week. We shall reach Boston that evening, & will make you out very soon. I suppose you could not come up to us that evening.

You write about sending my wife home as tho' she were as free from impediments in this world as your happy self. She has a house, and children & cows & horses and dogs & pigs—and all the stern necessities of an English home. Nor could a woman knock about in winter, as we have both done during the autumn. But we shall be a fortnight in Boston & I do hope we may have a good time of it. I can assure you that in looking forward to it, I do not count a little on you. I have been real angry with you this week for not turning up.

Yours always
ANTHONY TROLLOPE

153. To RICHARD HENRY DANA, Jr.[1] 22 November. *Massachusetts Historical Society.*

Tremont House
22 Nov. 1861

My dear Mr. Dana,

Mrs Trollope and I are very sorry that we are prevented from going to you on Monday evening. We dine that day with Mr Sturgis.[2] Mrs Trollope leaves, and returns home on Wednesday by the Cunard packet. She will however go out to Cambridge on Monday morning and will call on Mrs Dana. I am very sorry that we have been so unlucky in missing you—

Very faithfully yours
ANTHONY TROLLOPE

154. To ? 26 November. Boston. *Haverford College Library.*

Trollope complies with a request for an autograph, 'attaching very small value to the present'.

155. To CHARLES ELIOT NORTON.[3] 27 November. Boston. *Harvard College Library.*

Trollope asks for confirmation of the date of a dinner engagement.

---

[1] This is the first of a series of letters between Trollope and Richard Henry Dana, Jr. (1815–82), author of the famed *Two Years Before the Mast.*

[2] Probably William Sturgis (1782–1863), a wealthy Boston merchant and statesman. For thirty-two consecutive years he was either a member of the Massachusetts House of Representatives or state senator.

[3] Charles Eliot Norton (1827–1908), the famed Harvard professor of fine arts, intimate friend of great men of letters, and editor of Carlyle's letters.

156. To WILLIAM BARLOW LEE. 7 December.
Philadelphia. *Columbia University Library.*

Through the mediation of Dr. Lothrop,[1] Trollope negotiates with Lee
for rooms in Washington, where he arrives on the 17th.

157. To KATE FIELD. 17 December.
Boston Public Library. Sadleir, *Commentary*, p. 217.

305, I Street
Washington,
Dec 17, 1861

My dear Kate,

You will be surprised to hear from me again so soon, but I
want to know whether that lecture which we heard from
Everett at Roxbury has been published; and if so I want to get
it.[2] Can you let me know?

I am in a lamentable position. I have an anthrax on my forehead and can not get out of the house. I have been to see no one
since I came here and am all alone in my lodgings. A doctor has
chopped it across twice, as you see in the following picture.
[See p. 98.]
The cross means the two chops. But the chops will keep healing
and the thing which has collected itself inside will not come out.
Tomorrow it is to be chopped again and the chops cauterized to
prevent them healing. All this is pleasant especially as I am
anxious to get out and see the people before war is declared. I
wish you were here to condole with me and get yourself scolded.
There will be war if those two horrid men are not given up.[3]

[1] Dr. Samuel Kirkland Lothrop (1804–86), the clergyman at the Brattle
Square Unitarian Church, Boston. Trollope's private account-books for
the 1860s and early 1870s, preserved by Miss Muriel Trollope, frequently
indicate engagements as well as expenses. They show that he arrived in
Boston on 5 Sept. and dined at Dr. Lothrop's the next evening with Sumner,
Palfrey, *et al.* The following morning he went to Dr. Lothrop's church.

[2] Edward Everett (1794–1865), Harvard professor, editor of the *North
American Review*, congressman, governor of Massachusetts, senator, and
peerless orator in the florid style. His famous speech 'The Causes and Conduct of the Civil War' was delivered sixty-two times. Trollope's account-
book shows that he heard it at Roxbury on 22 Nov. It is to be found in
Everett's *Orations and Speeches on Various Occasions*, 4 vols. (Boston, 1868),
iv. 464–89. For Trollope's opinion of Everett's lecture see *North America*,
2 vols. (London, 1866), i. 279–82.

[3] Slidell and Mason.

you see in the following
picture.

my forehead

The cross means the two chops. But
the chops will keep healing and
the thing which has collected
itself inside will not come out.
So morrow it is to be chopped
afresh and the chops cauterised
to prevent their healing. All this
is pleasant certainly as I
am anxious to get out to see
the people before war is
declared. I wish you were here
to condole with me and enter

I wish Wilkes and his whole cargo had gone to the bottom.[1] I am no lawyer, but I felt from the first that England would not submit to have her ships stopped and her passengers hauled about and taken off. The common sense of the thing is plain, let all the wigged fogies of the Admiralty courts say what they will. Because you quarrel with your wife nobody else is to be allowed to walk the streets quietly! I expect we shall be in Boston before long, shaking hands with you & embracing and crying, as I get on board the Cunard boat with my head tied up in a huge linseed poultice—as it is now.

Tell me about the lecture.

Yours ever
A. T.

158. To SALMON P. CHASE. 31 December.
Washington. *Historical Society of Pennsylvania.*

Trollope writes a formal note in the third person arranging to meet Chase in a few days. (Salmon Portland Chase (1808–73), United States senator, governor of Ohio, was secretary of the treasury during the Civil War, thereafter Chief Justice of the Supreme Court.)

1 8 6 2

159. To FREDERIC CHAPMAN.[2] 1 January.
Parrish Collection.

Washington, 1 Jany 1861 [1862]

My dear Chapman,

Thanks for your letter. I did recommend marriage to you, and am glad you have been so docile. I hope you got my letter of congratulation.

I know nothing of the 'Public Opinion'[3]—never to the best of my belief having heard the name. Little[4] wrote to me asking leave to put the stories into some paper. He may have named

[1] Commodore Wilkes of the ship *Trent.*

[2] Frederic Chapman (1823–95), younger brother of Edward Chapman, became head of the firm in 1864 at the latter's retirement. This letter is published in Sadleir, *Commentary,* p. 231.

[3] Five of the stories from *Tales of All Countries,* Second Series, were first published in *Public Opinion.* See Sadleir, *Bibliography,* pp. 49–50.

[4] See letter No. 110, *supra.*

that. I sent his letter to R Bell;[1] and as I had before acted in the matter on Mr Bell's opinion, I gave him authority either to give or refuse the permission which Little requested. My im pression is that the stories have been published without any permission.

I have sent no articles to the Cornhill, and have told Geo Smith that I could not send any. I found that my doing so would interfere with other work.

You sent me an article on 'Mr Trollope', cut out of some paper. From what paper was it cut? The author of it criticizes my writings, pointing out their weakness, and in doing so follows the proper line of his profession. But he goes beyond that when he takes upon himself to analize my motives in writing. His charge is that I write for money. Of course I do;—as does he also— It is for money that we all work, lawyers, publishers, authors and the rest of us. If we do bad work we shall not get paid for it,—and I like others must feel myself to be governed by that law or else shall fall to the ground. If my work be bad let him so tell his readers and there his work should end.

But I have worse to say of this critic than that. He insinuates that I have published under my name the writings of other people. He does not dare to say this; but he says that which is intended to make his readers so believe. This is in every way un fair & cowardly. No man should insinuate such a charge, unless he has strong ground to believe it to be true. This man can have no such ground. To those who know me I need make no assurance that such a charge is false.

So we are to have no war. I for one am very glad— The Americans just at present are rather quiet on the subject; but they will not forget to tell us about it, when their present troubles are over.

I am greatly shocked at the Princes death.[2] The effect on the Queen will be terrible.

always faithfully yours
ANTHONY TROLLOPE

I am very sorry to hear of Edward Chapman's accident. Pray

---

[1] Robert Bell (1800–67), a prominent journalist best known for his editions of the English poets, was Trollope's close friend and literary associate.

[2] Prince Albert died 14 Dec. 1861.

remember me to him. Keep the cigars for me—like a true man.
I shall have none if not them. Thanks for paying. If you wish you
shall have some when I arrive. How many are there?

160. To KATE FIELD. 4 January.
Boston Public Library. Sadleir, *Commentary,* p. 221.

Washington 4. Jany 1862.

My dear Kate,

All manner of happy new years to you and to your mother.

Why no story? I fear you are idle—that you spend your time in
running after false gods—Wendall Philips [*sic*],[1] woman Doten[2]
& so on, seeking the excitement of ultra ideas and theoretical
progress, while you begrudge the work of your brain, and the
harder work of your fingers and backbone. Those lectures are
but an intellectual idleness, an apology for sitting without a book
to read or a skirt to hem or a shirt to fell[3] instead of with them.
You want to go ahead of other folk—you know you do; but you
wish to do it lazily;—or rather you are lazy in your mode of
wishing it. You would whistle for a storm like a witch; but
storms now a days will not come for whistling. You must sit
down with a trumpet and blow at it till your cheeks would split.
If you'll do that, something of a puff of wind will come at last.
Now I hope you will find yourself well rated, & will send me
your story off hand.

So Slidell & Mason are gone. I will not argue with you about
them in a letter. To do so fairly would take hours and pages.
Cobden[4] is no statesman—never even tried his hand at state-
craft. As for Bright[5]—of course, if he or any other man will

[1] Wendell Phillips (1811–84) was a prominent Boston Abolitionist.
For Trollope on Phillips see *North America,* i. 282–4.
[2] Elizabeth Doten (1829–?), a minor poetess and short-story writer who
attracted Kate Field because of her interest in spiritualism.
[3] To fell = to sew or hem.
[4] Richard Cobden (1804–65) was a statesman who achieved wide public
acclaim as perhaps the foremost leader of the Anti-Corn Law League. He
twice visited America, and with his friend Bright supported the Northern
cause in the Civil War.
[5] John Bright (1811–89), orator and statesman who with Cobden formed
'The Commons League' for financial and parliamentary reform in 1849
and who with Cobden signalled the emergence of the manufacturing class as
a force in British politics.

re-echo American ideas and American desires, Americans, and you as one, will return the echo again. But he has been alone in England. He did not even dare to make that speech in a large city. But the men are gone, & thank God we shall have no war. Do not think that I triumph because they are gone. I only triumph because I need not quarrel with you and yours.

The blaze on my forehead has gone out, & I have been starring it about with all my accustomed personal attractions. I have seen most of the bigwigs here except the President, but have not as yet been to the White House. I spent four days in the camp, (without washing) and had quite enough of it. I think of leaving this for Harrisburg[1] and Cincinnati on the 12th or 14th.

Yours always dear Kate—
Very affectionately
ANTH TROLLOPE

161. To JAMES T. FIELDS.[2] 4 January.
Massachusetts Historical Society.

My dear Fields.

You were to have given me Longfellows autograph—for my wife (She has just sent me the enclosed). Pray do— She had but a sorry passage home, but is now settled peaceably among her pigs and poultry.

I go hence to Cincinnati on 12th Inst. That at least is my programme. I shall beat you up about 15 of March on my way home. Heavens, how quickly the time goes.

I have been over in the lines spending some days. It was dull enough—& awfully cold!! I am not given greatly to military pursuits. I went down to Mount Vernon, where we might all have gone easily enough, & shed a metaphorical tear over the Great Mans grave. Ah me! that they should now be fighting over the spot.

Ch Sumner[3] told me to-day that Dana is in town but I have not

---

[1] Capital of the State of Pennsylvania.

[2] James T. Fields (1817–81) was editor of the *Atlantic Monthly* and a partner in the famous Boston publishing house of Ticknor and Fields.

[3] Charles Sumner (1811–74), a Boston lawyer who was one of the founders of the Republican party. As U.S. senator he strongly opposed the South before the war.

seen him. I shall try to do so— I am dining out & *teaing* out, & doing a deal of talk, but somehow the place is dull to me. I dont care for such convivialities if the people are merely strangers.

Yours always
ANTY TROLLOPE

305 I Street.   Washington.

Jany 4, 1861. [1862]

If you do not write before 12th address to Cincinnati. Fred Chapman writes in sombre strains as to trade— But that is the way with all you publishers when you write to us slaveys.

162. To KATE FIELD. 6 January.
Boston Public Library. Sadleir, *Commentary*, pp. 223.

Washington.   Jany 6. 1861 [1862]

Dearest Kate,

I am afraid my verdict about the enclosed will pain you. The lines are not manipulated—not cared for and worked out with patience and long thought as should I think be done with poetry. Fine poetry is not I think written by flashes. Take the ode to Liberty. 'Smile on,' and 'Union' surely form no rhyme. Nor do 'Freemen' and 'glee then.' But the thought and imagery of a poem is more important than the rhyme. Take the Susannah. 'Watch lady watch. Glow worms the night illume; Pulsating fire;—' So far, good, at any rate the idea is true if not new. But the fourth line upsets the metaphor altogether. The glow worm consumes nothing, & its fire is altogether innocent.

> Watch lady watch. Glow worms illume the night
> Pulsating fire. Your watching is as bright.

Then the image would have been entire throughout; tho the stanza would be not perhaps worth much.[1]

Jokes in poetry should be clear as crystal—& should be clear to all readers. But how many would catch the joke of the 'pragmatic sanction'? Besides the joke is untrue to itself, for the word pragmatic means nothing apart from the joke.

Poetry should be very slow work—slow, patient, and careless

[1] I have not been able to trace the publication of any of the poems which Trollope mentions.

of quick result. That is not your character. Philanthropical ratiocination is your line, not philandering amatory poetising. I will not say that poetry will not come. As you grow older and calmer, and as you learn to think slower and with less of individual blood in your thought, the gift of poetry may come to you. But I doubt that it is to be desired. Who but the very highest do anything as poets? What is the reputation of Poe or Holmes, or our own L.E.L.?[1] What good have they done? It is a mistake to suppose that prose is grander than poetry per se.[2] It may be so; and has been so. But it has been so in the hands of a few people on whom God has set a very special mark. Scott will be known by his novels & not by his poetry. As is Johnson also, by his prose. And also Irving. And also Landor.

Ah me. It gives me such pain to write this. I still believe in you as strongly as ever. I still think that if you will work, you will succeed. But I should have said, a priori, that you would do better as a writer of prose than of poetry. I still think so—and advise you accordingly.

I know how bitter this is. You'll say that it isn't, and you'll be good, and then you'll go about for a day or two with a heavy feeling of ill-treatment at your heart;—ill-treatment not from me, but from the world. I know from *much* experience how bitter are the sapient criticisms of one's elders on the effusions of one's youth! I too have written verses, and have been told that they were nought. I am very fond of you, and it grieves me to pain you. But that will be no consolation!

You will have understood that my late 'jobation' letter was written before yours came with the pieces of poetry. Take courage dear Kate, & stick to the story. If you don't like it, do it again. It is a great profession that of writing; but you must spoil much paper, & undergo many doubting, weary, wretched, hours. But I do think that you can write good nervous readable prose;— and I know that you have a mind capable of putting something into that vehicle.

Tom says. 'I *have* written to Kate Field.' Tom was [? has] no

---

[1] Letitia Elizabeth Landon (1802–38), a popular poetess of the pale sort, had been a friend of the Trollope family.

[2] Undoubtedly a slip of the pen; Trollope meant to write 'that poetry is grander than prose per se'.

special Florence news. I presume that you will by this have heard
from Rose. She said she should write to you. She had a bad time
going over:—but then she had made up her mind to have a bad
time.

My kind love to your mother. Do not let her be ill. I am trying
to manage to get South, but believe I shall fail.

Your affectionate friend

Thanks for woman Doten's effu-
sion. It is not bad; but not so good
to read as it was to hear.

A. T.

163. To Salmon P. Chase. 8 January.
Historical Society of Pennsylvania.

Private.   8 January 1862
305 I Street

Dear Sir—

Will you excuse me if I take up your time for a minute. Our
press in England has among other charges brought this accusa-
tion against you,—that you—(I do not mean the Secretary of
the Treasury but the United States people) are not willing to
take on yourselves any portion of the present cost of the war—
but are staving it off onto the shoulders of those who will follow
you. On my return to England I shall probably publish some
remarks referring more or less to the present state of the Country, and according to my views as at present taken, I shall endeavor to shew that this charge is not true. I do not myself think
that your present financial crisis will lead to any tremendous
future financial embarrassment:—but as far as I am at present
informed it seems that some change in your constitution must
be made before you can arrange the stock of your debt satisfactorily.

I venture to say this, not as supposing that my opinion can be of
any possible weight to you, but in order that you may be aware
of the subject on which I am very anxious to have an opportunity
of hearing you for five minutes. Should you however tell me that
you do not wish to speak to me on the matter, I shall not take it
the least in dudgeon; and shall quite understand that coming

from you such an answer will be in no way uncourteous. I can assure you that my views as regards your war in general are probably in accordance with your own.

Your faithful Servant

ANTHONY TROLLOPE

I shall do myself the honor of waiting on you on Saturday in accordance with your permission.

164. To KATE FIELD. 12 January.
   Boston Public Library.

Washington   12 Jany 1861 [1862]

My dear Kate,

I have put off your letter & have only one moment to tell you that my address will be St Louis. I shall be there 23 of this month, but shall not remain there. You had better now keep your story, as I shall be in a state of turmoil, and heaven knows where in regard to post offices. You speak of causes which prevent your working. Do you mean, your health? But you may have troubles and sorrows by the score of which I know nothing. It is so with our dearest friends. But God has been good to me and gives me no grievance of which I can not speak—unless it might be thought unmannerly to say that I have another horrible carbuncle on the small of my back (if my back has a small).

Your letter to me was written after receipt of my first, but before the receipt of my last. I fear I shall have pained you. The upshot of my criticism was meant to be this—that good work will require hard toil.

Rose writes in most lachrymose spirits, all my letters from the west having gone astray. I hope they have amused the Post office officials.

Yours always—just now in great trouble of haste.

A. T.

165. To JAMES T. FIELDS. 20 January.
   Henry E. Huntington Library.

Cincinnati.   January 20—1862.

My dear Fields. Many thanks for your note—and very many to Longfellow for his poem which Mrs Trollope will value much.

Who is the author of the enclosed? I want to know—also whether it is new or an old song? Did it appear in the Atlantic? Did Whittier write it?[1]

So you are going the whole hog for abolition. Well, it is consistent. But by Jove you are [a] bold fellow to do it now. I think it is a mistake. Abolition drove the South to Secession, & will make a return to [? former] times impracticable. You know I am no Southern or I should not venture to say so.

Fred Chapman is always in the dumps. If he do not make money hand over hand he thinks the world is coming to an end. Maybe it is.

I am just now going—God knows where. If you answer this at once address to St Louis. If not keep your answer till you hear again. But remember I want an answer about the nigger song;—which [?] if new, I will—'borrow.'

My kindest regards to your wife. I never saw a woman so ill used as she was that Sunday when you made her go down to dinner giving her only 30 seconds to brush her hair & do her fixings, —nor any woman who bore such ill usage so well.

Thanks greatly for your kind hospitality. I will write to you in full when I find myself returning,—if ever I return. I was not nursed in New England, & had no high schools in my diggings. So it is well that I can write at all,—let alone so unwriteable a name as my own.   Yours always

ANTHONY TROLLOPE

Should any letter come to you for me, keep it.

166. To MR. RUSSELL. ? January.
Not traced. From a photostat in the Parrish Collection.

At some length Trollope declines an engagement: 'I see that your dinner does not come off in presence of your own Lares, & you must therefore allow me to beg off. . . .' It is impossible to tell which of many persons named Russell in Washington at this time Trollope is addressing. Nor is it possible to establish the date more closely than that of Trollope's visit; *i.e.*, 14 December to 13 January. His account book shows that he dined with the Russells several times.

[1] The poem which Trollope enclosed is Whittier's 'Song of the Negro Boatmen'. It was published in the *Atlantic* (ix [Feb. 1862], 244) and became immediately popular. It was at once set to music by several composers. From the advertisements on the obverse of Trollope's clipping, I judge he found it in a Pittsburgh newspaper.

107

167. To KATE FIELD. 4 February.
Boston Public Library. Sadleir, *Commentary*, pp. 224–5.

My dear Kate,   Cairo.[1] 4. Febry. 1862

I was very glad to get your letter—and your pardon for my criticisms. As I hope to be in Boston by the end of this month, or quite early in March, I will not now say any more about the money. Miss Crow[2] says that you are not well. Is this so? I know that you are not a female Hercules. None but Englishwomen are. But I hope you are not really ill,—or, which is almost worse, —really ailing. If so I will not bully you again about writing.

M[r] Grew[3] was very civil to me at St Louis & also to a friend who was with me. D[r] Elliot[4] I also saw, but he was in affliction for the death of a child. I do not like the West. It is well to say it out at once. Boston I do like, and New York. I do not dislike the people at Washington, tho' the town itself is bad. At Phila-delphia I could get on very well. But I do not love the Westerns. They are dry, dirty, and unamusing. Till I came here I thought St Louis the dirtiest place in the world; but this place certainly bears the palm. The discussion of my military adventures I must put off till I see you. I am great in guns, bombs, shells, mortars and questions of gunpowder generally. Oh, what thieving, swind-ling, and lying there has been in the management of this war! How your unfortunate country has been plundered! Gunpowder that won't explode. Shells that won't burst. Blankets rotten as tinder. Water put up in oil casks. Ships sent to sea that can hardly hold their planks together! There have been crimes in the North worse than the sin of Buchanan & Floyd.[5]

[1] A town in Southern Illinois.
[2] Emma Crow was a close friend of Kate Field from childhood days in St. Louis. She later married the nephew of Charlotte Cushman, who was Kate's friend in Italy. Trollope had met them all in Florence. See Lilian Whiting, *Kate Field: a Record*, p. 33.
[3] I do not find such a person in Campbell & Richardson's *St. Louis Business Directory 1863*.
[4] Dr. William Eliot (1811–87) was a minister who became Chancellor of Washington University in St. Louis.
[5] James Buchanan (1791–1868), fifteenth President of the United States (1856–60), an ardent advocate of States' rights who appointed a number of Secessionists to important offices. One of these was John B. Floyd (1806–63), ex-governor of Virginia, who became Secretary of War, and who resigned from office to become ultimately a major-general in the Con-federate Army.

If you only want money to go to St Louis I will not pity your poverty. You are better at Boston. But if it was wanted to carry you to England, I would negotiate a loan for you under Mr Chase's wing among the Croesus's of Wall Street.

Write me a line, saying how you are, to Niagara Falls Post-office. My kind love to your mother.

Yours affectionately,
A. T.

I had some talk with Eliot about you. 'Let her marry a husband,' said he. 'It is the best career for a woman.' I agreed with him—and therefore bid you in his name as well as my own, to go & marry a husband.

168. To FREDERIC CHAPMAN. 13 February.
Berg Collection.

Cincinnati.   13 February, 1862.

My dear Chapman,

Mrs Trollope has written to me, asking me whether I would like to have a portion of my book on America printed on slips, ready for me when I return. I will tell you exactly how I stand about it, and leave you to decide as to the printing. I have finished two thirds of the whole, & shall have the MS completed by the middle of April. I propose that it shall be published by the middle of May.[1] You can have Vol I, ready for the printers, by April 3rd or 4th—and the second volume by instalments as quick as you may wish them. If under these circumstances, you think well to print, say half the first volume, on slips, you can write to Mrs Trollope for the first ten chapters. If you think you will have time after the 3rd or 4th April for the whole, so as to get it out by 15 or 20 May, you need not put yourself to the expense. I do not anticipate that there will be much change in the first chapters; tho there will doubtless be some.

Mrs Trollope says you are disappointed about the 1st vol of Orley Farm. Who the deuce buys the first volume of a book? As far as I can hear the novel is as well spoken of as any I ever wrote. I fear we made a mistake about the shilling.[2]

[1] It was.
[2] *Orley Farm* was published in two volumes at 11 shillings each instead of the usual 10.

For heavens sake pay my money in from month to month. If you do not I shall be overdrawing my account some fine morning.

I hope matrimony suits you. I shall be home by the 24 March.

Yours always
ANTHONY TROLLOPE

F Chapman Esq

169. TO RICHARD HENRY DANA, Jr. 1 April.
Massachusetts Historical Society.

Waltham House
Waltham Cross.
1 April 1862

My dear Mr Dana.

You know the old saying, Give an inch and you'll be asked for an ell. You have been so kind to me in that matter of judicial information that I am tempted to ask you to read two chapters of my book in order that any errors *in fact* may be corrected by your correct knowledge— They are on the Constitution and Judicature of your country. I take the written Constitution; and the mixed practice of your law Courts. You will perceive that my object is, not that of writing learned treatises on either subjects [*sic*], but of making representations which shall put them before Englishmen in a familiar light.

As to my opinions, of course they will not find favor with you. There must be much as to which in opinion any two men of the two countries must differ. You will disagree with me entirely as to the suspension of the writ of H. C.[1] (Can you tell me what is that H. C.?)—and probably also on other political conclusions to

[1] Trollope wrote, 'The executive [Lincoln] in suspending the privilege of the writ [of habeas corpus] without the authority of Congress, has committed a breach of the constitution' (*North America*, ii, 223). He contends that the suspension of the writ is a function of the Congress, not of the executive; that such action is a matter for deliberation and does not follow rebellion or invasion automatically; that in arbitrarily suspending the writ Lincoln and Seward were guilty of an unconstitutional act (*North America*, ii. 222–8). The constitutional problem raised here appears to be a very difficult one. The points at issue are by no means clear to-day. The leading authority, James G. Randall, says (*Constitutional Problems under Lincoln* [New York: Appleton, 1926], pp. 118–39) 'the weight of opinion would seem to incline to the view that Congress has the exclusive suspending power . . .'. Nevertheless, Lincoln acted and was not restrained by either Congress or the courts. For a further discussion see letter No. 171, *infra*.

which I have come. But perhaps your friendship will induce you to give me notice on the margin left for that purpose, of any *errors in facts* which I have made. You can write in ink as the MS sent to you will not go to the printers.

My book comes out on May 12—& you will therefore see that I want your corrections *at once*. Both chapters were written on my way home at sea—

It may be as well to divulge my political heresies & follies to none of my friends or enemies till I myself place myself in their power.

Oh—that my enemy would write a book.

With a grateful remembrance of your pleasant voice and a thoro' hope that I may soon hear it here I am

Dear Mr Dana

always faithfully yours

ANTHONY TROLLOPE

Do not prepay your parcel back to me. I have a few remaining privileges as a Post Office officer. Address. A Trollope

General Post Office

London.

I calculate the pages will come back by the Cunard of 23 April from N. York.

170. To GEORGE SMITH. 2 May. Waltham.
Not traced. Sadleir's transcript.[1]

*   *   *

I called this morning but I was a little too early. I will change the name, though I cannot as yet say what the name shall be. I will change it, as you don't like it, as I myself do not feel strongly in its favour. But I must say that your reason against it as touching Mrs B. Stowe's novel would not have much weight with me. Am I to eschew pearls because she has got one?[2] Not if I know it.

---

[1] The first paragraph of this letter is published in Sadleir, *Commentary*, p. 232.

[2] *The Small House at Allington* had been originally entitled *The Two Pearls of Allington*. Smith objected because Harriet Beecher Stowe's *The Pearl of Orr's Island* was then being serialized in England.

111

Can you tell me what was our agreement—or rather our understanding if there was no agreement—as touching the period up to which I was not to write any other serial. If I remember rightly I did make some offer to you in a note, saying that I would not do so for four, six, or eight months after the commencement of the Cornhill serial. But it has not been put into the agreement and I should like to know to what I am supposed to be bound. I rather think you suggested six months, and I, with my usual liberality, offered eight. I am willing to make it ten. But I am thinking of publishing (or rather of having published) a short story in Scotland in the latter half of next year.[1]

*   *   *

171. To RICHARD HENRY DANA, Jr. 10 May.
Massachusetts Historical Society.

(Waltham House,
Waltham Cross.)
May 10, 1862.

My dear Mr Dana,

I do not know how to thank you sufficiently for all that you have done for me. I only hope that you will believe me to estimate it not only as a valuable work but also as one of great friendship.

What you say as to keeping your name unmentioned in the matter is a thing of course. I should have been greatly gratified in owning all that I owe you; but in questions such as those under discussion, of course I cannot do so publicly, as in doing so I should seem to make you responsible for my heresies and also for my blunders.

As regards that one great question of the privilege of the writ of H. C. I must declare at once that you do not carry me with you. I have placed my own paragraphs, your notes, Storeys[2] com-

---

[1] *Rachel Ray.*

[2] Joseph Story (1779–1845), one of the foremost of American legal writers, associate justice of the Supreme Court at the age of 32, first professor of the Harvard Law School. His famous *Commentaries* were published 1832–45. Trollope undoubtedly refers to his three-volume work *On the Constitution* (1834).

mentaries, and Binneys[1] pamphlet in the hands of one of our best constitutional lawyers,—Spencer Follett,[2] a brother of the late W<u>m</u> Follett,[3]—and he declares my views to be in his judgement right, and also declares that such must have been Storeys views had Storey been alive. Of course I will not now trouble you with discussion of the matter. But I tell you so much in order that you may know that I have followed your advice in going to an English lawyer, and that I have not ventured to differ from you without support.

As regards other matters pointed out by you I think I have in every respect either adopted your suggestions, or modified my statements in accordance with your views. I have done this as to Madisons original opinions. As to the instructions to Senators. As to the introduction into Congress of Ministers. As to pledging (practical pledging) of Electors even before the time of Van Buren.[4] As to the conduct of Massachusetts with reference to the F. S. Law;[5] and in a certain respect as to my use of the words 'universal suffrage', explaining that I used them as they are generally used in this country. I have also altered a few words to which you have objected. 'Foul-mouthed.' 'Set' &tc.

But still there remains my great sin as regarding the H. C. (What is that H. C.?) And as to that you must put forth your energies and crush me in the Atlantic.

I will send you over a copy by the next Cunard if it be possible. Otherwise by the succeeding packet. In the mean time pray accept my expression of gratitude.

Most faithfully yours
ANTHONY TROLLOPE

[1] Horace Binney (1780–1875), the most distinguished member of the Philadelphia bar in his day, wrote in his series of three 'Habeas Corpus Pamphlets' a valuable constitutional treatise; that to which Trollope refers is *Privileges of the Writ of Habeas Corpus under the Constitution* (1862).
[2] Brent Spencer Follett (1810–87), barrister, chief registrar of the Land Registry Office.
[3] Sir William Webb Follett (1798–1845), solicitor-general under Sir Robert Peel and later attorney-general.
[4] Martin Van Buren (1782–1862), eighth president of the United States (1837–41).
[5] The Fugitive Slave Law of 1850 provided for the return to the South of escaped Negro slaves. It was widely ignored in the North.

172. To George Henry Lewes. 15 May.
Mrs. E. S. Ouvry.

(Waltham House,
Waltham Cross.)
15 May. 1862

My dear Lewes.

I know my letter will grieve you, but still I think I had better write it. They tell me at the Post Office that your son is not doing well. Nothing is said against his character,—i e against his character as to conduct or good feeling; but they say that he utterly fails in making himself useful. 'He is careless & very slow; and will not exert himself.' That is the report made to me, and I am moreover told that this has been so sharply felt that for this reason he has been sent back to the missing letter branch. I learn that his name has been taken off the list of candidates for the next step above him.

I fear that you will think me harsh to write in this way— But I am only doing so as I would be done by. I believe his defect to be this,—that he is more au fait in French or German than in English, and that he is awkward & slow in the use of his own language. If he wishes to remain in the office I would strongly counsel you to put him in the way of writing English quickly.[1] I need not tell you how such lessons are to be learned. The Secretary's Office at the G.P.O. is a very good office for a young man, if he can get his promotion in his turn. But it is anything but a good office if a man is to be continually passed over.

You should make him work at English in his after hours.

Very faithfully yours
Anthony Trollope

173. To ? 23 May. Wisbech.
Parrish Collection.

Trollope rejects a business proposition made to him by unnamed correspondents.

[1] Lewes apparently did so, for his son remained in the office until 1886, attaining the rank of Principal Clerk (Lower Section).

174. To MARY [? CHRISTIE]. 2 June. 193 Piccadilly.
Parrish Collection.

Trollope arranges a week-end party with Mary and Owen [? Grant]
to meet Tom Trollope.

175. To the REV. S. W. KING. 28 June. Norwich.
Parrish Collection.

Trollope plans to call on King when he returns to town. Samuel William
King (1821–68) was rector of Saxlingham-Nethergate, Norfolk. He was
an amateur entomologist and geologist whom Trollope had met at the
Alpine Club. There is a report of an amusing speech by Trollope at the
Alpine Club in *A Mid-Victorian Pepys: the Letters and Memoirs of Sir William
Hardman*, ed. S. M. Ellis (New York: Doran, 1923), pp. 143–4.

176. To GEORGE ELIOT. 28 June.
Mrs. E. S. Ouvry.

Waltham Cross   June 28—1862
My dear Mrs Lewes.

I have just read the first number of Romola and I cannot
refrain from congratulating you. If you can, or have, kept it up
to the end you will have done a great work. Adam Bede, M^rs
Poyser, & Marner [?] have been very dear to me; but excellent
as they are, I am now compelled to see that you can soar above
even their heads. The description of Florence,—little bits of
Florence down to a close nail, and great facts of Florence up to
the very fury of life among those full living nobles,—are wonderful in their energy and in their accuracy. The character of Romola
is artistically beautiful,—a picture exceeded by none that I know
of any girl in any novel. It is the perfection of pen painting,—
and you have been nobly aided by your artist. I take it for
granted that it is Leighton.[1] The father also of Romola is excellent.

Do not fire too much over the heads of your readers. You have
to write to tens of thousands, & not to single thousands. I say
this, not because I would have you alter ought of your purpose.

[1] The artist was Frederic Leighton (1830–96), later Baron Leighton of
Stretton, distinguished painter, President of the Royal Academy of Art, 1878.

That were not worth your while, even though the great numbers were to find your words too hard. But because you may make your full purpose compatible with their taste—

I wonder at the toil you must have endured in getting up your work,—wonder and envy. But I should never envy your success, or the great appreciation of what you have done that will certainly come,—probably today, but if not, then tomorrow.[1]

Yours very heartily
ANTHONY TROLLOPE

177. To OWEN GRANT. 10 August. Waltham Cross.
   Parrish Collection.

Trollope congratulates Grant on his approaching marriage. Owen Edward Grant (1831–1921), long a clerk in the Printed Paper Office of the House of Lords, was probably a grandson of Colonel Grant of Harrow.

178. To KATE FIELD. 23 August.
   Boston Public Library. Sadleir, *Commentary*, pp. 227–8.

(Waltham House,
Waltham Cross.)

August 23—1862—

My very dear Kate—

I forget when I wrote to you last, but I hope it was not very long ago, & that in writing now I display my own great merit rather than satisfy any just claim of yours. However I have a very nice long letter from you to answer, & therefore acknowledge that you are a fit *object* for my generosity.

You will be very glad to hear that Theo is improving very greatly and that Tom is becoming tranquil— At one time what with four doctors, & his determination to believe the worst, he was nearly crazed. He would bear her loss very badly. I begin to believe that he will not be called on to endure such sorrow.

---

[1] Of this letter George Eliot recorded in her journal under date of 30 June 1862: 'This morning I had a delightful, generous letter from Mr. Anthony Trollope about "Romola".' See *George Eliot's Life as Related in Her Letters and Journals*, ed. J. W. Cross (New York: Crowell, n.d.), p. 427.

You will not be glad to hear me declare that your dear friend (and my dear friend also) Miss Blagden is a plague. She has no idea of business, and in her shandiness greatly perplexes those who want to befriend her. She got me to sell a MS of hers—& then bargained about it with some one else, because she did not get from me a letter by return post,—she having given me no address! So I have to go back from my word with the publisher! Don't you tell her that I grumble, for I don't want to make her unhappy. But she is a plague.

Yes: I was mean not to give you my book. I wrote to you about it before you wrote to me,—blowing me up—which you did with a vengeance—! I was mean. I had to buy all the copies I gave, and did not think your beaux—(I cannot remember how to spell the word) worth 24/-. There! I have owned the fact, and you may make the most of it. But, dear Kate, I would give you ten times twenty-four shillings ten times over in any more pleasant way, fitting for yourself. One gives presentation copies to old fogies and such like. When you write a book, you will of course give one to me. You are a young lady.—A ring, a lock of my hair, or a rosebud would be the proper present for you; not two huge volumes weighing no end of pounds. Believe me, I would have been wrong to send it to you.

Your criticisms are in part just—in part unjust,—in great part biassed by your personal (—may I say love?) for the author. The book is vague. But remember, I had to write a book of travels, not a book of political essays—and yet was anxious so to write my travels, as to introduce, on the sly, my political opinions. The attempt has not been altogether successful. The book is regarded as readable, and that is saying as much for it, as I can say honestly. Your injustice regards chiefly abolition ideas; Freement [? Freedom] & such like; on which matters we are poles asunder.

What am I to say about your present state? I am not myself so despondent, as it seems to me are many of you Yankees. Things will go worse before you gain your object than I thought they would;—but still you will ultimately gain it. This conscription is very bad. Was it absolutely necessary? My feeling is that a man should die rather than be made a soldier against his will. One's country has no right to demand everything. There is much that is higher & better & greater than one's country. One is patriotic only because one is too small & too weak to be cosmopolitan. If a country can not get along without a military conscription, it had better give up—& let its children seek other ties. But I do not on this account despair. It was not to be supposed that in doing so much all should be done without a mistake.

Thanks for your newspapers. They are, however, very bad. I thank you as a friend of mine once thanked his God. 'I thanked God', he said, 'for a quiet night. But he did not give me one wink of sleep!' I say as much to you for the newspapers; but I can never learn anything from them.

We are not going to Italy this autumn. But in the spring. We are building a house,—or making ours larger, & it does not suit to be away. The bricklayers would run away with the forks.

I am now writing a letter to be published about that beast Harper.[1] But as I write it I cannot but feel that this is no time for such matters. Why don't they draught him & send him to New Orleans?

I was thinking to-day that nature intended me for an American rather than an Englishman. I think I should have made a better American. Yet I hold it higher to be a bad Englishman, as I am, than a good American,—as I am not. If that makes you angry, see if you would not say the reverse of yourself.

Tell me whom you see, socially, & what you are doing socially and as regards work. I didn't at all understand how you are living, where—with whom—or on what terms. But I don't know that it matters. How little we often know in such respects of those we love dearest. Of what I am at home, you can have no idea;— not that I mean to imply that I am of those you love dearest. And yet I hope I am.

I am not writing at home,—in spite of the great red words—[2] or Rose would send her love. I send mine to your mother & my kind regards to your aunt.[3] To yourself—full assurance of true friendship and love.

A. T.

Write often.

[1] See letter No. 180, *infra*.
[2] The engraved address on Trollope's stationery.
[3] Cordelia Riddle Sanford, wife of a Newport millionaire.

179. To W. HEPWORTH DIXON. 31 August. Cromer.[1]
Capt. F. L. Pleadwell.

Trollope promises Dixon a paper for the *Athenæum* in a few days.

180. To JAMES RUSSELL LOWELL. 2 September.
Not traced. The Athenæum, No. 1819 (6 September
1862), 306–7.

Instead of writing an angry personal letter to Fletcher Harper on the
piracy of *North America,* Trollope decided to give his views on international
copyright the wider currency of an open letter to Lowell in the *Athenæum.*

Waltham Cross
Sept. 2, 1862.

My dear Mr Lowell,

I do not know that the present moment is very opportune for
the discussion on your side of the water of such questions as that
of International Copyright. You have your hands rather full of
other matters, and may probably lack time just now to attend
to the niceties of civilization. But the subject is one of great
importance to your countrymen, and, as nobody is more fully
aware than yourself, is so esteemed by them. As regards myself,
if I did not moot the matter now, I should probably never do so.
I will therefore, in the teeth of the war, endeavour to enlist your
attention and your sympathy on the subject.

To you and me, and to men, who, like us, earn our bread by
writing, the question is, of course, one of pounds, shillings and
pence, or of dollars and cents; although there are those who
affect to think that an author should disregard such matters, and
that he should work for fame alone. For myself, I profess that I
regard my profession as I see other men regard theirs: I wish to
earn by it what I may honestly earn,—so doing my work that
I may give fair and full measure for what remuneration I may
receive. As to you, may I not presume that you also regard the
literary labourer as worthy of his hire? I say so much at once,
because I wish you to understand that I am pleading here for the
honest payment for goods supplied by me to your countrymen;

[1] Cromer: a charming seaside resort in Norfolk, 132 miles north of
London.

but I am pleading also for the honest payment for goods supplied by you to my countrymen. And in putting forward these pleas, I think I can show that such honesty on both sides will tend to the general advancement of literature for the two countries, and will injure none; or, at any rate, none whose interests are worthy of our care.

I must begin my argument by the story of personal injustice done to myself. Had I not suffered, or imagined that I had suffered, such injustice, I should not now trouble you with this letter. But I can assure you that in placing myself in my present position, I have thought more of the general justice of the question than of my own interests, and have been actuated in what I have done by an endeavour to prove, either that an English author may deal on fair and secure terms with an American publisher, or else that there exists good ground for international interference in the matter.

For some time past, the Messrs. Harper, of New York, have undertaken the speculation of reprinting my books. This they did without any reference to me; but they paid some small sum on, as I think, each work to my English publishers,—with which payment I, however, had then no concern. Nor had I any ground of complaint, seeing that I had sold all my immediate rights in those books to the publishers in London. In 1859 I was in New York; and I then offered to the Messrs. Harper the early sheets of a book I was writing on the West Indies. This they declined, saying the subject did not suit them. But they afterwards applied to my publishers in London as to that work, and paid them again a small sum for the privilege of reprinting. I had then parted with my immediate rights in the book, and perhaps had no ground for complaining that the Messrs. Harper had changed their mind. Soon afterwards I became engaged on a periodical novel called 'Orley Farm,' which is now being republished in *Harper's Magazine*. Having resolved to keep the privilege of the foreign market as regards this work in my own hands, I essayed to deal with the Messrs Harper's agent in London; but when I came to mention my price, I was told that if I did not accede to ⟨the⟩ Messrs Harper's price, the Messrs Harper could and would publish it without any terms. Thereupon I again made over my privilege to my London publishers, feeling that I was foiled, and that I myself in London had no mode of fighting the battle further. My publishers took Messrs Harper's price, and we are dividing the proceeds. That was the first time that Messrs Harper's republication of my works had produced for me a dollar. I was not contented with the bargain, I will confess; but I was specially discontented with the manner of the bargain. I was compelled to sell my wares to one man, and he had the power of naming his own price! I had it in contemplation, however, to visit the States again, and I still hoped to adjust these little matters of commerce to my satisfaction.

In the autumn of last year I did go to the States, and, among many other great pleasures, had that of making your acquaintance. I also renewed that which I before had made with Mr Fletcher Harper. I called on him in New York, and explained to him, with what courtesy I could use, that I did not quite like his mode of republishing my books. He was civil enough to assure me that the transactions had been gratifying to him. I then asked him whether in the event of my making an engagement with any other American publisher as to the reprinting of work of mine, he would take reprisal by reprinting it also. I did not mention any special work, or allude to my intention of writing about your country. He was again very civil, and told me that much as he should regret my doing so, he would not reprint any book under such circumstances.

You no doubt know the name of Mr Lippincott, publisher and bookseller of Philadelphia. After my interview with Mr Harper, I came to terms with him as to the republication of my then projected volumes on North America, and in compliance with those terms I supplied him with the early sheets of the work. Mr Lippincott has printed and published it; but the Messrs Harper had out an edition, unauthorized by writer or publisher in England, four days before Mr Lippincott had published his edition. This they are selling at a price—60 cents, or 2s. 6d.—which must, I believe, entail a loss upon themselves, increasing in amount in accordance with the magnitude of their sale. Either this, or else, by great commercial economy, they may be able to produce the article for the amount charged. I think I may say that any profit to them is out of the question.

May I not fairly call this literary piracy? It is piracy in the

121

spirit, though it may not be so by law. No doubt, American publishers have legally the power of republishing all foreign works of literature, and need ask the leave of no one. But they have found it better to deal with the English authors. The Messrs Harper have repeatedly assured the American public of the fact that they buy their English works from the English writers. But in this special case their *animus* is shown by the manner in which the thing was done. I have not learnt how the firm in New York was able to have out an edition, they having no copy supplied to them, before the firm in Philadelphia, to whom the early sheets were sent. As far as I can ascertain, the edition of the Messrs Harper was out within three days of the arrival of the earliest steamer which could have brought them a copy of the English book. They undoubtedly have been very smart; but I think you will agree with me that such smartness is not creditable to their trade or their country.

The question, however, between me and the Messrs Harper is not worth to you, or to the public of either country, the paper on which this is written. I have told the story because I could not otherwise illustrate the grievance under which authors lie in our two countries. It is not that tricks such as these are often played, but that the possibility of such tricks takes away all security both from the author and from the publisher. In the above case there was a determination on my part to escape from the trammels of the Messrs Harper, and a determination on their part, better based, that I should not escape. There was also on their part a determination that their brothers in the trade should be taught that they were not to be touched with impunity. It is against the exercise of such power that I make my protest.

Between no other nations can a copyright law be of the importance that it is to you and us, because no other two great reading people speak the same language. A small class only in France read English books, and a small class only in England read French books. But almost every man and woman in the Northern States reads our authors; and your authors are known at any rate as well in our country as they are in your own; and this interchange of literature has increased twenty-fold in the last twenty years, and may increase again twenty-fold in the next twenty. You yourself have thousands of British customers; and having indeed been blessed with a special British editor of your own, may probably have experienced no individual hardship; but you will not on that account be less alive to the interests of your profession. A friend and countryman of yours, whose name is with us a household word, but which I cannot mention, as I have not his permission, told me that the pecuniary results of the republication of his works in England was to him very slight. He made no complaint, but seemed to regard the fact as the natural consequence of there being no law of international copyright. Had he possessed the privilege which such a law would have given him, that alone would have afforded him a large income. For aught I know, he may be as affluent as he desires; but there are few of us who do not like to get the price of our wares. But perhaps the publishers are worse off in this matter than are even the authors. The republication of new English works is as important a branch of an American publisher's work as the publication of national literature. But at present he has no protection in this business. The first which is most unscrupulous and most powerful in its commercial operations has advantages over others against which they cannot contend. Mr Lippincott— who is, however, in a large way of business, and probably will not mind it—must have burnt his fingers by daring to publish my volumes. Various American publishers have assured me that they desired nothing so much as an international copyright with England, in order that they might undertake British works with some security. 'You are Mr Harper's property,' has been said to me, 'and we don't dare to touch you.' It was in vain that I declared that I had not made myself over to the Messrs Harper. 'He has put his hand upon you,' I was told, 'and we cannot inter- fere.' I should have but little doubt of obtaining an international copyright if the question could be carried by the votes of the publishers and booksellers in the States.

It has sometimes been argued that an international copyright would do a material injury, as it would raise the price of English books in the States. I will not now do more than notice the fact, that such an argument throws over all idea of honesty, and that it might as well be used against domestic copyright law in either of the two countries; but I will dispute the assertion. An inter- national copyright law would not enhance the price of English books in the States, or of American books in England. The security given to those concerned in the trade would fully compensate the privilege which the trade now has, in each country, of republishing works without special permission from the authors or owners. The proof of this is very simple, and easy to be understood. New works by American authors are not now cheaper in England than new works by English authors, nor, in New York, are new works by English authors cheaper than those by native authors.

Then why is there not an international copyright law? I think you will admit that the difficulty is on your side of the water, and that such a law would be sanctioned here without doubt or dissent. I have heard no literary man in the States defend the present state of the question, though I have discussed it with many. The answer to me has been that such a law would not be popular. Should it not be the work of such men as you to make it popular? For myself, I believe that if you and your brethren in Boston would put your shoulders to the wheel, the thing would be done.

Yours very sincerely,
ANTHONY TROLLOPE

181. To W. H. BLAKE. 23 September. Waltham Cross. *Parrish Collection.*

Trollope advises a candidate for a Civil Service examination. Blake lived in Cashel, county Tipperary, Ireland, and may have been the son of W. H. Blake, who was educated at Trinity College, Dublin, and became (1849–62) Chancellor of Upper Canada.

182. To the Editor of the *Athenæum.* 22 October. *Not traced.* No. 1826 (25 October 1862), 529–30.

Fletcher Harper answered Trollope in the pages of the *Athenæum*, and Trollope immediately replied.

Oct. 22, 1862.

I must trouble you with a few words of rejoinder to Mr Fletcher Harper's letter on the matter of American literary piracy.

In his first-numbered paragraph, he simply repeats what I had asserted with reference to my early works. I made that statement as a necessary beginning to my story. In his second paragraph he re-tells what I had told as to 'Orley Farm,' adding the price given by him, and taunting me with having at last grumblingly accepted a crown for my wares, having first asked a sovereign. But here he altogether omits the point. When I attempted to make my bargain, I was met by the threat that if I did not take the price offered, my wares should be taken from me without any price. Such, at the moment, was the nature of my agreement with my English publishers, Messrs. Chapman & Hall, that though I had the power of refusing Messrs. Harper's offer, I could not do so without injury to them. I was so intent on refusing that offer, that I proposed to pay to Messrs. Chapman & Hall the moiety which would accrue to them—amounting to £100— in order that I might rid myself of any dealings with the American house. This they generously declined; and I therefore felt myself constrained to allow them to deal with the Messrs. Harper, resolving that in future I would keep the foreign right entirely in my own hands. I have never pretended to say that the price named by me for the use of the novel in America indicated its real value more correctly than the offer made by the American publishers. I did not like the bargain, it is true; but, as I said before, it was the manner of the bargain that I specially disliked. The Messrs. Harper affect to deal with the English authors and publishers, but they do so with a threat in their mouth. 'If you do not sell to us at our price,' they say, 'we will take your goods without any price.' This is what we call piracy.

But it is in his third paragraph that I must now come to a distinct issue with Mr Harper. I gave, in my letter to Mr Lowell, the result of a conversation which I had with Mr Harper, and he states that my recollection of that conversation is incorrect. My inaccuracy, if I have been inaccurate, amounts to a total misrepresentation of the purport of what passed between us. I called on Mr Fletcher Harper with the express and single purpose of asking him whether, in the event of my dealing with another firm in America, he would reprint the work of which I would so dispose. 'You can, of course, answer my question or decline to answer it,' I said, thinking that in either case I should have his intention. He told me distinctly that in such a case he would not reprint my book. I repeat this assertion on my own personal credit, and I think that I shall be believed in England:

I am very sure that I shall be believed in America. As Mr Harper says, I made him no offer, seeing that I had determined not to deal with him on any terms.

In his fourth paragraph, Mr Harper defends his general practice of dealing; and in doing so he explains the risk incurred by him in paying anything to English authors. His firm have no protection against piracy!—no protection except the comity of trade, which is, as he says, enforced by reprisals! By this he intends us to understand that the American publisher who first ventures upon the works of an English author,—even though he has done so, as the Harpers did in my case, without any consent from that author,—has a vested right in his man. The comity of the trade, to be enforced by reprisals, is to guarantee these vested rights! The comity of publishers is to insure to each of them among themselves the power and privilege of taking at their own price, or without price, the works of authors, without any of that protection which the competition of an open market gives to the seller! I think that the readers of America, as well as those of England, will acknowledge that no stronger argument than this can be put forward in favor of an International Copyright Law.

Mr Harper twits me with being unwilling to name the terms on which the Messrs. Lippincott agreed to publish my work on 'North America.' I have no right to make them public without the permission of the Messrs. Lippincott. I can only say that those gentlemen are perfectly at liberty to publish them, if they please to do so; as is any publisher with whom I may have been concerned at liberty to make known the terms on which he has dealt with me. Such private matters are not generally considered as interesting to the public at large.[1]

Mr Harper has pointed out to me that I have called Russell Lowell by a wrong name. In your impression of September the 6th, he is unfortunately called William instead of James Russell Lowell. It was a clerical error, not of my own, for which I ask and confidently expect his pardon.

ANTHONY TROLLOPE

[1] Among Trollope's private business papers at the Bodleian Library is a letter from Lippincott's dated 11 Mar. 1862. In it they offer for the American rights to *North America* a royalty of 12½ per cent. after the first 2,000 copies have been sold.

183. To FREDERICK LOCKER. 9 November. Waltham Cross. *Harvard College Library.*

Trollope thanks Locker for the gift of a volume of his poems. Frederick Locker, later Locker-Lampson (1821–95), was the compiler of *Lyra Elegantiarum* and author of *London Lyrics*, which he extended and re-arranged through many editions. The reference is to the 1862 edition of *London Lyrics.*

184. To GEORGE SMITH. 21 November. *Not traced.* Sadleir, *Commentary*, p. 232.

* * *

I have been very remiss in not sending back to you the three numbers which you now have. I have been very busy. I have been trying to hunt three days a week. I find it must be only two. Mortal man cannot write novels, do the Post Office and go out three days.[1]

* * *

185. To GEORGE SMITH. 1 December. *Not traced.* Sadleir's transcript.

Trollope has just returned from a hunting campaign in Oxfordshire and has five days to write a Christmas story for *Good Words*. There is no trace of such a story.

186. ROSE TROLLOPE to KATE FIELD. 3 December. *Boston Public Library.*

3 Dec 1862.

Dear Kate,

Why dont you write to me? We are both really unhappy— I because I still think you are offended with me— My husband because he does not know why— I therefore will not wait for another week, and that will be certain to bring a letter—just as one takes out an umbrella & there will be no rain—but leave the thing at home & down it pours— He—my husband—not the rain nor the umbrella—has gone to hunt and on such days I always write heaps of letters because I dont like to be out of the way never knowing at what hour he may be in— Well at any rate if you are angry with me I am not going to care and shall torment you when the fit comes on. . . .[2]

[1] Mr. Sadleir's transcript.
[2] The rest of this letter deals with politics, meeting Americans in London, and other generalities scarcely relevant.

187. To George Smith. 4 December.
Mrs. Reginald Smith. Sadleir, *Commentary*, p. 233.[1]

(Waltham House,
Waltham Cross.)
4. December 1862.

My dear Smith.

Many thanks for the Cornhill. I did make your wife a promise to go down to Brighton, & I am a beast not to keep a promise, the keeping of which would be so pleasurable; but the fact is I have become a slave to hunting;—as men who do hunt must do at this time of the year. It is not that I would not willingly give up my hunting for the Wednesday—or even the Wednesday & Saturday; but that engagements get themselves made which will not have themselves broken. And so I have people here on the Wednesday—& indeed up to I dont know what day—Xmas I believe, who are all more or less in the boots & breeches line.

M[rs] Trollope bids me say that no further persuasion than your own would have been necessary—had she been a free agent. But she is not. A good wife always does head groom on such occasions.

Pray tell your wife from me that I own myself a beast—& humbly beg pardon. As things have arranged themselves it is too late now to do more than beg pardon.

Yours always
Anthony Trollope

188. To George Smith. 21 December.
Not traced. Sadleir's transcript.

* * *

Julia Cecilia Collinson,[2] whom I know to be a very nice person, she having been an intimate friend of my sister tho' I never saw her myself—writes to me saying that as I am editor of the Cornhill Magazine she humbly hopes I may have grace enough to return to her the MS. of a story which she sent to that magazine—for which she has since been bidden £20, but has no

[1] All but the last paragraph of this letter is published in Sadleir.
[2] Julia Cecilia Collinson De Winton Stretton, prolific novelist and biographer from 1855 to 1898.

other copy. The perplexing woman wrote the name of the tale on a separate bit of paper which I have lost. It was 'Don't you wish you may get it' or something like that. I know there was a 'get it' in it. Can you help her or me? Of course I shall undeceive her as to the high pinnacle of literary eminence to which she has erroneously exalted me.

*　　*　　*

189. To GEORGE SMITH. *23* December.
Not traced. Sadleir's transcript.

Trollope asks Smith to print two dozen copies of his lecture. This lecture was certainly 'The Present Condition of the Northern States of the American Union'. Trollope spoke 30 December and 13 January. It was published by Morris L. Parrish in *Four Lectures* (London: Constable, 1938).

1863

190. To JAMES T. FIELDS. 8 January.
Parrish Collection.

(Waltham House,
Waltham Cross.)
Jany 8—1863.

My dear Fields.

I send to you a lecture on the present condition of the Northern States which I have given once here in the provinces, & which I am to give again in London on next Tuesday. I think you will acknowledge that I am fighting your battles for you almost better than you are fighting them yourselves. I wish you to publish the lecture in the *Atlantic*, if you think well of doing so.[1] The small country audience received it well—what a larger audience in London may do, I cannot say. If you do publish it, do it with my name, & with *no alterations*. I am very strong in it against slavery, but I must not be made to appear what you call an abolitionist. If you do this take means to let me have a copy.

I send a few other copies for you to distribute by post or otherwise. We have no book post service to the States or I would not trouble you. I fear I may put you to some expense in this;—if so

[1] It was not published.

I will honestly pay you if you will condescend to tell me. By the bye I always fear that I put you to some expense about those books I sent, tho' I did all in my power to prevent it.

Give my very kindest regards to your wife & pray let me hear from you.

I have had no word from Lippincott as to the sale[1]—2500 have been sold here at 34/. At so high a price the sale is lower. In the spring it will come out in a cheaper form,—or perhaps later.[2]

Yours always very truly
ANTHONY TROLLOPE

191. To GEORGE SMITH. 11 February.
Mrs. Reginald Smith.

(Waltham House,
Waltham Cross.)

Feb—11—1863

My dear Smith,

I wrote this morning telling you that I meant to see you to-day. But the doctor came ordering me to bed—which was a bore as I was going to dine with our Postmr General. So I didn't go to town.

This is to tell you that the S. H. of A. is now finished—and as I always fear having it burned while the MS remains with me, shall be conveyed to you, very shortly. If it quite suits you to let me have the quid pro quo, I shall be very much obliged.

I wish you had my liver just for to-day.

Yours always
ANTH TROLLOPE

192. To GEORGE SMITH. 18 February.
Not traced. Sadleir, *Commentary*, p. 233.

*   *   *

Many thanks. All my interest in the S. H. of A. is now over. Just at this moment you fellows are beginning. I hope the great man Wilson[3] has been in a good humour. Ah me! If I could only have one of those spitted nests of oysters to remind me of what

---

[1] Of *North America.*
[2] The 'fourth and cheaper edition' (16*s.*) did not appear until Feb. 1864.
[3] Possibly one of Smith's employees.

you are doing. For myself, I had a bit of boiled mutton at three; and my wife remarked that she didn't think half a glass of sherry would do me any harm.[1]

*   *   *

193. To JOHN EVERETT MILLAIS. April.
Not traced. Sadleir, *Commentary*, p. 237.

[April, 1863]

*   *   *

X[2] (a Sunday magazine) has thrown me over. They write me word that I am too wicked. I tell you at once because of the projected and now not to be accomplished drawings. They have tried to serve God and the devil together, and finding that goodness pays best, have thrown over me and the devil. I won't try to set you against them because you can do parables and other fish for their net;[3] but I am altogether unsuited to the regenerated! It is a pity they did not find it out before, but I think they are right now. I *am* unfit for the regenerated and trust I may remain so, wishing to preserve a character for honest intentions.

*   *   *

194. To GEORGE SMITH. 9 May.
Not traced. Sadleir's transcript.

Trollope invites Smith to Waltham House and will not allow the Derby to interfere with their arrangements.

195. To JOHN TILLEY. 24 May.
General Post Office, London.

Among employees of the Post Office the following is known as 'Trollope's famous letter on promotion'.

Waltham Cross,
24 May 1863.

Sir,

I beg to acknowledge the receipt of your letter of the 8th Instant asking me whether I think that seniority coupled with

[1] Mr. Sadleir's transcript.
[2] *Good Words.* See letter No. 196, *infra.*
[3] Millais was at this time doing a series of drawings of the Parables for *Good Words.*

full competency for the duties of a higher class should be the condition of promotion throughout the entire Post Office Service.

I certainly do think so, as I have always thought; but my opinion has been much strengthened by watching the way in which the contrary system has worked. I feel very sure that the system of promotion by merit, as it is called, cannot in truth be carried out; and that it is injurious to the service and ever will be so, in so far as it can be or hereafter may be carried out.

It cannot be carried out, firstly because men will not commit the monstrous injustice which it enacts; and secondly because no weights and measures can be found by which merit can be weighed in the balance. The system demands that promotion shall be given to the best man, let the merits of those who are to be superseded be what they may,—and let the years of service and well-grounded expectations of the senior candidates be also what they may. A man may have worked his best for twenty years for the Crown; he may have amply deserved promotion; he may have married on the assured conviction that the merited reward would in due time be his; he may in all respects be fitted for the duties of the higher place; but by the system of promotion, now assumed to be carried out in the Civil Service, he is to lose it all if some better man than himself shall have come into the same class with him at the last moment! From the very wording of the rule it is apparent that no amount of excellence is safe, because a greater amount of excellence must always be possible. No extent of devotion to his duties will secure any man in his expectation of promotion, because some devotion, supposed to be more extended, may come after him. Such a system is so cruel in its nature that men will hardly attempt to work it.

The superior officer will certify that the senior man is the best man,—presuming always that he is a good and fitting man, —even tho' he be not the best or nearly the best. Such falsehood is very grievous to him; but it is not so grievous as the ruin which he would inflict on deserving men by the truth. But the attempt is sometimes made. It is made, I think, less frequently now than when the theory was in its first flush of triumph;—and it will, in course of time, cease to be carried out at all even tho' the rule should not be officially revoked, for such rules die of their own accord. The attempt however is still made; but there is absolutely wanted to those who make it any measure by which excellence may be meted. The reporting officer who is zealously anxious to work the new system, and who is resolved to throw all other considerations to the wind in carrying out a theory that sounds so well, can at last only depend on his own judgement. To know whether a man be absolutely fit or unfit for certain duties is within the capacity of an observant and intelligent officer;— but it is frequently altogether beyond the capacity of any officer however intelligent and observant to say who is most fit. Zeal recommends itself to one man, intelligence to a second, alacrity to a third, punctuality to a fourth, and superficial pretence to a fifth. There can be no standard by which the excellence of men can be judged as is the weight of gold.

Nor can I understand why the service should require more than actual competency. Indeed no service can require more than that, let its duties be ever so exalted. If a man be in all respects fit to do the work he has engaged to perform, no better man can be had. It has always seemed to me that the Civil Service can obtain nothing by the odious comparisons which this system institutes. But it undoubtedly loses very much. It is my opinion that the selected man is deteriorated by the act of selection;—that he is taught to imagine himself to be too great and too good for the very ordinary work which, in spite of the glory of his selection, he is generally called upon to perform; but, be that as it may, there can be no doubt that the men who are passed over are deteriorated. Very little experience in the Civil Service, or, as I imagine, in any other service, will teach an observer as much as that. The unfit man becomes more unfit;—so much so that even unfitness should not be measured too closely; and the man who was perfectly fit is made to be unfit by the cruelty to which he has been subjected. As to this there can be no doubt. The man who is competent and who has exerted himself and is yet passed over, cannot but be broken-hearted; and from a broken-hearted man no good work can be obtained.

The theory of promotion by merit,—that theory by which promotion is to be given not to the senior man who is fit, but to the man who is fittest, be he senior or junior—is thoroughly Utopian in its essence; but it has in it, as I think, this of special evil which is not inherent in most Utopian theories,—that it is susceptible of experimental action, and that the wider the action grows the greater is the evil done.

I am,

Sir,

Your most obedient Servant

ANTHONY TROLLOPE

The Secretary
General Post Office

196. To ALEXANDER STRAHAN.[1] 10 June.
Not traced. Sadleir, *Commentary*, p. 238.

Waltham Cross.
June 10, 1863.

Dear Sir,

I am sorry that you and D^r McCleod[2] have been forced to the conclusion at which you have arrived with reference to my story.[3] I claim for myself however to say that the fault in the matter is yours, & not mine. I have written for you such a story as you had a right to expect from me,—judging as you of course did judge by my former works. If that does not now suit your publication I can only be sorry that you should have been driven to change your views.

I have, as I take it, an undoubted right to claim from you the payment of £1,000 for the story. I do not however desire to call upon you for a greater sacrifice than must be made to place me in a position as good as that which would be mine if you performed your agreement & published my story during the next six months. If I publish that story in another form during the autumn,—as I shall do under the circumstances I am now contemplating,—I shall get for it £500 less than the sum which I should receive, when [? were] you to publish it in *Good Words*.

---

[1] Alexander Strahan was publisher of *Good Words*. Trollope was to have many business engagements with him in the future.

[2] Norman Macleod the younger (1812–72), chaplain to Queen Victoria, 1857–72, and editor of *Good Words*.

[3] The publishing history of *Rachel Ray* is chronicled fully in Sadleir, *Commentary*, pp. 234–43. Donald Macleod in his *Memoir of Norman Macleod* (London, 1876) quotes (ii. 149) two sentences from a letter written to him by Trollope about 1875: 'I need not say that Dr. Macleod's rejection of the story never for a moment interfered with our friendship. It certainly raised my opinion of the man.'

That sum of £500 I am willing to accept from you. But you will of course understand that in making this offer I reserve my legal right to demand the £1000, should you not accept the proposed compromise.[1]

A. T.

197. To G. G. FRERE.[2] 15 June. General Post Office.
Parrish Collection.

Trollope replies officially to a gentleman who complained that an important letter had not reached its destination within a reasonable time.

198. To EMILY ? 2 July. Waltham Cross.
University of Rochester.

Trollope promises to call, but is engaged at the moment, expecting daily the arrival of Tom Trollope and his family.

199. To LUCETTE E. BARKER.[3] 8 July. Waltham Cross.
Mrs. Arthur Helps.

Trollope sends his thanks for a drawing. 'I had originally intended to call the story The Two pearls of Allington and your drawing makes me wish that I had adhered to my original name.'

200. To GEORGE ELIOT. 10 July.
Parrish Collection.

(Waltham House,
Waltham Cross.)
July 10—1863.

My dear Mrs Lewes.

Not for your sake but for my own I must write you one line to thank you for your present. I will say nothing further of the book but this;—that were you now departing from us, as I trust you may not till you have added many another leaf to your wreath,— you might go satisfied that you had written that which would live after you.[4]

[1] I reproduce this letter from a copy preserved by Trollope among his business papers now at the Bodleian Library.

[2] Possibly George Frere (1810–78), one-time judge at the Cape of Good Hope.

[3] Lucette E. Barker was a sister-in-law of Tom Taylor.

[4] For Trollope's first impression of *Romola* see letter No. 176, *supra*.

I will get up to you as soon as I possibly can,—but you are regularly out (with a wise regularity) at the hour at which mortals call.

Yours most sincerely

ANTHONY TROLLOPE

You will know what I mean when I say that Romola will live after you. It will be given to but very few latter day novels to have any such life. The very gifts which are most sure to secure present success are for the most part antagonistic to permanent vitality.

201. To GEORGE SMITH. 19 July.
Not traced. Sadleir's transcript.

Trollope writes about making some slight changes in *The Small House*. He is just leaving for Switzerland.

202. To HERBERT JOYCE.[1] 22 August. Durham.
Fitzwilliam Museum.

Trollope writes about some correspondence on a 'new-fangled rule. There is too much of it, so that nobody will read it. And then some large part of it is hardly worth reading'.

203. To [? EDWARD] CHAPMAN.[2] 9 September.
Estate of Carroll A. Wilson.

September 9, 1863. (Waltham House,

Waltham Cross.)

My dear Chapman,

I had been thinking much about the novel[3] for the periodical before I got your letter and had intended to write to you. I dont think I can make my story shorter than I had intended;—that is I am not minded to do so— People will not have to wait longer, or so long, as for the monthly numbers. Indeed it may be [a]

---

[1] Herbert Joyce (1831–97) was Librarian of the Post Office.

[2] I take this letter to be written to Edward Chapman, since he, rather than Frederic, was managing the business.

[3] The novel to which Trollope refers is *Can You Forgive Her?* It appeared first in twenty monthly parts: Jan. 1864–Aug. 1865. In book form it was published in two volumes at eleven shillings each. The letter is discussed at some length in Norris Dresser Hoyt's unpublished Yale doctoral dissertation, pp. 58–60.

question whether it should not all be included in one year. In that case I should lessen the price as against the paper, and of course charge you separately as publishers for the republication— I think the object should be to bring it out in two volumes—such as the Orley Farm volumes for 20/. A sale of 4,000 or 5,000 in that shape is better than 1,500 in 3 volumes. If we make the weekly to consist of 40 or 48 pages without column (i e 36— or 44) could not the printing of the story be so arranged, that we could pull off from the same type the sheets for the subsequent volumes? Or we might have 32 pages on one sheet, and have the novel printed separately in similar type, and bring about together, say 32 pages of the periodical and eight or twelve of the novel. You will understand what I mean. Consider it well before you answer me— But let me have an answer. The thickness of the larger number of pages of the paper would not overweight us.

I should much wish the outside cover for the monthly numbers to be colored.

Of course you will enquire what would be the cost of weekly stitching. It would be very reasonable—

You must remember in considering the publication of my own novel, that I cannot sacrifice that. I can not make it shorter than it should be, in order that it might suit the periodical. If the novel as now arranged will do for the periodical, (as I think it will,) let it come out in that shape on 1st of January. If it will not it must come out alone, & the periodical be postponed.

Yours always
ANTHONY TROLLOPE

204. To [FREDERIC] CHAPMAN. 7 October.
Not traced. Sadleir, *Commentary*, p. 98.

(Waltham House
Waltham Cross.)
October 7, 1863.

My dear Chapman,

My mother died at Florence yesterday morning. I tell you this, that if you are intending to go to Florence, you may delay your journey for a few days.[1]

Yours always
ANTHONY TROLLOPE

[1] I can add nothing to Mr. Sadleir's perceptive comments on this note.

205. To C. W. Jones.[1] 7 October. Waltham Cross.
Historical Society of Pennsylvania.

Trollope replies indecisively to a lecture invitation. See letter No. 221, *infra.*

206. To Dr. John Doran.[2] 10 October.
Parrish Collection.

Waltham House
Oct 10—1863

My dear Doctor Doran,
I cannot but thank you again for the kindliness, heartiness, as well as excellent taste of your article on my mother.[3] And moreover there was no word that contained a mistake.

Yours faithfully
ANTHONY TROLLOPE

207. To George Eliot. 18 October.
University of Virginia.

(Waltham House,
Waltham Cross.)
October 18, 1863.

My dear Mrs Lewes,
Will you accept a copy of Rachel Ray, a little story which I have just published in two volumes. I have desired Chapman to send it to you.

You know that my novels are not sensational. In Rachel Ray I have attempted to confine myself absolutely to the commonest details of commonplace life among the most ordinary people, allowing myself no incident that would be even remarkable in every day life. I have shorn my fiction of all romance.

I do not know what you who have dared to handle great names

---

[1] C. W. Jones was an official of the Athenaeum, Bury St. Edmunds. See letter No. 221, *infra.*

[2] Dr. John Doran (1807–78), a prolific author on stage history, wrote widely for the *Athenæum* and acted as editor in the absence of Hepworth Dixon. He was subsequently editor of *Notes and Queries* from 1872 to 1878.

[3] The obituary notice of Frances Trollope referred to was published in the *Athenæum*, No. 1876 (10 Oct. 1863), 469.

& historic times will think of this. But you must not suppose that I think the little people are equal as subjects to the great names. Do you, who can do it, go on. I know you will not be deterred by the criticisms of people who cannot understand. Neither should you be deterred by internal criticism. That which you have in your flask you are bound to pour forth.

Yours always most truly
ANTHONY TROLLOPE

208. TO GEORGE SMITH. 29 October.
Mrs. Reginald Smith.

(Waltham House,
Waltham Cross.)
October 29, 1863.

My dear Smith.

My wife bids me say that she will like nothing better than to run down to Brighton for a couple of nights—if you will take us in for so long, & if you can make it within the first ten days of December. If so, will Mrs Smith fix the time within those ten days?

You spoke the other day to me about the Cornhill. Did you mean anything? I'll tell you why I ask, and you must not suppose that I mean to press you. A proposition has been made to me since I saw you, which very likely will come to nothing in any case, but which would certainly come to nothing if I were to write another novel for the Cornhill so early as 1865.[1]

I should not have thought of naming the matter had you not spoken, believing you to have enough on your hands with Thackeray and Wilkie Collins— But if you think you should like to have another of mine to commence about April 1865, and if you made me an offer which I could accept, I should then certainly decline the other proposition.

This is looking very far ahead and if you say it is too far ahead for you, I shall be satisfied.

Yours always
ANTHONY TROLLOPE

[1] *The Claverings*, Trollope's next novel for the *Cornhill*, was serialized from Feb. 1866 to May 1867.

209. To GEORGE SMITH. 5 November.
Not traced. Sadleir's transcript.

Trollope advises Smith that he is tempted by an offer from another publisher and would like to know Smith's decision about another novel fifteen
months hence. See letter No. 208, *supra*.

210. To [? EDWARD] CHAPMAN. 9 November.
Parrish Collection.

(Waltham House,
Waltham Cross.)
9. Nov. 1863.

My dear Chapman.

I'm sorry to hear of your rheumatics— I had no business when
I called the other day— I only came for a parcel of Mss from
Tom for the Victoria, which was lying at your place.[1]

I am glad to hear you are doing so well with R.R. After all
the old fashioned mode of publishing does very well now and
then as a change.[2]

I quite agree about the editions. Dont let them print at the
same time Nos 5—& 6— Whatever is printed at once let them
call it one & the same edition.[3] When anything is to be gained
by dishonesty there may be an excuse; but why be dishonest
when we don't want it?

Yours always
ANTHONY TROLLOPE

211. To GEORGE SMITH. 25 November. Waltham Cross.
Not traced. Sadleir's transcript.

Trollope prefers February or March for beginning *The Claverings*.
'Nevertheless, as you know, I always submit in all things.'

[1] Tom Trollope's novel was *Lindisfarne Chase*, published in the *Victoria
Magazine*, i and ii (May 1863–Aug. 1864).
[2] There was no serial publication of *Rachel Ray*.
[3] This letter supports Mr. Sadleir's contention (*Bibliography*, pp. 277–9)
that a single printing of *Rachel Ray* was being split into several 'editions'.

212. To GEORGE HENRY LEWES. 13 December.
   Mrs. E. S. Ouvry.

(Waltham House,
Waltham Cross.)
Dec. 13. 1863.

My dear Lewes,
   On returning home I have found your life of Goethe,[1] for which, I presume, I have to thank you. I do thank you heartily. I must get your name in it some day. I shame to say I never read the former edition. I have already been at work at this, and am charmed with it. Alas, me—for 11 years I learned Latin & Greek —nothing else—& know it now, you, who understand our English schooling, will know how superficially. Of German of course I know nothing. Shall I hereafter have an action against my pastors & masters?

Yours dear Lewes,
always yours
ANTHONY TROLLOPE

How excellent is your outside got up. Calico—we call it cloth when we want to be grand,—has thereon achieved its greatest biblical triumph.

213. To [? EDWARD] CHAPMAN. 25 December.
   Waltham Cross. *Parrish Collection.*

Trollope returns some corrected proof and illustrations for *Can You Forgive Her?* He adds, 'I have been greatly cut up by Thackerays death, which I only learned in the Times. It has not been a merry Christmas with us. I loved him dearly.'

214. To GEORGE SMITH. 25 December.
   Mrs. Reginald Smith. Sadleir, *Commentary*, p. 243.

(Waltham House,
Waltham Cross.)
December 25, 1863.

My dear Smith.
   I was going to write to you on another matter,—but I have been stopped in that, as in every thing, by Mr Thackeray's death. I felt it as a very heavy blow.

----

[1] This was the second edition of Lewes's *The Life and Works of Goethe*, 2 vols. (London, 1855). Trollope had an early copy, for the title-page of the new edition reads 1864.

You will of course insert in the next Cornhill some short notice of him. Who will do it for you? If you have no one better, I will do it gladly. Lewes, or Bell, or Russell[1] would do it better. I only make the offer in the event of your having no one better—

If you hear that anything is fixed about the funeral, pray let me know.

I have not the heart to wish any one a Merry Christmas.

Yours always
ANTHONY TROLLOPE

Of course you will know that what I offer is a work of love.[2]

215. To FOLLETT SYNGE.[3] December.
Not traced. Herman Merivale and Frank T. Marzials, *Life of W. M. Thackeray* (London, 1891), p. 215.

In the following letter Trollope describes Thackeray's death to one of Thackeray's close friends.

*   *   *

Dear old fellow—I saw him for the last time about ten days before his death, and sat with him for half an hour talking about himself. I never knew him pleasanter or more at ease as to his bodily ailments. How I seem to have loved that dear head of his now that he has gone.

I had better tell the story all through. It is bad to have to write it, but you will expect to be told. He had suffered very much on the Wednesday (23rd), but had got out in the afternoon. He was home early, and was so ill when going to bed that his servant suggested he had better stay. He was suffering from spasms and retching, having been for some months more free from this complaint than for a long time previously. He would not have the servant, and was supposed to go to bed. He was heard moving in the night. . . . It is believed that he must have gone off between

---

[1] William Howard Russell, later Sir William (1820–1907), long-time correspondent for *The Times* and the *Daily Telegraph*.
[2] See his 'W. M. Thackeray', *Cornhill Magazine*, ix (Feb. 1864), 134–7.
[3] William Webb Follett Synge, of the diplomatic service, was minister at Honolulu and a frequent contributor to *Punch* and the *Saturday*. Thackeray and Trollope had lent Synge a large sum of money. See letter No. 217, *infra*.

two and three, and I fear his last hours were painful. His arms and face were very rigid—as I was told by Leech who saw him in the morning afterwards.

*   *   *

1 8 6 4

216. To JOHN LEECH. 11 January. Waltham Cross.
   Parrish Collection.

Trollope invites Leech to join Millais and him in hunting. 'If you find it impracticable to send your own nag across I will contrive to mount you.' John Leech (1817–64) was the chief artist for *Punch*, 1842–64, and for many other magazines.

217. To [? HERMAN] MERIVALE.[1] 13 January.
   Berg Collection.

(Waltham House,
Waltham Cross.)
January 13.   64.

My dear Merivale.

John[2] asks me to let you know the particulars of a debt due from W. W. F. Synge to poor Thackeray.

Synge, who is now Consul at Honolulu, borrowed, before he went in May 1862, £900 from Thackeray & £900 from me. It was agreed that £100 should be paid off quarterly. The first quarter to Thackeray & the second to me,—& so on. We each received the first £100, but then there was a stop. Last year, in the spring, I think, Synge's father died, & there were some proceeds out of which Thackeray received £400 & I £400. It was then agreed that the remainder should be repaid by quarterly payments of £50 instead of £100. Whether Thackeray has had any such payment I cannot say. I have not. They were to be made by Messrs Bedwell & Alslop [?] the clerks of the F.O. who pay moneys for the consuls &c. They can tell you whether Thackeray has had any further instalment.[3]

---

[1] Herman Merivale (1806–74), elder brother of Trollope's friend John Merivale, under-secretary for India.

[2] John Merivale.

[3] Apparently the debt was not so quickly paid as Trollope's published

The debts were to bear interest at 5 per cent. Thackeray had a bond, prepared by Mr Gregory M. Wheeler in Bedford Row.

Yours faithfully

ANTHONY TROLLOPE

218. To GEORGE SMITH. 17 January.
Mrs. Reginald Smith. Sadleir, *Commentary*, pp. 243–4.

(Waltham House,
Waltham Cross.)
January 17, 1864.

My dear Smith.

I received together at Norwich on Friday your letters of the 13—& 14!! In the former you propose to insert my paper with papers & verse from Dickens & Lord Houghton, and in the latter you suggest a longer memoir for the March number.

I prefer the former plan. I do not feel up to writing a memoir, and I do not personally know enough, and tho' I might possibly borrow all that can be said from Hannays excellent article I do not care to borrow in that way.[1] More of criticism that [? than] what I have attempted would I think be almost out of place. I have said nothing that I do not think and believe, but if I were to say more I should perhaps run into rhodomontade or else cool down into ordinary eulogy.

You will see what alterations I have made. If you do not like what I have said,—a mere word—as to Hannays paper (which he sent me printed with his name) put it out.

I should be glad to see a revise—& let them print Anthony instead of 'A'. My brother is commonly called Adolphus.

Yours always

ANTHONY TROLLOPE

I have destroyed C.D's[2] paper—i e the copy you sent me. Why not put the name in the front—as with Dickens,—& so also with the other paper.

---

reference to the incident (*Thackeray* [New York, n.d.], p. 60) would indicate.

[1] James Hannay (1827–73), author and journalist, editor of the *Edinburgh Evening Courant*, where his *A Brief Memoir . . . of Mr. Thackeray* was first published.

[2] Charles Dickens.

219. To [? EDWARD] CHAPMAN. 26 January.
    Parrish Collection.

Trollope returns proof of *Can You Forgive Her?* with subjects marked for 'Mr. Brown': Hablot Knight Browne (1815–82), illustrator under the pseudonym of 'Phiz' of many of the novels of Dickens, Trollope, Surtees, &c. He illustrated Volume I of *Can You Forgive Her?*

220. To ? 26 January.
    John W. Watling.

Trollope arranges to meet a correspondent in Bury St. Edmunds, apparently on 2 February, some days *after* the lecture referred to in No. 221.

221. To GEORGE HENRY LEWES. 31 January.
    Mrs. E. S. Ouvry.

(Waltham House,
Waltham Cross.)
January 31. 1864.

My dear Lewes.

If I come to you at 5. pm on Thursday (or is it 5.30?), will you give me my dinner?

My lecture at Bury went off magnificently.[1] I went there in a carriage with a marquis, who talked to me all the way about the state of his stomach—which was very grand; and the room was quite full, and the people applauded with thorough good nature, only they did so in the wrong places;—and two or three Lady Janes told me afterwards that it was quite nice;—so that I was, as you see, quite in a little paradise of terrestrial gods & goddesses.

As you and your wife wouldn't come to see the wonders of Bury with me, I went off the next morning to hunt, 30 miles away, at 6. am

Yours
ANTHONY TROLLOPE

[1] Probably a revision of his lecture 'On the Present Condition of the Northern States'.

222. To GEORGE SMITH. 10 February.
Mrs. Reginald Smith.

(Waltham House
Waltham Cross.)
Feb. 10, 1864

My dear Smith,

Touching the article on our dear old friend[1] my wife is mer-
cenary, and requires payment. She wants you to give her a copy
of Esmond,—the 1-vol. Edit. of 1858. The book in that shape is
a great favorite with her, and we have used up our copy among
ourselves & friends.

There is a shop in the Rue St Honore devoted to Eau de
Cologne, and in which as my wife thinks is the only true fountain.
Will you bring her home the biggest bottle you can conveniently
do. I think they are about 12 francs. Tell your wife also that
Eau de Cologne if kept for a year or two, (as we always keep it)
is certainly the best I ever met. The shop used to be 333, but the
numbers have been changed. It is on the Rue Rivoli side, about
half way between the Palais Royal, and the street up to the Place
Vendome.

Thanks as to the printing.

My kindest remembrances to your wife. I hope your honey-
mooning will be all fresh and nice,—just as it was the first time.

Yours always
ANTHONY TROLLOPE

What is it the disciples of Banks do?[2] They eat every good
thing going, and then add two dry biscuits, and expect to be
saved by them. That is what I heard yesterday.

223. To GEORGE SMITH. 12 February.
Not traced. Sadleir's transcript.

Sarah Neale[3] having taken exception to the account of the brown silk
dresses in the first number of *The Small House*, Trollope, amused, forwards
the letter to Smith. 'I think Mrs. Smith should be asked for her opinion on

[1] Thackeray.
[2] Probably George Linnaeus Banks (1821–81), an eccentric journalist
and a miscellaneous writer who was interested in the social advancement of
the people.
[3] Sarah Neale was the wife of John Mason Neale (1818–66), the famous
hymnologist, warden of Sackville College, East Grinstead, and one-time
leader-writer for the *Morning Chronicle*.

this matter before any large number of the new edition are issued. My wife refuses to have any opinion, alleging that she has no pecuniary interest in the matter. I feel that my future literary reputation is at stake.'

224. To MARY CHRISTIE. 27 February.
Parrish Collection.

(Waltham House
Feb 27, 1864.   Waltham Cross.)
My dear Mary,

You know how the men answer the charges brought against them in the courts. I didn't take the man's money, or if I did I paid it back again, or if I did not pay it back again, I had very good reasons for keeping it. So I say to you, I got no letter from you. Or if I got one I answered it. Or if I didn't answer it, there must have been some good reason. I am, in an ordinary way, so good a correspondent, that I can never allow anyone like you to say that I have left a letter unanswered.

My dear mother died full of years and without anything of the suffering of old age. For two years her memory had gone. But she ate & slept & drank, till the lamp went altogether out; but there was nothing of the usual struggle of death. I think that no one ever suffered less in dying.

Of Charlie's[1] want of success, or of his success, we at present know nothing. It is not decided. But I greatly hope that if he be unsuccessful we can induce the Postergeneral [Postmaster] to employ him temporarily for—say—a year, and then give him another chance. I am writing to Kate today to tell her this.

The big looking glass has been put up, and we are very grand in our new room. Pray come & see it, & bring the girls so that they may ride. Tell Mary that Miss Vesey can go as quiet as ever.[2]

Very nice horses are scarce, but nice horses may be got. I wish we could get you to come & settle near us. I think we could find a place not dear; but it is so hard to find places that are perfect in every respect. My kind regard to Christie. Would he & you come to us here? We should be so delighted. My wife sends her love.

Yours always
ANTHONY TROLLOPE

[1] Charles Gould, son of Kate Gould, Mary Christie's sister.
[2] Mary Christie's daughter and Trollope's little riding-horse.

225. To Sir Rowland Hill. 2 March.
Not traced. The Times, 1 December 1883, p. 7.

(Waltham House,
Waltham Cross.)
March 2, 1864.

My dear Sir Rowland,
I have to thank you for your paper on the results of postal reform, the amended copy of which has just reached me.[1] I yesterday heard of your resignation. I hope that this has been caused rather by the fear that prolonged exertion might be dangerous than by existing ill-health, and that comparative leisure may restore your strength. As there is no longer any official connexion between us, I may perhaps say a few words which I could not have said while you were our secretary. I cannot but have felt for the last year or two since I was called upon to make one of a committee of inquiry during your illness, that you have regarded me as being in some sort unfriendly to your plans of postal reform. I am not going to trouble you with any discussion on that matter, but I cannot let your resignation from office pass without assuring you of my thorough admiration for the great work of your life. I have regarded you for many years as one of the essential benefactors, not only of your own country, but of all the civilized world. I think that the thing you have done has had in it more of general utility than any other measure which has been achieved in my time. And there has been a completeness about it which must, I should think, make you thoroughly contented with your career, as far as it has gone. There are national services, for which a man can receive no adequate reward, either in rank or money, and it has been your lot to render such a service to the world at large. I hope that you may live long to enjoy the recognition of your own success.[2]
Believe me, my dear Sir Rowland,

Very faithfully yours
ANTHONY TROLLOPE

[1] *Results of Postal Reform* (London, 1864).
[2] In his *Autobiography* Trollope's picture of Sir Rowland is highly unflattering. As if to show that he held two opinions, one public and one private, the *Postal, Telegraphic, and Telephonic Gazette* published (30 Nov. 1883, p. 274) the letter above. It was picked up by *The Times* and republished

226. To MR. ENOCH.[1] 2 March. Waltham Cross.
Mrs. Reginald Smith.

Trollope returns the title-page of *The Small House* with emendations.

227. To GEORGE SMITH. 4 March.
Mrs. Reginald Smith.

(Waltham House
Waltham Cross.)

My dear Smith.

The bearer of this letter of introduction is a distinguished
rebel from Maryland and my particular friend. I believe he has
done more in assisting Englishmen to get into rebeldom during
the war, than any other American out— And if he have not sent
South any contraband articles less innocent than Englishmen he
is a most libelled man.

He wants an introduction to an English publisher, and I have
much pleasure in giving him a line to you.

very faithfully yours
ANTHONY TROLLOPE
4 March 64

My friends name is Mr W. W. Glenn[2]

228. To JOHN EVERETT MILLAIS. 20 March. Waltham
Cross. *Paul Schoedinger.*

Trollope will join Millais and other painters for dinner. He promises to
contribute to their fund—'in a moderate way. I've spent all my money in
buying a dish at poor Thackeray's sale'.

the following day. Actually, of course, there is no discrepancy of judgement.
Trollope had a just appreciation of Sir Rowland's public services, which he
here expresses; but he did not care for him as a man, as he makes clear in
the *Autobiography* (chap. xv, p. 237). The two opinions, both fully justified
from Trollope's point of view, are easily reconciled.

[1] Mr. Enoch was manager of Smith, Elder & Co.
[2] William Wilkins Glenn (1824–76), journalist, part owner of the
Baltimore Exchange; arrested and imprisoned in Fort McHenry for asserted
treasonable activities on behalf of the Southern cause. This information has
been kindly supplied me by Mr. William D. Hoyt, Jr., of the Maryland
Historical Society.

229. To GEORGE HENRY LEWES. 21 March.
Mrs. E. S. Ouvry.

(Waltham House,
Waltham Cross.)

March 21, 1864.
My dear Lewes,

On Sunday I got your Aristotle[1] & went at it at once. It is wonderfully and deliciously lucid. Indeed I know no one so lucid —and at the same time so graphic—as you are. Your Goethe was charming to me as combining those two qualifications.

I shall get to you before long. I went to see Carlyle last week. Oh, heavens;—what a mixture of wisdom & folly flows from him!

Yours always,
A. T.

I have told George Smith to send to your wife the Small House at Allington. Ask her to receive it from me with my kindest regards.

230. To [?FREDERIC] CHAPMAN. 31 March. Waltham Cross. *Parrish Collection.*

Trollope sends corrected proof and discusses the publication of Tom Trollope's *Lindisfarne Chase.*

231. To W. H. B.[2] 22 April.
Parrish Collection.

(Waltham House,
Waltham Cross.)

April 22—1864
My dear Sir.

I do not quite understand who you are;—but in either position I should be very glad to shake hands with you;—and again to do the same with you as a brother Wykamist.

I remember John Tyler very well. I never in my life heard him

---

[1] *Aristotle: a Chapter from the History of Science* (London, 1864).
[2] A note at the bottom of this letter in another hand identifies the correspondent merely as W. H. B. I have not been able to trace the Tylers.

called Mr Tyler. I remember his marrying,—so you must be very young. I remember going to see his wife, as a boy,—when they were living at the junction of Davies Street and Mount Street, and thinking that she was very beautiful, and had as fine a taste in pound cake as I had ever met— And well I remember Aunt Charlotte. It is as good as 30 years ago,—nay, I suppose more, since I have heard of their whereabouts, and therefore you will excuse me for not understanding your exact connexion with our old & dearly loved friends.

My mother, whose death last year caused the black fringes around this paper, loved John & Charlotte Tyler very dearly.

Yours faithfully

ANTHONY TROLLOPE

232. TO OWEN GRANT. 1 May.
Parrish Collection.

May 1. 1864
(Waltham House,
Waltham Cross.)

My dear Owen.

I ought to have written to you before about Charlie Gould[1]— You know his position now. He is employed in the Postoffice, but is not on the establishment. The position is not a desirable one except so far as it affords him present employment & may make it easier for him to get a second nomination, or chance of competing. I have little doubt but that such other nomination may be had;—say in the course of the winter; but it would be of no avail, unless he can coach himself up in *arithmetic* and the writing of English. He should have lessons in that, & also in *writing*. Now I fear that Charlie, tho the best young fellow in the world, does not like the learning of lessons,—or indeed hard work of any kind. The question is whether you can and will keep his nose to the grindstone & make him do what is necessary. If he will work he will succeed, & then Tilley would see that in the office things were made for him as pleasant as they could be. I have not written to Kate since Charlie left us as I have not liked to say that her boy was idle— I saw no other fault in him at all.

[1] See letter 224.

He is quite a gentleman. Indeed how could her boy be anything else.

When you write to her tell her that I have written to you.

I hope she [? we] shall meet soon.

Yours always

ANTHONY TROLLOPE

233. To TOM TAYLOR. 5 May.
Mrs. Arthur Helps.

My dear Taylor,

There has come up a violent dispute which for the sake of a very pretty woman, you must take the trouble to decide. I have no doubt on the subject; but your decision must be had. Did Hawkshaw when shewing the handcuffs to the Tiger know that the Tiger was the Tiger?[1]

Yours always

ANTHONY TROLLOPE

Waltham Cross

May 5—1864

234. To MISS E. B. ROWE.[2] 16 May.
Miss J. Havell.

(Waltham House,

Waltham Cross.)

May 16, 1864.

My dear girls.

I have got your letter, but I do not know that I can tell you anything about Lily Dale & her fortunes that will be satisfactory to you. You were angry with me because I did not make my pet happy with a husband, but you would have been more angry if I had made it all smooth, and supposed her capable of loving a second man while the wound of her first love was still so fresh. Indeed the object of the story was to show that a girl under such circumstances should bear the effects of her own imprudence, &

---

[1] The reference is to *The Ticket-of-Leave Man,* Taylor's most famous play, which had been produced the previous year. The best discussion is in Winton Tolles, *Tom Taylor and the Victorian Drama* (New York: Columbia University Press, 1940), pp. 197–202.

[2] Miss Rowe wrote on behalf of herself and her sisters.

not rid herself of her sorrow too easily. I hope none of you will ever come to such misfortune as hers;—but should such a fate be yours do not teach yourself to believe that any other man will do as well.

Yours with much good will
ANTHONY TROLLOPE

235. To MRS. GEORGE TROLLOPE.[1] 24 May.
John W. Watling.

May 24, 1864.
(Waltham House,
Waltham Cross.)

Dear Madam,

For our names sake and I believe for some distant cousinship may I be forgiven in asking you to interest yourself for Miss Curwood, as to whom I send a paper. You I believe are a subscriber, & Miss Curwood's friends are very desirous of obtaining for her some annuity from the Governesses' benevolent institution. I see that Mrs Trollope of Christs Hospital also has a vote. Perhaps you might also interest her in the matter. If you or she could send a Proxy, would you send it to Mrs George Burns—Again asking you to excuse I am very faithfully yours

ANTHONY TROLLOPE

236. To MAJOR [? BENT].[2] 26 May.
Parrish Collection.

(Waltham House,
Waltham Cross.)
May 26. 1862

Dear Major.

Do I understand that you'll be up in London on June 6th? Of course I do. The fusiliers can't go to Exeter to eat their dinner. If it be so of course you will come to us. *Tom will be with us*—as also my boy Harry whom I should so like you to see;—a lad of 18 whom you will not be ashamed to call your cousin, I think.

---

[1] The name of the addressee has been pencilled at the top of the letter by another hand. There were a number of George Trollopes at this time, and it is not possible to identify these cousins positively. Nor have I been able to identify the other persons mentioned.

[2] Major Bent was the son of Mary Bent, first cousin to Frances Trollope.

We have lots of beds for you,—that is if one will not suffice;—
or if any of your young folk come with you.

Let me know what time would suit you best? I dine in London
on June 4—Saturday, but come home that night; and my wife
will dine at home. We shall be at home on the Sunday;—and as
far as we are yet advised on the Tuesday following. We live 11
miles out of town on the Great Eastern line of railway,—and
a good deal nearer to our station than you are to yours. I wish
I could think the strawberries would be ripe, but I fear all our
summer is over.

Give my love to all my cousins and to aunt Mary when you
see her.

Yours affectionately
ANTHONY TROLLOPE

237. To MRS. TROLLOPE.[1] 21 June 1864.
Bodleian Library.

(Waltham House,
Waltham Cross.)

June 21. 1864.
My dear Mrs Trollope

Here you have my brother and self.[2] You will perceive that my
brother is pitching into me. He always did.

Yours very sincerely
ANTHONY TROLLOPE

238. To GEORGE HENRY LEWES. 26 June.
Mrs. E. S. Ouvry.

(Waltham House,
Waltham Cross.)
June 26—1864

My dear Lewes,

There never was better criticism than that on Greek tragic
art in the two first pages of your chapter—called Iphigenia[3]
and I make you my compliments. I had felt it all before, but could

---

[1] Probably the wife of Charles Trollope. See letter No. 779, *infra.*
[2] Trollope enclosed a photograph of himself and his brother Tom.
[3] Lewes wrote of Goethe's *Iphigenie auf Tauris* in his *Life of Goethe.*

not have expressed it. Of course I speak of the Greek; not of the German which is to me a book altogether sealed. But how true are you to truth in your rhapsody as to dead bones. 'But—dead bones for dead bones—,' &c, page 287. You know you are only warming an idea. The history of mans mind must have in it more of poetry than the history of man's body,—even tho we throw you in the elephant's.

Yours ever
Anthy Trollope

I tried to see you the other day. Heavens, what pens and ink you do keep in your dining room! ! ! My kindest regards to your wife. I will if it be possible see you before long.

239. To George Smith. 1 July.
Mrs. Reginald Smith. Sadleir, *Commentary*, p. 248.

July 1—1864.   Friday
(Waltham House,
Waltham Cross.)

My dear Smith.

I got your letter this morning too late to allow of my answering it, so that you should get my letter before you left town. We have people staying with us,—a house full;—and I cannot therefore get away, as I should so much have liked to have done, to meet Mrs Gaskell.[1] If I were to ride over on Monday should I have any chance of finding her & Mrs Smith at home. I mean about 5 pm. I could then get back to my people by dinner time.

Laurence[2] seemed to think the black [? back] ground of the frame too dark; but I dare say he is wrong. *Pray do not have it altered.* I thought it very nice. I came upon it accidentally in the room when I came from the frame makers.

Such a week as I have had in sitting! Only that he is personally such a nice fellow, & has so much to say for himself, I should have been worn out. I have been six times, or seven I think,—& am

---

[1] Trollope did not meet Mrs. Gaskell. See letter No. 282, *infra.*
[2] Samuel Laurence (1812–84), portrait-painter of many illustrious nineteenth-century men of letters. There are two Laurence drawings of Trollope: one is in the possession of Miss Muriel Trollope; the other hangs in the National Portrait Gallery.

to go again. He compliments me by telling me that I am a subject very difficult to draw. He has taken infinite pains with it.
Of course I myself am no judge of what he has done.

Yours always

ANTHONY TROLLOPE

240. To GEORGE SMITH. 6 July.
Mrs. Reginald Smith. Sadleir, *Commentary*, pp. 248–9.

(Waltham House,

Waltham Cross.)

July 6. 1864

My dear Smith.

This morning we hung Thackeray up in our library,[1] and we
are *very much* obliged to you for the present,—not only in that
it is in itself so valuable, but more especially because it is one so
suited to our feelings. To-day we go into the Garrick Club, and
have an initiatory dinner at which as Chairman I shall propose his
memory. I heard yesterday from Shirley B[2] that the Dean of
Westminster has consented to put up a memorial (whether bust
or statue is not yet decided) & the subscription list is now opened.
I have been nervous about this lest the time should slip away.
The next thing will be to have a perfect edition of his works.—
for which we must look to you.

I hope it will not be long before you come & see the portrait.

Yours always very truly

ANTHONY TROLLOPE

241. To [? FREDERIC] CHAPMAN. 14 July.
Pierpont Morgan Library.

Trollope introduces Chapman to Mrs. Macquoid, who has a manuscript
novel for sale. Mrs. Katherine Sarah Macquoid (1824–1917) was a prolific
minor novelist.

[1] The Laurence portrait of Thackeray to which Trollope refers remained
in the Trollope family until 1946, when it was presented by Muriel Trollope
to Hester Thackeray Ritchie Fuller.
[2] Charles William Shirley Brooks (1816–74), a miscellaneous writer
and long-time editor of *Punch*.

242. To GEORGE SMITH. 16 July. Windermere.
Mrs. Reginald Smith.

Trollope is in the Lake country, but working harder than ever, making up for the time he lost while sitting to Laurence. His wife 'liked the portrait *very much indeed*. She seemed to have a fuller respect for me when she had seen it than ever before'.

243. To GEORGE SMITH. 12 August.
Not traced. Sadleir, *Commentary*, pp. 265–6.

* * *

I think you would possibly find no worse illustrator than H. Browne; and I think he is almost as bad in one kind as in another. He will take no pains to ascertain the thing to be illustrated. I cannot think that his work can add any value at all to any book.

I am having the ten last numbers of Can You Forgive Her illustrated by a lady. She has as yet done two drawings on wood. They are both excellent, and the cutter says that they will come out very well. She has £5: 5:—a drawing for them. Why not employ her? She is a Miss Taylor of St. Leonards.[1]

But of course the question is one for you to settle yourself. As for myself I can never express satisfaction at being illustrated in any way by H. Browne.

If you are going to bring out a cheap edition of The Small House, of course I should prefer the 5/- shape very much; as all those which Chapman has are in that form.

* * *

244. To OWEN GRANT. 14 August.
Parrish Collection.

August 14. 1864.   (Waltham House,
                                      Waltham Cross.)
My dear Owen.

The other day Kate wrote to me asking me about Charlie—& expressing a hope that he would by this time have made such an improvement as to justify his friends in putting him forward for another nomination. I was then away in Westmoreland, but

---

[1] Browne was dropped and Miss Taylor, whom I have not been able to identify, was engaged to do the illustrations for vol. ii.

immediately on my return I went to the Postoffice & enquired about him.

I do not find the account satisfactory. You know that he is employed on task work, and it seems that he does not earn above 4/ a day. The average of those employed as he is employed is nearer 6/. This comes partly from extreme slowness,—& partly from errors in his work. I fear he would be rejected if he were sent up again for competition at present— He has time enough for the next six months or more;—but unless he can work harder than he does at present, he will not do any good in the Post-office. I found that the men are well disposed to him, but they think he is idle.

I tell you this because I can not tell Kate so much. I can not bring myself to give her bad tidings of her boy. I shall tell her that I have written to you, & that it is clearly not expedient that another nomination should be procured for him quite im-mediately.

I send this to your office. No doubt you are out of town but it will be sent after you.

Yours always
ANTHONY TROLLOPE

245. TO GEORGE SMITH. 10 October.
   Mrs. Reginald Smith. Sadleir, *Commentary*, p. 249.

(Waltham House,
Freshwater   Waltham Cross.)
   Isle of Wight
10. October 1864
My dear Smith.

I suppose you are back from your Italian wanderings, & I write a line to thank you—in my wifes name chiefly,—but also in my own, for your gracious present to us of myself—done to the life, in a wonderfully vigorous manner. When I look at the portrait I find myself to be a wonderfully solid old fellow. The picture is certainly a very good picture & my wife declares it to be very like,—and not a bit more solid than the original. For your munificence we both thank you very heartily, and hope you and your wife will soon come to see it—& the others—in their places.

158

My brother says you would not go & stay with him after all. No doubt you feared that with the aid of some Italian bravo and dagger he would compel you to accept an unlimited number of articles for the Cornhill. I shall be very anxious to hear your account. I have heard that you did nurse maid to Bice[1] up at the convent.

Yours always faithfully
ANTHONY TROLLOPE

That stupid Mrs MacQuoid has written to me to ask to dedicate her novel to me.[2] I have written to decline, as I hate such trash. But she writes simply from Stanley place. What postman can be supposed to know where Stanley place is? Some of your people will know. Will you have the address completed? I enclose the letter.

I also send a Devonshire MS—& a letter from me, which you will find not to be very pressing.

246. To GEORGE SMITH. 4 November. Waltham Cross. *Not traced.* Sadleir's transcript.

Trollope wants to write eight or nine pages for Smith in reply to the Archbishop of York and to a leader in *The Times,*[3] pp. 130–56.

247. To GEORGE SMITH. 6 November. *Not traced.* Sadleir's transcript.

Smith apparently disapproved of the idea of the article, and Trollope agrees to drop it. His object was to answer the attack made on sensationalists by showing that all modern English novels present life decently and do little or no harm; that, indeed, they do good, taking poetry's place in cultivating the imagination; that they advocate those lessons of life which mammas teach, or ought to teach, to their daughters.

248. To GEORGE SMITH. 24 November. Waltham Cross. *Mrs. Reginald Smith.*

Trollope has taken the liberty of putting Smith's name down for a ten-guinea contribution to the Thackeray monument. 'Will you indemnify me?'

[1] Bice was the 'short' name of Beatrice Trollope.
[2] Mrs. Macquoid's novel was *Hester Kirton.*
[3] The Archbishop was William Thomson (1819–90). His remarks of 31 Oct. were reported in full in *The Times*, 2 Nov., p. 9. His supercilious tone was indeed provocative.

249. To GEORGE SMITH. 4 December.
Not traced. Sadleir's transcript.

Smith had apparently renewed the suggestion of an article on fiction, for now Trollope begs off on grounds of inadequate time.

250. To GEORGE HENRY LEWES. 24 December.
Mrs. E. S. Ouvry.

In the following letter Trollope refers to Lewes's decision not to accept the editorship of the *Fortnightly Review.* Apparently as a result of Trollope's pressure Lewes again changed his mind and accepted the post.

(Waltham House,
Waltham Cross.)

24 December 1864.
My dear Lewes
I cannot deny that I am disappointed and grieved by your letter; but you are not to suppose that I shall either find fault with you or argue with you. I know well how these things go, and do not think that a man is open to censure because he changes his views. I am not one of those who suppose that a mans mind should be subject to no hesitation,— to no vacillating influences. Men who are strong enough never to be so subject are distasteful to me. Haud ignarus dubitationis, dubitantibus succurrere disco.[1] So much I say, to quell any fear that you may have that I should condemn you,—believing that you would not wittingly be condemned by one who regards you as well as I do.

But having said this I must go on to declare that I greatly regret your defection. I have felt the necessity of the aid of some one who would know what he was about in arranging the work of such a venture as we propose; and I have also felt,—more strongly perhaps than I can explain to you,—that to make the affairs comfortable to myself the person selected for the above described purpose should be one with whom I could hold close friendly intercourse. I do not care to put myself at the beck of any one whom I do not know, or whom, when known, I may not like.

I would recommend you, for your own sake, to come to the meeting on Thursday. It would, I think, be better that you should

[1] See Virgil, *Aeneid*, i. 630: 'Non ignara mali miseris succurrere disco.'

state your own withdrawal, than that I should do so for you. As
to that, however, you can make up your mind and let me know
your intention.

Yours always faithfully
ANTHONY TROLLOPE

Give all kind remembrances of the season to your wife. I feel
that I ought to congratulate her upon your decision.

251. To GEORGE SMITH. 31 December.
Not traced. Sadleir's transcript.

Trollope's new novel *Harry Clavering* [*The Claverings*] is finished, and
the manuscript will soon be on its way. 'I tell you this in obedience to
your intimation regarding the little quid pro quo—as to which I am grateful
for your liberal readiness of purse.'

252. To GEORGE SMITH. [1864.]
Not traced. Sadleir's transcript.

Trollope is lecturing in Leeds soon but has not yet finished writing. Can
Smith print a few copies for him in twenty-four hours?

1865

253. To GEORGE SMITH. 9 January.
Mrs. Reginald Smith.

Trollope has nominated Smith for the Garrick Club. He asks for an opinion
of a manuscript.

254. To MISS TAYLOR. 7 February. Waltham Cross.
Parrish Collection.

Miss Taylor had intended one of her illustrations for *Can You Forgive
Her?* for Rose Trollope, but Trollope tells her that it has been lost at
Chapman's.

255. To GEORGE SMITH. 12 March. Waltham Cross.
Not traced. Sadleir's transcript.

Trollope sends the manuscript of 'How to Ride to Hounds', the last of
his series of eight hunting sketches for the *Pall Mall Gazette*.

256. To GEORGE SMITH. 15 March.
Not traced. Sadleir, *Commentary*, p. 251.

Trollope complains of publishers' emendations in his text. 'Will you kindly ask your assistants in Salisbury Street not to alter my MS. Let them send back or omit to use any paper that is unsatisfactory, and I will not even ask the reason. But don't let one be altered.'

257. To GEORGE SMITH. 31 March. Waltham Cross.
Not traced. Sadleir's transcript.

Trollope announces the arrival of a consignment of 12,000 cigars. How many does Smith want?

258. To GEORGE SMITH. 31 March.
Not traced. Sadleir, *Commentary*, p. 251.

*　　*　　*

The drawing which I return is very spirited, pretty and good. The horse is faulty. He is too long— Look at the quarters behind the girl's seat. And your artist has made the usual mistake of supposing that a horse goes at his fence in the full stride of his gallop. He does not do this, but gathers himself for his jump exactly as a man does. This horse could only have gone through the paling,—could not possibly have jumped it.

*　　*　　*

259. To GEORGE SMITH. 3 April. Waltham Cross.
Mrs. Reginald Smith.

Trollope invites Smith to a Garrick dinner with Billy Russell, Charles Taylor, and Mark Fladgate, 'in assistance towards which Taylor has bespoken up from his country quarters a young sucking pig. At any rate, whether sucking pig be or be not to your taste come & join us, & we will be very jolly'.

260. To GEORGE SMITH. 5 May.
Not traced. Sadleir, *Commentary*, pp. 251–2.

*　　*　　*

I went to a May meeting today at 11 am. punctual, and would not go to another to be made Editor of the Pall Mall Gazette!

You do not know what you have asked. Go to one yourself and try. You sit four hours and listen to six sermons;—and the sermons are to me (—and would be to you,)—of such a nature that tho' they are in their nature odious and so tedious that human nature cannot listen to them, still they do not fall into a category at which you would wish to throw your ridicule.

I will tomorrow morning write you an article (a Zulu at a May meeting), for which the materials arranged themselves not unhappily; but I *can do no more*. Suicide would intervene after the third or fourth, or I should give myself up to the police as the murderer of Mr. . . .[1]

In short I cannot bring myself to go through another May meeting—even tho' the object be to comply with your wishes.

I had thought perhaps my boy Harry might have done the attendance for me, but he,—having accompanied me today,—found so ready a resource in somnolence, that to him a May meeting would simply mean sleep for the future.

* * *

261. To GEORGE SMITH. 9 May.
   Mrs. Reginald Smith.

73 St Georges Square
   9. May. 1865

My dear Smith,

I hope I shall not offend you tho' I fear I may run some risk of annoying you by my present letter.

I am obliged [to] return the enclosed cheque as I cannot consent to be paid [at] the rate of two guineas and a half for articles about the length of a leader in the Times.

I know that on reading this your first feeling will be that I should be the last man to stand out for higher pay than you are disposed to give. But that is not what I do. If you will think of it I am sure you will perceive that tho' I may well afford to give you any little aid in my power from friendship, I cannot afford to work as a professional man at wages which I should be ashamed to acknowledge.

[1] The proper name here was apparently illegible. 'A Zulu in London' appeared in the *Pall Mall Gazette*, i (10 May 1865), 3–4.

I can easily understand,—and do understand,—that the sort of work I may do for you is not of value to you at all equal to that which others furnish who are more capable of supplying the wants of a daily newspaper; but that simply shews that a daily newspaper is not in my line.

I am so fond of the P. M. G.[1]—and so greatly admire your energy and skill and I may say genius in the matter—that I really dislike doing or saying anything which may terminate my connexion with it. If you will let me think that I may from time to time send you a letter,—all for love, I shall be delighted; and I pray you to accept those lately inserted in that light. Should you, on thinking over the matter, wish for three or four papers about tourists in the autumn, I will do them for you at the price you paid for the hunting sketches, which was I think 4 guineas a column. Or it may well be that you can get these done better by a younger hand at a lesser cost.

Pray tell me that you appreciate my motives, and that there is to be no ill will between us. I want you to understand that I can write for you without a view to income, but I cannot accept wages which if acknowledged would lower my position in my profession.

Yours always faithfully
ANTHONY TROLLOPE

262. To GEORGE SMITH. 11 May. Waltham Cross.
Mrs. Reginald Smith.

Smith wrote a mollifying note, and Trollope, cooling off, agrees to accept the cheque and forget 'that little difficulty'.

263. To GEORGE SMITH. 16 May.
Not traced. Sadleir's transcript.

*   *   *

I saw of course the notice in the P. M. G., but had not, and have not, seen the Saturday.[2]

---

[1] The *Pall Mall Gazette.*

[2] In the *Pall Mall Gazette* (i [5 May 1865], 4) Trollope had published a hitherto unrecorded article on Abraham Lincoln. The following week he was attacked in the *Saturday Review* ('Mistaken Estimates of Self', xix [13 May 1865], 564) because he had presumed to sign his name to the

I cannot but think such personal notices, in which the criticism is all on the man and nothing on the matter, to be in very bad taste.

*　　*　　*

264. To GEORGE HENRY LEWES. 30 May.
Mrs. E. S. Ouvry.

Glasgow 30 May 1865—

My dear Lewes,

As to putting Belton E. first in Nº 3, do just as you please.[1] I have a strong opinion against putting the novel always first as it indicates an idea that it is our staple;—which indicates the further idea that the remainder is padding. Were I Editor I think I should always give the novel a distinctive place just before the Chronique.[2] But that is a matter of small, or no, moment.

My revises were returned 4 days since,—& the non return up to then was not my fault. Indeed I had not asked for revises. But they were sent, and sent without the original proofs, and were therefore useless. I wrote for the original sheets and then returned the revises.

Touching the signing[3] I have been so driven by official work that I have not put a pen to it. But I will. I am not *at all* anxious as to the number in which it may appear. Indeed it would be too late now for the third. Fourth or fifth will do as well. I shall be with you in about a week. Who is to do your chronique? If you are in a difficulty *I will attempt it.* Only, could not the pages be less pressed? It is closer than we at first intended. Poor Billy![4] Why did he give up?

I have got, just got, Nº 2 & have only read your article.[5] It is beautiful, but, oh, so cruel. You are as hard almost as Carlyle;—

---

article. The *Saturday* implied that Trollope's views on such a subject were of no more interest than those of any other private citizen.

[1] Lewes varied the arrangement of his articles, but *The Belton Estate* continued normally to appear first.

[2] A series on 'Public Affairs' which was printed near the end of each number.

[3] Trollope's article, 'On Anonymous Literature', i (1 July 1865), 491–8.

[4] Probably William Howard Russell (1820–1907), later Sir William, ubiquitous war correspondent for *The Times* and the *Daily Telegraph.*

[5] *The Principles of Success in Literature*, chap. ii, 'The Principle of Vision', i (1 June 1865), 185–96.

165

without the salve which one has for Carlyle's blows, in the feeling that they are all struck in the dark, & may probably, after all, not be deserved. But it is very beautiful. Your style leaves nothing to be desired.

Enjoying myself! revising a post office with 300 men, the work and wages of all of whom are to be fixed on one's own responsibility! Come & try it, & then go back to the delicious ease & perfect freedom of your Editors chair!

Yours always
ANY TROLLOPE

265. TO GEORGE HENRY LEWES. 1 June.
Mrs. E. S. Ouvry.

Glasgow
June 1, 1865

(Waltham House,
Waltham Cross.)

My dear Lewes,

Beesly's[1] paper on Catiline is admirable.[2] It is written by a man leaning on his pen with delight, which leaning always gives a life to the work. But he writes too much like an advocate with a side to defend, to be perfectly convincing. I still believe that Cicero was more of a patriot than Catiline. That both were false and both cruel is to be assumed,—for they were Romans of that false and cruel time that began with Sulla and ended when there was no longer spirit enough in Rome either for falsehood or cruelty. That Cicero was constitutionally a coward,—tho he knew how to die,—& Catiline a man of nerve was little to the credit or discredit of either,—as little as having strong arms or long legs. Had Beesly been more historic & less enthusiastic he would have told us that Cicero, who was so loud against Verres was at any rate honest in his own province (a very rare virtue) and that he sought nothing from his countrymen at home beyond the objects of a fair ambition, & was therefore entitled to deal heavily with a demagogue.[3]

[1] Edward Spencer Beesly (1831–1915), a philosopher and educator, an authority on Comte.
[2] 'Catiline as a Party Leader', *Fortnightly Review*, i (1 June 1865), 167–84.
[3] Trollope discusses this point later in his *Life of Cicero*, 2 vols. (New York, 1881), i. 213–14.

That he did,—is as I have said a matter of course because he was a Roman; and equally a matter of course that he did successfully, because he was gifted with the use of words.

I however, am myself so given to rebellion in politics that I am delighted to see and hear any Catiline defended, and any Cicero attacked.

I am glad you have no difficulty about the chronique.

Yours ever
A. T.

Tom immersed in a lawsuit with a Russian—(in Florence!) which is like to keep him there all the summer,—as to the sale or non sale of his house!!!

266. To GEORGE SMITH. 3 June. Glasgow.
Parrish Collection.

Trollope regrets that he cannot attend a *Pall Mall* dinner.

267. To BEATRICE TROLLOPE. 8 June.
The Hon. Mrs. James Cecil.

Belfast.   8 June 1865.

Dearest Bice,

I got a letter yesterday from Mrs Lark, who was a great friend of your mama's, in which she said that she wanted to see you in London. She goes away on the 16th June. I was obliged to tell her that you would not be back so soon.

Your great aunt Mrs Clyde,—my mothers sister,—who is a very old woman living in Exeter has sent you a present of ten guineas. We must have a great consultation between you, and aunt Rose, and papa, and Barney,[1] and all the other wise people as to what you had better buy. What do you say to a new cow? Or perhaps ten guineas worth of chocolate bonbons? In the mean time you must write a pretty letter to Aunt Mary (that is her name) for the present, & send it to me to send it.

Remember me most kindly to M^r & Mrs Fell.

Your own affectionate uncle
T
(for Toney)

[1] Trollope's old Irish groom.

268. To Mrs. Anderson. 14 June.
   Estate of Carroll A. Wilson.

   Trollope invites Dr. and Mrs. Anderson to Waltham House for the week-end.

269. To R. S. Smyth. 21 June. *Not traced.* R. S. Smyth,
   'The Provincial Service Fifty Years Ago', *St. Martin's-le-Grand*, xiii (Oct. 1903), 375–6.

> (Waltham House,
> Waltham Cross.)
> June 21st, 1865

My dear Sir,—

That which is unsatisfactory to you in the nature of your position and prospects at Belfast, is owing to the fact that you find yourself to be possessed of better qualities for business than you had, when younger, given yourself credit for possessing, and not by any means to the inferiority of pay or rank which you have in the Belfast Post Office. If you will remember what were your expectations when you joined the Office some ten years since, you will find that this is so. Had you at that time been assured of the senior clerkship, with a prospect of an increase to the then rate of senior clerk's pay, you would have thought the place sufficiently alluring. That is now your position, and you are dissatisfied, not because you think that that is bad, but because you think higher of yourself. Such a condition is very common with men of energy, and such men must then decide whether they will begin the world again by placing themselves where a higher career may be open to them (in which there is always risk), or whether they will accept the moderate and sure advantages which they already possess. It may well be that you can do better for yourself, as you are still young, by finding service elsewhere; but I think you should endeavour, if you remain where you are, to teach yourself not to regard the service with dissatisfaction. That you will always do your work well I am sure, but it will be much for your own comfort if you can make yourself believe that the service in which you are has not been bad or hard to you.

> Very faithfully yours,
> Anthony Trollope

270. To GEORGE SMITH. 27 June.
   Not traced. Sadleir's transcript.

Trollope sends for the *Pall Mall* a letter about Lord Westbury.[1]

271. To GEORGE SMITH. 29 June.
   Not traced. Sadleir, *Commentary*, p. 253.

*   *   *

I only got your letter about the horse (altho' dated 27th) as also your other about that inferior animal the Lord Chancellor, this morning. Touching the horse, as we are going over to you tomorrow Barney shall ride him over and he can come back with us. He is quite right; but he has been having tares for the last three weeks, and is somewhat soft.

Touching Lord Westbury his fault (in my judgement) has been this,—that he has taught himself to think that intellect would do without moral conduct in English public life. He certainly ought to go, as no one can doubt that he has disgraced his position.

*   *   *

272. To GEORGE SMITH. 10 July. Waltham Cross.
   Mrs. Reginald Smith.

Trollope forwards a tentative list of nine tourist sketches.[2]

273. To WILLIAM DEAN HOWELLS. 13 July. Waltham Cross. *Harvard College Library.*

Trollope invites Howells to Waltham House for dinner. William Dean Howells (1837–1920) was American Consul at Venice in 1865 and just beginning his long and distinguished career as a man of letters.

[1] Richard Bethell, first Baron Westbury (1800–73), was Solicitor-General, Attorney-General, and, in 1861, Lord Chancellor. In 1865 he resigned when in the House of Commons a vote of censure was passed on him as being inattentive to the public interests. Trollope's letter was published on 28 June ('The Lord Chancellor', p. 4). The result was unfortunate. See Sadleir, *Commentary*, p. 253.

[2] All but one ('Tourists who enjoy themselves') appeared in the *Pall Mall* at intervals between 3 Aug. and 6 Sept. 1865.

274. To SAMUEL LAURENCE. 17 July. Garrick Club.
Parrish Collection.

Trollope writes on behalf of 'a Miss Hughes', who had been the victim
of a bogus art firm which offered positions to students who paid for lessons.
Will Laurence investigate?

275. To NORMAN MACLEOD. 10 August.
Waltham Cross. *Dr. Herman T. Radin.*

Trollope invites Macleod to Waltham House to meet Tom Trollope.
'What about Miss Anna Drury's manuscript?'[1]

276. To GEORGE SMITH. 24 August.
Mrs. Reginald Smith.

(Waltham House,
Waltham Cross.)

Augt. 24, 1865

My dear Smith.

I am almost ashamed to trouble you again about the S. H.
of A., having made such a mull of it before;—but there is being
made to me a proposition by C. & H. (with reference as I fancy
to a further proposition to them from Smith of the Strand) to
purchase from me for a term of years my copyright in certain
novels i e 10 or 11 in number. If I did not make any further
arrangement with you about the S.H., I should naturally include
it in the lump with the others, fixing my price accordingly. You
will understand that I by no means want to take it away from
your hands;—but perhaps you would tell me whether at the end
of your time for selling—i e in next spring,—you would make
me any & what offer.

Yours always
ANTHONY TROLLOPE

Geo. Smith Esq

[1] Anna Harriet Drury published *The Brothers* in 1865 and *The Three
Half-crowns* in 1866. Trollope's reference is probably to the earlier, since
The Three Half-crowns is a boy's book.

277. To [? JAMES] HUTTON.[1] 7 September.
Parrish Collection.

Sept. 7. 65.
(Waltham House,
Waltham Cross.)

My dear Mr Hutton.

I greatly regret your decision,—as regards ourselves. For yourself, of course I can say nothing further.

The MS you sent me I have left for Lewes as he will now be here in a day or two—and I am not interfering in his work more than has been necessary in his absence. It could not have appeared in the next number.[2]

It shall certainly either be used or returned.

Yours most faithfully
ANTHONY TROLLOPE

278. To GEORGE SMITH. 7 September.
Mrs. Reginald Smith.

This letter, like others from Trollope to his publishers, shows not only the many ways in which the Victorian novelist disposed of his property, but also how, without an agent, he had to fend for himself in the tricky business of managing his copyrights advantageously.

September 7, 1865.   (Waltham House,
Waltham Cross.)

My dear Smith.

I told you the other day that W. H. Smith was, (or was going to be,) in treaty with C & H. for my copyrights, & that C & H. intended to treat for a royalty on each copy printed. F. C.[3] now tells me that no such proposal has been made, but that W. H. Smith has suggested that I s^d name a price for the sale of my copyrights. This I have not done,—and do not think that I am disposed to do it.

Would you be disposed to buy them?— You will understand that my object is not immediate money, but a desire to make what I can of the property, and to put them into good hands—

---

[1] Probably the James Hutton who contributed a review of William Edwards's *Reminiscences of a Bengal Civilian* to the *Fortnightly Review*, vi (15 Oct. 1866), 510–12.

[2] The *Fortnightly Review* had been founded in May 1865 with G. H. Lewes as editor and Trollope as chairman of the Finance Committee.

[3] Frederic Chapman.

Of the following—I have the half copyrights, to be disposed of at once.

> The Macdermots
> The O'Kellys
> Dr Thorne ⎬ originally 3 volumes.
> The Bertrams
> Castle Richmond

> West Indies—   1 octavo
> North America   2   ,,
> Tales of all Countries ⎱ originally
> Rachel Ray   ⎰ two.

The North America has been reprinted in two smaller volumes; —all the others in one.

> Miss Mackenzie— 2 volumes.
>   has never yet been printed.

> Orley Farm
>   and
> Can You Forgive Her

have never been reprinted. The first would be sold say in twelve months time; the other in two years, so as to allow for selling the present 20/ edition.

> Belton Estate— 2 volumes

to be sold within a year after it has come out, which will be on 1 Jany next.

Chapman holds all these copyrights with me, and he is aware that I am going to write to you. If you can make an offer I can deal with him.

The other copyrights of books written by me are those of The Three Clerks—owned in entirety by Bentley—and of The Warden & Barchester Towers, owned between myself & Longman,—as to which I would do anything to assist you, if you wished to get them.

> Yours always faithfully
> ANTHONY TROLLOPE

279. To GEORGE SMITH. 13 September.
       Not traced. Sadleir's transcript.

Trollope sends Smith an itinerary of a month's trip through Germany and Austria. His son Fred is about to leave for Melbourne. Can Smith furnish him with any suitable letters of introduction?

280. To ?[1] 31 October.
       Estate of Carroll A. Wilson.

(Waltham House,
Waltham Cross.)
31. Oct 1865

Sir.

I found your letter of Sept 30 on my return yesterday from the continent. My absence from home has been the reason of my not earlier noticing and answering it.

I must in the first place beg you to believe that I do not write without thinking very much of what may be the effects of what I write,—and that I do my work with a most anxious wish & with much effort that what I produce may at least not do harm. Were I to believe that any young persons could be led into evil ways by what I have published I should be very unhappy.

The subject of adultery is one very difficult of discussion. You have probably found it so in preaching. It is a sin against which you are called on to inveigh, (—and I also as I think of my work,) —but as to which it is difficult to speak because of the incidents to adultery which are not only sinful, but immodest & in some degrees indecent. Of theft, lying, & murder you can speak openly to young & old, but against adultery or fornication you must caution those who are most in danger with baited [*sic*] breath. That I think is the cause of your letter to me.

But the bible does not scruple to speak to us of adultery as openly as of other sins. You do not leave out the seventh Commandment. The young girl for whom I or you are so tender is not

[1] Carroll A. Wilson, to whom the manuscript of this letter belonged, wrote me that he had been told it was addressed to Arthur J. Munby, 6 Fig Tree Court, The Temple, London. He did not know, however, on what authority this attribution was made. The *Post Office London Directory, 1865*, lists Munby at this address, but he was a barrister, not a clergyman, and therefore he can hardly have been the addressee.

ignorant of the sin;—and, as I think, it would not be well that she should be ignorant of it.

The education of our daughters is a subject on which at present many Englishmen differ greatly. Thinking as I do that ignorance is not innocence I do not avoid, as you would wish me to do, the mention of things which are to me more shocking in their facts than in their names. I do not think that any girl can be injured by reading the character whose thoughts I have endeavoured to describe in the novel to which you have alluded.[1] It is not probable that I shall carry you with me, but I may perhaps succeed in inducing you to believe that I do not write in the manner of which you complain without thought or without a principle.

> Your very faithful Servant
> ANTHONY TROLLOPE

Allow me to assure you that I accept as a very great compliment any criticism on my work from a man such as you—

281. To GEORGE SMITH. 2 November. Waltham Cross.
Mrs. Reginald Smith.

Having discussed with Fred Chapman the matter of selling his copyrights, Trollope now sets a price on the entire group. The enclosure on which the sum was named has not been preserved.

282. To GEORGE SMITH. 15 November.
Parrish Collection.

November 15—1865   (Waltham House,
                                     Waltham Cross.)

My dear Smith.

We have been most grieved to hear of the death of Mrs Gaskell. I do not know how often I was to have met her at your house, and yet we never did so. I regret it greatly now. It seems that she must [? have] gone quite suddenly. It will have shocked you greatly,—and your wife.

[1] The reference is probably to the Lady Glencora Palliser–Burgo Fitzgerald scenes in *Can You Forgive Her?*, publication of which in monthly parts had just been concluded. See Trollope's reference to the letter in *Autobiography*, chap. x, p. 153.

Are you going to print the clerical papers?[1] I have not gone on with them till I found what you were doing; but should do so if I get the proofs from your office.

Yours always
ANTHONY TROLLOPE

Geo Smith Esq

Had Mrs Gaskell finished her story for you?[2]

283. To ?[3] 17 November. Waltham Cross.
Parrish Collection.

Trollope is happy to be on the list of stewards and will try to be present at the dinner and support his friend Dr. McCleod [? Macleod].

284. To GEORGE SMITH. 3 December. Waltham Cross.
Parrish Collection.

Trollope forwards three of his clerical sketches and urges Smith to write to Tom Trollope.

285. To CHAPMAN & HALL. 20 December.
Parrish Collection.

In apparent disagreement with his publishers about the disposition of early sheets of *The Belton Estate*, Trollope writes them a severely formal letter, which they callously proceeded to disregard.[4]

(Garrick Club)
Waltham Cross.   December 20, 1865

Gentlemen:

With reference to the conversation I had with you today regarding the republication in America of my work, the Belton

---

[1] Trollope's ten *Clerical Sketches* were published at intervals in the *Pall Mall Gazette* from 20 Nov. 1865 to 25 Jan. 1866.

[2] The last number of Mrs. Gaskell's *Wives and Daughters*, published in the *Cornhill* for Jan. 1866, left the novel still incomplete.

[3] The name of the addressee is illegible.

[4] Carroll A. Wilson, in a letter to Mr. Parrish dated 25 Mar. 1929 and preserved in the Parrish Collection, points out that Lippincott's American first edition has an English imprint on the reverse of the title and on the last page.

Estate, by Messrs Lippincott of Philadelphia, I must beg you to
understand that I am altogether averse to the measure which
you propose to adopt in placing early sheets, or rather entirely
printed early copies, in the hands of Messrs Lippincott for publication in America.

I must remind you that you have no legal power to do that
which you propose to do, as, in my contract with you in reference
to the work in question, I have expressly kept the foreign rights
in my own hands. When the book is published by you, and has
found its way to the United States, it will of course be open to
any American publishers to republish it, and it is open to you
to sell to any firm, in the States or elsewhere, any copies of the
book as published by you. But it is not within your rights to sell
unpublished matter of mine to any one, or to place in the hands
of any publisher, at any time, volumes printed at your expense,
but bearing on the title page the name of an American firm of
publishers.

I must therefore request that you will not send out to the
Messrs Lippincott any copies of the work so prepared, and that
you will not place in their hands any copies whatever of the work,
till it has been published here.

I request also that you will be good enough to let me know
that the copies prepared with the title page I saw today, bearing
Messrs Lippincotts name as publishers, will not be sent to the
United States.

I am Gentlemen,
Your most obedient Servant
ANTHONY TROLLOPE

Messrs Chapman & Hall
193 Piccadilly

286. To GEORGE SMITH. 21 December.
Not traced. Sadleir's transcript.

Trollope suggests a scene for Mrs. Edwards to illustrate as a frontispiece
for *The Claverings.* The work of Mary Ellen Edwards is discussed briefly
in Forrest Reid, *Illustrators of the Sixties* (London: Faber & Gwyer, 1928),
p. 261.

287. TO JOHN [? TILLEY]. 31 December.
Parrish Collection.

(Waltham House,
Waltham Cross.)

31, Decr. 65.

Dear John:

I have told the publishers to send you a copy of a good book, called Belton Estate, which will improve your mind, and the minds of your children if you and they will attend to it.

Ever so many happy new years to you all

Thine A. T.

1 8 6 6

288. TO GEORGE SMITH. 3 February.
Not traced.[1] Copy in the Bodleian.

In January 1866 Trollope began *The Last Chronicle of Barset.* In a few weeks Smith wrote to offer him for his next novel £3,000 plus half profits from future cheap editions.

3. Feb. 1866

My dear Smith.

I do not think that I have any objection to make to the terms you propose about my new novel. I should wish there to be an understanding as to the period of publication—viz that it shall all appear in the course of 1867 & 1868;—also as to the payment, which you will probably not object to make by instalments of £150 a month from 1 Jany 67 to 1 Augt 1868,—on condition of course that so much of the MS is in your hands. I contemplate finishing the whole by next Xmas.

I will see you tomorrow for a moment at about 3.30 pm if you can spare me the time.

A. T.

[1] Both Smith's letter and a copy of Trollope's reply are preserved in the Bodleian Library.

289. To GEORGE SMITH. 6 February.
Not traced. Copy in the Bodleian.

The following letter well illustrates the difficulties and handicaps under which the Victorian novelist worked who wrote for serial publication in parts.

(Waltham House,
Waltham Cross.)
6 Feb 1866

My dear Smith.

I quite agree as to the enclosed and send a copy signed by myself. I return the original that you may insert the change of date, 1866—for 1865 inscribed in error.

But it is essential, in reference to the proposed 30 numbers, to be prepared for such a division if it be contemplated. It would not be practicable to divide 20 numbers into 30 equal parts, unless the work be specially done with this intent. I commonly divide a number of 32 pages (such as the numbers of 'Orley Farm') into four chapters each. If you wish the work to be so arranged as to run either to 20 or to 30 numbers, I must work each of the 20 numbers by 6 chapters, taking care that the chapters run so equally, two and two, as to make each four into one equal part or each six into one equal part— There will be some trouble in this, but having a mechanical mind I think I can do it. If you wish it I will do so. Had you made up your mind for the sixpenny venture I could of course do the work more easily and more pleasantly.

You will understand that I wish to suit your views altogether; but that it is necessary that you should say—Write it in 20 parts or in 30 parts—or in parts to suit either number. And you will also understand that if your mind be made up either to 30 or to 20, you need not put my mechanical genius to work.[1]

290. To ? GIBBON.[2] 12 February.
Parrish Collection.

A dinner invitation. 'I will have an old one-eyed Irishman to meet you. I am sorry that you should stay with me so short a time the first time I have you under my roof.'

[1] *The Last Chronicle of Barset* finally appeared in thirty-two sixpenny parts, published weekly from 1 Dec. 1866 to 6 July 1867.

[2] Possibly Charles Gibbon (1843–90), author of *Dangerous Connections* (1864) and some thirty other novels. But the formality of letter No. 483, *infra*, to C. Gibbon makes this assignment highly dubious.

291. To GEORGE SMITH. 25 February.
Not traced. Sadleir's transcript.

Trollope will write *The Last Chronicle* in 30 numbers of 21 pages each.
'I will put down Greenwood's[1] name tomorrow,—simply saying "Literature" as his profession. Pity it isn't his brother[2] as I should have had such pleasure in entering him as a "casual".'

292. To ? 8 March.
Parrish Collection.

(Waltham House,
March 8, 66   Waltham Cross.)
Sir.

The house which I had chiefly in my minds eye when I described Mr. Thornes house in Barchester Towers was a place called, I think, Montacute House,[3] belonging to Mr Phelips—not far from Yeovil in Somersetshire. But the house was not in all respects such as I described;—and indeed in some respects was very different. Ullathorne, if I remember,—(for I have not the book by me,)—was described as standing with two parlors, one at right angles to the other.[4] Montacute house is straight.

But for colour of stone, irregularity of design falling into and creating lines of architectural beauty, and for general picturesque forms of stone work without such magnificence as that of Longleat[5] or Hatfield,[6] Montacute House is the best example I know in England.

Your obt Servant
ANTHONY TROLLOPE

[1] Frederick Greenwood (1830–1909) succeeded Thackeray as editor of the *Cornhill* and with Smith was co-founder and editor of the *Pall Mall*. The reference is to Garrick Club candidature.
[2] James Greenwood wrote a sensational article for the *Pall Mall* descriptive of the London casual wards called 'Low Life Deeps'.
[3] Montacute House is an Elizabethan mansion erected 1580–1611 and arbitrarily attributed to John Thorpe. See Edward Hutton, *Highways and Byways in Somerset* (London: Macmillan, 1930), pp. 248–55.
[4] See *Barchester Towers*, chap. xxii.
[5] Longleat, seat of the Marquess of Bath, was erected in 1547–80. It is in Wiltshire, near Frome.
[6] Hatfield House in Hertfordshire is the property of the Marquess of Salisbury. Partly Renaissance but chiefly Jacobean in construction, it has many historical associations.

293. To GEORGE SMITH. 9 March.
Mrs. Reginald Smith. Sadleir, *Commentary,* p. 260.

Trollope's next novel was *Nina Balatka*, an experiment in anonymity which he here offers to Smith for the *Cornhill*.

9 March 66.   (Waltham House,
                                                    Waltham Cross.)

My dear Smith—

If you like to publish NB in the C. H. M. for £300 you shall do so. If you like to publish 1500 for £300 you shall do so. If you like to buy the copyright for £500—(undertaking not to disclose the name without my permission,) you shall do so.

Yours always
A. T.

294. To ROBERT BROWNING. 9 March.
Library of Congress.

(Garrick Club)

My dear Browning.

Our dinner is at St James hotel, Piccadilly, at 7–PM on Wednesday next. Do come to us. Your coming will not be taken, nor is our wish for you to come, intended as in anyway, [*sic*] binding you to anything more on our behalf than the light of your face on our little dinner. Not but that we are most *anxious* for your stouter assistance if at any time you can give it to us. I think we shall have a nice dinner.[1]

Yours always
ANTHONY TROLLOPE
9 March 1866

295. To CHOLMONDELEY PENNELL. 11 March.
Parrish Collection.

Trollope writes a formal third-person note inviting Pennell to dine with him at the Athenaeum Club. Henry Cholmondeley Pennell (1837–1915) was Inspector of Sea Fisheries, 1866–75, and author of many books on sport and natural history. Trollope's account-book shows that Pennell dined with him on 13 March.

[1] I have not been able to determine the group or organization for whom Trollope speaks, but Mr. Frederick Page has kindly established for me that Trollope attended a meeting of the Royal Literary Fund Society at Adelphi Terrace on that day.

296. To ?[1] 12 March.
    Parrish Collection.

March 12. 1866

(Waltham House,
Waltham Cross.)

My dear Sir

If it be not too late, let the words scandala magnata be altered
to scandals.

I have made search, and I believe after all I am wrong about
the word magnatum.[2] I cannot quite explain to you, all my reasons
for having supposed myself to be right.

Yours always
(in a penitential spirit)
ANTHONY TROLLOPE

297. To GEORGE SMITH. 21 March.
    Not traced. Sadleir, *Commentary*, p. 290.

Trollope passes off gracefully Smith's rejection of *Nina Balatka.* 'All
right about N.B. Would you kindly send her back;—to Waltham. She
won't mind travelling alone. Whether I shall put her by, or try another
venture with her I don't quite know. At any rate you are too much the gent
to claim acquaintance if you meet her in the street.'

298. JOHN BLACKWOOD[3] to TROLLOPE. 14 April.
    Bodleian Library.

This letter from John Blackwood to Trollope opens what was to be a long
and cordial business and social relationship.

Edinburgh
April 14/66

My dear Sir

It gives me very great pleasure to receive your letter to M^r
Langford[4] & to see the frank way in which you accept the remarks
I ventured to make on Nina Balatka.

---

[1] Possibly Mr. Enoch, manager of Smith, Elder & Co., who was seeing
the *Clergymen of the Church of England* through the press.

[2] *Magnatum* is a genitive plural.

[3] John Blackwood (1818–79), longtime editor of *Blackwood's Edinburgh
Magazine* and head of the famous publishing house.

[4] Joseph Munt Langford (1809–84), dramatic critic and head of the
London branch of Blackwoods for thirty-five years. Trollope knew Langford

I accept at once the alteration you propose in the terms I offered and accordingly agree to give you £250—for the appearance of the story in the Magazine and £200—for the remainder of the Copyright.

I agree with you that Nina herself is very much of a real character and there is a great charm & purity in the way she pours forth her love. This made me all the more savage at the Jew when he tried to disgrace such a mistress by making her purloin her fathers key & it was quite a relief to me when I found you got her out of the scrape which you do most ingeniously.

I am overdone with serials in the Magazine at present and I hope you will not care if I postpone the start of Nina for a month or two. Indeed it would not be a good plan to begin the story at a time when I have no doubt my readers think I have too many papers in parts going on already.

I intend to be in London about the middle of May when I look forward with much interest to making your personal acquaintance.

Hoping that the correspondence we have now entered into may prove a pleasant & advantageous one to us both

Believe me dear Sir

yours very truly

Anthony Trollope Esq   JOHN BLACKWOOD

299. To FREDERIC CHAPMAN. 11 May.
Parrish Collection.

Conway,[1]
May 11, 1866.   (Waltham House,
Waltham Cross.)

My dear Chapman,

I made attempts to see you on Monday, Wednesday & Thursday, but failed. I therefore went to W H Smith[2] on Thursday

at the Garrick Club and talked with him about *Nina Balatka*. As a result Blackwood read the manuscript, and in a letter to Langford dated 10 April, and preserved among the Trollope papers at the Bodleian Library, Blackwood wrote the lengthy criticism of the novel to which he refers in the first paragraph above.

[1] Conway: a town in Carnarvonshire, Wales.

[2] William Henry Smith (1825–91), statesman, established in 1858 the famous English railway bookstalls. By carefully choosing its novels this

morning,—as you will probably have learned from him. It was necessary to explain that two of the novels, Orley Farm and Can You Forgive Her can not well be brought out in one volume each and that they should be republished in two—at 6/ each.[1] I told him also that my price for my half copyrights was £2650— When I made them up, I found that this was the sum to which they would come. I suppose you would let me have your half for the same. I shall be back home by the end of next week.

Very faithfully yours
A<small>NTHONY</small> T<small>ROLLOPE</small>

300. To G<small>EORGE</small> S<small>MITH</small>. 19 May.
  Mrs. Reginald Smith.

Private

May 19, 1866.   (Waltham House,
                                        Waltham Cross.)

My dear Smith.

I was at your place today, and finding you out of town I made an appointment with Enoch for seeing you at ½ past 2 on Monday,—which appointment I will keep. I want to see you again about my copyrights. I have a dislike to suggesting to you again to buy them, but the circumstances are altered,—as I will explain, —and I think we are intimate enough for me to ask you to tell me, without fuss and in the way of friendship, whether it would suit you to have them.

Chapman wishes to part with them & to realise what he can get for them, and W. H. Smith has offered to buy the bulk of them, (I will tell you which when I see you) for £3000,—or to hire them all at a certain rate for 5 years. I will not sell my half of them he wishes to buy for £1500, but have no objection to

firm, together with Mudie's Circulating Library, did much to shape Victorian taste in reading. See Sir Herbert Maxwell, *The Life and Times of the Rt. Hon. William Henry Smith,* 2 vols. (Edinburgh, 1893); also G. R. Pocklington, *The Story of W. H. Smith & Son* (priv. ptd., 1921).

[1] *Orley Farm* and *Can You Forgive Her?* both appeared in two volumes in 1868 as 'yellow-backs' in Chapman & Hall's Select Library of Fiction. W. H. Smith & Son bought the copyrights and asked Chapman & Hall to put their imprints on the volumes. See Arthur Waugh, *A Hundred Years of Publishing: Being the Story of Chapman & Hall, Ltd.* (London: Chapman & Hall, 1930).

let them for the 5 years. But Chapman is willing to take the
£1500 for his half,—and has told me that if I can make any
bargain for the whole which will give me what I want for my
half, he will take that sum for his share. Perhaps this may enable
us to deal. Could you consider it again & let me know what you
can give? I send you the list. Those that have an L. before them
are electrotyped, & you would have the stereos.[1] The stock in
hand at cost price of all but the two first, (Can You Forgive Her
& Orley Farm) would come to £230—which would go to
Chapman. As regards those two he proposes that the purchaser
should give him 3/6 a copy for what he has. The books are in
two volumes, cost price 20/- and £95 should be paid for the
plates of the two, & the stereos of Orley Farm. The plates of
Orley Farm are by Millais. This all makes them come very much
cheaper than when I wrote before. I will take £2300 for my
share.[2] The whole price therefore would be £3800. I have been
away to Wales, & the thing has been delayed, & we must give
Smith an answer. Therefore I trouble you with this letter. Keep
the list till I see you on Monday.

Yours always faithfully
ANTHONY TROLLOPE

301. To RICHARD BENTLEY. 9 June.
Parrish Collection.

Trollope asks for a copy of the cheap edition of *The Three Clerks*. In 1860
The Three Clerks was issued as one of 'Bentley's Standard Novels' at *3s. 6d.*
In 1865 it appeared as No. 10 of 'Bentley's Favourite Novels' at *6s.*

302. To GEORGE SMITH. 24 June.
Not traced. Sadleir's transcript.

Trollope suggests a title for the novel subsequently published as *The
Last Chronicle of Barset*: 'The Story of a Cheque for £20, and of the Mis-
chief Which It Did.' Its short title would be: 'A Cheque for £20.'

[1] 'Electros' are not *now* called 'stereos'.
[2] Trollope ultimately sold his half-share in the copyright of 14 volumes
for £2,000. See Sadleir, *Bibliography*, pp. 245–6.

303. To GEORGE SMITH. 24 June.
Not traced. Sadleir's transcript.

Trollope sends an article for the *Pall Mall*. 'Use the enclosed or not as you like.¹ There is no doubt as to the truth. It was the Bishop of Oxford,² and he gave the living which fell vacant the other day,—Myddleton I think, —which had been held for fifty years by a scamp, a son of old Bishop Tomlin,³ to his own youngest son,—just in orders. I have a word or two to say to you about curates and church preferment some day.'⁴

304. To OCTAVIAN BLEWITT.⁵ 6 July.
Parrish Collection.

Trollope advises Blewitt about rewriting the Memorial for the Hon. Lady Wraxall.⁶

305. To LADY AMBERLEY.⁷ 6 July. Waltham Cross.
Parrish Collection.

Trollope refuses one engagement but accepts another.

306. To GEORGE SMITH. 21 July. Waltham Cross.
Mrs. Reginald Smith.

Trollope sends a note to the *Pall Mall* about the curate income question, 'feeling strongly that I am in the right. If you like to print it. If you do not, burn it. I am very keen about it, but I should not open the controversy elsewhere.' The article was published as 'Curate's Income', *Pall Mall Gazette*, iv (24 July 1866), 3–4.

¹ The article does not seem to have been published.
² Samuel Wilberforce (1805–73). His son Ernest Roland Wilberforce was given the living of Middleton Stoney. See Reginald G. Wilberforce, *The Life of Samuel Wilberforce*, 3 vols. (London, 1882), iii. 305.
³ Sir George Pretyman Tomline (1750–1827), bishop of Lincoln and dean of St. Paul's, 1787; bishop of Winchester, 1820. The son was Richard Pretyman (1792–1866). He and his brother George Thomas Pretyman each held at least six ecclesiastical offices, from which they derived an enormous income.
⁴ See letter No. 306, *infra*.
⁵ Octavian Blewitt (1810–84), secretary of the Royal Literary Fund, 1839–84. Trollope was treasurer.
⁶ Mary-Anne Herring Wraxall, widow of Sir Frederick Charles Lascelles Wraxall (1828–65). Trollope was apparently interesting himself in a pension for her from the Royal Literary Fund.
⁷ Lady Amberley was the wife of John Russell, Viscount Amberley. See letter No. 329, *infra*.

307. To George Eliot. 3 August.
   Parrish Collection.

(Waltham House,
August 3 1866.   Waltham Cross.)

My dear Mrs Lewes,

I must welcome you home with a word of thanks for Felix
Holt which I received from Mr Blackwood as a present from you.

I hope you are gratified by the reception which it has obtained.
I know how disdainful you are of ordinary eulogium,—being
perhaps led on to be somewhat more so than your own nature
would make you by the severity of G. H. L. But in spite of him
and his severity, and of your own disdain whether natural or
acquired, the unrivalled success of Felix Holt must have touched
you. For, as far as I can make an estimate of such things, I think
its success is unrivalled.

For myself I think it has more elaborated thought in it, and
that it is in that way a greater work, than anything you have
done before. With the character of Mr Lyon I am perfectly
satisfied, loving all his words dearly. Felix is very great as a
result of an admirably conceived plan of a character. With Esther
I feel sometimes inclined to quarrel because she seems to doubt,
after she knows that she loves the man. Mrs Transome is excellent and great. Mrs Holt is very good,—tho not equal to M^rs
Poyser[1] as being perhaps less like what I have seen with these
eyes of the flesh and heard with these ears. As to story Adam
Bede is still my favourite. For picturesque word painting Romola
stands first. To me the great glory of Felix Holt is the fulness of
thought which has been bestowed on it.

My kindest regards to the Master. If he wants any of the new
batch of 8000 cigars which I have just got over from Cuba let
him tell me at once how many. I called on Thursday and heard
from [? the] cook some feeble excuse about the weather. The
summer winds had detained you!!

Yours always most heartily
ANTHONY TROLLOPE

[1] In *Adam Bede.*

308. To GEORGE SMITH. 5 August.
   Mrs. Reginald Smith.

My dear Smith.   August 5—1866
   I am very sorry to hear what you say about your wife. I hope
you do not mean anything serious. Let me have a line to tell me.
   About the money, put it down for 1 Jany. I shall not want it
sooner and shall think that very good pay.
   I need hardly say how glad I am to hear that you like what
you have seen of the story.[1] When I have worked to order the
only criticism for which I care much is the criticism of the buyer
who has trusted me so far as to purchase what he has not seen.
   Millais was talking to me about certain illustrations. I said—
(after certain other things had been said)—'You know you will not
do any more.' He replied—'If you like it I'll do another of yours.'
   He is in Scotland. Shall I write and ask him?[2]
   I thought you had said that you wanted cigars— So many
people ask me that I forget who is a candidate & who is not.
                               Yours always
                               ANTHONY TROLLOPE

309. To JOHN BLACKWOOD. 17 August.
   Parrish Collection.

                               August 17, 66
                               (Waltham House,
My dear Blackwood,   Waltham Cross.)
   I send back Chap 8—corrected. Do just as you like about the
divisions. I have no doubt your judgement in such matters is at
the least as good as mine. It is easy to have too little of a story,
& *very easy* to have too much. I do not know whether you have
suggested to yourself any time for bringing out the whole. I see
that 8 chapters are just half, and if you thought of bringing out
the volume in January, you would probably make the story run
six numbers in the magazine.[3]
   But, as I said before, use your own judgement altogether in
this. I will promise to be satisfied.

[1] *The Last Chronicle of Barset.*
[2] Millais did not do the illustrations.
[3] *Nina Balatka* ran in *Blackwood's Magazine* for seven months: July
1866–Jan. 1867.

Your friend in the country is very clever.[1] But I find that appreciation of particular style is as peculiar a gift as appreciation of peculiar[2] music, or as the power of remembering faces. Some men who are always reading never acquire it. Some excellent critics do not hit it at all. Whereas other men who do not even think themselves to be critical, unconsciously recognize all the little twists and niceties of individual style. I hope you explained to your clever friend that as far as this matter went he had proved himself to be no where!

Yours always
ANTHONY TROLLOPE

M^r & Mrs Felix Holt[3] have returned blooming like two Garden peonies. I may be away from September 12—to end of October. I merely mention this as to proofs.

310. To JOHN EVERETT MILLAIS. 20 August.
Parrish Collection.

August 20, 1866

(Waltham House,
Waltham Cross.)

My dear Millais

A thousand thanks for the 'Grice',[4] which have been most welcome. I hope you are having good sport. I do envy you fellows— But then I think that my good time is coming in the winter.

But how about the illustrations. You promised me a further answer. Do *do* them! They wont take you above half an hour each.[5]

Yours always
ANTHONY TROLLOPE

I am obliged to send this to your house in town unless I were to address it simply

Grouseland

[1] Someone had been knowing enough to penetrate Trollope's anonymity at once.

[2] Dr. Chapman has suggested to me that Trollope is using this word in its etymological sense of 'individual'.

[3] Lewes and George Eliot.

[4] A facetious plural for 'grouse'.

[5] Millais persisted in his refusal, but illustrated *Phineas Finn* for Trollope the following year.

311. To JOHN BLACKWOOD.   7 September.
   Parrish Collection.

(Waltham House,
Waltham Cross.)

September 7, 1866.

My dear Blackwood

I send back the sheets corrected, and I think I never saw cleaner proofs go back.

Touching the breaks I cannot find that the requirements of the story make any difference. In the October month you can put 3 chapters (VIII–IX—& X) making 21 pages, or 2 chapters making 14. It must depend on your desire to finish the story in six or seven numbers. You will see that there will not be enough for eight. If you like to finish the story with the end of the year, there will be three chapters for each number. In that case you must let me have Chapter XIII to correct by the end of the month, as, I shall be in Italy from 1. to 31 October.

For myself I like Nina better in print than in MS, but the man comes out too black. I think I'll make him give her a diamond necklace in the last chapter.

To shew in what doubt critics may be as to authorship;— The Times critic held me out that ODowd was by Bulwer,[1]—he, probably having got some inkling of dead knowledge [?], & then unconsciously forming his critical opinion thereby.

With kind regards to your wife,
Yours always
A. T.

312. To GEORGE SMITH.   11 September.
   Not traced.   Sadleir's transcript.

Trollope asks Smith to send copies of *Framley Parsonage* and *The Small House* to Mr. Thomas[2] so that he 'should see the personages as Millais has made them'.

[1] Charles Lever's *Cornelius O'Dowd*, a series of miscellaneous articles, appeared anonymously in *Blackwood's* for many years, beginning in Feb. 1864.
[2] George Housman Thomas (1824–68), illustrator of *The Last Chronicle*, painted for the queen and is known for his illustrations for *Uncle Tom's Cabin, Hiawatha,* and other celebrated works. See Forrest Reid, *Illustrators of the Sixties*, p. 248.

313. To ? 13 September.
     Parrish Collection.

Trollope writes to an official of the National Association for the Promotion of Social Science and regrets that because he is going to Italy he cannot attend the coming Manchester meeting. 'I will write to Mr Clay[1] respecting the matter of International Copyright.'[2]

314. To ? HILL. 27 October. Paris.
     Parrish Collection.

Trollope cannot accept a dinner invitation.

315. To GEORGE HENRY LEWES. 9 November.
Mrs. E. S. Ouvry.

November 9, 1866

My dear Lewes.

I wrote to you last night an official letter at the request of the Committee; but I cannot let you part from us without saying with more of personal feeling than I could put into that paper how sorry I am that it should be so. I hate the breaking of pleasant relations; and am distrustful as to new relations. I have felt however for some time that it must be so; and that you would not hang on to us much longer. I have felt also that your time was too valuable to be frittered away in reading MSS, and in writing civil,—or even uncivil—notes.

Only two propositions as to the Editing are before us. 1st to ask Mr John Morley to undertake it.[3] 2^d that I should do it for 6 months, without Salary, keeping Mr Dennis[4] with perhaps a somewhat encreased Salary. No doubt a permanent arrangement

---

[1] The Rev. Walter L. Clay, secretary of one of the departments of the association. See *Transactions of the National Association for the Promotion of Social Science*, 1866, ed. George W. Hastings (London, 1867), p. xvi.

[2] Trollope prepared a paper 'On the Best Means of Extending and Securing an International Law of Copyright' which is printed in the *Transactions . . . 1866*, pp. 119–25.

[3] John Morley (1838–1923), later Viscount Morley of Blackburn, was thus launched on his distinguished career in literary criticism, history, and politics. The *Fortnightly* first appeared under his editorship in the number for 1 Jan. 1867.

[4] Probably John Dennis of Hampstead, an active miscellaneous writer, sub-editor of the *Fortnightly*.

will be best, & the second plan has little in it of advantage either
for me or for the Review. But it is supported by the desire which
many of us have to keep the employment for Mr Dennis as long
as it can be kept; and also by a feeling that we hardly know
enough of Mr Morley. This latter may be overcome by better
information; and I shall be very glad if you will tell me your
opinion. Do you think that Mr Morley is competent for the
work? And do you believe that his opinions as to politics and
literature are of a nature to support those views which we have
endeavoured to maintain? If I found that the Review had drifted
into the hands of a literary hack who simply followed out his
task without any honesty of purpose, I should wash my hands
of it.

When you want a new pair of boots it is pretty nearly enough
for you to know that you are going to a good bootmaker. But this
going to an Editor is a very different thing. A man may be a most
accomplished Editor,—able at all periodical editing work,—and
yet to you or to me so antipathetic as to make it impossible that
the two should work together. You will understand what I mean
when I say that should I find I dont like the nose on our new
Editors face, I must simply drop the Review; and that therefore
I cannot but be very anxious.

Let me know what you think about Morley.

Give my kindest regards to your wife.

Yours always
ANY TROLLOPE

Address Waltham Cross
I am to see Mr Morley on Tuesday

316. TO GEORGE SMITH. 11 November.
Not traced. Sadleir, *Commentary*, p. 265.

Trollope was not entirely satisfied with Thomas's illustrations. 'I sent
back the proofs with the lettering. It is always well if possible to select a
subject for which the lettering can be taken from the dialogue. Because this
cannot be done as to No. 1 the lettering is poor. As to Nos. 2 and 4 it is all
right. In No. 3 the scene is sufficiently distinct to dispense with the rule.
The best figure is that of Miss Prettyman in No. 2. Grace is not good. She
has fat cheeks, and is not Grace Crawley. Crawley before the magistrates is
very good. So is the bishop. Mrs. Proudie is not quite my Mrs. Proudie.'

317. To Frederic Chapman. 2 December.
Waltham Cross. *Pierpont Morgan Library.*

Trollope hopes he was right in telling Morley to give the twenty guineas
(presumably for a *Fortnightly* article).

318. To Thomas Adolphus Trollope. 24 December.
Parrish Collection.

Trollope introduces his friend 'Mr W. G. Clark—Public orator at Cambridge, & late tutor at Trinity. He is now going to Florence and I wish for
both your sakes that you should be acquainted.' William George Clark
(1821–78), Public Orator at Cambridge, 1857–70, joint editor of *The
Cambridge Shakespeare.*

319. To Miss Heston. 27 December. Waltham Cross.
Parrish Collection.

Trollope sends something, probably one of his books. 'I dare say you
have forgotten it, but I like to keep my promises.'

320. To Lord Houghton.[1] 1866.
Not traced. Reid, ii. 155–6.

(Waltham House,
Waltham Cross.)
(1866)

My dear Lord Houghton,
 I send you a copy of 'The Warden,' which Wm. Longman
assures me is the last of the First Edit. There were, I think,
only 750 printed,[2] and they have been over ten years in hand.
But I regard the book with affection, as I made £9 2s. 6d. by
the first year's sale, having previously written and published
for ten years without any such golden results. Since then, I have
improved even upon that.

Yours always faithfully
Anthony Trollope

[1] Richard Monckton Milnes, Baron Houghton (1809–85), miscellaneous
writer on literary, political, and social questions, editor of Keats, and intimate
of many distinguished men of letters.
[2] Longman's accounts show that 1,000 copies were printed. The sales
record is fully described in Sadleir, *Bibliography,* p. 262.

1867

321. To JOHN BLACKWOOD. 1 January.
National Library of Scotland.

> (Waltham House,
> Waltham Cross.)
> Jany. 1, 1866 [1867]

My dear Blackwood.

All the good wishes of the season to you and your wife.

Thanks for the money for which I send a receipt. Send me the volumes when they are out.[1] I trust you may do well with them, & that we may have a further bit of business some day. Touching the weekly,[2] the period of its coming out was Smiths idea & not my own, & frightened me when I first heard of it. How far it answers I do not know. It is his own speculation, & he is a man of such pride of constancy that I should not dare to propose to him any change. He will never complain to me, being in that respect made of the same stuff as yourself. As regards the workmanship of the story I believe it to be as good as anything I have done. A weekly novel should perhaps have at least an attempt at murder in every number. I never get beyond giving my people an attack of fever or a broken leg.

Many thanks for continuing to me the Magazine. I hope we may see you & Mrs Blackwood in the Spring.

> Always yours
> ANTHONY TROLLOPE

322. To MR. HARDCASTLE. 8 January. Wisbech.
Parrish Collection.

Trollope cannot accept an invitation. Hardcastle was probably Joseph Alfred Hardcastle (1815–99), M.P. for Bury St. Edmunds.

[1] *Nina Balatka* was published 1 Feb. 1867.
[2] *The Last Chronicle of Barset* was published in weekly numbers, beginning 1 Dec. 1866.

323. To Virtue & Co. 24 January.
  Not traced.[1]

I reproduce Trollope's ratification of the agreement for the publication of *Phineas Finn*, because it represents the summit of his career, financially speaking.

January 24, 1867
Gentlemen

I beg to say that I agree to terms for the sale of a novel by me to you—contained in your letter of the 21st inst.

Viz. That the novel shall consist of not less than 480 pages—(such pages as those of the Cornhill Magazine)

That it shall be shipped to you not later than the end of September next.

That it shall be published in your magazine[2] in continuous monthly parts to begin 1st Oct, and that the entire copyright for that and subsequent publication shall be your own.

That you shall pay me for the copyright £3200 in monthly instalments of £160 per month—on acct from 15 October next.

                    I am
                              Gentlemen
Messrs Virtue & Co.   your most obedient Servant
  294 City Road   Anthony Trollope

324. To Sir Charles Taylor.[3] 26 January.
  Parrish Collection.

                              January 26, 1867
                                        (Waltham House,
                                        Waltham Cross.)
My dear Taylor,
  The difficulty of the position of Mme Blaze de Bury[4] as a

---

  [1] I print from Trollope's copy of the letter (Bodleian).
  [2] Plans were afoot for the launching of *Saint Pauls Magazine*, with Trollope as editor.
  [3] Sir Charles Taylor (1817–76) was a close friend of Thackeray and Trollope at the Garrick Club. He was a brilliant, though sarcastic, conversationalist and an authority on sports. Edmund Yates (*Recollections and Experiences*, i. 237) quotes Trollope's estimate of Taylor: 'A man rough of tongue, brusque in his manners, odious to those who dislike him, somewhat inclined to tyranny, he is the prince of friends, honest as the sun, and as open-handed as Charity itself.' See *Autobiography*, chap. viii, pp. 126–7. Yates remarks that this characterization is equally true of Trollope himself.
  [4] Marie Pauline Rose Stewart (or Stuart), Baroness Blaze de Bury, was

novelist consists in this—that having many years ago made a reputation, she has not maintained it. It is, I should say, over 15 years since M. Vernon came out.

Has she the pluck to stand the chance of failure,—or rather of failing which is not exactly the same thing. If so let her write her novel entire & send it over to you. I would have it read,—or read it; and no doubt could get it sold if it was liked. She must not however expect a long price, as she would come out almost as a new novelist.

There is no novelist in the Cornhill. Geo Smith makes his bargains from time to time with one writer after another, as he finds it expedient. He buys the novels unwritten, but generally with the proviso that tho he is to be bound to pay the specified price, he is not to be bound to use the novel in the magazine unless he likes it.

I fear your friend is likely to be disappointed in her desire to sell a novel from a sample. Had she been writing novels for the last 10— or 5— or even 3 years, continuously, she could probably sell one without any sample; but I fear the publisher would not regard her past successes.[1]

I shall be in town and at the Club on Wednesday,—perhaps you will delay your answer till you have seen me.[2]

Yours always

A N T H O N Y   T R O L L O P E

325. To TOM TAYLOR. 8 February. Waltham Cross.
J. H. *Spencer*.

Trollope thanks Taylor for volumes of Browning and Charles Kingsley, and for kind words about *Saint Pauls*. He mentions a sitting, apparently for Elliot & Fry, photographers.

an authority on the French classic drama and a desultory novelist. Her husband, Baron Henri Blaze de Bury, was a distinguished Goethe scholar. I have not been able to identify 'M. Vernon'.

[1] Curiously enough, Trollope published Mme Blaze de Bury's novel himself. It was called *All for Greed* and appeared in the early numbers of *Saint Pauls* from Oct. 1867 to May 1868.

[2] Taylor forwarded Trollope's letter to Mme Blaze de Bury with the following note: 'I send you a letter from Anthony Trollope, to whom I wrote on your subject. I am sure his is the best opinion going.'

326. To MR. LOVEJOY. 27 February. Waltham Cross.
     Not traced. Catalogue of Wm. Smith & Son, Reading,
     Autumn 1946.

Trollope writes regarding a deed said to have been sent to him by the
Dean of Bristol. Mr. Lovejoy was the proprietor of a well-known bookstore
and lending library in London Street, Reading.

327. To ALEXANDER STRAHAN.[1] 10 March.
     Not traced.[2]

The forceful letter to Alexander Strahan which follows shows again that
if, as Trollope's critics charge, he was a business-man novelist, he had more
integrity than his publishers and stoutly resisted their typographical
chicanery.

March 10—1867—

My dear Mr Strahan.

On my return home yesterday I found your letter of the 7th,
and I regret to say that I cannot allow the tales in your hands to
be published in two volumes— I want you to understand that I
altogether refuse any suggestion to such an arrangement—

I have always endeavored to give good measure to the public—
The pages, as you propose to publish them, are so thin and
desolated, and contain such a poor rate of type meandering thro'
a desert of margin,[3] as to make me ashamed of the idea of putting
my name to the book. The stories were sold to you as one volume
and you cannot by any argument be presumed to have the right
of making it into two without my sanction to the change—
Your intention is to publish the book as an ordinary two volume
novel for I presume 20/- There is enough for a fair sized vol to
be sold at 10/6—

I enclose a page of one of the former series, and ask you to
compare it with the pages, which I return from your own
printers—

[1] Strahan, with whom Trollope had become acquainted during the *Rachel
Ray* fracas, had become proprietor in 1866 of *The Argosy*, to which Trollope
had contributed.
[2] I print from Trollope's copy of this letter (Bodleian), which has an end-
note in the hand of H. M. Trollope: 'This must refer to *Lotta Schmidt and
Other Stories*.'
[3] Cf. *The School for Scandal* (I. i): '. . . a beautiful quarto page where a
neat rivulet of text shall meander through a meadow of margin.'

I am grieved that the expense of second printing should be thrown upon you. Tho' I have not been in any way the cause of this, I will share the expense of this printing with you on condition that you break up the type and print the stories afresh.[1]

328. To LADY AMBERLEY. 11 March. Waltham Cross.
Parrish Collection.

Trollope will be in the gallery of the House the following afternoon, but will be delighted to go to Lady Amberley in the evening.

329. To LADY AMBERLEY. 29 March. Waltham Cross.
Parrish Collection.

Trollope will dine with Lady Amberley on 9 April.[2] 'I was very sorry to hear from Arthur Russell that Lord Russell had lost a friend.'[3]

330. To ?[4] 29 March.
Parrish Collection.

March 29, 1867
(Waltham House,
Waltham Cross.)

My dear Friend.

I wrote you a horrid scrawl yesterday, having just received a petition from Strahan for some means of giving illustrations of the Marlyn [?] churches.[5] I doubt it cannot be done.

Have there not been other 'Representative Women' so called?

---

[1] An extract from this letter is published in Sadleir, *Bibliography*, p. 288.

[2] For an amusing account of Trollope at Lady Amberley's dinner see *The Amberley Papers*, ed. Bertrand and Patricia Russell, 2 vols. (New York: W. W. Norton, 1937), ii. 27.

[3] Arthur Russell (1825–92), son of Lord George William Russell and secretary to Lord John Russell, 1849–54. He was a nephew of Lord John, a brother of Odo William Leopold Russell, and an Athenaeum friend of Trollope. Lord John Russell, earl Russell (1792–1878), was a younger brother of Lord George William Russell (1790–1846), and Lady Amberley's father-in-law. She was the daughter of Lord Stanley of Alderley.

[4] Trollope's correspondent was probably either Anna C. Steele or his distant relative Cecilia Meetkerke.

[5] I am not certain of my reading of the proper name, but at any rate I can find no such article in *Saint Pauls*. The reference may possibly be to something by Thomas Waddon Martyn, a poet friend of Austin Dobson who was a contributor to *Saint Pauls*.

I have some such notion—but whether it is only so because of the 'Representative Men,' or whether it be a fact, I cannot say. If it be no fact I would make it a fact by doing a lot of them. I liked both those you sent me, but the lady the best.[1] I may say I generally prefer ladies.

Apollonius of Tyana has been done very well lately, by one McCall, (I think) in the Fortnightly.[2] Of Julian the world is very ignorant. But I always regarded his apostacy as good old fashioned conservatism, but Xtians have always been so very bitter mouthed against those who have left us or would not come to us. My wife will read the MS. She has not as yet, because I have hardly been at home since I was with you. I write now from the town post.

Yours always
A. T.

331. To GEORGE SMITH. 12 April.
Mrs. Reginald Smith.

April 12, 1867   (Waltham House,
                                              Waltham Cross.)

My dear Smith

You know probably that dear old Robert Bell died this morning. I send a notice of him which I hope you may find yourself justified in inserting in the P.M.G. tomorrow.[3] He was a very manly fellow. I loved him well. And I should be sorry that he should pass away without a word of record.

Yours always
Geo Smith Esq   ANTHONY TROLLOPE

332. To EDMUND ROUTLEDGE. 13 April. Waltham Cross.
Parrish Collection.

Trollope is too busy at the moment to do anything for Routledge's new magazine. Edmund Routledge (1843–99) was the second son of the publisher George Routledge. His new magazine, the *Broadway*, appeared in September 1867.

[1] Trollope probably refers to the following: 'Women of the Day', *Saint Pauls*, ii (June 1868), 312–14; and 'Madame de Sévigné', *ibid.*, 319–27.
[2] W. M. W. Call, 'Apollonius of Tyana', *Fortnightly Review*, ii (15 Sept. 1865), 488–503.
[3] 'Mr. Robert Bell', *Pall Mall Gazette*, v (13 Apr. 1867), ii.

333. To Mr. Dennis.[1] 15 April.
Parrish Collection.

April 15, 1867

(Waltham House,
Waltham Cross.)

My dear Dennis.

Do not forget to return the lecture, as I have no other copy.[2] I find that committees appreciate best a mode of arrangement in regard to lectures, which I have twice suggested. I offer to give a radical lecture, or to subscribe £10— They always take the £10 —saying that the radical lecture is too much for their strength.

Bell will be buried at Kensall Green as I understand on Thursday. I shall be there certainly.

He edited the Home News for India & Australia for the Mess[rs] Grindlay.[3] But of the circumstances I know nothing, nor do I know anything of the Mess[rs] Grindlay. I have not the slightest idea who will succeed him.

Yours always faithfully
ANTHONY TROLLOPE

334. To James Virtue.[4] 19 April. Waltham Cross.
Parrish Collection.

Trollope sends a title-page for the new magazine. The title: The Whitehall Magazine.[5]

[1] Probably John Dennis of Hampstead. See letter No. 315, *supra*.
[2] Probably 'Higher Education of Women', published recently in Morris Parrish's *Four Lectures*, pp. 68–88.
[3] *Home News for India* was a weekly, published 1847–98; *Home News for Australia* was a monthly, published 1853–98.
[4] James Sprent Virtue (1829–92) was an enterprising and highly successful printer turned publisher.
[5] There was a friendly scrimmage between proprietor and editor over the title. This one is not among the discards mentioned in Sadleir, *Commentary*, p. 270.

335. To JOHN MURRAY.[1] 9 May.
   Parrish Collection.

9. May. 1867

(Garrick Club crest)

My dear Sir.

I presume that you knew something of the late Robert Bell, from your connexion with the Corporation of the Literary Fund. A memorial is to be presented to Lord Derby[2] by Lord Stanhope[3] asking for a pension for his widow, and it now lies at the office of the Literary Fund, 4 Adelphi Terrace. The Memorial contains the circumstances of the case. Will you call at the office and sign it.

Yours very faithfully
ANTHONY TROLLOPE

John Murray Esq

336. To WILKIE COLLINS. 9 May. Waltham Cross.
   Parrish Collection.

Trollope asks Collins for a contribution to the Bell fund. 'Poor Bell worked hard at letters for over 50 years.'

337. To GEORGE SMITH. 31 May.
   Not traced. Sadleir's transcript.

Trollope voices a strong negative to Smith's suggestions about *The Last Chronicle.* 'No dedication and no preface. It is all nonsense. I never wrote a preface and never dedicated a book.'[4]

338. To LADY WESTERN. 3 June. Clovelly, Devonshire.
   Parrish Collection.

Trollope will still be absent from town and cannot accept a dinner engagement. Lady Western was the wife of Sir Thomas Burch Western (1795–1873), M.P. for North Essex.

[1] John Murray (1808–92) was son of and successor to the John Murray who published for Mrs. Trollope. He continued his father's guide-book series and successfully published a large group of illustrated travel-books.
[2] Edward George Geoffrey Smith Stanley, fourteenth Earl of Derby (1799–1869), distinguished statesman.
[3] Philip Henry Stanhope, fifth Earl Stanhope (1805–75), Viscount Mahon, naval historian and statesman.
[4] Almost immediately, however, Trollope wrote a preface to *The Vicar of Bullhampton.*

339. To FREDERIC CHAPMAN. 13 June.
Parrish Collection.

June 13, 1867   (Waltham House,
My dear Chapman,   Waltham Cross.)

I wanted to see you yesterday to ask you to assist me in getting Bell's books down to me here. I have bought the lot. I am told there are nearly 4,000. Could you not put me in the way of getting them down here. I should like to have this done early next week. I will call on you tomorrow evening about 5. I have another subject on which I wish to speak to you.

Yours always
ANTHONY TROLLOPE

340. To JOHN BLACKWOOD. 10 July.
National Library of Scotland.[1]

(Waltham House,
Waltham Cross.)
July 10, 1867

My dear Blackwood

I sent you the novel by this days post, registered, to the same address as this letter. I sent it a few days earlier than I said because I do not quite know when you will want to use it; and I shall be abroad from July 17 to August 20th. When shall you want to have the first number corrected? If for the September number, which is not probable perhaps, you must either let me have the sheets before I go, or send them to Mrs Trollope to bring after me. She does not start till the 21st. If the story will not be used till October I can correct the sheets after my return.[2] Touching the name, I find that "Linda Tressel" is the most suitable, as you will say when you read it. The other however is not unsuitable, and you can take your choice.[3] Do *not* take the two.

Let me have a line to acknowledge receipt of the novel.

Yours always
ANTHONY TROLLOPE

[1] An excerpt from this letter is published in *Parker*, p. 58.
[2] *Linda Tressel* was serialized from Oct. 1867 to May 1868.
[3] Trollope's work-sheet for this novel, preserved among his papers at the Bodleian, does not show an alternative title. The novel was written in five and a half weeks.

341. To Austen Henry Layard.[1] 15 July.
British Museum.

July 15, 1867
Address, Waltham Cross.

My dear Mr. Layard,

Thanks for the kindness of your letter.

After what you have said I will look elsewhere for papers on home politics, as we should certainly wish to have the subject treated consecutively—& not less than every other month. I feel though that I cannot press the matter on you.

I hope in every other month also to have an article on foreign politics—and these articles would not necessarily be written by one & the same person. Could you, do you think, write such an article for me for the November number.[2]

Yours very sincerely
Anthony Trollope

342. To Mr. Lucas. 24 July. Glasgow.
Bodleian Library.

Trollope writes in the third person, giving a mailing address for Mr. Synge. Lucas was possibly Samuel Lucas (1818–68), journalist and barrister, founder of *The Shilling Magazine*.

343. To Miss Dunlop. 22 August. Waltham Cross.
Parrish Collection.

Trollope sends a photograph of himself and Tom Trollope. 'I need hardly say with how much pleasure!—only that my big brother is getting so much the best of me.'

344. To John Blackwood. 2 September.
Waltham Cross. *National Library of Scotland.*

Trollope has been out of town, but is now returned and ready for his proofs.

[1] Austen Henry Layard, later Sir Austen (1817–94), was a distinguished archaeologist and statesman. He excavated Nineveh, then in 1852 entered politics, becoming Under-Secretary for Foreign Affairs, 1861–6, and later Minister at Madrid and Constantinople. He contributed a number of papers to *Saint Pauls.*

[2] The November political article, 'The New Electors', is probably not by Layard, but the December article probably is his. See 'England's Place in Europe', i (Dec. 1867), 275–91. Note letter No. 348, *infra.*

345. To JOHN BLACKWOOD. 16 September.
National Library of Scotland. Sadleir, *Commentary,*
p. 262.

(Waltham House,
Waltham Cross.)
September 16, 1867

My dear Blackwood.

I will return the proof today or tomorrow; but I write a line
at once to say that you are quite at liberty to give up the story if
you do not mind the expense of having put it into type. Do not
consider yourself to be in the least bound by your offer;[1]—only
let me have the MS back at once without going to the printers.
What has been with them must of course be recopied.

Let me have a line from you at once,—and feel quite sure that
your returning it to me will moult no feather between you & me.

Yours always faithfully
ANTHONY TROLLOPE

346. To ? 18 September.
Not traced. Maggs Catalogue 421 (Spring 1922).

Trollope writes to a woman who wishes to submit a manuscript novel
that he has one appearing currently and two to follow.

347. To RICHARD SAMUEL OLDHAM.[2] 22 September.
Waltham Cross. Myers & Co.

Only a few of Trollope's letters to this old friend and correspondent appear
to have survived. 'I send the enclosed in re Tommie. I wrote a long preach-
ment to your wife the other day, & therefore will be concise with you to day.
I suppose you are back in the land of cakes.'[3]

---

[1] Blackwood had written 16 July offering £450 for *Linda Tressel.* 'On
looking into the matter I was disappointed to find that we had not sold 500
copies of Nina which is a great shame & a heavy loss but I trust that the
well-earned reputation which could not help poor Nina herself will help
Linda.'(Bodleian.)

[2] Richard Samuel Oldham (1823–?), who belonged to the small Episco-
palian community in Scotland, rector of St. Mary's, Glasgow; later dean
of Glasgow. See *Crockford's Clerical Directory for 1870* (London, 1870),
p. 832.

[3] Scotland.

348. To Austen Henry Layard. 5 October.
British Museum.

(Waltham House,
October 5, 1867   Waltham Cross.)
My dear Mr. Layard,

I write not knowing at all where you are. In your last note
you spoke of an article which you wd write for us,—not for the
November number, but for the one to follow. I have consequently
arranged for two articles on home politics for our two first
numbers, (—of which you may perhaps have seen the first,)—
and shall be glad, if it suits you, to have yours for the December
number. If so it should be with me quite early in November. You
probably know that the magazine-mongers insist on having
these periodicals out some days before the end of the month;—
and that in order to fit the articles any one intended for special
publication in a particular month should be early.

Yours always
Anthony Trollope

349. To John Blackwood. 5 October. Waltham Cross.
National Library of Scotland.

Trollope thanks Blackwood for his cheque for £225.

350. To John Blackwood. 11 October. Waltham Cross.
National Library of Scotland.

Trollope asks why he has had no proof for the second number of *Linda
Tressel.*

351. To Mountstuart Elphinstone Grant Duff.[1]
17 October. *Lady Grant Duff.* Not seen.

(Office of the St Pauls Magazine,
294, City Road, London.)
Dear Sir,

You may perhaps have seen the first number of the Saint
Paul's Magazine, which is being edited by myself. If so you will

[1] Mountstuart Elphinstone Grant Duff, later Sir Mountstuart (1829–
1906), was Under-Secretary of State for India, Governor of Madras, and
Lord Rector of Aberdeen University.

have noticed that it is our object to make the magazine a vehicle for political articles on the Liberal side. I am not at liberty to mention the names of those who are already writing for us, but I believe you would find the matter such as you would approve in point of feeling and line of argument.

I trouble you now to ask you whether you would give us occasionally the advantage of your assistance in reference to foreign politics. If you could do so we should much like to have an article from you on the present condition of Prussia with regard to France for the number to be published in November. In this case your MS should be with us by the 7th* of this month, in order to give you time to revise your own proofs. The length should be 12 or 14 pages. Should this not be within your power I am sure you will excuse my troubling you.[1]

> Yours very faithfully
> ANTHONY TROLLOPE
> address:—Waltham House,
> Waltham Cross.

M. E. Grant Duff, Esq., M.P.

* i.e. by 7th November to be ready for publication by 24th or 25th of that month.

352. To WILLIAM HENRY GREGORY.[2] 21 October.
Not traced. Sadleir's transcript.

> (Office of St Pauls Magazine
> 294, City Road, London)
> Oct. 21. 1867—

My dear Gregory,

F. Lawley[3] has mentioned to me that he has had some communication with you about an article which he thinks you might

[1] The article was probably 'Prussia, Germany, and France', *Saint Pauls*, iii (Nov. 1867), 147–62.

[2] William Henry Gregory, later Sir William (1817–92), M.P. for Galway, 1857–71; Governor of Ceylon, 1871–7. Sir William was one of Trollope's acquaintances at Harrow. In his autobiography he wrote vividly of Trollope's school-days. See *Sir William Gregory, K.C.M.G., an Autobiography*, ed. Lady Gregory (London, 1894), pp. 35–8.

[3] Francis Charles Lawley (1825–1901), journalist, one-time secretary to Gladstone, U.S. correspondent for *The Times*. He wrote widely on sport.

write about poor Lord Dunkellin,[1] who as I hear from him was a close friend of yours. I have no doubt if you have the necessary papers at command you could make a charming paper on the subject. If you like to do this we shall be delighted to take it from you. We are as liberal as others in our payment & will not cut down your little honorarium. Let me have a line to say if you can do it, & if so at about what length. It should be about 12 pages. If intended for the December number it should be with me by December 7.[2]

Yours always

ANTHONY TROLLOPE

353. To AUSTEN HENRY LAYARD. 21 October.
British Museum.

(Office of the St Pauls Magazine,
294, City Road, London.)

October 21 (186)7

My dear Layard,

Thanks for your note. It seems now almost sure that the Emperor will find himself driven to send troops to Italy.[3] If so, he will surely have committed the worst blunder. You ask for a late date;—but we are forced to be very early in type. You will of course choose to correct your own proof. The whole thing has to be stereotyped— And they will insist on having the magazine ready for distribution by the 24th Will you let me name the 10th as the last available day.

I will bear in mind what you say about not mentioning your name. Not but what these things always get out.

Yours faithfully

ANTHONY TROLLOPE

354. To MR. MARTEN. 22 October. Waltham Cross.
Bodleian Library.

Trollope asks for information about a woman who has applied for financial assistance. 'The letter reads like that of a person in the begging letter trade.' Marten was possibly Alfred George Marten, barrister, of Lincoln's Inn.

[1] Ulick Canning de Burgh, Lord Dunkellin (1827–67), military secretary to Lord Canning when Canning was Governor-General of India. He was the son of the Earl of Clanricarde.

[2] The article does not seem to have been written, but Gregory described Dunkellin in his autobiography.

[3] When Garibaldi threatened Rome, Napoleon III, yielding to the anger of the Catholics, again sent troops into the city.

355. To ?[1] 23 October.
Parrish Collection.

(Waltham House,
Waltham Cross.)

My dear friend.

I could not possibly have come to Brighton before Oct 31, when I am clear of the Post Office—and now I do not like, (indeed at present cannot) get out of this dinner to Dickens.[2] I am sorry that it should turn out so,—& of course did not anticipate that it would be so when we were talking over the matter at the hotel. I thought you wd have stayed there longer.

If you leave Brighton on Monday 4th. would you come here that day? We have no cook, ours having gone blind, but it doesnt seem to make much difference. Let us have a line to say whether you & Cecil will come?

About Dickens' dinner the dean should write to Charles Kent,[3] (whom I do not know or never heard of till I got the enclosed). This will tell him all I can tell. You & he know that I am not specially in that set, but having been asked I did not like to refuse.

Oct 23   67

Yours always
A. T.

356. To ? 27 October.
Parrish Collection.

Cambridge

October 27. 1867

(Waltham House
Waltham Cross.)

Dear Madam.

I wish I could say anything that might encourage you; but I cannot advise you to take the offer of Messrs S & O.[4] I feel certain

---

[1] I cannot identify this correspondent. The 'dean' suggests Charles Merivale, dean of Ely. If so, the addressee might be his sister.

[2] A farewell dinner was tendered to Dickens on 2 Nov. in honour of his leaving for the United States. Trollope was one of the principal speakers. See 'Addendum ', letter No. 351a.

[3] William Charles Mark Kent (1832–1902), editor and proprietor of the London *Sun* and intimate friend of Dickens, for whose periodicals he wrote.

[4] Saunders, Otley & Co., London publishers.

if you do so that the publication of the book will not bring profit to you. What you will do is to ask your friends to subscribe,—which they may probably do to the number of the 40 copies. But they will feel that they are subscribing for you,—while they will in truth be subscribing for Messrs S & O.

Should you finally determine to publish, I shall be happy to put my name down for a copy.

Very faithfully yours
A N T H O N Y T R O L L O P E

357. To Mr. Benthall. 30 October.
Parrish Collection.

Trollope promises to write to a Mr. Howes. 'His cantankerousness can't hurt me. I shall be very happy to shake hands with you tomorrow.' Benthall was probably A. Benthall, who according to Post Office records was in 1857 a first-class clerk in the Secretary's office. I have not been able to trace his later career.

358. To Anna C. Steele. 30 October.
Parrish Collection. Bradhurst, p. 260.

October 30. 67   (Waltham House,
                                          Waltham Cross.)

My dear Mrs Steele

Regarding you as a wicked rival who are springing up to take the bread out of my mouth, and who have just committed the sin of having four columns in the Times, I wonder how you can have so cruel a heart as to write to me at all, for you must be sure that I hate you. Nevertheless I shall be most delighted to go to Belhus, if only to shew you with what an outward shew of equanimity I can bear your triumphs.

But, I am sorry to say I am engaged all next week,—having promised to go to Brighton on Tuesday. Any day after Sunday the 17, I should be most happy.

I would congratulate you heartily on your success,[1] which I regard as very great, were I not sure that you would not believe a word that I said.

Yours very faithfully
A N T H O N Y T R O L L O P E

[1] Mrs. Steele's novel *Gardenhurst* had just been published by Chapman & Hall.

359. To Austen Henry Layard. 7 November.
British Museum.

(Office of the St Pauls Magazine,
294, City Road, London.)

November 7, 1867

My dear Layard,

I send you your article in type— I have read it with very thorough satisfaction. I do not quite think as you do as to the future of Prussia, but I am quite aware that you have better grounds for thinking than I have.

At Page 15, line 6, would you object to softening the scorn conveyed in the "limited capacity."— I hardly think such [an] expression, well as it may be deserved, tends to . . . .¹

And in the last line of the article would you object to soften the assured threat of destruction held out against the "Tory" order & class. I think you hardly mean it to [,] yourself. It is somewhat antagonistic to what you have already said, and is certainly antagonistic to what you feel.

You will see that you run to 17 pages,—with a space for insertion of 20 or 25 lines if you please.

I have therefore arranged that your article *shall* take 17 pages.

Again thanking you & assuring you that I like the paper very much I am

Most faithfully
Anthony Trollope

You must put a name to the article. I shall be here on Saturday, & may perhaps get it back then corrected.

360. To Cecilia E. Meetkerke. 7 November.
Parrish Collection.

Nov. 7, 1867   (Waltham House,
Waltham Cross.)

My dear Mrs Meetkerke.

I must be at Brighton on Saturday or I would have been most happy.

If any changes were made in the poem that were wrong, you are responsible for certainly not a word was changed after the

¹ One word illegible.

proof was sent to you.[1] You could have objected then,—& it
would not have been too late.

Yours always most sincerely
A. T.

361. To AUSTEN HENRY LAYARD. 9 November.
British Museum.

Trollope forwards proofs. 'I shall see you no doubt in London during the
short Session coming & I will say a word to you about the Eastern article.'

362. To AUSTEN HENRY LAYARD. 30 November.
British Museum.

(Waltham House,
Waltham Cross.)

November 30
   1867

My dear Layard,

I see by the debate on the Great Beke case[2] that you are out
of town for 10 days. Perhaps that may be as mendacious as some
other things;—but as I had hoped to have seen you, & suppose
you are now gone, it may be as well to write you a line. Will
you like to write for us the article of which you spoke, so as to be
in my hand Feb 9—for the number to be published on Feb 25th?
—or would you write on any other subject of foreign affairs?
You shall take the East: Question if you like;—but of course, as
you know, we are all of us a little afraid of you on that steed.

---

[1] There are no signed poems by Mrs. Meetkerke in the relevant issues of
Saint Pauls at this time, but the reference may be to 'Secrets', i. (Nov.
1867), 172.

[2] Charles Tilstone Beke (1800–74) was an Abyssinian explorer, author
of *The Sources of the Nile* (1860) and of *Discoveries of Sinai in Arabia*. In 1864
King Theodore of Abyssinia imprisoned Capt. Cameron and other British
subjects and missionaries. Beke secured their temporary release, but was
imprudently defiant, and the Abyssinian war resulted. He performed a
valuable service, however, in supplying information to the army and the
government. The debate arose over the government's failure to publish all
Beke's correspondence in its blue books. See *Hansard's Parliamentary Debates*,
third series, clxxxix (26 July 1867), 244–9; cxc (6 Dec. 1867), 649–50,
667–73. See also an exchange of letters between Beke and Layard in the
Pall Mall Gazette, v (26 Feb. 1867), 4–5; v (27 Feb. 1867), 3; v (8 Mar.
1867), 4–5.

210

But you shant be baulked; after the very excellent paper you have given us.

Could I get you to come to us here for a couple days during the next month? Do you hunt?

Yours always
ANTHONY TROLLOPE

A H Layard Esq

363. To AUSTEN HENRY LAYARD. 5 December. *British Museum.*

(Waltham House,
Waltham Cross.)

Dec 5, 1867.

My dear Layard,

I had no intention of letting you off, but did not write before, as one has to make various arrangements.

As you can not write your East: article in time for publication in February, will you let me have it for publication in April?—say by April 3—or 4th.[1] I will then keep the space for it— My purpose is to alternate articles on Home & Foreign questions.

Yours always
ANTY TROLLOPE
Dec 5— 1867

364. To JAMES VIRTUE. 7 December. Waltham Cross. *Parrish Collection.*

Trollope regrets that because of his bad throat he cannot go into London to meet Virtue's men.

365. To ? WILLIAM ALLINGHAM. 10 December. London. *Robert H. Taylor.*

Trollope asks a contributor to omit the dedication to a 'little poem on Squire Curtis. It is unusual, and I think ugly in a magazine.' 'The Ballad of Squire Curtis', *Saint Pauls*, ii (Apr. 1868), 77–8, is signed 'W. A.', and appears in William Allingham's *Songs, Ballads, and Stories* (London, 1877), pp. 179–83.

[1] See 'The Panslavist Revival in Europe', ii (Apr. 1868), 18–33.

366. To AUSTIN DOBSON.[1] 24 December. London.
G. F. C. Dobson. Not seen.

Trollope accepts for the *Saint Pauls* Dobson's '*very pretty* lines on La Belle Marquise'.[2]

1 8 6 8

367. To MRS. POLLOCK.[3] 12 January. Stilton.[4]
Parrish Collection.

Trollope sends thanks for a manuscript[5] and accepts an invitation.

368. To MESSRS. BRADBURY AND EVANS. 3 February.
Not traced.[6]

In response to an invitation from a publishing house Trollope wrote as follows:

Feb 3. 1868

Gentlemen.

Thanks for your letter of Feb 1, respecting the proposed novel for next year.[7] It is my intention that it shall be in your hands

---

[1] Henry Austin Dobson (1840–1921), poet and biographer who became Trollope's most regular contributor of verse. Trollope gave the young aspirant a hearing, and he responded with the best work which the magazine published. The two men did not become personally acquainted, however, until some years later.

[2] Published as 'Une Marquise: A Rhymed Monologue in the Louvre', i (Mar. 1868), 709–11.

[3] Julia Pollock, wife of William Frederick Pollock (1815–88), afterwards Sir William, barrister and queen's remembrancer. He was a long-time friend of Trollope, who is frequently mentioned in Pollock's *Personal Remembrances* (London, 1887).

[4] Stilton: a small town in Huntingdonshire about 75 miles north of London.

[5] Probably 'Columbus (A Dramatic Fragment)', *Saint Pauls*, ii (May 1868), 179–84. This work is signed 'J. P.'

[6] I print from Trollope's copy (Bodleian).

[7] The proposed novel was *The Vicar of Bullhampton*. The story of the difficulties of its publication has been well told in Sadleir, *Commentary*, pp. 296–9.

before 1 May 69—so that its publication will be commenced at that date. Of course it is understood that it is intended for your periodical, Once a Week.

Very faithfully yours,
ANTHONY TROLLOPE

Messrs Bradbury [*sic*] Evans

369. TO FREDERICK LOCKER.[1] 24 February. London. *Harvard College Library.*

Trollope thanks Locker for a contribution.[2]

370. MR. BRACKENBURY.[3] 2 March. Waltham Cross. *Parrish Collection.*

Trollope writes a letter of introduction to Trevelyan.[4]

371. TO AUSTIN DOBSON. 7 March. *G. F. C. Dobson.* Alban Dobson, *Austin Dobson: Some Notes* (London: Oxford University Press, 1928), p. 78.

7 March 1868

I return your poems, though I like them much, especially that of the dying knight, because, as it seems to me, they are not sufficiently clear in their expression for the general readers of a magazine. The general reader would have no idea for instance

---

[1] Frederick Locker, later Locker-Lampson (1821–95), a talented writer of vers de société, author of *London Lyrics*, a volume which he extended and rearranged through many editions. The two men were to become good friends, and Trollope ultimately presented Locker with the manuscript of *The Small House at Allington.*

[2] Probably 'A Nice Correspondent', *Saint Pauls*, ii (June 1868), 328–9. It is signed 'F. L.'

[3] Probably Captain Charles Booth Brackenbury (1831–90), military writer, who is mentioned in the *Autobiography* (chap. xv, p. 240) among the contributors to *Saint Pauls.*

[4] Probably Sir Charles Trevelyan (1807–86), Governor of Madras and responsible for many economic and financial reforms in India. In 1853 he introduced the system of competitive examination into the civil service. Trollope bitterly opposed this move and in *The Three Clerks* caricatured Sir Charles as Sir Gregory Hardlines. But see *Autobiography*, chap. vi, p. 94.

why "There is no bird in any last year's nest" nor would the . . .[1]
be at all understood.

I think it is indispensable that poetry for a magazine should be
so clearly intelligible that ill-instructed, uneducated, but perhaps
intelligent minds can comprehend it. I hope you will forgive me,
if you do not agree with me.

372. To GEORGE SMITH. 20 March.
   Mrs. Reginald Smith.

March. 20. 1868.   (Waltham House,
                                              Waltham Cross.)

My dear Smith.

I have read Bosworth's pamphlet[2] carefully. It seems to me
that he has in his warfare against you, fallen into three great
faults. He has published a statement saying that with you your
word is not as good as your bond; he has applied the term
"Rattening"[3] to your mode of truth [? trade], (the meaning of
which word we all know) and he has published an advertisement[4]
in the Athenaeum respecting one of your publications in terms
which are wilfully false in their signification. If you answer him
at all, you should do so I think on these headings.

I do not know how far he may be right in saying that his order
for the copies of the Queens Book[5] could have been enforced,
had the value of the books ordered been under £10;—but no
doubt you could shew that you had no intention to recede from

---

[1] Two words illegible. I have not seen the originals of the Austin Dobson
letters, but they have been copied for me through the kindness of Dobson's
son, the Rev. G. F. C. Dobson. The reference at this point is to an early
version of 'The Dying of Tanneguy du Bois'.

[2] Thomas Bosworth (? 1823–99), bookseller and small publisher, had
attacked Smith in a pamphlet called 'On "Rattening" in the Book Trade'.
Bosworth had been price-cutting, selling at cost books called for by name
at his counter, making his profit on deliveries and on a service charge on his
clerks' time for advice. Naturally, the big houses moved against him.

[3] Destroying an employer's machinery; in this instance, interfering with
normal trade practices.

[4] In the *Athenæum* of 29 Feb. 1868, p. 306, col. i, Bosworth advertises
his own pamphlet, but I find no such advertisement as Trollope suggests
between June 1867 and June 1868.

[5] *Leaves from the Journal of Our Life in the Highlands*, ed. Arthur Helps,
2nd edition (London: Smith, Elder, & Co., 1868).

any contract made by you;—and that his statement imputing to you dishonest motives is baseless. It would be very easy to shew that the peculiarly objectionable word "Rattening" has been used with a malicious object, and that there is not the slightest ground on which any man,—let his opinions on the subject of the sale be what it may,—can impute fairly to you, or other publishers acting with you, any of those modes of action which have been called Rattening.

As to the advertisement, which is so worded as to appear to emanate from the publisher & proprietor of the work in question, there can be no doubt of the falseness of the intention of the advertiser.

Touching the question itself, I am disposed to think that you are right in refusing the sale of your books to men reselling on the terms and in the mode in vogue with Mr Bosworth. I think I would use strong if not conclusive arguments to shew that the public would in the end suffer if the regular Retail booksellers were put out of the trade by the underselling of such as Mr Bosworth. But this at any rate is clear. That as long as you & other publishers confine yourselves to legal steps—(such as selling when you please and refusing to sell when you please)— such attacks as those made in this pamphlet are libellous in spirit if not in law.

I think I should get this put forth in a newspaper article, if I were you. It would be easily argued in a column and a half or two columns.

Yours always
A. T.

373. To GEORGE SMITH. 16 May. New York.[1]
Not traced. Sadleir's transcript.

*   *   *

I wrote a ballad yesterday on N. Y. Womanhood, intending to send it you. But it is spiteful, and I will only shew it you when I get home.[2]

---

[1] Trollope had again gone to the United States on an official postal and copyright mission.
[2] There is no trace of this ballad.

374. To KATE FIELD. 19 May.
  Boston Public Library.

                                        (Waltham House,
                                          Waltham Cross.)
My dear Kate,
    I send the enclosed from my brother,—hoping that you will
be able to understand them. What a very wicked woman Mrs. P.[1]
seems to be! I returned here through N.Y. the other day without
stopping an hour; and I heard the verdict of acquittal given on
Saturday.[2] I hope you like the way in which your party interfered
to stop the judgment in the middle when they found that it was
going against their wishes. I thought it disgraceful.
                                        Yours affectionately
                                              A. T.

                                    Washington May 19 68

375. To KATE FIELD. 24 May.
  Boston Public Library. Sadleir, *Commentary,* pp. 375–6.

Washington 24 May 1868   (Waltham House,
                                          Waltham Cross.)
Dear Kate,
    I got your letter on my return to W. from Richmond,[3] whither
I have been to look after memorials of Davis[4] & Lee[5] and the
other great heroes of the Secession. The MS. of which your letter
speaks has not reached me. The printed story, "Love and War"
(which I return as you may want it), I have read.[6] It has two
faults. It wants a plot, and is too egoistic. Touching the second
fault first, it is always dangerous to write from the point of "I."
The reader is unconsciously taught to feel that the writer is

    [1] Possibly Mrs. Theodore Parker. See letter No. 377, infra.
    [2] Trollope refers to the impeachment trial of Andrew Johnson. On
16 May 1868 Johnson was acquitted on the eleventh article of the impeachment.
    [3] Capital of Virginia and seat of the Confederate government during the
Civil War.
    [4] Jefferson Davis (1808–89), President of the Confederacy.
    [5] Robert E. Lee (1807–70), leader of the Confederate forces.
    [6] 'Love and War' was first published in *The Public Spirit* and reprinted
in *The Springfield Republican,* 4 Jan. 1868.

glorifying himself, and rebels against the self-praise. Or otherwise the "I" is pretentiously humble, and offends from exactly the other point of view. In telling a tale it is, I think, always well to sink the personal pronoun. The old way, "Once upon a time," with slight modifications, is the best way of telling a story.

Now as to the plot;—it is there that you fail and are like to fail. In "Love and War" there is absolutely no plot—no contrived arrangement of incidents by which interest is excited. You simply say that a girl was unhappy in such and such circumstances, and was helped by such and such (improbable) virtues & intelligences. You must work more out of your imagination than this before you can be a story-teller for the public. And I think you could do it. In spite of Dogberry, the thing is to be done by cudgelling.[1] But you must exercise your mind upon it, and not sit down simply to write the details of a picture, which is conveyed to you, not by your imagination, but by your sympathies. Both sympathy and imagination must be at work—and must work in unison—before you can attract.

Your narration as regards language and ease of diction is excellent. I am sure that you can write without difficulty, but I am nearly equally sure that you must train your mind to work, before you can deal with combinations of incidents. And yet I fully believe that it is in you to do it.

If I give you pain, pray excuse me. I would so fain see you step out & become one of the profession in which women can work at par along side of men. You have already learned so much of the art,—and then you are so young.

Most affectionately yours
A. T.

The end of your story should have been the beginning.

I will tell you of the last scene of the impeachment when it is over.

---

[1] 'God hath blessed you with a good name; to be a well-favour'd man is the gift of fortune; but to write and read comes by nature.' *Much Ado About Nothing*, III. iii. 12–15.

376. To KATE FIELD. 28 May.
     Boston Public Library. Sadleir, *Commentary*, pp. 276–7.

Washington.   May 28, 1868.

My dear Kate.

I have received your MS. & return it. Of course, as it is a fragment, I cannot tell how far the plot might be successful. It is much more pretentious than the printed story, and is for that reason worse;—but I should say of it that the author ought to be able to write a good story.

As a rule young writers,—(I speak, of course, as [? of] writers of fiction,)—should be very chary of giving vent to their own feelings on what I may call public matters. If you are writing an essay, you have to convey of course your own ideas and convictions, to another mind. You will of course desire to do so in fiction also, and may ultimately do so (when your audience is made) more successfully than by essay writing. But your first object must be to charm and not to teach. You should avoid the 'I' not only in the absolute expressed form of the pronoun, but even in regard to the reader's appreciation of your motives. Your reader should not be made to think that *you* are trying to teach, or to preach, or to convince. Teach, and preach, and convince if you can;—but first learn the art of doing so without seeming to do it. We are very jealous of preachers. We admit them at certain hours and places for certain reasons. We take up a story for recreation, and the mind, desirous of recreation, revolts from being entertained with a sermon. Your story about the Artist is intended to convey your teaching as to what Americans and Americanesses should have done during the war.[1] You will hardly win your way in that fashion. Tell some simple plot or story of more or less involved, but still common life, adventure, and try first to tell that in such form that idle minds may find some gentle sentiment and recreation in your work. Afterwards, when you have learned the knack of story telling, go on to greater objects.

There's a sermon for you.   Yours very aff.
                                                          A. T.

---

[1] See Kate Field, 'A Moving Tale', *Harper's New Monthly Magazine*, xxxvii (Nov. 1868), 814–21.

377. To KATE FIELD. 3 June.
Boston Public Library. Sadleir, *Commentary*, p. 277.

[Washington]
3. June 1868

My dear Kate,

I hope you have not blown up Mrs. T. Parker[1] very badly; for if she says the money was paid to Chapman, it probably was so paid; and Chapman is the very man to forget to mention it. Indeed he never does mention anything. However I only did as I was told.

I don't seem to care much about Planchette.[2] However, I am mild and submit to be taken to Planchettes and Hume's[3] [*sic*] and Dotens[4]—(was that the name of the Boston preaching and poetising woman?). I should like of all things to see a ghost, and if one would come and have it out with me on the square I think it would add vastly to my interest in life. Undoubtedly one would prefer half an hour with Washington or Hamilton to any amount of intercourse with even Butler[5] or Charles Sumner. But when tables rap and boards write, and dead young women come and tickle my knee under a big table, I find the manifestation to be unworthy of the previous grand ceremony of death. Your visitor from above or below should be majestical,[6] should stalk in all panoplied from head to foot—at least with a white sheet, and should not condescend to catechetical and alphabetical puzzles.

I enclose a note for your great friend, Mr. Elliott.[7] He writes

---

[1] Mrs. Theodore Parker, widow of the famous Boston preacher. Parker died in Florence in 1860 while Kate Field was living there. His *Works* (1863–70), edited by Kate Field's friend Frances P. Cobbe, were published by Trübner, not Chapman & Hall. I cannot, therefore, explain the reference to Chapman.

[2] A planchette is a writing device used in spiritualistic séances. Kate Field was just publishing a little book called *Planchette's Diary*.

[3] Daniel Home (1833–86), a spiritualist medium who created a sensation in England. See Robert Browning's 'Mr. Sludge "The Medium".'

[4] Lizzie Doten delivered poems which she thought inspired by Shakespeare, Burns, Poe, and others. These *Poems from the Inner Life* (1863) had reached a seventh edition by 1869. See letter No. 160, *supra*.

[5] Benjamin Franklin Butler (1818–93), congressman who led the campaign for Johnson's impeachment.

[6] See *Hamlet*, I. i.

[7] Charles Wyllys Elliott (1817–83), architect, folklorist, historian, and novelist.

(apparently) from No. 44 Bible Bower. But as I cannot believe that there is as yet in New York any so near approach to the Elysian Fields, I think it better to send my note to you, than to trust it so addressed to the post. I do not know when I shall be in N.Y. I won't say that I might not be there tomorrow. This place is so awful to me, that I doubt whether I can stand it much longer. To make matters worse a democratic Senator who is stone deaf and who lives in the same house with me, has proposed to dine with me every day! I refused three times but he did not hear me, and ordered that our dinners should be served together. I had not the courage to fight it any further, and can see no alternative but to run away.

If you are going out of town, let me know when you go, and whither. I have half a mind to take a run to Niagara for the sake of getting cool in the spray

Address as below if you write again.

Yours always
A. T.
Wormley [?] I Street
Washington

378. To KATE FIELD. 10 June.
Boston Public Library. Sadleir, *Commentary*, p. 278.

Washington 10 June, 1868

(Waltham House,
Waltham Cross.)

Dear Kate,

I got a telegram on yesterday (Wednesday) morning which took me away from N.Y. at 10—instead of 12—and so I do not know whether that horrid little Silenus[1] sent the photographs or no. I guess he didn't. At any rate he was bound to send them before & I hope he may be drowned in Burgundy and that his deputy with the dirty sleeves will photograph him in his last gasp,—piteously. If they ever reach you, tell me whether they are good for any thing. I should like one of you standing up, facing full front, with your hat. I think it would have your natural look, and you can't conceive how little I shall think of the

---

[1] Silenus, a satyr, was the foster-father and attendant of Bacchus. He is usually represented as intoxicated.

detrimental skirt of which our Silenus complained. I have got letters from England, & such letters. My wife says in reference to her projected journey over here—"Don't I wish I may get it." Had I told her not to come, woman-like she would have been here by the first boat. However, she is quite right, as Washington would kill her. For myself I shall write my epitaph before I go to bed to-night.

Washington has slain this man,
By politics and heat together.
*Sumner alone he might have stood
But not the Summer weather.
* Very doubtful.

My letters tell me that I should have received a telegram from England before I got them, which will enable (or would have enabled me) [*sic*] really to begin my work. But no telegram has come. As I must remain, I shall run for the V.-Presidency on the strictest Democratic ticket—which I take to be repudiation of the debt and return to slavery. I shall pass the next two months in reading Mr. Elliott's various Mss. which have arrived in a chest.[1]

Yours ever
A. T.

379. To RHODA BROUGHTON.[2] 28 June. *Michael Sadleir*. Sadleir, *Commentary*, pp. 340–1. Not seen.

Washington
28 June 1868

Dear Madam,

I have just read your novel *Not Wisely but too Well* and wish to tell you how much it has pleased me. I should not write you on such a matter if I were not also a novelist and one much interested in the general virtues and vices, shortcomings and

[1] Elliott's miscellaneous work was being widely published in *Harper's* and elsewhere. Under the pseudonym of Thom White he published this same year a novel, *Wind and Whirlwind*.

[2] Rhoda Broughton (1840–1920), a talented minor novelist who outlived her reputation for audacity. She said of herself, 'I began my career as Zola; I finish it as Miss Yonge.' The two novels Trollope mentions were published in 1867.

excellences of my brethren. Some months since I was told by a
friend,—a lady whom I know to be a good critic,—that *Cometh
Up as a Flower* was a book that I ought to read; that your later
published novel was also very clever, though not equal to the
one which was earlier given to the public. This lady, who is an
intimate friend of mine, told me either that she knew you or
that some mutual friend created an interest on her behalf in your
writings. I do not often read novels, but I did the other day,
here in America, purchase, and have since read, the one I have
named. I must tell you also that I have heard that your stories
were written in a strain not becoming a woman young as you
are—not indeed becoming any woman. I tell you this without
reserve, as doubtless the same report must have reached your
ears.

In the story which I have read there is not a word that I would
not have had written by my sister, or my daughter—if I had one.
I do not understand the critics who,when there is so much that is
foul abroad, can settle down with claws and beaks on a tale
which teaches a wholesome lesson without an impure picture or
a faulty expression. I will not say that your story is perfect.
Having been probably ten times as many years at the work as
you have, I think, were I with you, I could point out faults here
and there against nature. You fall into the common faults of the
young, making that which is prosaic in life too prosaic, and that
which is poetic, too poetic. The fault here is of exaggeration. But
I read your tale with intense interest. I wept over it, and formed
my wishes on it, and came to the conclusion that there had come
up another sister [? writer] among us, of whose name we should
be proud.

Yours with much admiration
A N T H O N Y   T R O L L O P E

380. To KATE FIELD. 8 July.
    Boston Public Library. Sadleir, *Commentary*, p. 279.

Washington July 8, 1868.

My dear Kate,

I have put off answering your note of the 2nd till I could say
certainly what my movements would be—but even now I

can say nothing of the kind. The Post Genl[1] is away, electing a democratic candidate for the White House, and consequently I am still in suspense. Oh, Lord what a night I spent—the last as ever was,—among the mosquitoes, trying to burn them with a candle inside the net! I could not get at one, but was more successful with the netting. I didn't have a wink of sleep, and another such a night will put me into a fever hospital.

I still hope to leave here in time for the boat home on this day week. As I do not know where you are or where M[rs] Homans[2] is, I do not think I shall go on to Boston at all. If I had a day or two I would either run to Niagara or to Lake George. I am killed by the heat, and want to get out of a town. If you'll go down close to the sea, & near enough for me to get at you, I would then go to you.

I don't quite understand about the photographs, but I'll do as you bid me, pay the bill, (including the drink) and send you one of the two. I have got your section framed down to the mere hat and eyes and nose. It is all I have of you except a smudged (but originally very pretty) portrait taken from a picture.

Thanks for the account of myself taken from the 2 papers,[3] which describes me as being like a minie ball with gloves on. If I saw the writer I should be apt to go off and let him know that I never wear gloves. What fools people are. I saw in some paper an account of you amidst other strong-minded women— Janet L. Tozer, Annie B. Slocum, Martha M. Mumpers, Violet Q. Fitzpopam etc.[4]—I observed that every one except you had

[1] Postmaster General.
[2] Wife of Charles D. Homans, physician, of 4 Temple Place, Boston. See the *Boston Directory for 1868* (Boston, 1868), p. 309.
[3] I have been able to find only one account. In the Boston *Daily Evening Transcript* Trollope is thus described (16 June 1868, p. 2): 'He is a strange looking person. His head is shaped like a minnie ball, with the point rounded down a little, like the half of a lemon cut transversely in two. It is small, almost sharp at the top, and bald, increasing in size until it reaches his neck. His complexion and general bearing are much like Dickens's. His body is large and well preserved. He dresses like a gentleman and not like a fop, but he squeezes his small, well-shaped hand into a very small pair of colored kids. He "wears a cane," as all Englishmen do.' Four days later another item appeared in the same paper (20 June 1868, p. 2): 'Anthony Trollope, the brother of Thomas Adolphus, remarked to a friend in this country, "I cannot understand why my novels are reprinted in the United States while Tom's are not, for his are better than mine, especially his Italian ones." '
[4] I cannot trace these 'strong-minded women'. Is Trollope being facetious

an intermediate initial—I really think that with a view to the feelings of the country you should insist on one. It is manifestly necessary to success. Kate X. Field would do very well.

Of course I will do what you ask me about the proofs of the Dickens paper.[1] You must send them to the Brevoort House. If you could have got Dickens to do it for you in London it would have been better.[2]

What do you think your friend Elliott has proposed? That I should have his novel[3] published in England with my name on the title-page—and with any slight alterations in the vol. which I might be pleased to make!!! That I call cool—and peculiarly honest, & so clever too, as no two people were ever more unlike each other in language, manner, thought, and style of narrative.

Give my kindest love to your mother. The same to yourself dear Kate—if I do not see you again—with a kiss that shall be semi-paternal, one third brotherly, and as regards the small remainder, as loving as you please.

A. T.

381. To KATE FIELD. 13 July.
　　Boston Public Library. Sadleir, *Commentary*, p. 281.

Brevoort House N. Y.
　　13 July, 1868　　Monday

My dear Kate,
Here I am, and I start for England on Wednesday. Last night, I came from Washington. To-night I go to Boston. Tuesday night I come back here. I shall therefore be within 12 miles of you but shall not see you. I could not possibly get back to you, as you will see from the above programme. I shall be at the Parker House at Boston, but shall spend the morning & probably

---

[1] Kate Field heard Dickens's Boston lectures of Jan. 1868. In Feb. she wrote and published her little volume, *Pen Photographs of Charles Dickens's Readings*. Dickens, who had met and apparently been charmed by the girl, praised her work warmly. See relevant entries of her interesting diary in *Kate Field: a Record*, pp. 175, 186. Trollope refers to a revision for an English edition.

[2] Dickens at first offered to see that Chapman & Hall undertook an English edition, but later he said that it was too late for republication in London. See letter No. 389, *infra*.

[3] *Wind and Whirlwind*.

the day with the Homans at 4 Temple Place. I wish I could have seen your dear old face once more, (before the gray hairs come, on the wings of which you will arrive in heaven)—but I do not see how it is to be.

I have got the photographs, & have paid for them—$11.50. I wish I could have paid for yours at the same time.

The letter from Theodore P's widow I sent to Tom, (not to you). I could do nothing else with it. If Tom be not a fool he will let the thing pass as an account settled. I will do as you bid me about the Dickens papers if I get hold of them. On Wednesday morning if they be not here I will send for them. I think I will ask D. to speak to C & H—or at least consult him.

Your friend who lives in the Bible hotel has written me a most polite letter to say that my answer to him was just what he expected.

Touching the story for the Saint Pauls[1]—remember that it is to go into one number and be not more than from 14 to 16 pages —each 520 words. I say this because Tom writes to ask me whether you are not going to write a longer kind of story. I should have no room now for a longer story. Address.

> A. Trollope Esq
> 294 City Road
> London.

Touching the black phantom, I hope he has winged his way to distant worlds. He did not hurt me,—but a man is tough in these matters. It vexed you and teased my wife.

God bless you dear,—I wish I thought I might see your clever laughing eyes again before the days of the spectacles;—but I suppose not. My love to your mother.

> Yours always
> A. T.

[1] Trollope had suggested in June that Kate Field should write a story, and, flattered, she had planned to try. See *Kate Field: a Record*, p. 183. But the one or two stories in the next six issues of *Saint Pauls* could hardly be hers.

382. To THOMAS ADOLPHUS TROLLOPE. 6 August.
Parrish Collection.

(Waltham House,
August 6—1868.   Waltham Cross.)

My dear Tom,

I got home here at 12 on Monday night after a most disagreeable trip to America,—so much so that I do not intend to
go on any more ambassadorial business. However I made the
treaty, have been duly thanked by the P.M.G. and no doubt will
be duly paid.

I hope Bice is getting strong again. Somebody told me that
she saw her at Geo Smiths, & that she looked well.

Touching your articles, Vieusseux comes out in the next number, Parini will appear about 3 or 4 afterwards—Goldoni in its
turn,—similarly.[1] It does not do to bring such subjects on too
rapidly. I wrote to you about Fanny's first number.[2] I have not
yet read the second, as I have been very busy; but I will do so
very shortly.

My love to Fanny. I send this as directed to Salzburgh
Yours always affect.
ANTHONY TROLLOPE

383. To E. S. DALLAS.[3] 22 August.
Parrish Collection.

22 August 1868   (Strathyrum[4]
St. Andrews
N.B.)
My dear Dallas.

Many thanks for the Clarissa.[5] I quite admit that you have
improved the book greatly and that it ought to be read in its

[1] 'Giampietro Vieusseux' appeared in September, 'Parini' in November,
and 'Goldoni' in the following July.

[2] Tom's second wife, Frances Eleanor Ternan Trollope (? 1834–1913).
Trollope refers to her novel *The Sacristan's Household*, published in July 1868
and the following months.

[3] Eneas Sweetland Dallas (1828–79), editor of *Once a Week* and staff
writer for *The Times*.

[4] The letter is addressed from John Blackwood's country home near
St. Andrews, where Trollope was visiting.

[5] Dallas had just published an abridgement of Richardson's *Clarissa
Harlowe*. See also 'Clarissa', *Saint Pauls*, iii (Nov. 1868), 163–72.

improved form;—but I do not think that even what you have done will make the novel popular. It is not in concord with the present and growing tastes of the country.

Nor do I think that Clarissa deserves all the praise you give to the work. Its pathos is so exquisite that probably we may be justified in saying that in that respect it excels all other novels. And it may perhaps be the case, that of all attributes to prose fiction, pathos is the most effective. But then Clarissa is to my idea so defective in most other respects as to be far from the first of English prose tales. The vehicle in which the narration is given is awkward and tedious,—so much so as to be to the majority of readers repulsive. The fact that the writing of such letters is impossible wounds one at every turn. The language used by the writers, is unnatural,—especially that used by Lovelace. Clarissa is unnaturally good. The other Harlowes unnaturally bad. Lovelace is a mixture such as no one ever met. And then the language of the writers, so different in their characters, is quite similar in style and unnatural throughout. I agree that for an intelligent reader the pathos carries all this down;—only that the reader must be patient as well as intelligent. The ways of the present age are effectually impatient.

The French are infinitely more patient than we are. And then the pathos is as open to them as us;—not so the awkwardness of the language.

Yours always
A N T H O N Y T R O L L O P E

384. To E. S. D A L L A S. 1 September.
Berg Collection.

Broadford[1]
  Skye.
Sept 1, 1868.

My dear Dallas,

I return the article with thanks. The truth of the story was this:—I wrote a play over twenty years ago, which I called the "Noble Jilt." It was done before my novel writing days. This I sent to my old friend Bartley who was then manager at Covent

---

[1] Broadford: a village on the isle of Skye, the largest of the Hebrides.

Garden, and he returned it with a most heart-breaking letter, saying that it had every fault incident to a play and no virtue. It went away into darkness for some fifteen years, and then was brought out & turned into a novel. After all old Bartleys criticism, I believe it to be a good play.[1]

I read that remonstrance from C. R. in the number of O. a W. that you gave me.[2] Do you not think that he was very wrong to write it? I think you were almost wrong to publish it. Why should he notice what was said in the Mask? If he be conscious of right in the matter, such a flap from the tale [*sic*] of so small a fish should not hurt him at all. Does he not know that men who are above the line must always bear little stings from men who are below, —and that there should be no flinching and in truth no suffering from such stings? Who is there, that has not been so attacked? But other men do not notice such attacks, and thus the attackers lose their object.

Touching the papers on sympathy[3] what you say is true, no doubt;—but it is a truth in words rather than in facts. The same idea as to sympathy is made very clear in the matter of patriotism. Patriotism is the virtue of a limited & confined sympathy. A truly cosmopolitan feeling is a much grander condition of mind. But you may preach for ever without being able to teach men that they should love all the world as well as their own country.

Yours always
ANTHONY TROLLOPE

385. To MR. FARRAR. 23 September.
    Parrish Collection.

Trollope replies to a *Saint Pauls* contributor who had apparently become a bit huffy over not hearing promptly from the editor.

(Waltham House,
Waltham Cross.)

Mr Trollope
presents his compliments to Mr Farrar. The MS was sent to Mr Farrar immediately on receipt of Mr Lyttons letter,—which had

[1] See *Autobiography*, chap. v, pp. 71–2.
[2] Charles Reade, 'Foul Play', *Once a Week*, xix (22 Aug. 1868), 151–5. Reade replied to critics who accused him of plagiarizing *Foul Play* from the French play *Le Portefeuille rouge*.
[3] 'The Critical Temper', *Once a Week*, xix (22 Aug. 1868), 146–8.

been long in reaching Mr Trollope in consequence of his absence from home. If it have been received Mr Farrar will perhaps write a line to Mr Lytton to say so. If not, Mr Farrar will no doubt let Mr Trollope hear to that effect.

23—Sept. 1868.

386. To MR. TAYLOR. 25 September. London.
Myers & Co.

Trollope is not enthusiastic about a proposed paper for *Saint Pauls* on Darwin: 'I am afraid of the subject of Darwin. I am myself so ignorant on it, that I should fear to be in the position of editing a paper on the subject.'

387. To MISS EDWARDS.[1] 26 September. Waltham Cross.
Parrish Collection.

At the suggestion of Mrs. Eliot,[2] a friend of Trollope and Miss Edwards, Trollope writes to ask if he may call.

388. To KATE FIELD. 30 September.
Boston Public Library. Sadleir, *Commentary*, p. 282.

(Waltham House,
Waltham Cross.)

30 Sept 1868

My dear Kate—

I have just got your letter. I thought you had one of the photographs. You had said something of taking one from the intoxicated little party. However, I now enclose one, as I understand from your letter that I am scolded for going away without leaving it.

And now about your MS.—as to which I should doubtless have written with more alacrity had I had good news to send. I lost not a moment in applying to Dickens after my return home, but I found that he was opposed to the publication altogether;— and I also found, as I was sure would be the case, that without

---

[1] Probably Amelia Ann Blandford Edwards (1831–92), novelist and Egyptologist.
[2] Probably Frances Minto Elliot (1820–98), a prolific social historian of Italy and France who published many of her books through Chapman & Hall. See letter No. 523, *infra*.

his co-operation the publication with any good results would be altogether impossible. You may take it for granted that he would not like it. I greatly grieve that you should have had so much fruitless labour in preparing the paper for publication here.[1]

On that Tuesday Mrs Homans told me that she expected you, I had gathered that you were already too far from Boston to make it possible that you should be there. It was a melancholy day as I felt quite sure that it would be my last day in America. But I was better pleased to spend it in Boston than elsewhere. Whether I shall ever see again you or her must depend on your coming here. I am becoming an infirm old man, too fat to travel so far.

Let me have the story when it is ready. I will do the best I can with it—for indeed I would willingly see myself in some little way helping you in a profession which I regard as being the finest in the world.

God bless you—my kindest love to your mother.

Most affectionately yours,
A. T.

389. To GEORGE HENRY LEWES. 3 October.
Mrs. E. S. Ouvry.

(Waltham House,
Oct 3—1868   Waltham Cross.)

Dear Lewes,

Thanks. The paper has not come to me, but has no doubt gone to the office.[2] I will order a proof to be sent to you as soon as I get there. I have no doubt all good smokers will express their lasting gratitude in some substantial form;—a pyramid of cigar ashes—or a mausoleum for, long-delayed, future use, constructed of old pipe stems and tobacco stoppers.

In regard to the Spanish Gypsy[3] my regret is that the poet

---

[1] After Dickens's death Kate Field published in England a 'new and revised edition' of her book (London, 1871). She subsequently lectured widely on Dickens. Her lecture on 12 Apr. 1872 at Willis's Rooms was an unqualified success. See the *Graphic*, 13 Apr. 1872, p. 339. Another lecture is reported in *The Times*, 6 May 1872, p. 14.

[2] 'The Dangers and Delights of Tobacco', *Saint Pauls*, iii (Nov. 1868), 172–84.

[3] A dramatic poem by George Eliot.

departed in portions of her work from the dramatic form. The departure would seem to imply,—which is certainly not the case, —that she had lacked power to say all her story in that which is certainly the most efficacious and I think the most perfect form of expression. I think too that the strictly dramatic portions of the poem are stronger than those in which she recedes to narrative, —as would be naturally the case.

Fedalma, Zarca & Juan are perfect. Sylva [*sic*], no doubt intentionally, is so much inferior as a creature to these, that the character, or words attributed to the character, are less striking.

Yours always
A. T.

390. To AUSTIN DOBSON. 8 October.
G. F. C. Dobson. Not seen.

(Waltham House,
Waltham Cross.)

8 Oct 1868

My dear Mr Dobson,
Certainly we will have Boucher,[1]—which is admirable, and not a stanza too long. The feeling of it is excellent, and the execution generally very happy. There is no doubt about our having it.

Then of course come the less agreeable remarks, a criticism or two as to parts,—which however I will leave to your own judgement. 1st I do not quite like the bit of Chaucer which the reader does not expect—and fails altogether to understand till the subsequent explanation comes.

2^d I dislike the word 'weigh' in Stanza XVI—the simple change to 'play' would be an improvement.

3^d Blessed as the blind &c—Stanza XXI—I may be stupid, but I see no idea in this. The blind, if they bless, bless without seeing. But the blind are not specially given to the conferring of blessings. Stanza XXXII— 'That only love informs'—is I think weak.

'Knew in her cheek a little colour burn'

---

[1] 'The Story of Rosina. An Incident in the Life of François Boucher', *Saint Pauls*, iii (Jan. 1869), 460–6.

Stanza XXXIV—is certainly involved—and I think so much so as to be generally unintelligible.

But in regard to all these objections, I will give way to you if you object to them.

As to L'Envoy—I hope you will not object to omit it altogether.[1] It adds nothing, as the story is told so plainly that the lesson wants no elucidation, and the reference to the Magazine is altogether objectionable. You will want to reprint this some day. I return the MS,—but will have it printed as soon as you have looked to these things.

I know I am sticking pins into you by my remarks;—but what is an editor to do?

Yours always,
A. T.

391. To ? 17 October.
Parrish Collection.

I have been asked to express an opinion as to a novel by Lady Wood[2] called Sorrow by the Sea.[3] I am informed that this novel has been suppressed by the Publishers and that payment of the stipulated price has been refused by them on the ground that the book is immoral and injurious in its tendency. I have therefore read the novel in question.

I presume I am justified in supposing that the publishers found their denial of payment on a criticism on the book which appeared in the Athenaeum of May 2nd.[4] I have read that criticism, and I can understand that publishers should say that if that be just, they are bound to withhold the book from circulation; and that, so withholding it through fault of the author, they must decline to pay the stipulated price. Whether or no a jury would maintain them in such a course, if the criticism were justified by evidence,

[1] The 'Envoy' was not printed.
[2] Emma Caroline, Lady Wood (*c.* 1820–79), widow of the Reverend Sir John Page Wood, vicar of Cressing, subsequently published widely with Chapman & Hall novels and anthologies. She was the mother of Trollope's good friend, Anna C. Steele.
[3] Trollope is slightly inaccurate. The book was called *Sorrow on the Sea.* It was published in three volumes by Tinsley.
[4] No. 2114, pp. 623–4. It was a blistering review, of which the following sentence is typical: 'The details of these volumes are literally unfit for presentation in any language.'

I am not lawyer enough to say;—but it is manifest that the burden of justifying the criticism must be on the publishers. It cannot be sufficient for them to say that this or that paper has condemned the book, and that therefore they will retreat from the bargain. If this were so no author could be safe.

I have no hesitation in saying that the criticism in question is manifestly unjust, unfair in its severity, and untrue both in its deductions and assertions. It begins with very heavy censure against the author, accusing her of having applauded the conduct of a certain lady of quality in that she caused her memoirs to be published in Peregrine Pickle.[1] What the author has done is to applaud the conduct of the lady in question, as narrated by Smollett, in that she resorted to strong exercise to deaden her sense of grief in periods of misfortune. It is hard to believe that the mistake on the part of the writer of the criticism has been accidental and not malicious. The whole article is very heavy in its censures, mentioning certain points in the authors tale & the manner of telling them; and then asserting that the bad parts of the book were too bad to be quoted by them. As far as I have been able to form a judgment the reviewer has quoted the very worst in words or sentiments which were to be found in the book. It is then said in the last line of the criticism that there are passages in this book, which ought not to be produced in any language. In answer to this it must first be stated that that which is unfit for publication in one language, must be unfit for publication in any other. But the intention of the writer is to make English readers believe that the author of the novel, an English lady, has written in English that which would be held to be disgraceful even in the literature of countries which are less severe on such matters than are we in England. No evidence whatever is given in the article to support this statement.

I am of opinion that there is nothing in the book to justify the criticism, or the action taken on that criticism by the publisher. I do not think that the book is injurious to morals or likely to do evil. I assume that there was no adequate cause for suppressing it, and I think that the criticism in the Athenaeum to which I

[1] See 'The Memoirs of a Lady of Quality' in *Peregrine Pickle,* chap. lxxxi. This long narrative is thought to be the work of Lady Vane, revised by Smollett.

have alluded was manifestly unjust. I am willing, should there be occasion, to support the claim of the author of the book by public testimony to this effect.

ANTHONY TROLLOPE
Oct 17, 1868

392. To MRS. E. L. YOUMANS. 20 October. London.
New York Historical Society.

Trollope arranges to receive a visitor at his *Saint Pauls* office. Catherine E. Newton Lee Youmans was an American Bluestocking who put her literary talent at the service of her husband, Edward Livingston Youmans (1821–87), a writer, editor, and promoter of scientific education. Youmans was a popular lecturer on science and the chief American disciple of Herbert Spencer.

393. To MISS EDWARDS. 18 November
Waltham Cross. *National Library of Scotland.*

Trollope returns a manuscript and arranges for an appointment.

394. To CECILIA MEETKERKE. 2 December.
Waltham Cross. *Fitzwilliam Museum.*

Trollope apparently refuses an invitation. 'Alas me, I am so driven about just now, that I hardly get time to have a days hunting anywhere. . . . I have just been beaten standing for Beverley, and am now going to petition.' (See *Autobiography*, chap. xvi, pp. 242–53.)

395. To H. B. WHEATLEY. 4 December.
Waltham Cross. *Parrish Collection.*

Trollope subscribes for two years to the Early English Text Society.[1]

396. To ? 17 December. London.
Parrish Collection.

Trollope invites a potential contributor to forward his translation of a story by Heine. I cannot discover that the story was published.

[1] Trollope's knowledge of and interest in early English literature, particularly the drama, is not generally recognized. Few professional scholars of his day had read so many plays. An edition of his critical commentary on some 275 pre-Elizabethan, Elizabethan, and Jacobean dramas has been prepared for the press by Bradford A. Booth and Hugh G. Dick of the University of California, Los Angeles, but still wants a publisher.

1 8 6 9

397. To E. S. Dallas. 5 January.
Not traced.[1]

With this letter the stormy career of *The Vicar of Bullhampton* was begun.[2]

Jany 5—1869

My dear Dallas

A novel such as The Claverings—i e a novel in 3 volumes would run through 32 numbers of Once a Week giving 7 pages a week. A novel such as the Small House or Phineas Finn, i e equal in amount to 4 volumes would give 9 pages for 32 weeks. I should not care to spread a story into a greater number of divisions.

My price for the former would be £2800—for the latter £3200; for the copyright. These are the prices which I got for the Claverings and Phineas Finn— I should ask two thirds of these prices for the publication in the periodical alone,—specifying in such case that I should be enabled to publish the whole simultaneously a full month before the terminating of the whole. Otherwise I should find the property cruelly lessened by the power of the libraries to let out the whole in the copies of your periodical.

I would commence the publication in the first week of May 1869. My purpose wd be not to publish any novel along side of it for the first six months. I would not bind myself to the letter of this arrangement, but I should keep to it in the spirit.

Yours ever
A. T.

[1] I print from Trollope's copy (Bodleian).
[2] Everything went awry with the business arrangements for this novel. The story of Dallas's excuses and Trollope's anger is told in Sadleir, *Commentary*, pp. 296–9; and Sadleir, *Bibliography*, p. 295.

398. To ARTHUR HELPS.[1] 7 January. *Not traced. Correspondence of Sir Arthur Helps*, ed. E. A. Helps (London: John Lane, 1917), p. 269.

(Garrick Club)
Jan. 7, 1869.

My dear Mr. Helps,

I am very much obliged to you for your book[2] and your kind letter, which I have this moment received. When I have read it, which I will do at once, I shall write to you again and tell you what I think about it—in very truth. I was surprised when I heard that you had descended into our arena, feeling that you had fought your battles on a nobler battlefield. With me, it often comes to me as a matter, I will not say of self-reproach but of regret, that I can express what I wish to express only by the mouths of people who are created—not that they may express themselves, but that they may amuse. You have gained your laurels after a more manly fashion.

Most faithfully,
ANTHONY TROLLOPE

399. To ARTHUR HELPS. 26 January.
Parrish Collection.

January 26. 1869.   (Waltham House,
Waltham Cross.)
My dear Mr Helps.

At last I have read *Realmah.* You can perhaps understand how a man may be so pressed, as to lack time from week to week to give a day to such a book.

I often tell my brother, who knows more than any man I know and who is [a] man desiring to communicate his knowledge and convictions, that he is too didactic, too anxious to teach, to write a good novel. I will not say the same to you, as yours is not a novel. It is a most suggestive work, full of speculation and thought; doing just what Friends in Council[3] did, only in another

---

[1] Arthur Helps, later Sir Arthur (1813–75), was clerk of the privy council, revised works by Queen Victoria, and published widely on diversified subjects and in all the literary forms.

[2] The reference is to Helps's novel *Realmah*. See letter No. 399, *infra.*

[3] *Friends in Council* (London, 1847–59). This work appeared in several series.

form. I will confess that in the volumes themselves I prefer Milverton and Ellesmere to Realmah, and can get more from them. In Realmah I am always trying to fathom a mystery, a double entendre, as to which I am not quite sure whether it exist or no, and which, at last, I think I perceive not to exist with the completeness which I first imagined. I looked even for a recondite meaning in every name, but did not find it.

The records of a presumed early civilization have always been very alluring. There is no form in which one's own political and social tenets can be put forward with more clearness, and in which satyre can be better conveyed without any personal sting. Utopia was a great attempt in this way. I do not know whether you know Helionde,[1]—which was far fetched. In Realmah, you have been very politic, very reasonable, very true—& very readable. You will have conveyed your ideas to men of your own class; but, judging from the book only and knowing nothing of what may have been its fate as to readers of the magazine, I should doubt your hitting the mere devourers of novels. But that is what one wishes to do,—to pour thoughts upon thoughtless men under the guise of amusement.

Very faithfully yours
ANTHONY TROLLOPE

There is at page 263—a proverb, with its interpretation[2]— which quite comes home to me after reading your book

400. To ANNA C. STEELE. 27 January.
Mr. and Mrs. Maurice Fitzgerald. Bradhurst, p. 188.

(Waltham House,
Waltham Cross.)

My dear Mrs Steele,

Of course we will come. Will you get 3 stalls for myself, wife and one of the boys— I send a guinea, hoping I dont intrude. You can, perhaps, send me the tickets.

[1] See Sydney Whiting, *Helriondé; or, Adventures in the Sun* (London, 1855). Whiting was a barrister with an active literary avocation.

[2] 'Nero fiddled while Rome burned.' Helps says that if he fiddled at all, it was not during the fire, but after the fire, to collect subscriptions for the sufferers. Preceding this passage there is a dialogue discussion of *The Last Chronicle of Barset*. One of the speakers says of Lily Dale, 'She is more real to me than many a character I read of in history.'

I don't care twopence about the lifeboat. I wish you could take the money to buy hunters for yourself and two brothers. Only Charley[1] mustn't ride home first when the fox is found.

Could we see you for a moment to settle when you would come to us in February. Come on a Tuesday—say Feb 16—hunt on Wednesday—would be the nicest. I'll mount you, & take you out, and find you in everything except whip & spurs,—including sherry, sandwiches, & small talk.

Yours always

Wednesday   A N T H O N Y   T R O L L O P E
27 Jan. 69

401. To A N N A C. S T E E L E. 31 January.
Mr. and Mrs. Maurice Fitzgerald. Bradhurst, p. 188.

Jan 31, 1869.   (Waltham House,

My dear Mrs Steele   Waltham Cross.)

We will get our little place in order by degrees. Won't your brother bring you on the Tuesday? Let me know. If that will suit you, I'll write to him. If you will not ride my sons mare— to which you would be very welcome,—you must send your own, not here which would be quite out of the way, but to Tylers Green, where my horses stand, where your horse should have the warmest stall and grass from the hand of fellowship. But you must stay the Wednesday night,—& your brother.

However we shall all be wiser about it when we know the meet for the 15th.

Yours always faithfully

A N T H O N Y   T R O L L O P E

Thanks for the tickets.

402. To P R O F E S S O R F A W C E T T. 4 February.
National Women's Service Library, Oxford.

Trollope will read Mrs. Fawcett's paper on Fox, but asks her to 'remember that the impatience of ordinary magazine readers will not endure long articles'. The reference may be to W. J. Fox (1786–1864), author, liberal preacher, and M.P. for Oldham, 1847–63. Henry Fawcett (1833–84) was M.P. for Brighton and professor of political economy at Cambridge, 1863–84. According to *D.N.B.* Millicent Garrett Fawcett 'shared his intellectual and political labours'.

[1] Charles Page Wood of Scrips, Kelvedon. He was Mrs. Steele's younger brother.

403. To PROFESSOR FAWCETT. 11 February.
Parrish Collection.

Trollope rejects the article: 'I am afraid that the memory of Mr Fox has so far died out that we should hardly succeed in resuscitating it by the article you so kindly sent me.'

404. To MESSRS. LOVEJOY. 27 February.
Waltham Cross. *Bradford A. Booth.*

Trollope denies ever receiving any such deed as that referred to by the Dean of Bristol. There is not sufficient information to determine what this business concerned.

405. To MACMILLAN & CO. 8 March.
Not traced.[1]

Thanks for your note. I think that you[2] and Mr Grove[3] will like the story. You can have the MS. when you please.[4] It will be for you to make what arrangements you please in America,— the foreign copyright being yours. Of course it must not be published in America before it is published here for all our sakes.

A. T.

March 8, 69.

I observe on reading your note that you say the story is to run about 14 or 16 of your pages. I dont know the length of your pages. It would run about 10 Cornhill pages,—i e something over that rather than under; but the pages have been written to that measure.

---

[1] I print from Trollope's copy of this letter (Bodleian).
[2] Probably Alexander Macmillan, brother of Daniel Macmillan (1813–57), who was the founder of the firm. It is difficult to determine who actually edited *Macmillan's Magazine* at this date. David Masson, the first editor, resigned in 1867, and Grove is said not to have assumed the editorship until 1873. See Charles Morgan, *The House of Macmillan (1843–1943)* (New York: Macmillan, 1944), p. 84.
[3] George Grove, later Sir George (1820–1900), a Macmillan editor and compiler of the famous *Dictionary of Music and Musicians.*
[4] The novel referred to is *Sir Harry Hotspur of Humblethwaite*, serialized in *Macmillan's Magazine*, May–Dec. 1870.

406. To GEORGE SMITH. 15 March. Waltham Cross. *Not traced.* Sadleir's transcript.

*   *   *

I think I mentioned to you that I was thinking of extracting the material of a comedy from the story of The Last Chronicle of Barset. On commencing the absolute work I encounter an idea that as you have half the copyright of the novel I should have your permission. I don't quite know the law in that respect. But will you have the kindness to let me know whether you have any objection to my work. The name I have at present in my mind for the play is

Did He Steal It?[1]

*   *   *

407. To MR. ANDERSON.[2] 29 March. Waltham Cross. *Parrish Collection.*

Trollope knows nothing of Kelly's projected return.

408. To the Editor of the *Daily Telegraph.* 31 March. *Daily Telegraph,* April 1, 1869, p. 3.

To the Editor of 'The Daily Telegraph.'
Sir—Will you allow me to ask insertion in your columns for a few remarks which will be made with the fullest sincerity and in perfect good humour.

In a leading article of your impression of today[3] you charge me with having drawn portraits of the leading politicians of the time in a novel of mine lately published,—and you refer especially to a presumed portrait of Mr. Bright.

You say 'Is it gentlemanlike to paint portraits thus?' 'Is it right for any novelist to put into a novel of the day malignant little touches professing to lift the veil of private life or to depict a public man as he appears in private society or at his own fireside?'

[1] See *Autobiography,* chap. xv, p. 231.
[2] I have not been able to identify either Mr. Anderson or Kelly.
[3] 31 Mar. 1869, p. 4.

Certainly it is neither gentlemanlike or right to do these things, and I protest that I have [not] done them. In the character of Mr. Turnbull to which allusion is made, I depicted Mr. Bright neither in his private or public character; and I cannot imagine how any likeness justifying such a charge against me can be found. The character that I have drawn has no resemblance to the chairman of the Board of Trade in person, in manners, in character, in mode of life, or even in the mode of expressing political opinion. It was my object to depict a turbulent demagogue;—but it was also my object so to draw the character that no likeness should be found in our own political circles for the character so drawn. I have been unlucky,—as the charge brought by you against me shows; but I protest that the ill-luck has not been the result of fault on my part. I intended neither portrait or caricature, and most assuredly I have produced neither.[1]

Your obedient servant

March 31, 1868 [1869].   ANTHONY TROLLOPE

409. To MISS EDWARDS. 2 April. Waltham Cross.
Parrish Collection.

Trollope is glad to have received a letter. He had hoped to call but 'was kept among the haunts of printers, publishers & the like'.

410. To ? 5 April.
Estate of Carroll A. Wilson.

April 5—69
(Waltham House,
Waltham Cross.)

Madam

I am most happy to send you my autograph—small as must be its value. I fear from the tone of your letter,—that you ask me for more than this,—for something written, an ode, sonnet, or some original matter. Unless I were to write you a novel in 3 volumes, (which is my only mode of performance) I should not know how to furnish you with this.

Your faithful Servant

ANTHONY TROLLOPE

[1] For an interesting discussion of matters treated in this letter see R. W. Chapman's 'Personal Names in Trollope's Political Novels', in *Essays Presented to Sir Humphrey Milford* (Oxford University Press, 1948), pp. 72–81.

411. To AUSTIN DOBSON. 18 April.
Not traced. Sadleir, *Commentary*, pp. 288–9.

*   *   *

I will use both your poems[1]—on the condition that you will ease a prejudice on my part by expunging the joke about Gibbon's 'Decline and Fall'.

*   *   *

412. To JOHN EVERETT MILLAIS. 20 April.
Waltham Cross. *Parrish Collection.*

Trollope will be happy to dine with Millais and his artist friends.

413. To MISS HOLMES.[2] 24 April.
Parrish Collection.

April 24—1869   (Waltham House,
                                                  Waltham Cross.)

My dear Miss Holmes,

I am almost ashamed to answer your letter and I do not know that I can do any good by doing so. When I got a letter from you ever so long ago,—more than two years I think, I went to work to find whether I could do anything towards getting up the outside scene-work of a concert for you;—asking noblemen to lend their rooms and the like,—of all which I felt ashamed

---

[1] 'The Death of Procris', *Saint Pauls*, iv (June 1869), 319–20; and 'Ad Rosam', *Saint Pauls*, iv (July 1869), 428–30.

[2] Mary Holmes (*c.* 1815–78) was to be Trollope's most regular correspondent over the next nine years. She was a friend of Thackeray's cousin, Mary Graham Carmichael. In 1852 she began a correspondence with Thackeray himself, later acting as governess to his children. See Gordon Ray, *The Letters . . . of William Makepeace Thackeray*, i. cxxxix–cxli. She had literary and musical enthusiasm and worked hard, but there was no real talent. Her life was solitary and frustrated, but, becoming a Catholic convert, she solaced herself with the consolations of religion and with her long correspondence with Newman. After Thackeray's death she began to write to Trollope, who treated her with unfailing courtesy, even when she did not respond in kind. At her death he was moved to write feelingly of her virtues. See letter No. 714, *infra*. A brief account of Miss Holmes is given by Robert F. Metzdorf, for many years curator of the R. B. Adam Collection of the University of Rochester, in *The Month at Goodspeed's*, xvi (May–June 1945), 206–9.

while I was making the attempt, and failed altogether at last. But in the failure months went by, and then I had not even an address at which to write to you to tell you that I had failed. You thought, no doubt, that I was cruel, and I thought that I had endeavoured to take a work in hand with which I ought never to have meddled.

And now I write simply to say that I am utterly powerless in the matter of music. I know well that it is not so much my absolute aid you require, as a touch of sympathy from somebody of whose sympathy you would be glad. But still, I, knowing that sympathy will make fat neither the man nor woman would be so glad to help you if I knew how. But we all have our own circles, our own ways and fashions, and the paths to which our feet are familiar. My feet know nothing of musical paths. I can only wish you success, & promise you that I will come & call on you if you are settled in London.

faithfully yours
ANTHONY TROLLOPE

414. To MRS. JOHN EVERETT MILLAIS.[1] 1 May.
Waltham Cross. *Parrish Collection.*

Trollope has read Mr. Anderson's paper about the gold-diggings in Scotland. 'It was very well written, & interesting to those who will interest themselves about the subject,—but I fear that the subject would not be of sufficiently general value, to be of use to a magazine. People however vary so greatly in their ideas, that it is very probable that either Mr Froude for Frasers Magazine or Geo Smith for the Cornhill, would be glad to have it.'

415. To MARY HOLMES. 3 May. Waltham Cross.
Parrish Collection.

Trollope writes to say that Annie Thackeray is in Italy. Anna Isabella Thackeray, later Lady Ritchie (1837–1919), was Thackeray's eldest daughter. In her own right she was a talented novelist and essayist.

416. To FREDERIC CHAPMAN. 8 May. Waltham Cross.
Parrish Collection.

Trollope returns a manuscript. 'It is by far too diluted to be published in numbers. It could not be divided into parts which would of themselves have any interest.'

[1] Euphemia Gray had married Millais in 1855, two years after receiving a decree of nullity of her marriage to Ruskin.

417. To MRS. FIELDS,[1] 18 May. Skipton.[2]
Boston Public Library.

Trollope will call as soon as he returns to town.

418. To JOHN HOLLINGSHEAD. 23 May. Waltham Cross.
Maggs Catalogue 386 (Christmas 1919).

Trollope had undoubtedly received an unfavourable response from Hollingshead on *Did He Steal It?* 'I dont doubt about [? but] what you are right about the play.'

419. To FREDERIC CHAPMAN. 10 August.
Not traced.[3]

(Beauport,[4]
Battle.)

10 August 1869.

Dear Chapman,

If you do anything about my tale[5] with that American publisher,[6] do not let him have the right of publishing it in his Magazine for less than £500—as I do not think you can make more than £200 out of a one-volume novel. If he should take it on these terms, which I doubt, you could republish it for £200 to me, on the understanding that I am to have the first £200 out of the profits;—so that you should not lose by it, or be called on for your money before you have received it.

Yours ever
A. T.

I will not ask you to pay £200 to me till you have made it out of the profits; so that you should be at no loss.

The copyright will be mine.

---

[1] Wife of James T. Fields, the Boston publisher.
[2] A small town in Yorkshire.
[3] I print from Trollope's copy (Bodleian).
[4] Battle: a small town near Hastings in Sussex and the home of Trollope's great friend, Sir Charles Taylor.
[5] *The Golden Lion of Granpère.* This is the letter described in Sadleir, *Bibliography*, pp. 300–1.
[6] Appleton.

420. To GEORGE HENRY LEWES. 13 August.
Mrs. E. S. Ouvry.

(Waltham House,

August 13—1869   Waltham Cross.)

My dear Lewes,

Your news about your boy is very bad. I can only tell you how strongly I feel for you.

I do admire Horne[1] as a poet,—that is I think highly of his Orion;—but I do not know of what nature is his prose, or how the man who wrote Orion in 1839 (or thereabouts) would write now in 1869. Nor am I specially wedded to serial articles (to use an abominable word). Readers of magazines skip them when on dry subjects. Seebohm[2] did answer with you,—but then they were very good. Bell's[3] did not. But they were very bad. If he has ought written and will send it to me, I will read it;—but I will not pledge myself.

And now I have a bit of news for you of the domestic kind which will surprise you. My eldest boy Harry has gone into partnership with Chapman. I pay £10000—(of course this is private)—and he has a third of the business. I have had an immense deal of trouble in arranging it, and will tell you details when we meet. It is a fine business which has been awfully ill used by want of sufficient work and sufficient capital.

Do not let me intrude on you;—but if you are disengaged and Thornie[4] is not too ill, I will come up to you next week some evening. My wife is away,—in Paris,—or rather goes tonight. I go with her, but return. Address Athenaeum Club.

Yours always affectionately

A. T.

---

[1] Richard Henry (Hengist) Horne (1803–84), miscellaneous writer, friend of and collaborator with Mrs. Browning, commissioner in Australia, 1852–69. His epic *Orion*, praised by Poe, was published in 1843. No serial articles appeared in *Saint Pauls* at this time.

[2] Frederic Seebohm (1833–1912), historian of Anglo-Saxon and medieval England. He published two articles in the *Fortnightly Review*: 'The Black Death and its Place in English History', ii (1 Sept. and 15 Sept. 1865), 149–60; 268–79.

[3] Robert Bell wrote three articles at the same time on 'Social Amusements under the Restoration'.

[4] Thornton Arnott Lewes (1844–69). He died shortly after Trollope's visit.

421. To JOHN BLACKWOOD. 19 August.
National Library of Scotland.

> (Office of St Pauls Magazine
> 294, City Road, London)
> August 19, 1869.

My dear Blackwood,

After your kindness on the subject I cannot but tell you that the partnership between Chapman and my son is completed;— i e they are now partners and I have paid the money.[1] The exact extent of Chapman's capital is to be fixed on 31 Decr. 1869 by Bell & Langford with power of naming a referee. The deed of partnership exacts that. Langford has been most kind & useful.

> Yours always
> ANTH TROLLOPE

422. To ALFRED AUSTIN.[2]
Not traced. Autobiography of Alfred Austin, 2 vols. (London: Macmillan, 1911), i. 6.

> (Waltham House,
> Waltham Cross.)
> 3rd Oct. '69.

My dear Austin,

It seems that the 'Vindication'[3] is having a considerable sale. . . .

I find both from the American Press and from letters from

---

[1] Trollope had been looking for a position for Henry in a publishing house, and Blackwood had expressed an interest in the young man. Henry remained with Chapman only a few years, however.

[2] Alfred Austin (1835–1913), poet laureate, 1896; for thirty years leader-writer for the *Standard*, editor of the *National Review*, author of twenty volumes of verse, as well as much miscellaneous writing. Austin had met, grown fond of, and, in fact, been sponsored by Tom Trollope in Florence. In England he looked up Anthony, and they became fast friends. *The Garden that I Love*, one of the most charming of his later works, is said to describe Trollope's last home, at Harting, near Petersfield, Sussex. Austin was present at Trollope's funeral, and later wrote an appreciative essay, 'Last Reminiscences of Anthony Trollope'. See *Temple Bar*, lxx (Jan. 1884), 129–34.

[3] Harriet Beecher Stowe had published in the September number of the *Atlantic Monthly* 'The True Story of Lady Byron's Life'. Alfred Austin's pamphlet, 'A Vindication of Lord Byron', was one of many answers to Mrs. Stowe's sensational article, in which the main features of the *Astarte* story were first described.

correspondents that Mrs. Stowe is much more hardly handled there than she is here.

I still feel that no more outrageous piece of calumny—in the real sense of the word—was ever published; or, as I think, with lower motives. . . .

I am, yours always,
ANTHONY TROLLOPE

423. To JOHN BLACKWOOD. 13 October.
National Library of Scotland. Parker, p. 58.

(Waltham House,
Waltham Cross.)
Oct 13, 69

My dear Blackwood.

Yes. I am going to lecture at Edinburgh but not till Friday the 28 January;—a long day, my lord, and I shall be very happy to be your guest; am indeed most thankful to you for asking me. Some learned pundit,—at least he was a doctor,—kindly offered to give me the 'hospitality of the city,' which, as it means a half-formed introduction to the pickled snakes and a visit to the public library & the like I viewed with horror and did not accept.

I will lecture about novels,[1] and shall expect Mrs Blackwood to go and hear me. I will not be so hard upon you, because you must know more about novels than I can tell you. Whether Mrs Trollope will go with me I do not yet know. It is a long journey for a lady to make in the middle of the winter & that only for a day or two. I give the same lecture at Hull on the 24th and at Glasgow on the 27th.

Henry is hard at work and comes home freighted with Mss. What he does with them I don't know; but I feel glad that I am not an author publishing with Chapman & Hall as I fancy he goes to sleep over them with a pipe in his mouth.

Yours always
ANTH TROLLOPE

[1] 'On English Prose Fiction as a Rational Amusement.' Printed in Morris L. Parrish, *Four Lectures*, pp. 94–124.

424. To AUSTIN DOBSON. 8 November.
Not traced. Austin Dobson, *The Drama of the Doctor's Window* (London: priv. ptd., 1872), pp. 20–21.

The poem referred to in the following letter was for some time the object of a heated controversy.[1]

(Waltham House,
Waltham Cross.)
Nov. 8, 1869.

My dear Mr. Dobson,—

Here, as always (I mean in regard to your juveniles which I send back by the same post as this) I like your idea, and manner, and current of thought, and versification:—but think that you have omitted that for which you have taken credit when you say that 'you do not think you can do more to the verses.' I mean that you are somewhat too quick, and apt to send out your work without attaining the amount of verbal perfection at which you are aiming.

Such a poem as your 'Pyramus and Thisbe' should be as clear as running water. No one should have to pause a moment to look for interpretation. If it is not fit to be read aloud so as to catch the intellects of not very intellectual people, it does not answer its professed object. But I have found myself compelled to unravel passages. This I am sure you will acknowledge should not be. I will venture, at the risk of calling down curses, to point out a few words I would alter. 'Desire for green' is surely left there because a clearer expression would take trouble to find. Why 'emphatic *terra firma*?' 'Sniffed' should be sniffing, but I don't insist upon that. 'Ulysses' rest' is, I think, very far-fetched, and almost misses your point. 'After', Part III., Scene I., you

---

[1] 'Pyramus and Thisbe' is a section of a longer poem called 'The Drama of the Doctor's Window', which Dobson published in *Saint Pauls* (v [February 1870], 557–61). Shortly thereafter an acquaintance of Dobson, a solicitor named R. E. Webster, accused the poet of plagiarism from a young lady. In spite of every proof Webster persisted in his delusion. Dobson then published the whole story, including all pertinent correspondence, in a privately printed pamphlet, *The Drama of the Doctor's Window*. This excessively rare piece (only one copy has ever come up for sale) I have been allowed to see, through the courtesy of Alban Dobson, in the University of London Library, where Mr. Dobson has deposited his incomparable collection of his father's works. The controversy is discussed in Alban Dobson, *Austin Dobson: Some Notes*, pp. 23–6.

mean 'then.' 'Wide, blue, and tired' I do not understand. I do not know with what they act. What is blue and tired? 'Fled.' The word should be in the other stanza;—would, only the rhythm is troublesome. 'Spelled!' Spell and spellbound I know; but not spelled except in regard to orthography. 'With' should, I think, be 'while.' 'Cultured caution' is far-fetched, and 'sought' in the same line should be 'found.'

In fact, could you not look over it again and alter where you yourself doubt. Your criticism will be better than mine; and allow me to ask you to remember that did I not like the piece much, I should not descend to such picking of holes—which is unpleasant work. Pray let me have it again.

Yours always
ANT TROLLOPE

425. To AUSTIN DOBSON. 15 November.
  Not traced. Austin Dobson, *The Drama of the Doctor's Window*, p. 21.[1]

(Waltham House,
Waltham Cross.)
Nov. 15, 1869.

My dear Sir,—
  I have directed a proof of your 'Pyramus and Thisbe' to be sent to you.

You were right to put out the *terra firma.* The expression should not, I think, be used unless there is some, however far-fetched reason for calling that 'terra' especially 'firma.'

Yours always
A. T.

426. To MRS. BENT.[2] 18 November.
  Parrish Collection.

(Waltham House,
Waltham Cross.)

Nov. 18—1869.

My dear Mrs Bent.
  I have received the book and I have written to thank my aunt.[3]

---

[1] See letter No. 424, *supra.*
[2] Mrs. Bent was the wife of Trollope's cousin, Major Bent. See letter No. 236, *supra.*
[3] Mary Milton Clyde.

I think the book must have belonged to her grandmother,—for it bears the name

Mary Gresley[1]

1740—

Now Mrs Clyde's mother could have owned no book, & could not indeed have been alive in 1740.[2] I fancy it has come down to the fourth generation. Many thanks for the trouble you have taken.

My wife sends her kind regards to you and the Major & the girls—to which I add my own.

Very sincerely yours

ANTHONY TROLLOPE

427. To WILLIAM SETHBRIDGE. 19 November.
Waltham Cross. *Myers & Co.*

Trollope is engaged and cannot accept an invitation. Sethbridge was manager of the firm of Bradbury and Evans.

428. To RICHARD BENTLEY. 20 November.
Waltham Cross. *Parrish Collection.*

On behalf of Mrs. Pollock and *Saint Pauls* Trollope asks for a review copy of 'a life of my chief favourite among novelists, Jane Austen'. (The book was J. E. Austen-Leigh's *A Memoir of Jane Austen* (1870). Mrs. Pollock's article was 'Jane Austen', v (March 1870), 631–43.)

429. To ANNA C. STEELE. 21 November.
Mr. and Mrs. Maurice Fitzgerald.

(Waltham House,

Waltham Cross.)

My dear friend,

My back is not in the least broken,—except by my trot home to-day— I was out to-day & yesterday for the first time, and am like an old porter. But as for the election, I let that run like water

---

[1] Trollope used the name at once, his story 'Mary Gresley' appearing in the November number of *Saint Pauls*. It is now found in *An Editor's Tales*.

[2] The book must have belonged to Mary Milton Clyde's great-aunt, for her grandmother Gresley was Cecilia Leeson Gresley.

off a ducks back. I have somewhat of a grievance as to South Essex,—as I offered to contest the division before the bill was passed, when the expense would not have been £2,000, and when A. J.[1] not only would not come forward but was most prominent in urging me to do so. But in politics I take all these things as Fate may send them. A walkover for the county was too good a thing for me to expect. I shall have another fly at it somewhere some day, unless I feel myself to be growing too old.

What about your mothers book? Why do you say not a word about it?

When will it suit you to come to us?

Dont be a shrivelled leaf, before you have come to summers colour. At present you have but the green of spring struggling against the chills of infancy.

Yours always
A. T.

21 Nov 69

I want to make you *write* a novel in serial parts. I know all you have to say against it, & it is all nothing.

430. To FRANCIS BLACK. 24 November.
Waltham Cross. *Parrish Collection.*

Trollope is staying with John Blackwood in Edinburgh, and he therefore cannot accept Black's invitation. Francis Black was an Edinburgh publisher and president of the Edinburgh Booksellers' Association.

431. To MRS. BROOKFIELD.[2] 3 December. London.
Parrish Collection.

Trollope has so many novels on hand for *Saint Pauls* that he cannot take advantage of Mrs. Brookfield's kind offer.

432. To TOM TAYLOR. 7 December. Waltham Cross.
J. H. Spencer.

Trollope must reject for *Saint Pauls* an article on art criticism which had come to him from a lady on whose behalf Taylor had spoken.

[1] Andrew Johnston, first chairman of the Essex County Council and M.P. for South Essex, 1868–74.

[2] Jane Octavia Elton Brookfield (1821–96), Thackeray's great friend. She wrote a number of indifferent novels, beginning with *Only George* (1864), which went through several editions. The manuscript which at this time she was trying to sell was probably that of *Influence*, which was finally published in 1871.

433. To AUSTIN DOBSON. 8 December.
G. F. C. Dobson. Not seen.

8 December 1869

*   *   *

I lunched yesterday with my dear friends George Eliot and
G. H. Lewes,—as to whom you will at any rate know who they
are. I regard them as the two best critics of English poetry (or
prose) whom I know. They were very loud in their praise of
your Autumn Idyll, and George Eliot asked me to let the author
know what she thought of it.[1]

*   *   *

434. To GEORGE HENRY LEWES. 13 December.
Mrs. E. S. Ouvry.

(Waltham House,
Waltham Cross.)

Dec\[r] 13. 1869

My dear Lewes,

What can I do for you about cigars? If you liked that one I left
with you, (which I think very mild though perhaps a little large,)
I can send you a hundred of them,—strictly commercial—4\[d] a
peice. I have a large parcel of unopened cigars,—12 hundred,—
of which you shall have a box on trial instead if you prefer them.
They are of course 12 months younger. I think they are probably
quite as good a cigar, but a little stronger. Would you like a box
of each?

I write as I was led to believe you were getting short of baccy.

Yours always

ANTH TROLLOPE

You said a word as to the impossibility of inferring God's
intentions with created things, from the observed habits of the
creatures. Is this not a fair mode of argument for our own
guidance. We know that there have been men who think it
wrong to eat flesh; but may we not argue that we are intended

---

[1] Published in Alban Dobson, *Austin Dobson: Some Notes,* p. 79.

to eat flesh, by seeing that certain animals do so, who from their nature cannot act against the Creators intentions?

> But you may [? have] the cigars
> without answering
> all this

435. To RICHARD SAMUEL OLDHAM. 18 December.
Parrish Collection.

> (Waltham House,
> Waltham Cross.)

December 18, 1869

My dear Oldham,

I purpose being in Glasgow on the 25th January—Tuesday—at some hour, viz as soon as I can get there from Hull—(at which place I lecture on the Monday.) I have engaged myself to go to George Burns[1] on the Wednesday, & shall stay there Wednesday & Thursday. On Friday I go to Edinburgh. All this you will see leaves me my Tuesday evening in Glasgow, and I have so left in order that I might have an evening with you to discuss Test[2] abolition, Oecumenical Council,[3] Dr Temple,[4] and the state of things generally. Shall you be prepared? At what hour I shall get to Glasgow I cannot learn without an amount of continued study of Bradshaw[5] for which I have neither strength nor mental ability [? agility]. But it must be before the hours of discussion are gone. Let me have a line to say whether we can meet as purposed.

> Yours always
> ANTHONY TROLLOPE

[1] George Burns, later Sir George (1795–1890), was co-founder of the steamship company which became the Cunard Line.

[2] The Test Act: an act to prevent Roman Catholics from holding office in England. Most of its provisions were finally abolished in 1828, the rest in 1926.

[3] Oecumenical Council: a convocation of the constituted authorities of the whole church.

[4] Frederick Temple (1821–1902), headmaster of Rugby whose rationalism provoked a flurry of opposition, especially in 1869 when he was nominated bishop of Exeter by Gladstone. He later became archbishop of Canterbury.

[5] George Bradshaw (1801–53), a map-engraver and printer, began in 1841 to publish his famous 'Bradshaw's Monthly Railway Guide'.

1 8 7 0

436. To JOHN BLACKWOOD. 10 January (dated in error 10 January 1869). Waltham Cross. *Parrish Collection*.

Trollope arranges to stay with the Blackwoods over the week-end of his lecture, 28–30 January.

437. To STATION MASTER, Peterborough.[1] 16 January. *Parrish Collection*.

Trollope arranges for the transportation of his horses to two hunts.

438. To E. B. NICHOLSON.[2] 22 January. *Parrish Collection*.

(Office of the S[t] Pauls Magazine, 294, City Road, London.)

Jan. 22, 1870

Dear Sir,

I am constrained to return your poem, and am prohibited by your letter from giving any reason for doing so.

You propose prose articles on certain subjects named by yourself of very various shades of interest, and add an offer to *write on any other subject*. You will perhaps believe me, and perhaps will not, when I say that I am led by the culture and intellect shewn in your poem to regret that you should not have a clearer insight into your powers. Such insight will no doubt come in time; but till it does come I fear you will have to suffer the sorrow of an unfulfilled ambition.

Yours very faithfully
ANTHONY TROLLOPE

E. B. Nicholson Esq

[1] Peterborough: a railway centre and cathedral city 75 miles north of London.
[2] Edward Williams Byron Nicholson was at this time an Oxford undergraduate who amusingly overestimated his versatility. He became librarian of the London Institution, 1873–82, and subsequently Bodley's Librarian. He published many poems, stories, and scholarly articles.

439. To Miss Bond.[1] 3 February. Waltham Cross.
Estate of Carroll A. Wilson.

Trollope sends his thanks for a very pretty drawing.

440. To CHARLES KENT. 6 February.
Parrish Collection.

Feb 6, 1870 (Waltham House,
Waltham Cross.)
My dear Sir,
   I have considered closely the matter which we discussed the other day in Piccadilly and I feel myself obliged to decline your kind offer with reference to the Sun newspaper. I should be troubling you too much with affairs which are simply my own were I to give you the various reasons which make me feel myself bound to abandon the project, but I may as well state to you candidly that in carrying out the scheme I should find myself under an obligation of giving more personal unpaid labour than I could afford to supply.   Very faithfully yours
                                    ANTHONY TROLLOPE

441. To ?[2] 19 February. Waltham Cross.
Parrish Collection.

Trollope recommends Mr. Galloway of the firm of Morgan & Galloway[3] to the further protection of the British government in connexion with a grievance which 'has no doubt come from the want of bribes administered to the Peruvian authorities'.

442. To OCTAVIAN BLEWITT. 24 February.
Berg Collection.

24 Feb. 1870 Waltham House,
Waltham Cross.
My dear Mr Blewitt,
   I have this moment got your MS. & hasten to explain to you that I give up the editorship of the Saint Paul's Magazine in

   [1] Miss Bond was a Birmingham artist who had previously sent Trollope drawings of 'birds & Little Red Riding Hood'. In the *Cornhill* of Oct. 1867 there is a Little Red Riding Hood illustration, but it is not likely to have been the work of Miss Bond.
   [2] The name of the addressee, apparently a government official, has been obliterated by a water stain.
   [3] I do not find any such firm listed in the *Post Office London Directory 1870*.

June next, and am almost full up to that date. I doubt whether I have room for so long an article. I will read it and then will write again;—but I write at once to assure you that any thing coming from you to me would be treated with the utmost respect. If I cannot use it myself, I may perhaps leave it as a legacy to Strahan's people. I will tell you all about it, however, before long.[1]

Pray believe me that it gives me great pleasure to see you employed at such work again.

Yours always faithfully
ANTHONY TROLLOPE

443. To JOHN BLACKWOOD. 6 March.
National Library of Scotland. Parker, p. 59.

(Waltham House,
Waltham Cross.)
March 6, 1870

My dear Blackwood

I should have been happy to have read Miss Hassell's[2] paper on Browning,[3]—whom I regard as a very great poet,—were it not for that decision on the part of the proprietors of Saint Pauls Magazine which I communicated to you. I cannot answer for what the magazine may see fit to do when it edits itself,—as does another periodical we know of.

I have matter to last me up to the end of my reign,—& more I fear than I can use. I fear to leave MSS to Strahans tender mercies, knowing that he has already on hand many tons of contributions which, if not accepted, are not rejected.

I have written to Miss Hassell explaining this as well as I can.

Yours always
ANTHONY TROLLOPE

[1] It is impossible to trace this article. During Trollope's editorship articles in the *Saint Pauls* were published anonymously. Only after Jan. 1871 were they generally signed. I find nothing by Blewitt.

[2] Miss E. J. Hassell was a frequent contributor to *Blackwood's Magazine*.

[3] 'Euripides in Modern English—Browning's Balaustion', *Saint Pauls*, xii (June 1873), 680–99; (July 1873), 49–66.

444. To JOHN BLACKWOOD. 10 March.
National Library of Scotland. Sadleir, *Commentary*,
p. 300; *Parker*, p. 59.

(Office of St Pauls Magazine
294, City Road, London.)
Address Waltham Cross   March 10, 1870

My dear Blackwood.

Since I got home from my lecturing expedition I have been at
work on the Caesar,[1]—and find it very hard work. However I
have done the first and longest of the two Commentaries.
Before I attack the other, I should like to know what you & Mr.
Collins[2] think of the one I have done. Caesars remaining work is
so clearly divided into two parts, that there will be no difficulty
in this. The whole, if completed will make a volume about the
length of the Iliad;—(I mean of course Mr. Collins' Iliad).
Would you let me send you the 7 chapters done, and then would
you let me know what you think of it. There will be also an
introductory chapter, (nearly done already,) but I will not send
trials as it cannot be completed till the second commentary has
been taken in hand. I do not like, myself, sending a half completed work; but the job is so very stiff a one, and so much
subsidiary reading is necessary, that I would spare myself six
week[s] labour on the second Commentary if, as may be probable, you or Mr. Collins do not like what I have done. If you
approve of that I will go to work again with a will.

MS to you or to him? If to him give me the address
Yours always faithfully
ANTHONY TROLLOPE

[1] Trollope's *The Commentaries of Caesar* was published in June 1870 as a
volume in Blackwood's series of 'Ancient Classics for English Readers'.
[2] William Lucas Collins (1817–87), rector of Kilsby and later of Lowick,
editor of the 'Ancient Classics' series.

445. To John Blackwood. 14 March.
National Library of Scotland. Parker, p. 59.

(Waltham House,
Waltham Cross.)

March 14, 1870

My dear Blackwood.

I send the MS of the Caesar in two parcels. You will understand, and Mr Collins will understand, that there is to be an
introductory chapter,—which is indeed three parts done, but
which I cannot complete until I have read the De Bello Civ.

I am exceeding glad that you will print it before reading it,
because, though parts have been rewritten thrice, the whole has
not been recopied, and the MS, though very good copy for
printers, is a little too much interlined for comfortable reading.

Yours always

Anthony Trollope

446. To John Blackwood. 29 March. *National Library
of Scotland.* Sadleir, *Commentary*, p. 300; *Parker*, p. 60.

(Waltham House,
Waltham Cross.)

March 29. 70

My dear Blackwood

I am very pleased that you are satisfied with my little endeavour. According to the way in which that which is printed
goes there will be about 150 pages of your printing when the
whole is done:—or something more, if anything be added to the
first part.

I will do as you suggest in adding a few short scraps of Caesar's
own words translated. As to battle peices I tried it & found that
any intelligible description of any one battle would be an
addition which the volume would hardly bear. You can hardly
guess how great was the necessity for condensation. A reader
never sees this. I am bound to give some analysis of the seven
books, and was driven to measure myself by lines at last;—to get
the thing said in the pages I had allowed myself.

As to that last book written by Hertius Pansa[1] I will own to

[1] Book VIII of the *Gallic Wars* is said to be by Aulus Hirtius. Hirtius
and Caius Vibius Pansa were consuls after Caesar's assassination. Trollope
apparently did not distinguish between the two.

you I have never read it. It never used to be printed with the
Commentaries when I was young: nor is it now in the edition
which I chiefly used. I will however, see what I can do to make
the finale of the first Commentary seem less bald.

Yours always
ANTHONY TROLLOPE

447. To W. LUCAS COLLINS. 6 April.
   National Library of Scotland. Sadleir, *Commentary,*
   p. 301; *Parker,* p. 60.[1]

(Waltham House,
Waltham Cross.)

My dear Sir.   April 6, 1870
   I am very glad that you like the Caesar.

Blackwood sent me but one copy of the printed sheets which I
returned with certain additions as asked by him,—so that I have
no copy by me. I have not even a manuscript. I did add certain
translations of small paragraphs which seemed to be telling,—
fearing however to add much as I find the difficulty to be chiefly
in reducing the matter on hand to a proper compas [*sic*].

The printers errors I corrected, i e those noted by you, such
[as] 'finer' to 'fewer,' 'suffeing' to 'suffering' and various others.
As to the phrases which strike you as too colloquial—'thick as
blackberries' &c, you will, I do not doubt, understand the spirit
in which they were used. The intention is to evoke that feeling
of lightness which is produced by the handling of serious matters
with light words, & which is almost needed in such a work. I
would not admit slang, but such phrases as may be held to be
admissible in ordinary easy conversation do not seem to me to be
objectionable. 'As fast [as] he could lay leg to ground' seems a
fair colloquial translation for 'quam magnis itineribus.' But let
the phrases go if they displease you.

Does Caesar use the word ligatos? I do not find it. I speak
of his anger against the Veneti in the second book. He calls the
officers whom P Crassus had sent 'legatos,'—and afterwards
speaks with horror of the breach of the 'ius legatorum'—and he
says that they were 'in vincula conjectos'—which answers the

---

[1] Short excerpts, only, in Sadleir and Parker.

purpose of your argument just as well. But to a modern reader the joke is on the assumption by Caesar that all critics, let them be ever so barbarous, must have understood the Roman feeling— and also in this, that when it served his purpose to imprison German ambassadors he did not scruple to do so. The passage you quote from Cicero might be supported by the words which Horace put into the mouth of Regulus. 'Qui lora restrictis lacertis sensit iners timuitque mortem.'[1]

I thought I had translated all the Latin phrases. It can easily be done.

I do not know Lewin's books. My books have been Long's Caesar, Merivale's Roman Empire, Napoleon & Plutarch. The less one allows oneself to be tempted into would-be learned disquisitions the better I think in such a work.

I quite agree with what you say as to criticism. I am keenly alive to the gratification and discomfort it may produce and acknowledge . . . .[2]

448. To JOHN BLACKWOOD. 7 April. Waltham Cross.
National Library of Scotland.

Trollope calls for 'a copy of the Caesar, as far as it is printed, either corrected or uncorrected, does not matter. I have no copy by me to work with.'

449. To KATE FIELD. 15 April.
Boston Public Library. Sadleir, *Commentary*, pp. 283–5.

(Garrick Club)
April 15, 1870

Dear Kate,

I am not a grumbler, and you are very—impertinent. All the same I am delighted to think that you should have made $8000 —and I congratulate you with all my heart. I am sure of this; that in whatever way you earn money, it will be both honest and honourable, that the money will represent hard work mental culture and much thought; and that as you have never been depressed by poverty, so will you never be puffed up by your wealth.

[1] See Horace, *Odes*, Book III, 5, ll. 35–6.
[2] The rest of the letter is missing.

You write as though I should find fault with your lecturing. I am not in the least disposed to do so. I think writing nicer for either man or woman;—but that perhaps comes from the fact that I am better paid for writing than for lecturing. I like your account of yourself,—with your handsome dress, looking as well as you can, and doing your work colloquially. I have no doubt you look very well. You could do that when you were not handsomely dressed;—and I should like to hear you lecture amazingly. Only I should want to go home to summer [? supper] with you afterwards & be allowed to express my opinion freely. But in truth I am not patient under lectures, and much prefer lecturing myself,—as I dare say you do also.

As for your lecturing here, I do not doubt you would have very large audiences;—but they do not pay well. £10 a lecture is about the mark if you can fill a large room—600 or 700— for our rooms are not so large as yours,—and our lectures are chiefly given to audiences who do not pay for tickets, but pay by the year. So that the managing committees cannot afford to pay much. I had a word to say the other day about fiction, and I lectured in four places, receiving £15 in two and £10 in two. All of which information may I hope be useful to you soon, as I should so greatly delight in having you here.

I don't in the least understand why you fly out against me as to matrimony,—or as to what I have said on that subject in regard to you. I have said and say again that I wish you would marry. But I have never advised you to marry a man for whom you did not care. You tell me I don't know you. I think I do— as to character and mind. As to the details of your life of course I do not.

You may at this moment be violently in love with some impossible hero, and I know nothing about it. What I have meant to say in the way of council [*sic*] is this;—that you should not so bind yourself to an idea of personal independence, as to allow that feeling to operate in your mind against the idea of marriage. I think that it does so, and has done so;—not that I have any notion of any individual sent about his business on those grounds, but that I think such to be the tendency of your mind. As I think that, at any rate in middle life, married people have a better time than old bachelors and spinsters, I do not like that tendency in you. Now I think that is all very straightforward and decorous, and I don't know why I am to be flown at.

I never said you were like W. Petrie.[1] I said that that young woman did not entertain a single opinion on public matters which you could repudiate,—and that she was only absurd in her mode of expressing them— However we'll drop W. P. now.

I have given up, or rather am now just giving up my magazine, and therefore have no longer any power in that line. But in truth I myself hate Fechter[2] as an actor, and I think the people here are sick of him. To me he was never a pleasant actor.

I would tell you all about the magazine but that I am at the end of my letter. Our chief news is that early next year we go out to Australia to see a son of ours who is settled there. I hope to induce my wife to return via San Francisco. With kindest love to your mother.

Very affectionately yours,
A. T.

450. To JOHN BLACKWOOD. 16 April. *National Library of Scotland.* Sadleir, *Commentary,* p. 301; *Parker,* p. 60.

(Waltham House,
Waltham Cross.)
16 April 1870

My dear Blackwood.

I think I can promise that the remainder of the MS shall be in your hands by May 1. I have done the two first books of the Civil War, and have nearly finished the introduction. It has been a tough bit of work; but I have enjoyed it amazingly, and am very much obliged to you for having suggested it. It has been a change to the spinning of novels, and has enabled me to surround myself for three months with books & almost to think myself a scholar.

I sent back the revise you sent me to Collins, with further corrections as suggested by him, and think that I incorporated

---

[1] Wallachia Petrie, the Republican Browning. Introduced in chap. lv of *He Knew He Was Right* (1869).

[2] Charles Albert Fechter (1824–79), a celebrated actor on both the French and the English stage. At the time of Trollope's letter he had just become manager of the Globe Theatre, New York.

nearly all (I may perhaps say all)—that was proposed either by you or him. He I presume will send those sheets on to you.

I find from Herodotus how very much depends on the touch of the man who does it. And the Herodotus is certainly not the equal of the Homer; though it no doubt leaves the conviction that the man who did it understands his author.[1]

Very faithfully yours

ANTHONY TROLLOPE

We have a blaze of summer here all at once!

451. TO LORD HOUGHTON. 22 April.
Not traced. Reid, ii. 224–5.

Waltham House,
Waltham Cross,
April 22nd, 1870.

My dear Lord Houghton,

I hardly gather from your letter whether you meant that an offer made in 1848 (if the fact of the offer be genuine, and the offer ever was) supplies an answer to the question that was in dispute between us. Were we not discussing an affair of the day? But I was clearly wrong in this, that I did not limit my assertion by any stipulation as to the solvency of the offerer. I might offer you half a million for Fryston,[2] and you would thereby be justified in saying that so much money had been offered for that property; but if you were thinking of selling Fryston, my offer would have no weight with you, because you would know that the half-million was not forthcoming. Twelve years ago—not to talk of twenty-two—novels were worth almost double what they are now; but I think that no novel has ever been sold for £10,000, and no novel would be worth it, except by Dickens, whose prices, by-the-bye, are much more moderate. However, if you think I have lost my bet, I will pay it with a happy heart. I hope you will dine with me on May 4th.[3]

Yours always,

ANTHONY TROLLOPE

[1] In the 'Ancient Classics' series the Herodotus was written by George C. Swayne, the Homer by W. Lucas Collins.
[2] Lord Houghton's country seat.
[3] For the sequel see letter No. 459, *infra.*

452. To EDMUND ROUTLEDGE. 22 April. *Not traced.*
F. A. Mumby, *The House of Routledge* 1834–1934
(London: George Routledge & Sons, 1934), pp.
112–13.

> (Waltham House,
> Waltham Cross.)
> April 22, 1870.

My dear Sir,

I would not undertake to make the story more than 20 of your pages. That was the length I mentioned when I had the pleasure of seeing you. I have never been willing to bind myself to any publisher not to do other work than what I may undertake to do for him. Indeed I have never done it and will not do so now. I do not think that there is any probability of my writing another Christmas story, but I should prefer to be free.[1] As I told you, the entire copyright would be yours. I would not specifically bind myself to a day for the delivery.

I am a punctual workman, and should be anxious to accommodate any publisher for whom I worked. I do not doubt the story would be ready by the time named. The day of payment would be indifferent.

As I have been obliged to decline so many of your stipulations, I shall suppose the matter is off until I hear again.

> Very faithfully yours,
> ANTHONY TROLLOPE

453. To EDMUND ROUTLEDGE. 23 April. *Not traced.*[2]

> (Waltham House,
> Waltham Cross.)
> April 23rd, 1870.

Dear Sir,

I enclose the agreement signed and suppose you will send me a duplicate. There is no probability that I shall write another

---

[1] The story was 'Christmas Day at Kirkby Cottage', published in *Routledge's Christmas Annual 1870*; reprinted in *A Cabinet of Gems*, ed. Bradford A. Booth (Berkeley: University of California Press, 1938), pp. 293–332.

[2] Published in Mumby, pp. 113–14, together with the memorandum of agreement for 'Christmas Day at Kirkby Cottage' (£100).

Christmas story, as I have very much work on hand,—and stories do not come as thick as blackberries. But I fear mine for you will not exceed the 20 pages, as your pages are so long; and I have always found that a short story does not require above 10 or 20 pages to tell itself. You shall however have full measure, and I will endeavour to give it to you by the first week in August.

Yours faithfully
ANTHONY TROLLOPE

454. To ALFRED AUSTIN. 2 May. *Parrish Collection.*

(Waltham House,
Waltham Cross.)

May 2—1870

My dear Austin,

I have read the satyre.[1] As to the spirit shewn in it, the authors capacity for versification,—and for poetry also as shewn in one or two pieces,—and all those points which depend on the use of language, there can I think be no doubt. The frequent alliteration offends me somewhat, but offends but slightly.

As to the stuff of the satyre, its truth or absence of truth,—or what we may better call its justification by the state of things or wanting such justification,—you and I differ so much about the condition of mankind generally, that we should hardly agree. Of satyre such as is yours,—unmixed satyre,—satyre written solely with the object of censuring faults in the world presumed by the satyrist to be so grievous as to oppress the virtues,—I doubt the use, and generally doubt the truth. The age of which you write I believe to have been better than preceeding [*sic*] ages, and the class of women which you represent to be bad, I believe to be good. There are exceptions; bad, heartless, worldly women,—& always have been. And of such the doings are more visible than are the doings of the gracious. But that, (which must always be the case,) hardly justifies general satyre. I have known very many men who have believed women of their own class to be bad and deserving of satyre;—but they have always excepted their own mothers, sisters, wives, and daughters.

You will say that this is a judgment against all satyre; and I think it is a judgement against all satyric writings written only

[1] The poem referred to is *The Season* (revised 1869).

as such. I do not believe that such writings have ever done good, or have left other impress than that of the cynic disposition, and power, of the writer. I doubt whether Juvenal ever aided at all in the suppression of vice;—but Horace, who was not a satyrist by profession, & who is playful and even good-natured in his very satyres, did probably teach men to be less absurd in their manner of writing, of speaking, and of eating than they would have been without him. Byron as a satirist was wholly powerless on vice, simply leaving the impression that he, a man gifted with strong powers of description, had to avenge himself upon a world that had injured him. And satyre runs ever into exaggeration, leaving the conviction that not justice but revenge, is desired. The exaggeration probably may come from no such feeling, but from the natural tendency of the writer to seek ever for strong and still stronger modes of expression; till at last all truth is lost in the charm of heaping epithet on epithet and figure on figure;—as the eater loses the flavour of his meat through the multiplied uses of sauces and pepper.

So much as to satyre in general. In judging you as a satyrist I feel myself called on to say that you are too prone to throw forward your own person;—and in this satyre you do so on what I regard as the weakest ground an author can take to stand upon;—namely your youth. Youth is an immense advantage because it has itself, and has maturity before it also. Maturity has nothing better to look at. But, for all work, maturity must be better than work [? youth]; and is so much better that it may be doubted whether youth is justified in making public its work by any other consideration than that of the doubt whether maturity may come. But youth, I think, should never claim special strength as its own. I altogether deny your implied assertion that youth should speak truth aloud, because age is prone to falsehood. As seen by my experience Age is truer than Youth, juster, clearer, more merciful, less selfish, and infinitely more capable of teaching the lessons which satyre is intended to convey. In common parlance, no doubt, we hear of the generosity of youth,—of its noble impulses, and the like. But I think we only hear of this because such qualities, when seen in the young, are more striking,—by reason of their comparative rarity—than when found in the old. And selfishness in the old is specially noticed—because it specially disgusts. We hardly expect the young to be other than selfish.

You will justify the repeated allusion to yourself, as a special person in your satyre, by the example of Horace. But in Horace's days literary men were so few in number that one who had made a name for himself was justified in the use of the 'I'—by the absurdity of ignoring it; as with us is a Prime Minister, or a chief Justice, or an Archbishop. And Horace was already Horace when he wrote his satyres. And, moreover, he was goodnatured, —almost I may say a trifler,—in his satyres; and the 'Videar nimis acer' is less ambitious than are you when you declare that 'To conflict called you abdicate your ease.'

There is my Sermo—and I hope you will not think that I have carried it beyond the bounds of friendship.

Yours always most sincerely
ANTHONY TROLLOPE

I may assert that I should not have written so to one of whose great intellectual capacity I was not convinced.

455. To JOHN BLACKWOOD. 7 May.
Not traced.[1] Sadleir, *Commentary*, pp. 301–2.

(Athenaeum Club)
[May 7, 1870]

*   *   *

I send down the whole work corrected, having, as I think, complied with every suggestion made by you or Collins. It is a dear little book to me and there is one other thing to be said about the little dear. I think the first of June is your birthday. At any rate we'll make it so for this year and you will accept *Caesar* for a little present.

*   *   *

456. To ? 11 May. London. *J. A. Waley Cohen.*

Trollope sends for correction to an unknown contributor the manuscript of 'It Ghelmez'. (For which see *Saint Pauls*, vi (June 1870), 304–12.)

[1] The original of this letter is not among the Blackwood papers in the National Library of Scotland, and I have not been able to trace it elsewhere.

457. To John Blackwood. 12 May.
National Library of Scotland.

(Waltham House,
Waltham Cross.)
May 12, 1870

My dear Blackwood

I send back the revise, as I hope for the last time. I have added to the note to page 158, and if I could see a proof of that I should like it.

Your printer has made two most unnecessary blunders. At pages 87—and 130 he has omitted two half pages, and has added pages numbered 87x—and 130x; but by doing so he has upset altogether the headings of the subsequent pages.

As regards the first I had proposed, as you will see, to have cut the story of Pulfius and Varenus, so as to bring in the half page;—either to do that or to add a line to the 12 preceeding [*sic*] pages. But in doing that I had not known that there would be a second error of the same kind.

As it is I must leave it to you to arrange.

Will you allow Langford to send me 25 copies for friends of my own.

Yours always most faithfully
Anthony Trollope

We shall be back in town at any rate by the end of May, i e 28th May. I write a line to your wife about poor Sunbeam.[1]

458. To Miss Chapman. 15 May. Waltham Cross.
Parrish Collection.

Trollope cannot accede to a request (i.e. accept a contribution) because he is giving up the editorship of *Saint Pauls*. Mary Frances Chapman (1838–84) was a novelist who published widely under the pseudonym of J. C. Ayrton.

[1] Mrs. Blackwood's favourite horse. See Mrs Margaret Oliphant, *The Annals of a Publishing House: William Blackwood and His Sons,* 4 vols. (Edinburgh, 1898), iv. 364.

459. To Lord Houghton. 19 May.
Not traced. Reid. ii. 225–6.

Waltham House,
Waltham Cross,
May 19th, 1870.

My dear Lord Houghton,

We will have no compromise; and as I do not in the least doubt the truth of every word you say, I enclose a cheque for £10. But my conviction is not in the least altered; and I look upon the offer—which, it seems, was made two years ago, not for 'Lothair,' but for some other novel not then known to be written—to be of the same worth as would be an offer from me to you of half a million for your property at Fryston. Whether you might wish to sell Fryston or not, you would discard the offer, coming from a man who clearly could not pay the sum offered. Two years ago Dallas was editing the paper called *Once a Week*; and, as it happened, I sold a novel through him to the proprietors of that paper, just at that time for publication in the paper. My price was not exorbitant—that is, it was exactly at the rate I was being paid for the article from other sources. I found that he was running amuck among novelists, offering to buy this and that—buying, indeed, this and that; and in the meanwhile the paper had to be disposed of as worthless. It was sold, I believe, for all but nothing. My bargain had been made *bona fide* with the proprietors, and my novel was written for them; but I was obliged to assent to another mode of publication, and to abate my price.[1] Therefore I regard an offer made by Dallas as no genuine offer, even though his offer were for 'Lothair;' and, again, I know fully well the value of these articles in the market, and I think that I know that no novel would be worth £10,000 to a publisher by any author: no house could afford to give such a sum. Dickens's last novel (which, I do not hesitate to say, is worth three times the value of 'Lothair' in a simple pecuniary view) has been sold for a considerably less sum—not indeed the entire copyright, but the immediate publication, and half-copyright afterwards. I have heard you quote as to other works sums reputed to be paid, but which were fabulous.

[1] Compare Sadleir's account of the publication of *The Vicar of Bullhampton* (*Commentary*, pp. 296–8).

For a novel published as 'Lothair' is published, and sure of a large circulation, a publisher could offer to give an author about 10s. a copy for all copies sold by him at the cost price, nominally 31s. 6d., for which he gets about 17s. 6d. The other 7s. 6d. would pay the cost, the advertising, and give the publisher a small profit. —— told me the other day that 6,000 copies had been sold—that would make £3,000 for the author; and the market has been so glutted with the work, that the publisher cannot hope to sell above another thousand. Where could he possibly recoup himself in an expenditure of £10,000?

I do, however, believe that Dallas made the offer two years since.[1]

Yours always,

ANTHONY TROLLOPE

460. To AUSTIN DOBSON. 21 May.

G. F. C. Dobson. Not seen.[2]

(Waltham House,
21 May 1870   Waltham Cross.)

My dear Mr Dobson,

I will do as you desire with your poem[3] which I have read with much pleasure. I cannot as yet miss [? dismiss] the old habit and would ask you whether 'overgrow' in the third line satisfies you in the sense in which you use it—you mean—overlay. Again 'look' in the first line on page 3 hardly pleases me;—or the phrase lower down of 'arousing the quiet.' We disturb the quiet and arouse the echo— To say that a hound's yell would not, as a term in venery, be accepted by hunting men, may be hypercritical. Pray excuse me, and if you will return the MS with or without alteration I will hand it over to Mr. Strahan with some very few others when in the course of next month I give up the seals.

And now I will descend from poetry to prose. In my endeavour to establish the Saint Pauls on what I considered to be a good literary footing, I insisted on myself naming the remuneration

[1] Reid says (p. 224) that the exact sum offered Disraeli was known to Houghton, 'a fact which did not prevent Mr. Trollope from insisting that it was impossible that any such sum could have been paid'.

[2] Excerpt published in Sadleir, *Commentary*, p. 289.

[3] See letter No. 462, *infra*.

to be paid. It has not been very great, but it has been fairly good. The object now is to make the magazine pay. What may be the result of that resolve to contributors in the way of remuneration will never be known to me after June. I fear it may not be altogether satisfactory.

I cannot refrain from saying how much gratification I have had during the last two years and a half in meeting with two or three contributors whom I have not known before,—(in your case have not even yet known in the flesh) and as to whom I have felt that they would grace our literature hereafter. But I must own to a corresponding vexation of spirit when I have found that literary work which I have known to be good, has not made that mark under my editorship, which I have known that it has deserved. As to your poems I have heard that praise from some few whose praise is really worth having,—from a man or two and also a woman or two, who in speaking of poetry speak of that which they understand; but I have been disappointed at finding as regards yourself and others, that good work has not been more widely recognized.

But it is perhaps well for literature that good work should not attain its recognition easily, and that perseverance at the back of it should be needed. I am sure that you will succeed if you persevere.

My Caesar will be a little thing,—but it has been a great delight to me to do it, as giving a break to the constant writing of prose fiction and taking me back to the books which I read when I was young.

Very faithfully yours
ANTHONY TROLLOPE

461. To ANNA C. STEELE. 25 May.
Mr. and Mrs. Maurice Fitzgerald.

Bolton Bridge
May 25—70

(Waltham House,
Waltham Cross.)

My dear Mrs Steele,

One word in answer to your nice note, though it be on a subject very difficult to speak of.[1]

[1] The subject is Carry Brattle, the 'castaway' of *The Vicar of Bullhampton*.

271

Of course one's sympathies are with the fathers and mothers & brothers,—and should be so; but not the less should one have mercy on the most terrible sufferers of this age;—on a class who suffer heavier punishment in proportion to their fault than any other, and who often have come to their ineffable misery almost without fault at all.

It would be quite against the grain with me to represent such a woman as interesting, charming, fit for diamonds, and a thing to be adored.

The whole Formosa business[1] was to my thinking detestably false. But a poor creature may fall,—as we call it—and yet be worth redeeming. Fathers & mothers will forgive anything in a son, debauchery, gambling, lying—even the worst dishonesty & fraud—but the 'fallen' daughter is too often regarded as an outcast for whom no hope can be entertained. Excuse all this enthusiasm, and believe me

Yours always
A. T.

This is the prettiest spot in England. We have been here ten days & go homewards tomorrow. I hope Lady Lennard[2] is not ill again by your hurry to go to Brighton.

462. To AUSTIN DOBSON. 29 May.
G. F. C. Dobson. Not seen.

29 May 70
(Waltham House,
Waltham Cross.)

My dear Mr. Dobson,

I have just read Leisure's epitaph[3] aloud to my wife and family —and we are charmed with it. It is very good indeed. Should Strahan, who may be is not given to the Muse, hesitate, shall I try it elsewhere?

Yours
A. T.

[1] The tempest over Boucicault's play. See 'Formosa', *Saint Pauls*, v (Oct. 1869), 75–80. This article is probably by Trollope.

[2] Emma Wood, Mrs. Steele's sister, married Sir Thomas Barrett Lennard.

[3] Probably a revision of the poem mentioned in letter No. 460, *supra*. It was published as 'A Gentleman of the Old School', *Saint Pauls*, vi (July 1870), 367–9. As a headnote it carries a motto from George Eliot: 'Leisure is gone . . . fine old Leisure.'

463. To JOHN BLACKWOOD. ? May. Waltham Cross.
National Library of Scotland.

As Trollope leaves for Yorkshire he forwards a number of textual emendations.

464. To ANNA C. STEELE. 6 June.
Mr. and Mrs. Maurice Fitzgerald.

(Waltham House,
Waltham Cross.)

June 6—1870

My dear Mrs Steele

Thanks for your kind letter. I have not seen the article in *The Times*,[1]—nor had I heard of it till I got your note— It was, I find, in the Supplement, which in this house usually gets thrust away, and so it escaped notice. I shall not care to search it up now.

Not that, as a rule, I am indifferent to criticism on my own work. I fancy that I am too anxious, like other authors, to see what others say about me. But now, as I know it to be hard, I will pass it by.

But I do profess so much in my own behalf;—that I never ask who has criticised me, and that I am above animosity against those who blame, as I am above gratitude to those who praise me. Whatever may be the motive of the critic, I presume that it has been that which alone can be honest—that namely of giving a just judgement. If it be so, the writer who gives it can deserve neither thanks or blame from me. I am sure the matter should be so regarded.

Do not, however, suppose that I profess myself to be indifferent. I know, as well as any man, or woman, the value of a favourable review in the Times.

Yours lovingly
A. T.

[1] A review of *The Vicar of Bullhampton* appeared in *The Times*, 3 June 1870, p. 4. The critic wrote, 'We do not think that either in construction or development this novel will add much to Mr. Anthony Trollope's reputation.'

465. To AUSTIN DOBSON. 15 June.
G. F. C. Dobson. Not seen.

(Garrick Club)
June 15. 1870

My dear Mr. Dobson,
 The last day of my rule over the magazine has been deferred for a month,—and I am inserting your poem, which is I think almost the best we have had. I am going out of town for a few days, but I hope to make your acquaintance when I return.

Yours always
AN TROLLOPE

466. To OCTAVIAN BLEWITT. 28 June. Waltham Cross.
Royal Literary Fund. Not seen.

Trollope, who has been applied to on behalf of Mrs. D., a widow, promises to attend the committee meeting to discuss her case.

467. To JOHN BLACKWOOD. 30 June.
National Library of Scotland. Parker, p. 60.

(Athenaeum Club)
June 30—1870

My dear Blackwood
 I yesterday met W. G. Clark,[1] and was speaking to him about the Ancient Classics. He is, I think, I may say, undoubtedly, the first Aristophanic scholar of the day, and is certainly of all men the one most connected at present with the name of Aristophanes. He is moreover in every respect well qualified to do what you want to have done with the Greek comedian. He was tutor at Trinity and public orator at Cambridge till he resigned those offices,—and is well known to all literary men.
 He said yesterday that he would much like to do the work.[2]

 [1] William George Clark (1821–78), public orator at Cambridge, 1857–70; joint editor of *The Cambridge Shakespeare*.
 [2] W. Lucas Collins, the editor of the series, prepared this volume himself (1872).

I had sent him the Caesar. If I would send you or Collins to apply to him you had better address him as W. G. Clark Esq

Trinity

Cambridge,

—for though he is in orders, he is struggling to get out of them.

Yours faithfully

ANTHONY TROLLOPE

468. TO JOHN BLACKWOOD. 8 September.
National Library of Scotland. Parker, p. 61.

Brougham Hall

Sept 8. 1870

My dear Blackwood

I have been here for the last three days reading the MS of the first Vol of Lord Brougham's Autobiography,[1]—having undertaken the task with the view of suggesting to the present Lord Brougham any steps that might be well taken towards preparing the work for publication; and I now write to you at his request as it appears that there is an intention that you shall publish the book.

It is intended that there should be three volumes. It may be a question whether it should not be compressed into two. I have only seen the first,—which it is intended to publish before the other two. That such a work will excite considerable interest there can be no doubt. In the first volume there is very much of interest;—especially in regard to the establishment of the Edinbro' Review, and Brougham's early correspondence with Lord Grey. But the whole matter, as it now exists, is unconnected, confused, very incomplete, and altogether unchronological. It is also full of errors, from ignorance on the part of copiers.

I have given it as my opinion to Lord Brougham that he must do one of two things;—he must either consent to put forth a bad book to the public, which will be confused and incomplete,—explaining in a short preface from himself that the somewhat

[1] Henry Peter Brougham, Baron Brougham and Vaux (1778–1868), was one of the founders of the *Edinburgh Review*, founder of London University, chancellor of the University of Edinburgh, and a writer and statesman. His autobiography was published as *The Life and Times of Lord Brougham*, 3 vols. (Edinburgh, 1871).

heterogeneous mass of matter is given to the public in that shape, because it was so left by Lord Brougham,—excusing, (without absólute acknowledgement of fault,) the shortcomings of the work by the fact that it was arranged when the author was past 80 years old;—or else he must put the whole of the MS into the hands of some competent Editor, with full editorial power, so that the errors may be corrected, and the confusion reduced from the present Chaos to fair literary order.[1] I have told him that if he intends to do this he must consult with his publisher as to such Editor, and that he cannot expect to procure such work without liberal payment. I am far from saying that he could certainly get such work even for liberal payment.

In regard to the MS which I have read I have advised the present Lord Brougham to omit a long journal of a tour in Sweden, which for various reasons I think ill adapted for such a work as is intended. If this be omitted I doubt whether the MS now apportioned for the 1st volume would suffice.[2]

The matter as handed to me was continuous. I have divided it into chapters, and have prepared headings for the chapters.[3] But I have done this rather as shewing what is needed, than as supplying the actual words which should be used for the headings. Even should it be thought well to publish the book without any Editor, (and Lord Broughams feeling rather lies in that direction,) there would be needed a not small amount of correction, as to which the care of an instructed person would be required. You will find that this is so, when you look yourself at the MS.

I myself think that for the reputation of the late Lord Brougham, for the comfort of the present owner of the MS., & for the sake of the public who will read the book, the whole work should be regularly edited.

I have told Lord Brougham that you would no doubt write to him after receiving the letter from me. He will then see you, taking the MS of the first vol to Edinburgh with him, if it shall appear by your letter to him that you wish to see it with the view of publishing it.

Most faithfully yours
ANTHONY TROLLOPE

[1] Apparently no further editorial assistance was sought.
[2] The journal of the Swedish tour was not omitted.
[3] Trollope's chapter headings were retained.

469. To GEORGE SMITH. 28 September.
Not traced. Sadleir's transcript.

Trollope insists that the title-page of *Brown, Jones and Robinson*, now
first being published in book form, shall carry the legend: 'Reprinted from
the Cornhill of 1862.' 'It must, of course, appear as a reprint.'

470. To ANNA C. STEELE. 7 October. Waltham Cross.
Mr. and Mrs. Maurice Fitzgerald.

Trollope thanks Mrs. Steele for some favour unnamed, mentions his four
hunters, and adds, 'I am so sick of the war! Are not you? And I hate the
French,—and ever did. But I wish now that they could be spared further
suffering.' He concludes with a postscript about *Sir Harry Hotspur*:
'Humblethwaite is too gloomy and wretched.'

471. To ALEXANDER MACMILLAN. 18 October.
Parrish Collection.

18. October 1870   (Waltham House,
                                     Waltham Cross.)

My dear Mr Macmillan,

I am sorry that any thing to do with my tale should be less
advantageous to you than you had expected. But the fact is that
as one pound of tea wont make two by any variance in packing the article—so neither will a one-volumed tale make two
volumes.[1] You will say that in one case the quantity is fixed,
and in the other not. But in regard to the latter article the quantity is too well and too nearly fixed to admit of such violent
stretching. The real pound may be, and often is, lessened by an
ounce in the packing;—but to make two pounds out of one is
more than can be done even in Marlbro Street. I am quite sure
that you agree with me.

You tell me that the trials of authors have their mitigations.
I have had none to complain of, but what have come from a dull
brain and relaxed application.[2]

                              Yours always faithfully
                                ANTHONY TROLLOPE

[1] The novel in question was *Sir Harry Hotspur of Humblethwaite*.
[2] There is a full discussion of this letter and the issues involved in Sadleir,
Bibliography, p. 119.

472. To CHARLES KENT. 22 December.
Parrish Collection.

December 22, 1870

(Garrick Club crest)

My dear Mr. Kent,

Many thanks for your kind letter,—which should have been answered sooner but that the copy of the paper which you sent me went astray and I had to procure it. Such praise as yours is always most pleasant to an author[1]—I only hope it may have been deserved. I am always most doubtful about my work;—and in some moods am altogether beyond doubt.

Most faithfully yours
ANTHONY TROLLOPE

1 8 7 1

473. To W. H. DUIGNAN.[2] 20 January.
Parrish Collection.

Stourbridge[3]   20 Jany 1871

(Waltham House,
Waltham Cross.)

My dear Sir,

I think I left my umbrella in your hall;—one with a large knob;—if so perhaps some one coming up to London would leave it for me either at the Atheneeum [*sic*] Club in Pall Mall, or at Chapman & Hall 193 Piccadilly. If not,—it will not matter.

But I have done a stupider thing than this. I have left (or lost)

[1] In the *Sun* Kent had said in a review of *Sir Harry Hotspur* (15 Dec. 1870, p. 2): 'It is not only a brilliant example of Anthony Trollope's powers as a novelist, but it is in a very striking manner a radiant specimen of English imaginative literature.'

[2] W. H. Duignan was the author of a pamphlet called 'Land Laws: a lecture given at Walsall, Jan., 1878'. He edited *The Charter of Wulfrûn*, 1888, and published three books on the place-names of Staffordshire, Warwickshire, and Worcestershire, 1902–12; also *The History of Rushall Hall*, 1924. He died in 1936. Walsall is a town eleven miles north-west of Birmingham. Trollope's account book shows that he lectured there on 19 Jan.

[3] Stourbridge: a manufacturing town just west of Birmingham, where according to his account book Trollope lectured on 20 Jan.

my purse somewhere. It may have been left in my bedroom at your house. I had no occasion for it to day, having silver in my pocket, and have only found my loss this moment. It was an old brown port-monnaie, and in it there was £25 in bank notes and some gold,—£6—or £7—but I do not know how much. I think there were cards in it with my name. I had it in the lecture room, because the notes were paid to me there by Mr Stephen, and I think I had it when I went to bed. If you hear of it perhaps it would not be too much to ask you to telegraph to me

> Garrick Club,
> Garrick Street
> Covent Garden, London.

—I beg to apologize very much for all the trouble I am giving you.[1]

> Very faithfully yours,
> ANTHONY TROLLOPE

474. TO MARY HOLMES. 20 January.
   Parrish Collection.

Stourbridge. 20 Jany 1871

> (Waltham House,
> Waltham Cross.)

My dear Miss Holmes,

Your letter has followed me into the country, where I have been for the last week, lecturing at one town and another.

Touching your novel,[2]—I can say many wise things to you, which have been said over and over again to beginners in their attempts to earn money by literature; but I doubt whether you will not know them all without my saying them; and I doubt also whether the saying of them, wise as they may be, ever does any good. Of all modes of making money literature is the most precarious. For one attempt that succeeds, hundreds fail. And of

---

[1] Maggs Catalogue 405 (Summer 1921) which lists this letter mentions a pencil note from Duignan which does not appear in the Parrish Collection. It reads: 'My dear Willie took the umbrella and the purse and contents to Mr. Trollope at Stourbridge and he gave him a sovereign for his trouble, which mightily pleased Willie.'

[2] The novel, as will be seen from letters that follow, was rejected by Chapman & Hall and seems never to have been published.

all failures it is the most agonizing, because the wound is to the amour propre. Knowing well how probable and how bitter the disappointment is, I always hear such statements as yours, from persons for whose welfare I am anxious, with something of sorrow. It is hard to say why one educated person should succeed with a novel, and another not; especially as some have succeeded at the first attempt. It may be, and I trust it will be, that you may do so;—but do not let your hopes run high. The novels which get money for their writers are but a small percentage of those printed;—and the novels printed but a very small percentage of those written with a view to publication.

If you will, (after all this sermonizing) send your MS when finished to Chapman & Hall of 193 Piccadilly,—the publishers,—I will endeavour to have it read for you and an answer given without delay.

Very faithfully yours
ANTHONY TROLLOPE

475. TO MARY HOLMES. 27 January.
Parrish Collection.

27 Jan 1871
(Waltham House,
Waltham Cross.)

My dear Miss Holmes,

You are altogether in error about the tendency of the firm of Chapman & Hall to positivist and socialist principles because they are the Editors of the Fortnightly Review. The two things have no connexion together. They publish very many novels, besides those in the Fortnightly Review. I should tell you that Chapman & Hall are in truth Chapman & Trollope, and that the Trollope is my son,—who, as it chances, is a very staunch Churchman

But I mention C & H not as offering any peculiar advantages, but because I thought I could [? have] your MS read for you there without delay. I shall be very happy to give you a letter of introduction either to Mr Strahan—or to Mr George Smith (Smith & Elder)—or to Mr Macmillan,—or to Mr. Blackwood, the proprietor of the magazine. They are all friends of mine.

I quite agree with you about Lothair.[1] To me it is the most snobbish book I ever read;—but I may assure you, (as far as the money is concerned) that when you have been Prime Minister, you will be able to get almost any price for a novel

Most faithfully yours

ANTHONY TROLLOPE

476. To CHARLES [? MARLLEN]. 30 January.
Parrish Collection.

30 Jany. 71   (Waltham House,
                                              Waltham Cross.)

Sir.

I was born in Keppel Street, London in 1815. I published three novels in 1846—1847—& 1848—but had no success. I published again in 1856 another novel, The Warden, which was the forerunner of those which have made my career,—such as it is.[2]

Yours faithfully

ANTHONY TROLLOPE

Mr Charles Marllen

477. To GEORGE SMITH. 10 February.
Parrish Collection.

                                    (Waltham House,
                                          Waltham Cross.)

10. Feb. 1871.

My dear Smith,

Thanks for the copy of the letter. I do not think that anything on that subject can be useful!!!

I do not know that there will be any need of looking through the reprint of the Claverings. Your reader will see that the old text is correctly repeated.

I had forgotten all about the conditional £200 in reference to

---

[1] See *Autobiography*, chap. xiii, pp. 216–17.
[2] Printed in *The Colophon*, New Graphic Series, Number Two, and reprinted in the *Princeton University Library Chronicle*, viii (Nov. 1946), 10. John Carter has pointed out (*loc. cit.*) that among all the dates given only the first is correct.

the Claverings, and therefore, am not, on my own account, disappointed by what you say.[1] But there is another half profit arrangement between us as to which I look for better results. The Last Chronicle of Barset is a joint property between us from the commencement of the cheaper edition. I presume that there will be something to divide. I forget when the edition was brought out, but perhaps you can let me know the amount before I start.[2]

Yours always faithfully
A N T H O N Y   T R O L L O P E

478. To JOHN BLACKWOOD. 20 February. *National Library of Scotland.* Sadleir, *Commentary*, pp. 263–4; *Parker*, p. 61.

(Waltham House,
Waltham Cross.)
20. Feb. 1871

My dear Blackwood.

Lord B.[3] wrote me word that I was to receive a volume of the autobiography a day or two since. I have not got it. Probably he was too quick in his anticipation as to its being ready.

Will you purchase of me for your magazine a third story after the manner of Linda Tressel and Nina to run through any eight numbers you please of 1872, and to be republished in 1872?[4] I shall have no other work published entire in that year. I would propose that it should come out with my name, and that you should then have my permission to publish my name with the other two, should it suit you to do so.

If such an arrangement would suit you, I would offer the novel at a price to you, or you should propose a price to me as you pleased.

[1] Trollope had been promised an additional £200 if Smith, Elder made £400 from the two-volume original edition in three years. See Sadleir, *Bibliography*, p. 287.
[2] Trollope sailed from Liverpool to visit his son Fred in Australia on 24 May.
[3] Lord Brougham.
[4] Blackwood rejected *The Golden Lion of Granpère*. It was subsequently serialized in *Good Words* (Jan.–Aug. 1872) and published by Tinsley.

It was matter to me of great regret that I did not see you when you were in London.

Give my kindest regards to your wife.

Yours always
ANTHONY TROLLOPE

The story in question does not end unhappily as do L.T. & N.B;[1]—but is otherwise of the same class.

479. To JOHN BLACKWOOD. 12 March.
National Library of Scotland.

(Waltham House,
Waltham Cross.)
March 12. 71

My dear Blackwood.

Thanks for your letter. I am afraid we cannot deal about the tale,—which I regret.

There was some misunderstanding about the old lords book, as to which I must write to him again today. I had supposed that it came at last from Edinburgh;—I wrote to tell him I had got it from you. However it will be all right now.

I am very sorry to hear that you have been so far from work as to have knocked off MSS. It must be hard with you when you do that. I have been trying to do what hunting I could with a half fear that I may never hunt any more. I may find myself old and worn out when I get back (if I do get back) from those distant diggings.

Give my kindest regards to your wife and accept them yourself. I hope at any rate that I may live to see you both again

Most sincerely yours
ANTHONY TROLLOPE

If you think of it, will you kindly send the other volumes of the Brougham, and the classics as they come out to Harry at 193 Piccadilly.[2]

---

[1] Trollope had forgotten his own story! *Nina Balatka* does *not* end unhappily—but it should have done so.
[2] The office of Chapman & Hall.

480. To FREDERIC CHAPMAN. 1 April.
Estate of Carroll A. Wilson.

(Waltham House,
Waltham Cross.)

1 April 1871

My dear Chapman,

I have received the enclosed letter from Morley to Harry, with extreme disgust. It seems to me that the redundancy of Fanny Trollope's work is entirely owing to his own carelessness in not having seen that a proper proportion was inserted in each number of the Review. I do not know how to ask her to leave out 100 pages, which would I imagine utterly destroy her narrative.[1]

As regards my own novel I have told him that I must insist on its being commenced on 1st July, and I look to you without any doubt to see that this is done.[2] Should it not be done my indignation would be very great. What does he mean by saying that two novels can not be published at the same time? Why should not this be done, for two months, if Fanny's novel cannot be completed in the appointed time? If necessary you could allow him an additional sheet.

At any rate the property is yours & not his; and I am sure you will not break an engagement with me, as to which I have made all other arrangements to agree. You must tell him that the novel must appear according to contract.

Most sincerely yours
ANTHONY TROLLOPE

481. To OCTAVIAN BLEWITT. 13 April. Waltham Cross.
Royal Literary Fund. Not seen.

Trollope forwards a letter of inquiry from an applicant for a grant.

[1] Frances Eleanor Trollope's novel *Anne Furness* was published in the *Fortnightly Review* from July 1870 to Aug. 1871.
[2] Trollope won his point. *The Eustace Diamonds* began in July 1871 and thus overlapped for two months with *Anne Furness.*

482. To JAMES T. FIELDS. 22 April.
  Berg Collection.

(Waltham House,
Waltham Cross.)

22 April 1871

My dear Fields

Your letter of the 4th has reached me in a moment of great bustle and perturbation. I and my wife start for Australia next week[1] to see our boy who is established there. Had I a short story ready written you should have it with a will;—but I have not. If I could send you one written on the voyage, I would write it on the voyage; but it could not possibly reach you in time. I have only about ten days before starting, and they are so completely pre-occupied with business and farewell visitings, that it would not be in my preserve to get it done in the time. I much regret this as I do not like to refuse a request of yours,—but, as you will acknowledge, I have no alternative.

We intend to return via San Francisco—and I hope that we may see you and your wife in the course of next year.

Very faithfully yours,
ANTHONY TROLLOPE

483. To C. GIBBON.[2] 5 May.
  Parrish Collection.

Trollope refers to Strahan & Co. a request to publish an extract from one of his novels in *Saint Pauls.*

484. To ALFRED AUSTIN. 5 May. *Not traced. Autobiography of Alfred Austin*, 2 vols. (London: Macmillan, 1911), ii. 19–20.

(Athenaeum Club)
May 5, 1871.

My dear Austin—

Very many thanks for your introduction and kind farewell letter. Alas for us, the wretched ambition which wrecked the

[1] The sailing was postponed eighteen days. See letter No. 484, *infra.*
[2] Charles Gibbon (1843–90), author of *Dangerous Connections* (1864) and some 30 other novels. The extract appeared in *The Casquet of Literature*, ed. Charles Gibbon and Mary Elizabeth Christie, 6 vols. (London, 1873–4). I have not been able to see this work, but through the kindness of Professor Florence Brinkley I learn that in another edition (1895–7) the extract is chap. xxx of *Barchester Towers.*

'Queen of the Thames' on its homeward journey has caused our vessel to be postponed eighteen days,[1] and we do not sail till the 24th—which is an incredible nuisance to us, busy as we homeless wanderers are. We are in all the misery of living about among friends and pot-houses, going through that very worst phase of life which consists in a continuous and ever-failing attempt to be jolly with nothing to do. I cannot believe the Old Testament because labour is spoken of as the *evil* consequence of the Fall of Man. My only doubt as to finding a heaven for myself at last arises from the fear that the disembodied and beatified spirits will not want novels. For your sake I will trust that there may be left enough of the prevailing spirit of our present nature to make satire still palatable.

A most faithful adieu to you and your dear wife! I hope you may go on and prosper, and earn all the success and renown which your honesty and intelligence deserve. I write to Tom today.

Yours most faithfully
ANTHONY TROLLOPE

485. To FREDERIC CHAPMAN. 25 September.
Pierpont Morgan Library.

(Waltham House,
Waltham Cross.)

Brisbane 25 Sept. 1871

My dear Chapman,

I was very glad to get your letter about the cheap Dickens,[2] and to have part 1. I like the paper and print and general look very much. I do not care so much about the woodcuts. You and Harry give different accounts as to the sale. You say the greater sale is of the numbers,—which I should prefer as being the more likely to last. Harry says the greater sale is of the parts. But, in

---

[1] *The Queen of the Thames* was wrecked near Cape Agulhas on the south coast of Africa on 18 Mar. But, according to a passenger's account in *The Times* (22 May 1871, p. 6), the disaster occurred not from a reckless desire to break a record (as Trollope apparently supposed) but from the captain's negligence in setting his course.

[2] The reference is to the new 'Household Edition' of Dickens. It could be purchased in monthly parts, penny numbers, or bound volumes.

either case, 200,000 will do very well indeed. I shall be very anxious to hear what is the highest number reached, and also whether it is maintained.

If J. Forster[1] and Ouvry[2] allow you £1875 for E Drood, I shall be very well contented. Mr Harding[3] expected more. I am delighted to hear so good an account of the business generally. I suppose that long before you get this you will have settled the Dickens account for the June half year.

My wife is with Fred in New South Wales, and I have been up here alone for six weeks, hammering away at the Colony.[4] On the whole I have enjoyed it very much. I think however very often of the next winters hunting which I am going to lose. You say nothing about the little horse. I hope that he is doing well with you, and that you intend to mate him. I have had some good kangaroo hunting; but it does not amount after all to very much.

One of the 'Australian'[5] people—Editor, manager, or owner,[6] told me that he had bought *from you* the right to republish my book about Australia. What is the meaning of this? I have never spoken a word of an Australian novel to any one.

Write again like a good fellow, and send me all the news about the business & other things. You can send your letter to John Tilley Esq GPO. Give my very kindest love and a kiss to your wife. You need not be jealous as I should give it myself if I were at home.

Yours always most faithfully
ANTHONY TROLLOPE

[1] John Forster (1812–76), Dickens's most intimate friend and biographer.
[2] Frederic Ouvry (1814–81), Dickens's lawyer; president of the Society of Antiquaries.
[3] Robert Palmer Harding, later Sir Robert (1821–90), accountant, head of Harding, Whinney & Co. He specialized in bankruptcy cases and founded the Imperial British East Africa Co.
[4] That is, gathering information for his book on Australia and writing a series of travel letters for the *Daily Telegraph*. See Bradford A. Booth, 'Trollope in California', the *Huntington Library Quarterly*, iii (Oct. 1939), 118.
[5] *The Australian Magazine*.
[6] Probably Marcus Clarke. See letter No. 530, *infra*.

486. To GEORGE WILLIAM RUSDEN.[1] 27 September.
Trinity College Library, University of Melbourne. Not
seen.

Brisbane 27 Sept. 1871

My dear Mr. Rusden,

Many thanks for the compliment of the dedication.[2] Shall I
see the pamphlet before I get down to Melbourne. My address
will now be Post Office Sydney. I think I shall be back in
Melbourne about the end of November.

Very faithfully yours
ANTHONY TROLLOPE

487. To GEORGE WILLIAM RUSDEN. 29 October.
Trinity College Library, University of Melbourne. Not
seen.

Mortray Station
29 Oct. 1871

My dear Mr. Rusden,

Your letter of the 9th. followed me here. No copy of your
pamphlet has reached *me*, but I found here a copy which you had
kindly sent to my son. This he has allowed me to read; but as
I cannot take it away, you will have to give me another copy. I
agree with you in much but not in all that you say. When you
go to history you are unassailable,—but in your opinions you
seem to me to fall into the fault, general throughout the Colonies,
of thinking that England is indifferent, and weak in her present
policy—Laudator temporis acti;[3] you seem to believe that she
is no longer great and fostering. Speaking as a colonist you seem
to think, as sons so often think of their fathers, that enough has
not been done because the father wishes the son to thrive by
dint of his own mettle. I know you will forgive this from me,
and will be prepared for an argument in which I shall delight,—
and shall listen.

We purpose going hence to Sydney on 9th November, and

[1] George William Rusden (1819–1903) was clerk of parliaments in Australia for twenty-five years. He subsequently wrote three-volume histories of
Australia and New Zealand.
[2] Rusden dedicated to Trollope his *The Discovery, Survey and Settlement
of Port Phillip.* See Trollope's *Australia and New Zealand* (London, 1875),
i. 5. [3] Horace, *Ars Poetica*, l. 173.

making our way to Melbourne about the 7th December. Then we purpose taking an expedition up into the mountains some time towards the end of that month. Can your goodness secure me right of enjoyment of the Club on the date I have mentioned? Mr. Forster[1] I have not seen, but will see. Martin[2] I saw, but not the Chief Justice who was absent on the Assizes. Mr. Knox[3] I met more than once. I thought the Victorian resolution worded harshly towards Lord Kimberley,[4] whom I like and respect.

The wool news is good, very. I am sure you will be glad to hear that I find my son all that I could wish—steady, hard-working, skilful and determined.

Yours ever faithfully
ANTHONY TROLLOPE

488. To GEORGE WILLIAM RUSDEN.   6   December. Sydney.

Trinity College Library, University of Melbourne. Not seen.

Trollope writes to verify Saturday the eighteenth as the date for a dinner, apparently in his honour, at the Yorick Club in Melbourne.

1872

489. To CAPT. EASTWICK.[5] 15 January.
Parrish Collection.

Hobarttown Tasmania.   15 January, 1872.

My dear Captain Eastwick

I dare say you forget having written to me on 13 May last a letter respecting your niece Mrs Arland Anderson and her family.

---

[1] William Forster (1818–82) was for twenty years a prominent figure in parliament, where he held at one time or another virtually all the important offices. See the *Australian Encyclopedia*, i. 485.

[2] Sir James Martin (1820–86) was premier and attorney general, 1870–2. See ibid., ii. 44–5.

[3] Edward Knox, later Sir Edward (1819–1901), was chairman of the directors of the Colonial Sugar Refining Co. and of the Commercial Bank. See ibid., i. 703–4.

[4] John Wodehouse, first Earl of Kimberley (1826–1902), a prominent statesman, was Colonial Secretary, 1870–4.

[5] There were two brothers Eastwick, Edward B. and William J., both

As I and my wife spent a week with them at Fairlie House before we came over here, I now answer your letter to tell you how very kind they have been to us, and how much we enjoyed our sojourn with them.

They have two boys and two girls, the girls the eldest,—all very nice children; though I doubt whether I should so speak of Mary Anderson who is as tall as her mother. They have two houses on a large peice of ground about 2 miles from Melbourne, and live, as you say, after a clannish fashion. The modern house is very large, & there live the two Colonels, father & son, & Mrs Arland's mother. In the old house there is always one or two families,—the sisters of your neice's husband. Their husbands are squatters in different parts of Victoria. Colonel Anderson is Commander in Chief of the Victorian Army; and it may come to pass, if their Prime Minister do not become more civil than he has been, that Anderson will have to take the field against the forces of Great Britain and the other Colonies combined.

We have just heard very bad news of the health of the Prince of Wales;—but it has reached us via California; and it is the rule here to discredit anything that reaches us by that route. My experience hitherto tells me that the rule is right.

With many thanks for a most agreeable introduction I am
very faithfully yours
ANTHONY TROLLOPE

490. To GEORGE ELIOT and GEORGE HENRY LEWES. 27 February. *Mrs. E. S. Ouvry.*

Melbourne. 27. Feb. 1872.

Dear Friends,

I was so glad to get a letter from Priory! I ought to have written sooner myself;—but I am hurried from place to place, and have no rest for my foot, and do not do the things I ought to do. I am beginning to find myself too old to be 18 months away from home. Not that I am fatigued bodily;—but mentally

captains. *Kelly's London Post Office Directory 1872* lists William J. as the occupant of 12 Leinster Terrace, the address on the envelope containing this letter.

I cannot be at ease with all the new people and new things. And I find myself asking myself that terrible question of cui bono every morning. I am struggling to make a good book, but I feel that it will not be good. It will be desultory and inaccurate;— perhaps dull, & where shall I be then?

Forsters first volume is distasteful to me,—as I was sure it would be. Dickens was no hero; he was a powerful, clever, humorous, and, in many respects, wise man;—very ignorant, and thick-skinned, who had taught himself to be his own God, and to believe himself to be a sufficient God for all who came near him;—not a hero at all. Forster tells of him things which should disgrace him,—as the picture he drew of his own father, & the hard words he intended to have published of his own mother; but Forster himself is too coarse-grained, (though also a very powerful man) to know what is and what is not disgraceful; what is or is not heroic.

Cigars! Yes, indeed, you in your comfort smoke cigars I dont doubt, and drink coffee, and look on the pleasant faces of books, and write with good ink at a comfortable table,—and are civilized. I am reduced to the vilest tobacco out of the vilest pipe, and drink the vilest brandy and water,—very often in very vile company. But perhaps I shall live to get home whcn,—not the noctes cenae [que] Deum[1]—but the pleasant morning table may be spread for me again with just that sufficiency of the divine aura which rescues an hour of sensual enjoyment from any touch of reproach.

My best & kindest love to both—

Yours always
A. T.

491. To George William Rusden. 1 May. Adelaide.

Trinity College Library, University of Melbourne. Not seen.

Trollope and his wife will arrive on the fifteenth or the sixteenth at Colac, where they will be 'refreshed' by Mr. Robertson. John Robertson, later Sir John (1816–91), was for thirty years one of Australia's most prominent political figures, serving as premier several times. He long opposed Henry Parkes. See letter No. 498, *infra*.

[1] Horace, *Satires*, ii. 6. 1. 65.

492. To GEORGE WILLIAM RUSDEN. 7 May. Adelaide.
Trinity College Library, University of Melbourne. Not seen.

Trollope writes at some length, describing his itinerary and urging Rusden to meet him at Colac.

493. To GEORGE WILLIAM RUSDEN. 16 May. Colac.
Trinity College Library, University of Melbourne. Not seen.

Trollope has just arrived. He plans to go to Melbourne in a few days and asks for privileges at Rusden's club.

494. To GEORGE SMITH. 20 May.
Parrish Collection.

Melbourne, Victoria—20 May 1872

My dear Smith.

The enclosed will in part explain itself. Charles Reade has written to me saying that he has concocted a play out of one of my novels, Ralph the Heir,—and that he intends to have it acted.[1] He then makes a great merit of his purpose of putting my name on the play bill as the author,—I presume in conjunction with his own. To all this I have given no consent whatever; nor has there ever been between me and him a single word suggestive of such a proceeding!!

For myself I cannot understand how any author can act in such a way. It is monstrous that I should be made to appear as a writer of plays without my own permission,—or that I should be coerced into a literary partnership with any man. If the play has appeared with my name to it, or if it be advertised to appear with my name, will you kindly insert the enclosed in the Pall Mall

[1] The play was *Shilly-Shally*. Out of its production arose a furious, and somewhat comical, misunderstanding between Trollope and Reade. The troubled history of this play has been described at length in Bradford A. Booth, 'Trollope, Reade, and *Shilly-Shally*', *The Trollopian: A Journal of Victorian Fiction*, i (Mar. 1947), 45–54; ii (June 1947), 43–51.

G.[1]— I have sent a copy of the letter to C. Reade,—who is by way of being an intimate friend of mine. I think you will do as much as this for me, and excuse the trouble.

I have been journeying about from Colony to Colony till I am heartily homesick. I seem to regret greatly last years hunting,— feeling that there can be but few more years of hunting left to me & that I should lose none of it. I have interested myself with these colonial people,—as to habits, wages, ways of life & the like; but in regard to social delights I cannot cotton to them thoroughly.

If you will write me a line in answer send it to Harry— 193 Piccadilly,—and I shall get it either in New Zealand or in California on my return. I hope to be back about the first week in December.

Remember me most kindly to your wife,—and to Dolly[2] if she will condescend to remember me. I suppose Dolly is a young woman now. It seems to be so immensely long a time since we were dining with you up in the rooms in Waterloo Place.

Always yours sincerely
ANTHONY TROLLOPE

495. To GEORGE WILLIAM RUSDEN. [May] Menzies. *Trinity College Library, University of Melbourne.* Not seen.

Trollope arranges to meet Rusden at Ballarat. He suggests that they drop formal modes of address.

496. To GEORGE WILLIAM RUSDEN. 4 June. Melbourne. *Trinity College Library, University of Melbourne.* Not seen.

(Melbourne Club)

June 4. 72.

My dear Rusden. Of course I admit your theory of government upon which all our parliamentary practice is founded,—but in this as in many other matters our Constitution is worked by usage in direct opposition to the theory. The Crown by its

---

[1] Published 16 July 1872, p. 5.
[2] Elizabeth Smith, later Mrs. Yates Thompson.

prerogative is the controlling power of the Army, but the Army is controlled by Parliament—and it is because these apparent contradictions are admitted, so that a gradual development of the power of the people is enabled to go on without abrupt changes in our traditional theories, that we have no revolutions and remain loyal and contented.

Sir Rt. Peel in the words you quote states that he 'offered' his advice to the Crown. I believe it to be notorious that he was asked for advice and gave it. In his subsequent words he is desirous, as Conservative Ministers have ever been, to maintain his devotion to the theme [? throne], but when uttering them he knew that the Queen must delegate the authority of choosing a Ministry to some one, as she can not be responsible herself for any act of government.

But the progress of men's minds on this subject has been great even since 1846. The loyalty which thinking men at home are able to feel for and to show to the Crown, rests on the knowledge that the sovereign can do no act of government. Were it not so, the loyalty would be impossible, because we are all agreed not to entrust the power of governing us to any one person. Could the Queen act on her own responsibility, ten [*sic*] of thousands of us who pride ourselves on our loyalty would be rebels to-morrow. But, in regard to this great act of choosing a responsible minister, we know that the sovereign asks advice and acts upon it. No one dreams that were Gladstone to resign tomorrow the Queen would do other than ask his advice as to what she should do upon his resignation.

I do not maintain that the system is yet equally near perfection in the colonies. The Governor has responsibility and is bound to obey instructions from Sectry. of State at home. In regard to the present question I only say that were our system of government fully carried out in the Colony, then Mr. Duffy's[1] advice should be taken. I do not say that in the present condition of things the Governor ought to take it.

Yours ever,
A. T.

[1] Charles Gavan Duffy, later Sir Charles (1816–1903), was an Irish nationalist who became a colonial politician. He was Prime Minister of Australia, 1871–2.

497. To GEORGE WILLIAM RUSDEN. 17 June. *Trinity College Library, University of Melbourne*. Not seen.

Mortray. June 17   72

My dear Rusden. As to the law for payment of Victorian Members of Parlt.

Is it not the fact that the arrangement commenced with this Parliament, at the beginning of the last session, and that, unless renewed, it will expire with this Parliament at the end of next Session?

If renewed—as I presume is probable—will it be renewed in this Parliament—and if not can it be renewed by the next Parliament which would thus vote itself its own payment?

Let me have a line to answer these questions, addressed to Petty's Hotel, Sydney.

We hope to have A. Dickens[1] here this evening.

> Yours always
> ANTHONY TROLLOPE

498. To HENRY PARKES.[2] 2 July. Melbourne. *Mitchell Library, Sydney*.

> (Australian Club)
> 2 July 1872.

My dear Sir,

My friend Mr Macintosh[3] has told me that he has spoken to you as to putting my son on the roll of land magistrates in the Forbes district—He has become a zealous hard-working squatter, and I shall be much obliged to you if you assist him in this way to enter the position which I should be glad to see him occupy. I feel sure that he will not disgrace the bench.[4]

> Very faithfully yours
> ANTHONY TROLLOPE

---

[1] Alfred Tennyson d'Orsay Dickens was sent out to Australia by his father in 1865.

[2] Henry Parkes, later Sir Henry (1815–96), a distinguished Australian statesman, was Prime Minister of New South Wales, 1872–5.

[3] I have not been able to identify Mr. Macintosh. He is not listed in the new *Dictionary of Australian Biography*.

[4] He apparently did not get the appointment.

499. To GEORGE WILLIAM RUSDEN. 3 August. Melbourne. *Trinity College Library, University of Melbourne.* Not seen.

Off the Bluff   3 August 1872

My dear Rusden,

I have been using my time on board writing 2 short preparatory chapters respecting your colony, in which I have often used your name and your work. I would send them to you were not the work of copying so terrible. I contest with you the point as to the 'shabbiness' of any ministers 'frittering away' the colonies —thinking the idea that such shabbiness exists to be a mistaken idea. Your facts I take implicitly in rebus Flinders, Henry, Batman and Fawkner—and put forward, under your name, your advocacy of H. Hume.[1]

Now answer me these questions.

Is not Henty, (or if not Henty ipse, Henty in his immediate descendants,) still flourishing in the neighbourhood of Portland. He was in truth the first and I should be glad to say so, if such be the fact.

Can you say when and by whom the name of Melbourne was given?

When and by whom the name of Victoria was given? When was the railroad opened out of Geelong to Ballarat [*Pencilled in* Ap. 1862]

When out of Geelong to Melbourne?

Was the population of Geelong ever greater than that of Melbourne?

Who founded Geelong?

Was not Geelong once regarded as the coming capital of Port Phillip?

If you can answer this in time for the last mail of this month to New Zealand, address to Wellington, N.Z. if not address to 193 Piccadilly, London.

One word to say how much unaffected pleasure I have had in making your friendship.

                                        Yours always
                                        ANT TROLLOPE

[1] See *Australia and New Zealand*, ii. 1–28.

500. To A. LOCKER. 27 August.
Wellington, New Zealand. *Not traced.*[1]

In reply to a publisher's invitation Trollope offers the manuscript of *Phineas Redux*. Arthur Locker (1828–93), novelist and journalist, editor of the *Graphic*, 1870–91. *Phineas Redux* ran in the *Graphic* from 19 July 1873 to 10 January 1874. The contract is described in Sadleir, *Bibliography*, p. 302.

501. To THE EDITOR of *The New York Herald*. 26 November. *Not traced. New York Herald*, 25 November 1872, p. 3.

Brevoort House,
New York, Nov. 26, 1872.

To the Editor of The Herald:—

Sir— On my arrival here yesterday morning I was surprised to see in your paper a statement[2] that I had compromised my lawsuit with Baron Tauchnitz, the Leipsic publisher.[3] I have never had any lawsuit or any difference whatsoever with Baron Tauchnitz. Perhaps you will do me the kindness of inserting this letter.

I am, sir, your very obedient servant,
ANTHONY TROLLOPE

502. To BARON TAUCHNITZ. 26 November. *Not traced. Fünfzig Jahre der Verlagshandlung Bernhard Tauchnitz, 1837 bis 1887* (Leipzig, 1887), p. 150.

Brevent [Brevoort] House
New York
Novbr. 26, 1872.

My dear Baron Tauchnitz,

On arriving here yesterday I found by the *New York Morning Herald* that I had *compromised my long law-suit with you* by accepting from you an enormous sum of money which made my mouth

[1] This letter exists only in Trollope's copy (Bodleian).
[2] The *Herald* had said: 'Anthony Trollope has compromised his long law-suit with Mr. Tauchnitz, the Leipsic publisher, by accepting from him the sum of £3,000 sterling. On his subsequent writings he is to receive from Mr. Tauchnitz a copyright of three percent.'
[3] Christian Bernhard von Tauchnitz (1816–95) began in 1841 his famous series of inexpensive reprints of popular English books. He followed with a series of English translations of German books.

water. . . . Of course, I have written to the paper to say that I never had a lawsuit or any difference whatsoever with you. . . . It is odd that they should now for a second time pick me out as the object of your litigation or you of mine,—as I never had any contention with any publisher though, either on my own account or that of others, I have perhaps had more dealings with publishers than any man living. I am with the most sincere esteem

Yours faithfully
ANTHONY TROLLOPE

503. To BARON TAUCHNITZ. 17 December.
Not traced. Tauchnitz, p. 150.

3, Holles Street
Cavendish Square
London
Decbr. 17, 1872.

*   *   *

Latterly in order that I might avoid the trouble of many bargainings I have sold my novels with all the rights of copyright to the English purchaser—and have, therefore, given over to him the power of doing what he pleases as to foreign editions. . . . As to the future I will arrange that the German republication shall be with you. I am so fond of your series that I regret to have a work of mine omitted from it.[1]

*   *   *

504. To AUSTIN DOBSON. 17 December.
Alban Dobson. Not seen.

(Garrick Club)
17 Dec. 72

My dear Dobson

As to my name you were quite justified,[2]—or at any rate may hereby be put at ease on that matter. I don't see what good the name has done you,—but that is your affair.

---

[1] The reference is to *The Eustace Diamonds*. See Sadleir, *Bibliography*, pp. 133–4.

[2] In his pamphlet *The Drama of the Doctor's Window*. See letter No. 424, *supra*.

As to the claim against you I see it all, & have suffered the same thing—a young lady once told all her friends that she had written a novel of mine, and stuck to it till her father absolutely took her into the publisher's shop and asked for a price for his daughter's work—! The father believed his daughter absolutely. So probably did Mr W believe his claimant.

Yours very sincerely
ANTHONY TROLLOPE

A man when he has been led into such an error by a loved one, has a hard card to play. The father of my young lady was brought to great sorrow.

505. To CHARLES PAGE WOOD. 24 December.
Mr. and Mrs. Maurice Fitzgerald.

3, Holles Street
24 Dec. 1872.

My dear Wood,

Many thanks for your care about the horses. Will you let me know what I owe you. I fancy you have bought a lot of things for me, though I hardly know what I owe you. However, I have a desire to get out of debt before all my money is gone in this sinful metropolis.

We had 2h. 45 min. after the same fox on Saturday, the biggest bellyful of hunting I ever had in my life, almost without a cheque [*sic*]; first 30 minutes very fast and a kill. I never had such a day before. Buff carried me through it all as well as ever. But was *very tired*. He and a second horse I had out were both too tired to be got home.

You will be sorry to hear that Banker and another of my small lot are laid up with coughs. I have four in all.

Where is your sister, Mrs. Steele? Tell her I am back and ask her when she will be in town. My kindest regards to your mother.

Yours gratefully,
ANTHONY TROLLOPE

1873

506. TO MARY HOLMES. 3 January.
Parrish Collection.

3, Holles Street
Cavendish Square   3 Jany 1873

My dear Miss Holmes,

It is true that we have got home again after wandering around the world for twenty months,[1]—and now I am in the agony of endeavouring to get my book about Australia out before the end of the month,—which however I shall not do, such wretches are the printers.[2]

I was very glad to see your handwriting and to hear that you are fairly well,—as I gather from your letter that though you have been ill, you are so no longer.

I like your enthusiasm about the fiddle,—for in spite of all that you say I will keep to the old word which is much older than the french violin—Fidibus[3] was the term in the time of Augustus. I do not agree with you in your depreciation of the every-day piano,—not from any love which I bear it myself, or from liking to hear the ordinary playing of ordinary ladies, but from the conviction that they as regards themselves and their own minds and souls, are better with it than they would be without it. It is said that a little learning is a dangerous thing. I entirely differ from the intended meaning of the proverb. A little learning is very much more dangerous than extended learning, but infinitely less so than utter ignorance. I think the same of music. Any awakening is better than lifeless somnolence.

I have always felt that the fiddle in some of its forms was the finest instrument yet known. I remember well, when I was quite

---

[1] Actually, slightly under nineteen months. Trollope left England 24 May 1871 and returned 20 Dec. 1872.

[2] The exact date of publication is not known, but *Australia and New Zealand* was advertised in *The Times* on 4 Feb. 1873 and may have appeared a few days earlier.

[3] The term in the time of Augustus was *fides*. But Trollope may have been led to use a dative plural form by his memory of Horace ('Aeoliae fidibus puellae').

a young man, being moved to weeping by hearing a solo on the violinchello by Lindley.[1]

I have been for 18 months in Australia and New Zealand and have seen quite a new life,—and, as I think, a very much better life than we have here. There a man who will work has enough of all that he wants— The horror of this country is that let men work as they will there is not and cannot be enough for them all. A man who is not properly fed cannot be a man fit either for God's work or for man's work. But this is a subject infinitely too big for a letter.

Very faithfully yours
ANTHONY TROLLOPE

507. To LADY RUTHVEN.[2] 6 January.
Parrish Collection.

Lady Ruthven had written asking Trollope to locate for her the scene in which Lady Dumbello artfully regains her husband's affections and discourages the advances of Plantagenet Palliser. Trollope replies in a formal third-person note, identifying the scene as from *The Small House at Allington*, ii, chap. xxv. 'Mr. Trollope feels much flattered by the enquiry.'

508. To AUSTIN DOBSON. 18 January. Garrick Club.
G. F. C. Dobson. Not seen.

Trollope thanks Dobson for dedicating to him *Vignettes in Rhyme*, his first collected volume. 'Of course I cannot but accept so flattering a compliment.'

509. To FREDERIC CHAPMAN. 1 February.[3]
Pierpont Morgan Library.

Trollope asks for 'a bill at 30 days for £1250 on account of Eustace Diamonds' to pay the premium on the house at 39 Montagu Square which he had just purchased. 'I want this quite at once. Let me have it on Monday like a good fellow.'[4]

[1] Robert Lindley (1776–1855) was the greatest violoncellist of his time, principal violoncello at the opera, 1794–1851, and professor at the Royal Academy of Music. It will be remembered that the violoncello was Septimus Harding's favourite instrument.

[2] Caroline, Lady Ruthven, wife of Walter James Hore-Ruthven, 7th Baron Ruthven.

[3] Trollope dates the letter 1875, but his business accounts and the known date of his moving to Montagu Square make it certain that 1875 is a slip of the pen for 1873.

[4] Trollope was asking for only a 30-day advance, the sum being due to him from Chapman & Hall on 1 Mar.

510. To ANNA C. STEELE. 1 February.
Mr. and Mrs. Maurice Fitzgerald.

3. Hollis Street
My dear dear friend,   1 Feb. 1873.

I have been such a brute to you! When I got your letter I had intended to fix a day when I could propose to come to Rivenhall; but one thing and another has come up and has gone by, and I have never done so. I am trying to hunt down at Leighton, but now there is this infernal frost. I have had two very good days with the Baron,[1] and two very bad with Selby Lowndes.[2] I hope things will mend.

And I have been looking for a house and have [? found one at] last,—at least I think I have got it,—in Montagu Square,—not a gorgeous neighbourhood, but one which will suit my declining years and modest resources.

And I have been bringing out a book on Australia of which I corrected the last sheet of the index yesterday. I dont [? know] whether in literature you have ever as yet been brought to the making out of an index— It is of all efforts in letters the meanest, the most enervating, and at the same time the most difficult.

Give my kindest love to your mother. I hope I shall see you all before long. You are coming to town often. Let me know some day that I may meet you. I can manage to give you a lunch in Piccadilly if you can go up two pair of stairs.

Affectionately yours
ANTHONY TROLLOPE

511. To GEORGE WILLIAM RUSDEN. 3 February.
Trinity College Library, University of Melbourne. Not seen.

3 Holles Street,
Cavendish Square,
London
My dear Rusden,   Feb 3, 1873

By the same mail with this, or I should perhaps say by the

---

[1] Baron Meyer is mentioned in the *Autobiography* (p. 291) as a master of the hounds in Essex.

[2] William Selby Lowndes (1807–86), master of the Whaddon Chase hounds. See *Autobiography*, p. 291.

same boat—will go out to you my book. I care more for your criticism on it than for that of any other colonist. You will see that I fight you staunchly respecting separation; but that I do not differ from you—I think—very widely on other points; except it be in regard to the extent of ministerial responsibility. I know that in many matters I must be inaccurate. The necessities of the work,—which had to appear not as a history or a grave treatise to which unlimited time could be given, but as the rapid work of a traveller,—demanded that it should be written quickly. I can not accuse myself of having spared myself labour in writing it; but I found myself driven to attempt details which should have received more work in verifying them, than the time allowed me to give them. I send also a copy to Sir James Martin. I believe that the book will come out here tomorrow.

My eldest boy has gone out on a visit to his brother. He will have travelled direct to Sydney, and I did not therefore give him a line to you. You have been down at the Garrick for the last six months and will come up as I fancy some time this spring.

We have had terrible weather here,—unremitting rain for months, and now intermitting snow, frost and thaw, which is abominable. The hunting is cut up terribly.

We are taking,—I hope have taken, a house in London, and are going to enter into the ruinous pleasures and necessary agonies of furnishing it. I remember I used to hear that a modest man might supply himself with beds, tables and a chair to sit on for £200. Now I am told that £1500 for the rough big things is absolutely indispensable, and that prettinesses may be supplied afterwards for a further £500.

I hope you have got into the collar with your opus magnum. There is nothing like an opus magnum for thorough enjoyment of life, and in this case the work is really required. There is much to be told of which even well-informed men are absolutely ignorant. *Macte* nova virtuti, puer[1]—and I trust you may *get to stars*.

But you never will, unless you feel that that concluding line in the Sapphic stanza can not begin with x.[2] I fear the last pipes ordered were never sent. I cannot, however, be certain, as Harry

---

[1] See *Aeneid*, ix. 641.
[2] See Horace, *Odes*, i. 2, 19–20.

went before I got your letter and I had not thought of asking
him. You shall have it when you come,—which coming may not
I trust be postponed for any Greek kalends.

Yours always *most sincerely*

ANTHONY TROLLOPE

512. To WILLIAM FREDERICK POLLOCK.
18 February. *Parrish Collection*.

Trollope refuses an invitation, having just returned to London from a
trip to Lincolnshire.

513. To GEORGE WILLIAM RUSDEN. 18 February.
Trinity College Library, University of Melbourne. Not seen.

18 Feb. 1873

Garrick Club

My dear Rusden,

You have been elected here without a single black ball. Perhaps that was because no one knew you. Omne ignotum pro
magnifico.[1] I send you the printed list of rules. I have done
nothing as to paying the money as you see that being out of the
country you need not pay for twelve months. Perhaps you will
write home to your cousin about it before that. It seems useless
to pay the money 12 months before it is wanted. I hope you will
have got my book by the same mail with this. I am more afraid
of your criticisms than of any others as you are critical by nature
and thoroughly understand the subject—on any matter of fact if
you say I am right, I will be right;—or if wrong, wrong. That
we should disagree in certain speculative matters of politics is
a matter of course.

God be with you, dear friend, and come over and teach the
Garrickers billiards as soon as you can.

Yours always

ANTHONY TROLLOPE

[1] See Tacitus, *Agricola*, xxx.

514. To JOHN HOLLINGSHEAD. 14 March.
Henry E. Huntington Library.

193 Piccadilly.   14 March 1873

My dear Hollingshead,

I beg to assure you that I have never felt any bitterness against you in regard to the play adapted from my novel, and very bitter against Charles Reade. He did what I think was wrong. Had he asked my consent to the use of my plot I should have taken it as a compliment.[1] But he was utterly unjustified in taking my name without consulting me. I cannot at all understand his action. But the whole matter is quite trivial,—though I felt myself obliged to deny participation in a work as to which I had never been consulted.

Yours always
ANTHONY TROLLOPE

515. To ALFRED AUSTIN. 31 March.
Parrish Collection.

This letter and the succeeding refer to Austin's poem *Madonna's Child* (1873), later incorporated as Act II in *The Human Tragedy* (1876).

193. Piccadilly, 31 March 1873

My dear Austin,

I ought to have acknowledged before this the receipt of your book;—but you have probably felt with me that there are two modes of acknowledgment of such gifts,—that which is carefully made before the reading has been possible, and that which has been deferred till an opinion can be given. Like you I have not chosen the former. I have been out of town hunting, all the last month, and have had time to read nothing. I shall venture to tell you what I think when I have awaked myself to better pursuits.

You know that you and I are not quite in accord as to the opinion of others respecting your works. Your praise of mine would be delightful to me. Mine of yours would be nothing to you. And vice versa as to censure. This knowledge on my hand

[1] Hollingshead was testing Trollope's reaction to Reade's unauthorized dramatization of *Ralph the Heir* in connexion with his campaign in support of copyright legislation.

does not debar me from the privilege of telling you what I think, but it makes me aware that I may put off doing so— I shall write to you again when I have read your poem.

Many thanks to you for sending it to me. All the same I wish that Langford had not repeated to you a word that was certainly not intended for repetition—

> Yours always
> Most affectionately
> ANTH TROLLOPE

516. TO ALFRED AUSTIN. 4 April.
   Parrish Collection.

4. April 1873   (Garrick Club crest)

My dear Austin—

I have read your poem with I cannot tell you what delight. It is, to my taste, infinitely better work than any other I have seen from your hand. There is an injustice in satyre which always offends me, and robs the work of my perfect sympathy,—and this feeling may perhaps have made me hypercritical to former poems of yours, as poems. This one has greatly charmed me,—chiefly perhaps by the versification,—but in a very great degree by the perfect sympathy which it creates with the girl. This feeling is perhaps unconsciously enhanced by the conviction (conviction on my part, I mean, not on that of readers at large) that you as author had to imbue her with all the charms of a pietistic faith in which you do not yourself have a part. There would I think be left in the mind of a general reader an assurance of the ecstatic faith of the author.

> Yours always faithfully
> ANTHONY TROLLOPE

Tom got his cheque. It was indeed money out of the fire.

I think you might have put a few more words into the girls mouth at parting

Hunting over—nothing to do beyond the writing of a novel or two till November next. In some coming perfect world there will be hunting 12 months in the year.

517. To THOMAS WOOLNER.[1] 21 April.
Mitchell Library, Sydney.

21— April 1873
(10, John Street, Adelphi.)
My dear Woolner
We are very anxious to make a good list of stewards for our
Literary Fund Dinner.[2] Gladstone is to be in the chair. I think
you got a card. Can you oblige us by allowing us to add your
name to our list?

Yours very faithfully
ANTHONY TROLLOPE
Thomas Woolner Esq

518. To MOUNTSTUART ELPHINSTONE GRANT DUFF.[3]
21 April. *Parrish Collection.*

Trollope asks permission to add Grant Duff's name to the list of stewards
for the Royal Literary Fund dinner.

519. To JOHN HOLLINGSHEAD. 21 April.
Henry E. Huntington Library.

193 Piccadilly. 21 April 1873.
My dear Hollingshead,
There can I think be no doubt as to the justice of the extended

---

[1] Thomas Woolner (1825–92), sculptor and poet, was one of the original
Pre-Raphaelite Brethren. He became a member of the Royal Academy in
1874.
[2] The 84th anniversary dinner of the Royal Literary Fund was held in
Freemasons' Hall, 28 May. A most distinguished gathering was present,
and *The Times* next day ran a four-column verbatim account of the proceed-
ings. Mr. Walter, in replying for the House of Commons, said: 'I do think
it may well make the humblest member of Parliament content with his lot
and console those who are most oppressed with the cares of office, to be
told, as we have lately been by a distinguished member of this Brotherhood
—Mr. Anthony Trollope—in his interesting work on our Australian
colonies, that he looks on a seat in the House of Commons as the highest
honour which can be conferred on an Englishman.' *The Times*, 29 May
1873, p. 12.
[3] Grant Duff had given Trollope some assistance in the early days of the
Saint Pauls. See letter No. 351, *supra.*

copyright which you are demanding.¹ If a dramatist have a property in the plot of his play or a novelist in the words of his story,—why should not the novelist have a similar property in his plot? As regards myself I cannot imagine myself to feel much injured by the adaptation to the stage of any novel of mine. Indeed I do not think that I should refuse the use of a plot to any respectable dramatist who might pay me the compliment of asking for it. But I do feel very bitter against those who endeavour to palm off as their own the work of others.

Very faithfully yours

ANTHONY TROLLOPE

520. TO LADY WOOD. 21 June.
Parrish Collection.

Trollope answers an objection to *Lady Anna* that continues to be heard.

(39, Montagu Square,)
21 June 1873—

My dear Lady Wood,

Of course the girl has to marry the tailor. It is very dreadful, but there was no other way. The story was originated in my mind by an idea I had as to the doubt which would, (or might) exist in a girls mind as to whether she ought to be true to her troth, or true to her leneage [*sic*] when, from early circumstances the one had been given in a manner detrimental to the other—and I determined that that [*sic*] in such case she ought to be true all through. To make the discrepancy as great as possible I made the girl an Earls daughter, and the betrothed a tailor. All the horrors had to be invented to bring about a condition in which an Earls daughter could become engaged to a tailor without glaring fault on her side. The story, from first to last word, was written on board ship on my way out to Melbourne.

I was very sorry to miss you when you were in London.

Affectionately yours

ANTHONY TROLLOPE

¹ Hollingshead's persistent lobbying for an extended copyright law ultimately resulted in the appointment of the Royal Copyright Commission, Apr. 1876, of whose fifteen members Trollope was one.

521. To KATE FIELD. 5 July.
Boston Public Library.

(39, Montagu Square,)
5, July 1873.

Dear Kate,

My wife has written to ask you to come and dine here.[1] If you
will come, (which pray do) we will discuss the album—[2] But in
truth I know nothing about it. As he is generally so good a correspondent I am surprized that he should not answer you. If you
like I will write to him.

Two of the wildest of your countrymen, Joachim Miller[3] &
Mark Twain, dine with me at my club next week.[4] Pity you have
not yet established the rights of your sex or you could come and
meet them, and be *as jolly as men.*

Yours always
ANTH TROLLOPE

522. To FREDERIC CHAPMAN. 13 July.
Parrish Collection.

39 Montague[5] Square,   Sunday
13 July 1873

My dear Chapman,

I am off to Scotland tonight for ten days.

I took the three first numbers of my tale[6] to Virtue, and saw
Virtue who promised in the course of this week to let me have
three or four proofs.

[1] At Trollope's dinner Miss Field met Wilkie Collins for the first time.
See *Kate Field: a Record*, p. 306.

[2] Probably Kate Field's book of travel and character sketches, *Hap-
Hazard* (1873).

[3] Cincinnatus Heine Miller (? 1841–1913), known as Joaquin Miller,
was a romantic American of the far West ('the Oregon Byron') who had
drifted to London and there privately printed two volumes, *Pacific Poems*
(1870) and *Songs of the Sierras* (1871), which brought him immediate and
enormous popularity. For Miller on Trollope, see *Joaquin Miller's Poems*,
Bear edition, 6 vols. (San Francisco: The Whitaker & Ray Co., 1909–10),
iv. 154.

[4] Mark Twain wrote an amusing account of this dinner. See Bernard De
Voto, *Mark Twain in Eruption* (New York: Harper, 1940), pp. 332–3.

[5] Trollope's spelling of Montagu Square (even on his stationery) is not
consistent.

[6] *Lady Anna.*

I have promised to dine with Pain on the 24th.— Fawkes,[1] his nephew, is to breakfast with me on the 23rd. Would it be worth your while to come and meet him?

I have sent a cheque to Christie & Manson[2] for the books I bought—

I wish you would send young Pollock[3] a cheque for that money. Pray do this.

Some time since I left a novel with you written by Mr Woolriche,[4] the police magistrate, who is an uncle of Fred Clays.[5] You promised to have it read. Has it been read. Would you have this done, and let Fred Clay know—

Yours always faithfully

ANTHONY TROLLOPE

My address will be

Divart Cottage
Drumnadrochet
Inverness

523. To MR. LOVEJOY. 23 July. Athenaeum Club. *Not traced*. Unidentified Catalogue of Wm. Smith & Son, Reading, probably October–November 1946.

Trollope writes on behalf of Mrs. Elliot, whose balance from Chapman & Hall was to have been paid to Lovejoy. Frances Minto Elliot had published with Chapman & Hall her two-volume *Diary of an Idle Woman in Italy* (1871), a new edition of her *Pictures of Old Rome* (1872), and her two-volume *Old Court Life in France* (1873–4).

[1] Lionel Grimston Fawkes (1849–1931), a colonel in the Royal Artillery. See Michael Sadleir, 'Luke Fildes', *Times Literary Supplement*, 5 Apr. 1947, p. 157; 19 Apr. 1947, p. 183. See also Hilda F. Finberg in *TLS*, 19 Apr. 1947, p. 183.

[2] Christie, Manson & Woods, art auctioneers.

[3] Probably Walter Herries Pollock (1850–1926), whose article at Trollope's death (see *Harper's Magazine*, lxvi [May 1883], 907–12) Mr. Sadleir has called the best of its kind.

[4] Edmund Humphrey Woolrych (1839–88), barrister and police magistrate, 1861–79. His novel does not seem to have been published.

[5] Frederick Clay, a well-known London printer.

524. To FREDERIC CHAPMAN. [24 September.]¹
Killarney. Wednesday. *Parrish Collection.*

Trollope has had 'one drawing from Fawkes. It is with slight exceptions very good. I shall be back on 1ˢᵗ October and will shew it to you. It is time something should be decided.'²

525. To ? LADY WOOD. 9 October.
Parrish Collection.

9 October 1873
(39, Montagu Square.)

Dear Friend,

Your last letter reached me at Killarny when I was wandering about. We have now been home a week and I ought to have written sooner. But I have been troubled and in some sort unhappy. I fear I have lost the hearing of one ear for always.³ For such troubles a man ought to be prepared as he grows old; and this is comparatively so small a trouble, that I ought not to feel it a grievance. But for a time it frets me, and confuses me. I fancy that I am always going to be run over, and everybody seems to talk to me on the wrong side. I am told that a bone has grown up inside the orifice. Oh dear! One does not understand at all. Why should any bones grow, except useful, working, bones? Why should anything go wrong in our bodies? Why should we not be all beautiful? Why should there be dread?—why death?— and, oh why, damnation? The last we get out of by not believing it, but when a man has a bone in his ear, so that everything makes a rumbling noise and nothing is heard distinctly, he does believe it. But why;—why is it there? I suppose I have done something or left undone something, which if left undone or if done, would have saved me from the bone. But for the moment I cannot get it out of my head. I wish I could! When are you coming home? The Square is desolate without you.

¹ This is one of very few undated Trollope letters. His working calendar (Bodleian) shows that he was in Killarney from 20 Sept. to 1 Oct. and in that period Wednesday was the 24th.

² Trollope probably has reference to *The Way We Live Now*, the monthly parts for which began in Feb. 1874. But the artist finally chosen was Luke Fildes, not Fawkes. That there was great uncertainty about the illustrations is shown in the fact that the cover-drawing is not by Fildes, but by 'J. B.'

³ Faulty hearing was a Trollope family failing. Tom Trollope was quite deaf.

Touching the form of rule in France I do not feel sure that I quite agree with you. I dont want a king with divine right. I do not want to undo whatever little may have been done in France. But I do think that a monarchy such as would come after Henri V would be the best mould on which to model a Government for France.

With kindest regards to your people

Yours affect.

A. T.

526. To Arthur Locker. 17 October.
Not traced. Sadleir's transcript.

(39, Montague Square.)

My dear Mr. Locker, October 17, 1873.

I have written a good many novels,—more I believe than any man alive,—and I have thought much of the names of them. I think the name I have given to the tale for the Christmas number of The Graphic is a good name, and I do not wish to change it.[1] The question of the name of a novel is one which must be left to the author. No one else can be in a condition to give a name to his story. I must trust you will not think me stiff-necked,— but there are matters in which a man must go by his own judgment.

Yours very faithfully

Anthony Trollope

527. To Austin Dobson. 21 October.
G. F. C. Dobson. Not seen.

(Garrick Club)

My dear Mr Dobson, Oct 21. 1873.

Very many thanks for your volume.[2] You know so well what I think of your poetry that I need not now express my opinion. But I will wish you God Speed and trust you may have early that success which so seldom comes early, but which generally comes at last if it be deserved.

Yours always

Anthony Trollope

[1] *Harry Heathcote of Gangoil.*   [2] *Vignettes in Rhyme.*

528. To MR. ELMORE. 21 October.
Parrish Collection.

Trollope sends a dinner invitation. This was probably Alfred Elmore (1815–81), a well-known painter.

529. To ARTHUR.[1] 26 November. Montagu Square.
Parrish Collection.

Trollope has asked George Smith to notice Arthur's newspaper in the *Pall Mall.*[2] He likes Arthur's 'bar-dining' article; hopes he will make a fortune out of it and found a new college.[3]

530. To MARCUS CLARKE.[4] 27 November.
Public Library of Sidney.

Nov—27—1873

(39, Montagu Square.)

My dear Mr Clarke— Many thanks for your book[5] which I have read with great pleasure. I am so much out of the way of reviews, —always avoiding any personal contact with critics as critics, because of my own business as an author,—that I fear I can hardly assist you. But I will do so, should it come in my way.

Most faithfully yours

ANTHONY TROLLOPE

531. To MR. GRIMSTONE. 16 December.
Montagu Square.

Trollope sends a dinner invitation. 'Some men are coming who play whist afterwards. I dont know whether you are that way given. There will be no compulsion. . . . I have had some good runs this month, but am at present laid up from a sprained foot, got from a fall.' From a reference in the letter to Mount St., the addressee can be identified as Robert Grimston (1816–84), sportsman and chairman of the International Telegraph Company.

[1] Probably Arthur Augustus Tilley (1851–1942). Mr. Sadleir suggests that the newspaper was some short-lived undergraduate effort; but Arthur Tilley's half-brother, Sir John Tilley, knows nothing of it.
[2] I can find no notice of a newspaper.
[3] Mr. Sadleir suggests that the article, which I have not been able to trace, described a ceremonial dinner given as part of the ritual for aspirants to the bar. Arthur Tilley subsequently gave up the bar and returned to Cambridge as a fellow.
[4] Marcus Andrew Hislop Clarke (1846–81), Australian novelist and journalist. See the *Australian Encyclopaedia*, i. 271–2.
[5] Clarke's well-known prison novel *For the Term of His Natural Life* (1874), of which Trollope had an advance copy.

313

1 8 7 4

532. To R. P. Harding. 1 January. London.
Cyril A. Munro. Not seen.

Trollope and Chapman arrange for a conference with Harding.

533. To Kate.[1] 13 January.
Dr. Silvain Brunschwig.

January 13. 1874
(39, Montagu Square.)

My dear Kate,

In your letter you have taken the very last way to get a middle aged man like me to come to your ball. You only offer to put me in a corner to play cards! If you had promised to dance three round dances with me, I should have come at once.

But, my dear, to own the truth there are ever so many reasons against my coming. I shall be hunting that day and shall be so tired I shan't be able to move. There will be no room in the carriage. And I should be in a fret to bring everybody back home just when the real fun was beginning.

You must not be angry. You know I would do any thing for you: but I *hate* balls!

Yours very affectionately
Anthony Trollope

I mean I hate them for myself. I like them very much for other people,—like you and Flo.

Give my kindest remembrances to all your party.

534. To Mr. Schlesinger. 8 February.
Parrish Collection.

Trollope informs Schlesinger of his unanimous election to the Garrick Club. (Max Schlesinger (?—1881). I have this identification through the kindness of Lt.-Col. Baddeley, Secretary of the Garrick Club. Schlesinger is not listed in the *Post Office London Directory 1874*.)

---

[1] Not Kate Field, but some unidentifiable acquaintance of Trollope's niece, Florence Bland, who lived with the Trollopes and acted as her uncle's amanuensis.

535. To E. E. HALE.[1] 23 February.
Estate of Carroll A. Wilson.

(Garrick Club)
23 Feb 1874

Dear Sir,

Since receiving your letter I have seen Mr Chapman of the firm of Chapman & Hall, and I find that he has already given permission for the sale of the limited number of your magazine which came here for circulation.[2] I think however, that in your letter to me you do not notice the one real objection to such sale. It is this,—that any publisher here could pirate the work from your pages, if your pages circulate here as containing American authorship. In the very unsatisfactory state of the present law there is danger in yielding any point.[3]

Yours very faithfully
ANTHONY TROLLOPE

536. To LADY STANLEY. 25 February. Montagu Square.
Parrish Collection.

Trollope accepts a dinner invitation for 10 March. Lady Stanley was the wife of Edward Henry Stanley (1826–93), later fifteenth Earl of Derby.

537. To W. DONALD. 27 February.
Not traced.
Maggs Catalogue 320 (January–February 1914).

* * *

Literature is very wide, have you made up your mind what you mean by devoting yourself to it? Do you know what books you propose to yourself to write, or what you would do with them when written? . . . . Though the profession of Literature

[1] Edward Everett Hale (1822–1909), Boston Unitarian minister, author of *A Man Without a Country*, and editor of *Old and New*, to which reference is made.
[2] Apparently Chapman & Hall sold American rights on a story to *Old and New*, and then objected to the magazine's circulation in England.
[3] On the back of Trollope's letter Hale copied his reply, which in part reads: 'The point still unintelligible to me is why Mr. Chapman sells us the story,—knowing that we have an English circulation,—if, after he has sold it he does not wish us to publish it.'

is very pleasant to those who are successful, it is very precarious, and as full of peril as of allurements. Out of ten who make the attempt—nine fail to earn their bread at it.

*   *   *

538. To ? 10 March. Montagu Square.
Parrish Collection.

Trollope will be in Essex on the 16th and thus cannot vote for the addressee's friend.

539. To Mrs. De La Pryme.[1] 15 April. Montagu Square. *Parrish Collection.*

Trollope cannot accept an invitation for 5 May because he is going to Paris on 17 April.

540. To Mary Holmes. 1 May.
Parrish Collection.

(39, Montagu Square.)

1 May, 1874

My dear Miss Holmes,

I've a deal to explain. I sent the verses to Annie Thackeray because her brother-in-law Leslie Stephen is now Editor of the Cornhill,—thinking, & expressing a hope to that effect, that he might put them into that magazine. Annie wrote to me in answer, but said nothing about the verses. For aught I know they may go into the Cornhill,—and, for aught you now know, into Macmillans at the same time.[2] This is improbable,—but would make a trouble were it so— However let them take their chance.— I suppose that had L. Stephen intended to use them, she would have told me. About the guinea and the book I understand nothing. I hope I have not done wrong. But, like many another fool I can only defend myself on the plea of good intentions.

---

[1] Probably the wife of Charles De La Pryme (see letters No. 551 and 559, *infra*), who may have been a son of the Mr. De la Prime of Bruges who was a friend of Frances Trollope. See Frances Trollope's letter of 29 Aug. 1835 to John Murray, the original now in the possession of Sir John Murray, who kindly permitted me to examine the Trollope correspondence in his files.

[2] The verses do not seem to have been published in either magazine.

316

I should explain that at present I have not myself any interest or influence in any periodical, and could therefore only apply to a friend who might have some. Editors are now so beset by applicants that I fear they often give way, not to the greatest merit, but to the strongest pressure.

I wish you every success with your novel. Heaven knows that there ought to be room for any thing fairly good. I feel my own to be very bad often; but, I feel others to be much worse,—with an authors natural bias.

The Macdermots had its merits,—truth, freshness, and a certain tragic earnestness being the list [? best] of them. The execution was *very bad*. The best novel I ever wrote was the Last Chronicle of Barset. But I do not answer your letter with the object of talking about myself.

What you say of illustrations is all true,—not strong enough in expression of disgust. But what can a writer do? I desire, of course, to put my books into as many hands as possible, and I take the best mode of doing so.

I am very glad to find that you enjoy the liberty of your present life. I hope you may be able to live without ever returning to the quasi slavery of living in other peoples houses.

Yours always
ANTHONY TROLLOPE

Again I apologize if I have wounded you by sending your letter to Annie Thackeray.

541. To GEORGE SMITH. 3 May.
Parrish Collection.

3 May 1874
(39, Montagu Square.)

My dear Smith,

Tom Taylor, Millais, Frith,[1] & I are acting together to get up some sum to assist the widow of Shirley Brooks,[2] who after 35 years of literary work has died leaving an insurance of £4000 & nothing else. She is in great immediate want, & we wish if

---

[1] William Powell Frith (1819–1909), the distinguished artist and biographer of John Leech.

[2] Charles William Shirley Brooks (1816–74), a staff writer for *Punch* from 1851; editor, 1870–4. Tom Taylor succeeded him as editor.

possible to prevent any diminution of her capital and to add something for the assistance of her boys. Are you tender-hearted towards his memory?

At any rate excuse my begging,—which is not much in my line. In this case I am acting as Treasurer.

Yours always
ANTHONY TROLLOPE

542. To ALEXANDER MACMILLAN. 3 May. Montagu Square. *Bradford A. Booth.*

Trollope asks Macmillan to contribute to the Shirley Brooks Fund: 'I am Treasurer & I fear beggar-in-chief.'

543. To MR. SIMPSON. 3 May. Montagu Square. *Parrish Collection.*

A note on behalf of the Shirley Brooks Fund. Simpson was probably John Palgrave Simpson (1807–87), dramatist and novelist.

544. To MR. COLLINS. 3 May. *Parrish Collection.*

Another Brooks Fund note. Probably Wilkie Collins (1824–89), author of the popular novels *The Moonstone* and *The Woman in White.*

545. To GEORGE HENRY LEWES. 3 May. *Mrs. E. S. Ouvry.*

3 May 1874
(39, Montagu Square.)

My dear Lewes,

This is a begging letter, and I hate begging. It is intended for you and your wife alike. Shirley Brooks, who had been engaged for 35 years in literature, has died leaving a life insurance for £4000 with a wife & two sons, and not a penny else. His friends want to save the assurance for permanent income & if possible to add something,—also to raise a sum for immediate wants. I am acting as Treasurer. Dont be angry, and if you disapprove merely say so.

God bless you
Yours
A. T.

546. To GEORGE SMITH. [May]
Parrish Collection.

Trollope thanks Smith for his 'liberal donation for Mrs Shirley Brooks'.

547. To G. H. LEWES. 4 May.
Parrish Collection.

Trollope thanks Lewes for his subscription of ten guineas for the Brooks Fund.

548. To ? 7 May. Montagu Square.
Parrish Collection.

Another Brooks Fund letter. The goal of the solicitors is £2000.

549. To TOM TAYLOR. 30 May.
Parrish Collection.

Private   30 May, 1874—
                                              (39, Montagu Square.)
   I send you an account of my stewardship,—which keep as I do not wish to have to do it again. I have it in rough, but only in rough. I shall get another £10 from a good man who has promised me, but told me that he had to wait till he got his rents. Pender[1] promised me £10– 10/- I have dunned him once, but he has not sent it, and I cannot bring myself to dun him again. I suppose he did not mean it. Millais said he would get me some subscriptions,—but chances are doubtful. Perhaps you may have some others.
   What shall we do now? I shall be glad to get rid of it, and it will be as well for Mrs Brooks that we should do so. Tell me what you suggest.
                         Most faithfully yours
                         ANTHONY TROLLOPE

---

[1] Sir John Pender (1815–96), M.P. for Wickboroughs, chairman of the Telegraph Construction and Maintenance Company.

550. To ? [May.]
    Parrish Collection.

(39, Montagu Square,)
39, Montagu Square
(1874)

Dear Sir

Many thanks for your £5. Were I to meet you I would answer
as best I could your observations as to the propriety of a mans
providing during his life for his wife & children, an obvious duty,
—and as to the probable causes of insufficiency of such provision.
But the subject is too long for a letter,—especially as I have to
write some hundreds about this business.

Yours faithfully
ANTHONY TROLLOPE

551. To MR. DE LA PRYME.[1] 4 June.
    Parrish Collection.

4 June 74
(39, Montagu Square,)

My dear Mr Dela Pryme,

I had forgotten all about the Reform Club. I forget now how
it was that you seduced me to declare myself willing to incur the
expense of another club; probably by patriotic incentives, *nothing
else could have done so!* As it is I will recede— I belong to 3 clubs,[2]
which are two more than a man needs.

Yours with many thanks
ANTHONY TROLLOPE

552. To ? 3 July. Montagu Square.
    Parrish Collection.

Trollope makes an appointment with an unknown correspondent. 'I apolo-
gise for the delay but have been out of town.'

[1] Probably Charles De La Pryme (1815–99), barrister, political econo-
mist, chairman of the Ramsey board of magistrates. See letter No. 539,
supra.
[2] Garrick, Athenaeum, and Cosmopolitan.

553. To Mary Holmes. 6 July.
    Parrish Collection.

July 6, 1874
My dear Miss Holmes—   (39, Montagu Square.)
    I have two long letters of yours by me,—the first having been kept, not because I did not mean to answer it,—but because I meant to write more fully & comfortably than the manner of life one falls into allows one to do.

    But I defy any one to answer your letters, because they leap,— as all good letters should do. Correspondence should only touch upon the past things said,—just enough for compliment,—and then rush off into new pastures. But you've trod on ever so many of my most favourite corns. Lady Anna is the best novel I ever wrote! Very much!! Quite far away above all others!!!— A lady ought to marry a tailor—if she chanced to fall in love with such a creature, and to promise him, & take his goodness, when she was not a bad lady. That is all! Will you deny it?

    How am I to go on? Mr Alf's staff are real enough;[1] so real, that there is a dullness in the description of them, as they are devoid of caricature. The parish priest I knew myself, & loved, & opened my house to him, and fed him when he was fearfully, horribly, hungry, from sheer want,—and he was a gentleman at all points; but I could not go on with him, not because he was intent on converting me, for which I did not care; but because he would say nasty things of my religion which could only be answered by nasty things as to his, which I could not say to any guest, or to any sincere Christian. But yet he was a man who will certainly go to heaven, if a mortal may presume to say so much of any man.

    In what you say as to young ladies, (taking exception to the sister Longestaffes)—you must remember that no satirist can take the exact state of things and represent it. If he do he will be altogether inefficacious. The man whom he sees stealing a shilling he would accuse of stealing two shillings,—or a sovereign— It is the proclivity and not the depth of sin which he handles. No satirist will redeem a man from the lowest pit,—only the man who is going thitherwards.

---

[1] Trollope here speaks of characters in *The Way We Live Now.*

You ought to know girls more accurately than I do, of course, and I should be very much averse to hold an argument against you on this point or that. But I have had to endeavour not only to know what women are in describing them, but also to learn to write of them in language that people would read. No doubt the second attribute is as effective as the former. I often think that my young ladies have been popular, not because they have been true to nature, but because they have been lively.

You say nothing of your own novel, of which your former letter was full—why is that? . . .[1]

554. To MARY HOLMES. 18 September.
Parrish Collection.

Sept. 18, 1874
(39, Montagu Square.)

My dear Miss Holmes,

On returning from the continent two days ago I found two letters from you, both of which had been waiting here a long time, one written on 22 July, the day before we started! My son has got back today, having also been absent though not with us, —and he also has found two letters from you. You will therefore regard this as an answer to the two sets of letters. He is no longer in Chapman & Halls house,—having taken himself and his money out of it twelve months ago. It did not suit him, and since that he has been living chiefly abroad. He is now with us for a week or two, after which he goes back to Germany.

I will go at once to your novel. If it be completed, you had better send it to my address at Messrs. Chapman & Halls. Though Harry (my son) has left the house, I have still much to do with it, and am there almost daily. I will have the novel read there by their reader if you like it. They will not probably pay you for it, but may perhaps publish it on half profits. I found, when beginning the business, that the difficulty was not so much to get a novel written as to have it published. And after that there was the still greater difficulty of having it paid for. It was ten years after the first book published before the beginning of that happy consummation was reached. If you like to send the

[1] The remainder of this letter is missing.

MS to any publisher in preference to Chapman & Hall, do not hesitate to say so, and I will see that it is delivered.

I do not quite agree in all your criticism, touching A. Thackeray and G. Elliot;—not that I do not like Annie's work, but that I prefer George Elliots very much. She is sometimes heavy —sometimes abstruse, sometimes almost dull,—but always like an egg, full of meat.

Yours always most sincerely
ANTHONY TROLLOPE

555. TO MARY HOLMES. 28 September.
Parrish Collection.

28 Sept 1874
(39, Montagu Square.)

My dear Miss Holmes,

I got your letter today in which you lament the falling off in the condition of the poor, in that churches and gaols,—you might have added schools,—have been substituted for alms-houses. I can't tell you how much I disagree with you, because it is past 12 oclock, and the subject is very long, and my hand is tired with much writing. But I ought to have told you before that your MS reached Chapman safely, was unpacked by me, and has been consigned to his reader.

Yours always
very sleepy
ANTHONY TROLLOPE

556. TO MARY HOLMES. 7 October.
Parrish Collection.

7. October 1874
(39, Montague Square.)

My dear Miss Holmes,

I have only a moment to scrawl a line to say that as you interest yourself about W. W. L. N.[1] I have desired that the back numbers may be sent to you. And the future numbers will also be sent.

Paul Montague is all right. He is not a hero. But men are

[1] *The Way We Live Now.* The characters named are from this novel.

seldom heroes. He is as good as our brothers and sons and friends.
He does not vacillate really, after he knows Hetta C.

Yours most truly
A. T.

557. To ALFRED AUSTIN. 1 November.
  Parrish Collection.

(Waltham House,
Waltham Cross.)

39, Montagu Square
Novr. 1, 1874

My dear Austin,
  Both Johnson (Todds Johnson which taken for all in all I
regard as the best Eng Dict) and Webster give 'Ye' as the
nominative plural of Thou, and both give authorities out of the
bible only. The Imperial, which is a poor book, follows Webster
word for word. Richardson, which is a very good book, gives
'Ye' only as a nominative plural,—but he cites none but
Chaucerian literature throughout. You may take it as proved
that 'Ye' *was** only a nominative.[1] Byron has I think never been
known as a correct writer;—but he has so far made himself a
classic that I think he *may be taken as sufficient authority* for intro-
ducing a new use of a word.
  I cannot find Ye ever used in the accusative case by Dryden
who was certainly a great master of English—

Yours always
A T.

* i e in, say, ante Johnsonian literature

558. To HENRY REEVE.[2] 3 November.
  Parrish Collection.

(Garrick Club crest)
3 Nov. 1874

My dear Mr Reeve.
  I think there is a small error in your statement as to D of
Richmond,[3] page 67 vol 2. of the Greville Memoirs.[4] The Duke,

[1] Trollope was wrong. See the *O.E.D.*
[2] Henry Reeve (1813–95), editor of the *Edinburgh Review*, 1855–95.
[3] Charles Gordon Lennox (1791–1860), fifth Duke of Richmond; post-master general, 1830–4.
[4] Charles Cavendish Fulke Greville (1794–1865), clerk to the council,

I think, did take the salary of the PostmGeneral, having been advised that his declining to do so might raise a disagreeable precedent. He certainly did come in on the understanding that he was not to do so, and on that account did not pay for his patents. But, I think, you will find that he drew his salary from the first.[1]

I do not speak with confidence but it was in my mind that such was the fact.

Yours always

ANTHONY TROLLOPE.

I was a post office clerk, not quite in those days, but soon afterwards, and remember many years afterward talking over the matter with Lord Stanley of A— when he was Postmaster General.[2]

559. To CHARLES DE LA PRYME.
[? October–November.] London.
Parrish Collection.

Trollope refuses an invitation because he will be in hunting quarters.

560. To CHARLES DE LA PRYME. 7 November.
Montagu Square. *Parrish Collection.*

Trollope acknowledges receipt of a communication.

561. To MARY HOLMES. 9 November.
Parrish Collection.

Nov 9, 1874
(Waltham House,
Waltham Cross.)

My dear Miss Holmes—

I have seen Mr Chapman the publisher today and he tells me that his reader has said that your novel in its present form will

1821–59. Reeve edited his diary, valuable for intimate sidelights on statesmen, particularly Wellington and Palmerston. The first three of the eight volumes were published in 1874.

[1] The House of Commons had disapproved gratuitous service in the case of the Lord Privy Seal, and the Treasury put pressure on the Duke. He relented but 'managed to draw as little of the arrears of salary as possible'. See Herbert Joyce, *The History of the Post Office* (London, 1893), p. 413.

[2] Lord Stanley of Alderley was postmaster general, 1860–6.

not do, but that he thinks that, with certain alterations, it might do. I presume the novel has been sent back to you. It will be for you to decide whether you will make the alterations which will have been proposed to you—

I did not look at the MS myself. In such a case I can do no good by my doing so. Should I not like it, it would break my heart (as it has done in similar cases) to have to say so; and should I like it my opinion would go for nothing with a publisher who would regard my opinion simply as that of a friend.

If you have *not got* your MS back with an answer from Mr Chapman, let me know. What I have told you is what he told me today.

> Yours always faithfully
> ANTHONY TROLLOPE

562. TO MARY HOLMES. 11 November.
Parrish Collection.

Chapman has assured Trollope that Miss Holmes's manuscript has been sent. 'But publishers are deceitful.' If she does not receive it, she must let Trollope know.

563. TO MARY HOLMES. 23 November.
Parrish Collection.

23, Nov. 1874   (39, Montague Square.)

My dear Miss Holmes,

Your letter has made me unhappy; because I feel that you feel that you have been ill-used. I feared that it would be so. It generally is so when some little assistance is wanted by literary aspirants. One cannot give the help that is needed. One can only try, and fail, and suffer in the failure.

You think that Chapman and his reader have illused [*sic*] you,— but I believe you to be wrong in so thinking. I know them both well and would not have put your MS into their hands had they been unworthy. The firm is existing (you suspect that there is no such firm). It is doing a very lucrative business (you imagine the contrary). Mr Chapman is not deterred by the need of publishing the works of either his friends or his relatives from publishing yours. He has in truth done with your MS as he does with others,—but has done this somewhat quicker than he usually does under my instance. He sent your MS to his reader, and acted on his opinion.

A publisher in such a business as his gets perhaps two or three hundred novels a year. Of course there must be 19 disappointments for one success, and they who are disappointed naturally think as you do,—that they have been ill used. Of course a reader does not read the whole, except in a few cases. It is his duty to read till he is able to advise his employer, who has to act on such advice with reference solely to his own chance of making or of losing money by the transaction.

You write,—(and not only you but many others with whom I become acquainted, and who use my services because, being an old stager, I am supposed to be able to give assistance,)—as though it were the publishers business to publish your work and as though he injured you by not doing so. Of course he would be willing to publish if you or any other author were willing to bear the cost; but otherwise he can only look to his own interest, and you have no ground of complaint against him because he grounds his opinion on a partial reading. If he were to have all Mss thoroughly read he would incur an expense which the matter would not justify.

Do not think that I am hard because I write thus. I suffer much on account of your disappointment. I did what I could. I pressed the matter very much. I have not seen the reader, who lives in the country. Chapman gave me to understand that the reader thought the work might be made available, but with *very great alterations.* I certainly understood that he would be able to give some cue to the nature of the alterations required. But I am aware that such a task is very difficult,—almost impossible. A book has to be written about the book before this can be done.

For myself I may say that the task of dealing with the MS of other persons is so painful,—the necessity of explaining to an aspirant that his or her aspirations must be disappointed is so grievous,—that I have often been tempted to say, that I would never again incur the punishment. I can hardly bring myself to tell a friend that he or she cannot do that which I by chance can do myself— But I remember how often I failed myself before I succeeded,—how Vanity Fair and, as you say, Jane Eyre were carried here and there before they were accepted. I would suggest that you should read your own MS carefully and see if you yourself think it capable of improvement—and,—let me say this in pure friendship, without giving offence,—do not allow yourself to be tempted to think evil because the thing does not go as you wish it. Forgive even the tobacco.

Yours very sincerely and with true friendship
ANTHONY TROLLOPE

564. To MARY HOLMES. 29 November.
Montagu Square. *Parrish Collection.*

Trollope has forwarded Miss Holmes's note to Chapman's reader.

565. To NICHOLAS TRÜBNER.[1] 15 December.
Parrish Collection.

(39, Montagu Square.)
15 December 1874

My dear Mr Trübner

I propose to leave England on March 1, to go to Ceylon, remaining there two or three weeks, then to proceed to Australia where I shall remain about three months, and to return either by Bombay (in which case I should visit Calcutta) or by San Francisco. I cannot now say which might be my route home.

If it would suit you and your associates in the undertaking of which you were speaking, I would write your house a series of letters as to the countries I shall visit,—say 20 in number,—the earliest of which would reach London on the 12th April,—a Monday, in time for publication on the following Saturday, and would keep you supplied weekly from that time till August 28th— If it would suit you as well, it would suit me better to date the arrangement a week later,—that is from 24 April—to 4, September. But in this I will leave the choice to you.[2]

---

[1] Nicholas Trübner (1817–84), a prominent London publisher. He was also an accomplished orientalist and bibliographer.
[2] The twenty letters were published in the *Liverpool Mercury* (and probably in other provincial papers as well) every Saturday from 3 July to 13 Nov. 1875. They were reprinted in *The Tireless Traveler*, ed. Bradford A. Booth (Berkeley and Los Angeles: University of California Press, 1941).

The letters I would propose to make about the length of two columns of The Times.

I should endeavour to deal chiefly with the social condition of the people among whom I found myself. The absolute incidents of travels, unless they happen to be abnormally peculiar, are hardly interesting enough for such a correspondence. The face of nature generally will of course put itself forward, and what nature under such circumstances produces. But among those products men and women as they may there be found, their doings, their aspirations, their successes, and their failures, will and must be to all readers and to all writers the most interesting. If this be done I presume you would wish that my name should be attached to the letters.

If it would suit you to call here any morning on the subject as you go to the city, I shall be most happy to see you. If so, perhaps you would let me have a line naming the day.

Very faithfully yours
ANTHONY TROLLOPE

566. To DR. SEWELL.[1] 16 December. Montagu Square.
Parrish Collection.

Trollope begs off an engagement. 'I had to sit last night for two hours in a white cravat in the coldest room I should think in London, and came home with a fixed sore throat. Here it is snowing hard, and I do not dare to venture out. I am very sorry to be deprived of the pleasure of visiting you and seeing your gaudy but I should I know be foolish to go.'

567. To MISS DUNLOP. 25 December.
Parrish Collection.

Xmas day. 1874

My dear Miss Dunlop

Very many thanks indeed for your present. I will neither put a lamp upon it, nor jugs; but I will have it fixed up conspicuously and decorously in my library,—as it is well worthy;—and as I have the portraits only of literary persons who are or have [been] my personal friends, this shall ever be considered to be the portrait of Sappho, whom I will henceforth presume to have been my tutelary literary genius, and I will always think that the [*sic*]

---

[1] Probably James Edwards Sewell (1810–1903), warden of New College, Oxford, 1860–1903. He was a brother of Elizabeth Missing Sewell, the novelist.

she is pouring out waters of inspiration over my head. Yours
with very many good wishes of the season and very much
obliged
                                        ANTHONY TROLLOPE

1 8 7 5

568. To JOHN BLACKWOOD. 6 January.
   Parrish Collection.

6 January 1875—

My dear Blackwood,   (39, Montagu Square.)
   I have been very ill or I should have sooner answered your
most kind letter. I wish you and yours all happy returns of the
season. Pray say so much for me to your wife & Mary with my
kind love. A wretched attack of bile, and deficient liver came on
me in the middle of all that cold & very nearly upset me. At
present I am so weak that I can only just crawl. But I am attaining to a slow but manly desire for mutton chops and sherry, and
am just beginning to think once again of the glories of tobacco.
   We never allowed ourselves to be happy enough really to
think that you would want the house,—but had it been so it
would have suited us well. As it is I must bar up the library!!
   My boy in Australia is all in the right way. If he dont succeed
in the long run I can no longer believe in honesty, industry, and
conduct. But I believe I can give him a helping hand by going out.
I can see what money I can advance to him out of my small means,
and settle certain things with him.
   Harry is coming out in the family line, having an article in
February's Macmillan on the French Stage, which of course I
regard as the best thing ever written on that subject.[1]
   Shall you be up before the end of February. If not I must
postpone the pleasure of seeing you till after I return.
                           Yours always most sincerely
                                        ANTHONY TROLLOPE
Private
   What a blackguard book is that collection of Greville Memoirs!
Tell me what you think.

   [1] 'The French Theatre under Louis XIV', *Macmillan's Magazine*, xxxi
(Apr. 1875), 522–32.

569. To Mr. Jones.[1] 8 January. Montagu Square.
Parrish Collection.

Trollope sends an enclosure.

570. To Alfred Austin. 12 January.
Parrish Collection.

12 January 1875
(39, Montagu Square.)

My dear Austin,

I have been very ill, or I should have sooner have written to you about the T. of B,[2] which I had read before I became ill. To my illness first,—being the greater subject! I had a very nasty liver attack, and for a time thought badly of myself;—but am now better and am hunting again, and do not mean to die this bout.

I like your poem very much indeed,—very much better than anything you have done before. The character-drawing in Noema & Afrael is excellent—the Irad also, but of course with less scope. It is a question whether in a dramatic point you might not have done better with your priests, astrologers, & philosophers, of whom you do not make very much. But the pride of the poem is in the fulness of the meaning throughout, and the perspicuity of the language, a virtue which I have always held to be necessary to really great poetry. I congratulate fully & am

Yours affectionately
Anthony Trollope—still very weak.

571. To George Bentley.[3] 17 January.
Montagu Square. *Parrish Collection.*

Tom Trollope is about to publish two volumes of stories.[4] On his behalf Trollope asks for permission to reprint 'Meo Varalla'.[5]

[1] Possibly Charles Edward Jones, solicitor, of Young, Jones, Roberts, & Hale. See *Post Office London Directory 1872*, p. 1002.
[2] *The Tower of Babel: A Poetical Drama* (London, 1874).
[3] George Bentley (1828–95), the son of Trollope's old friend Richard Bentley, edited *Temple Bar*, 1866–95.
[4] *Diamond Cut Diamond*, 2 vols. (London, 1875).
[5] 'How Meo Varalla Won His First Love', *Temple Bar*, xxxiii (Nov. 1871), 470–503.

572. To GEORGE BENTLEY. 22 January.
Montagu Square. *Parrish Collection.*

Trollope thanks Bentley for permission to reprint Tom's story and agrees to write a novel for *Temple Bar.*[1]

573. To MARY HOLMES. 26 January.
Parrish Collection.

(39, Montagu Square.)

My dear Miss Holmes.   26 Jan. 1875

I must say a word touching my priest in W. W. Live Now. In the first place he is a thoroughly good man, anxiously doing his duty according to his lights, at any cost of personal suffering,—one of whom one might confidently say that he was on the road to heaven. If so, you can hardly say that, in describing such a man, I am hard on the order. Then, let me, (—if I may do so without arrogance,)—refer you to a novel of my own which you yourself name in your letter, 'The Macdermots', and say that in the character of Father John there I have drawn as thoroughly good and fine a man as I know how to depict. Then going back to the priest in the later novel, let me say that, when at Waltham, I became acquainted with the R.C. priest there, & opened my house to him in full friendship. He was a thoroughly conscientious man, an Oxford man, what we call a pervert and you a convert, and a perfect gentleman,—so poor that he had not bread to eat. I & my wife were as good to him as we knew how to be;—but he would never desist for a moment from casting ridicule and opprobrium on my religion, though I would not on any account have hinted a slur upon his. I was obliged to drop him. He made himself absolutely unbearable.

I have lived much with clergymen of your church, & have endeavoured to draw them in their colours as I saw them. But, because they were the priests of a church which was not my church, I have never drawn one as bad, or hypocritical, or unfaithful.

You are quite right about Mortimer Collins.[2] He is the very dregs.

Yours always

ANTHONY TROLLOPE

The American Senator appeared in *Temple Bar*, May 1876–July 1877. Mortimer Collins (1827–76) was a writer of verses, humorous novels,

574. To GEORGE BENTLEY. 7 February.
Montagu Square. *Parrish Collection.*

Trollope is dissatisfied with Bentley's terms. 'I think I had better see you.'

575. To GEORGE BENTLEY. 10 February.
Montagu Square. *Parrish Collection.*

Trollope agrees to terms. 'I like ready money, but I hate to lower my prices, and will therefore take the monthly payments,—which after all is the fair way. . . . The novel, of which two thirds are already written,[1] is a tale of modern English life, just such as you describe. I cannot insert the name as I never fix on that till the book is completed.'

576. To MR. DENNIS. 12 February. Montagu Square.
Myers & Co.

Trollope has so little time before he leaves and is so pressed by engagements that he does not have a free night.

577. To OCTAVIAN BLEWITT. 14 February.
Montagu Square.
Royal Literary Fund. Not seen.

Trollope is studying the work of an applicant for a grant. He begs off an appearance at the committee meeting. 'My time is growing very short. There has been a great deal of frost. Horses are expensive joys—and I wish to get the few days that are left to me.' Records of the Royal Literary Fund show that Trollope attended no meetings between 10 February and November.

578. To OCTAVIAN BLEWITT. 14 February.
Montagu Square.
Royal Literary Fund. Not seen.

Trollope writes later the same day, asking for Miss A.'s bibliography. 'Since writing this morning I have been keeping the Sabbath holy with Miss A. But the work in the periodicals is not marked with her name, except as to two papers!!! You had better send me tomorrow a list of her tales. The papers are full of consecutive portions of novels some of which are doubtless hers.'

essays, and political squibs. He was an ardent controversialist and an ardent Tory. In his early days he was known as the 'King of the Bohemians', flouting many of the conventions.

[1] Trollope must have had *Is he Popenjoy?* in mind for Bentley. *The American Senator* was not begun until he arrived in Australia. The contract is described in Sadleir, *Bibliography*, pp. 305–6.

579. To OCTAVIAN BLEWITT. 16 February.
Montagu Square.
Royal Literary Fund. Not seen.

Trollope recommends a small grant for Miss A. on the ground that 'her literary merit, though not high, should be acknowledged. . . . The lady is evidently industrious.'

580. To NICHOLAS TRÜBNER. 23 February.
Montagu Square. *Parrish Collection.*

23, February 1875.
(39, Montagu Square.)

My dear Mr Trübner

I think you are right to fix the date of the first letter as appearing on July 3rd — I find that we might manage a week earlier, but that it would crowd us at last. I will therefore so far take the paper[1] as my guide.

But I think you have made the succession of letters unnecessarily rapid. Even in the beginning of August when the closest work would come you allow 33 days between the arrival and the publication. The effect would be to cause me to write my letters without the advantages which a somewhat prolonged sojourn would give. Instead of posting 4 letters on May 18 from Melbourne I would send 3—and on June 15—3 instead of 4—on July 13—3 instead of 4,—allowing 6 instead of 3 to come by subsequent Mails— I think you will find that this will amply fill your wants as to time—

Doubtless you have a copy of the table and your clerk will perhaps look at this, so that we may decide on Friday.

I generally write on paper such as I enclose. Could the envelopes you kindly propose to supply be made large enough to send this? Or would you suggest any other paper? You spoke of a manifold writer? That I presume would have paper of a peculiar size. Could you get one for me? I would willingly pay the cost? [*sic*]

Yours always
ANTHONY TROLLOPE

[1] Probably a schedule drawn up by Trübner.

581. To Nicholas Trübner. 26 February.
Montagu Square. *Parrish Collection.*

Trollope signs the agreement.[1] 'I trust you may get the full 20 subscribers.'

582. To Frederic Chapman. 26 February.
Parrish Collection.

26 Feb. 1875

(39, Montagu Square.)

My dear Chapman,

I have to day sent back for Press the last sheets of the Prime Minister. The work is to come out in 8 parts, and each part is to contain 10 chapters. The whole novel comprises 80 chapters. The first part is to appear in October.[2]

I think we had better arrange to do nothing about the other story,—'an Eye for an Eye,'—unless you can refer to me. I should not like it to be placed here or there without my sanction.

Affectionately yours

Anthony Trollope

583. To Rose Trollope. 4 March.
Parrish Collection.

Rome 4. March 1875

Dearest Love,

I have got here safely but not without distressing adventures. At Bologna we were snowed up & could not get any further that night. That was at 3.30 am. Then we were to start again at 7.am. In those four hours I had to make my way up to the hotel through the snow and go to bed & come down again,—that, or sit in the station. I did go to the Inn, but was almost snowed up in getting there. It was awful work, consequently I lost a day & a half in getting to Rome. I reached here at 10 this morning & start again tomorrow morning— Coming here I had altogether

---

[1] Trollope was to receive £15 for each letter, with an additional £5 per letter should the number of newspapers subscribing reach 18.

[2] *The Prime Minister* appeared in eight monthly parts, Nov. (not Oct.) 1875–June 1876.

4 hours of bed,—including Paris & Bologna, but was not very tired. I am writing now at 10 pm & rather long for bed.

Tom will send you the list of my mothers books. I do not care twopence about that Kingsley memorial.[1] The folk are very pressing & may wait. Grove[2] was the man who applied to me about it.

Give my best love to Harry & Flo.[3] God bless you. Keep up your heart & be as happy as you can.

Yours ever & always

A T

584. To Rose Trollope. 6 March.
Parrish Collection.

Naples.   Saturday 6 March 1875.

Night.   10 pm

Dearest Love,

I have got so far all right, and I write one line to say that I live in the hopes of reaching the boat at Brindisi on Monday morning. If I do not I shall take one plunge into the Adriatic. But I think I shall. I was at the P. O here today and there was no letter from you. I will call again tomorrow, but I know I shall have no time to write after coming back to the hotel from the pictures,—as I shall have to dine & leave at 4-pm.

Tom came here with me & we got here at 5—yesterday. Naples itself is by no means particularly interesting. The bay is not equal either to Dublin or New York. But there are fine views of it if you climb on a big hill as we did today. We went to Pompeeii [*sic*] today, and that is interesting,—very. The old Roman streets and houses as they existed 1800 years ago when Pompeii was destroyed by the erruption [*sic*] of Vesuvius, have now been almost all uncovered, and comprise a vast town of which the

---

[1] The Charles Kingsley Memorial Fund, organized in Feb. 1875, proposed the enlargement of Eversley Church and the erection of a bust of Kingsley by Woolner in Westminster Abbey. Trollope's name is listed among prominent people supporting the fund. See *Charles Kingsley: His Letters and Memories of His Life,* ed. by his wife (New York, 1887), p. 490.

[2] Sir George Grove.

[3] Florence Bland, Trollope's orphan niece, daughter of one of Rose Heseltine Trollope's two sisters. She lived continuously with the Trollopes after 1863.

ruins are perfect,—not tumbled down & in disorder, but the whole regular & still well built as regards the lower portion of the works. The streets are as clear as the streets of a modern town, and the separate houses, theatres, temples, forums &c as well marked. I had never before realised to myself what Pompeeii was. Tomorrow we go to see the pictures; and then I am off. As I said before Naples as a town is not interesting as Rome, Florence or Genoa— It is very much bigger than either, & I have been surprised by the enormous number of private carriages on the fashionable drive,—apparently as many as are in Hyde Park in June.

God bless you dearest. I hope I shall find a letter tomorrow. My best love to Harry & Flo. Of course I shall hear from all at Point de Galle.

I have been troubled with sore throat, which has made me weak & I have been very glad of the quinine. I shall get rid of it when I get to sea.

Yours ever & always
A. T.

Pray write & say that you are well & happy—if possible

585. To ROSE TROLLOPE. 10 March.
Parrish Collection.

Ship 'Nigani' 10 March 1875

(39, Montagu Square.)

Dearest Love,

I wrote a wretched scrawl when I got on board, which I trust was posted at Brindisi. Since then I have been three days at sea and have written my first letter to Trübner,—about Italy, having pumped Tom for the contents. Garibaldi & the brigands make up the subject. The world you will say has had enough of Garibaldi & the brigands. But then the world has had enough of every thing, and there is nothing left but rechauffes.

Tomorrow we reach Alexandria early & then have, I fear, a bad day, with a worse night to follow, in the cars across the desert. After that there is a fortnight at sea, and I hope that I shall get again to my novel.

I find the working with that multiplying apparatus is a bore, not but that it is easy enough while you are doing it, but that it is so long & troublesome to arrange, and then it dirties your fingers in a disgusting manner.

We have nobody particular on board except Captain Shaw,[1] the man who puts out the fires in London, and who is in his way a hero. But he is a prig, & awfully conceited,—having been manifestly spoilt by aristocratic admirers. I never like the P. & O Captains. They always give themselves airs as fine gentlemen, —a fault from which the Cunarders are free. But in this respect we only have 3 days. The Peshawar[2] will be the treat. I send a line for Harry & another for Flo— I suppose I had better address my next letter to you to John's care, at the P. O., as it will be from Ceylon on 3 April—& will not reach London till 26th of that month. This will be posted at Alexandria and it is of course possible that I may find letters from you at the Peshawar and be able to answer them at Suez;—but I believe the ship sails as quickly as possible after our arrival. Nor do I know that you intended to direct to me there. I ought to have had newspapers at Brindisi, but got none. I see, however, from a borrowed paper that Kenealy has begun to make a beast of himself.[3] They bore with him then; but I trust they will find that they will not bear with him long.

God bless you, dearest love— I do hope you will enjoy your trip on the continent. I doubt your liking Hamburg or Dantzig, but I do not doubt that you will like Dresden & the Dutch pictures.

Ever & always your own
A. T.

[1] Eyre Massey Shaw, later Sir Eyre (1830–1906), head of the London Metropolitan Fire Brigade, 1861–91.

[2] The ship which Trollope boarded at Suez.

[3] Edward Vaughan Hyde Kenealy (1819–80), leading counsel for Orton, the Tichborne claimant. His extravagant and abusive conduct of the case was such that he was dispatented by the Lord Chancellor and disbarred by Gray's Inn. In Feb. 1875 he was elected M.P. for Stoke and immediately made himself obnoxious to the House.

586. To Rose Trollope. 17 March.
Parrish Collection.

St. Patricks day.   17, March—75

Aden[1]

(39, Montagu Square.)

Though we ar'nt at Aden yet but only reaching it.

Dearest Love,

I have got so far, and have not as yet lost my luggage. I was in a great fret about it at Suez till the things turned up. We have had it hot enough down the Red Sea, altho' all the old Indians & Chinese folk swear that the Red Sea was never so cool before. The thermeter [*sic*] (to tell us how hot it is,) rises between 80 & 90. Luckily we have not a crowded ship & I have got a large cabin to myself with a regular desk fixed, as I had on board the Great Britain, and I have done my work very regularly. We were so hurried through Egypt that I could write no letter about that. I fear we shall reach Aden too late tonight to allow of my saying anything about that—but I shall try.

I shall send this letter to the Square, as the mail via Brindisi will be due in London on 12 April. From Ceylon I shall of course address to John Tilly. Our passengers are not very bright but by no means unpleasant. The food is abominable. I have read the first volume of Tennant's [*sic*] Ceylon,[2] and I almost doubt whether I can get thro the second. Nothing longer or duller ever was written.

I hope you are all getting on well, and that things go squarely. By the time this reaches you, you will be preparing for your own migration. I wish I knew whether the house was likely to be let, but of course I cannot know.

One great misfortune I have had. You remember my big bottle of ink. When I unlocked my desk I found the bottle smashed to pieces inside the case, which had not been opened, and the ink of course had covered every thing. There were three shirts on top put in to keep things steady. I wish you could see those three

---

[1] Aden: a fortified seaport and coaling station on the south-west coast of Arabia.

[2] Sir James Emerson Tennent (1804–69), statesman and traveller, author of *Ceylon* (London, 1859). He and Trollope were old friends, Trollope's account book showing that they dined together 12 Feb. 1868.

shirts, and there were 100 loose cigars. I have not yet tried how cigars, bathed in ink, smoke—but I shall try. Some wretch had pitched the desk down like a ball, and all my beautiful white paper!— However that is now simply black-edged.

God bless you, dearest, dearest love. I do so hope that you will be happy & enjoy yourself. Tell me every thing of your doings & goings, and of your travelling adventures. Best love to Flo— I send a line to Harry.

Ever & always your own
A. T.

587. To NICHOLAS TRÜBNER. 17 March. Off Aden.
Parrish Collection.

Trollope sends a duplicate of his first letter. 'We were so hurried through Egypt, that I could not (honestly) write anything about the country. We are now reaching Aden, but I fear will be there only by night. If I can see the place, which is curious in its way, I will write you a letter.'

588. To NICHOLAS TRÜBNER. 10 April. Galle, Ceylon.
Parrish Collection.

Trollope sends four letters. 'It is at this moment so hot I can hardly write this note.'

589. To NICHOLAS TRÜBNER. 13 May. Melbourne.
Parrish Collection.

Trollope sends letters 7–10. On 24 May he sends the duplicates.

590. To NICHOLAS TRÜBNER. 24 May. Australian Club.
Parrish Collection.

Trollope is travelling 'up the country' tomorrow, and sends letter 11.

591. To NICHOLAS TRÜBNER. 3 June.
Mortray, Grenfell, N.S.W. *Parrish Collection.*

Trollope sends letters 12 and 13, and briefs Trübner on his itinerary for the rest of the trip.

592. To MRS. NEVILL.[1] 21 June.
Harvard College Library.

Mortray, Grenfell, N. S. Wales.

                                        June 21, 1875.
My dear Mrs Nevill,   (39, Montagu Square.)

Your letter of the 7th April reached me here, at my sons
station in Australia, the other day. I did receive your telegram in
Ceylon, and wrote to you an answer to it from Galle— I was
then on my way out here having come from England with no
intention of going to India. I think you must have got my letter as
it was written to the address given in your telegram. I had heard
all about your marriage, and though I never met your husband,[2]
had often heard of him and his mother from both my mother and
brother.

I hope I need not say how very much I should like to see you
again and to have a talk of old days. I shall never forget the last
day I met your father, the evening before I started on my first
journey to Australia. We dined together and I little thought then
that I should never see him again.

How I shall go home from hence I do not yet know, but I
purpose being in London by the end of next October. If I should
go by India I will do my best to get to you: but I do not at all
know how that may be. Should I do so I will let you know before
hand.

                    Yours always most sincerely
                        ANTHONY TROLLOPE

593. To MARY HOLMES. 8 July.
Parrish Collection.

Mortray Station, Grenfell
New South Wales.   ⟨39, Montague Square.⟩
My dear Miss Holmes,   8 July, 1875

Your letter of 3 May has followed me hither, round half the
world. I left England on 28 February, having a son here whom
I am forced to visit as he with his wife and bairns and hands full

---

[1] Julia Lever Nevill (1833–97), the daughter of Trollope's old friend and
fellow novelist, Charles Lever.
[2] Colonel Nevill was commander of the forces of the Nizam of Hyderabad.

of work cannot visit me. I am living in the middle of the bush, as the primeval forest is here called, in most unsophisticated simplicity, eating mutton and drinking tea;—though perhaps the simplicity would be less sophisticated if I ate Kangaroos and drank nothing but muddy water.

Your criticisms on my own work always please me, though I know them to be too eulogistic. What you say of the faults of Montagu's[1] character is quite true,—though your strictures do not go far enough. The character is badly done throughout, and fails in interest. Hetta also is bad, and you are quite right in saying that Mrs Hurtle, (who is well done) is kept too long on the stage. But she was wanted to give an interest to the last chapters, as Hetta &c were uninteresting, all which you found out.

Melmotte however is good, and the Longestaffes, and Nidderdale & all the 'rowdy' lot. And I think I am right in presuming that such people as the Longestaffes would object to the desecration of a *Jew alliance*

I read Scotts novels also from time to time and marvel at the power of story-telling, at the infinite imagination, and 20-horsepower of vivacity— But there is an infinity of padding, and a great amount of very lax work. Taking them through I regard Ivanhoe and Old Mortality as the best. But he never wrote anything, in my mind, as good as Esmonde.

I hope to be back in November.

Yours very faithfully
ANTHONY TROLLOPE

594. TO NICHOLAS TRÜBNER. 15 July.
   Mortray, Grenfell, N.S.W. *Parrish Collection*.

Trollope sends letter 16 and tells of his plans to return via Fiji and San Francisco.

595. TO NICHOLAS TRÜBNER. 9 August. Sydney.
   Parrish Collection.

Trollope sends letter 17. He will be in London by 30 October.

[1] This and the following criticisms relate to *The Way We Live Now*.

596. To NICHOLAS TRÜBNER. 3 September.
Auckland, New Zealand. *Parrish Collection.*

Trollope sends letter 18. The last he will bring with him. 'You will observe that the one I send now is written half on the multiplying paper and half on other paper. The black paper has become unfit for use. I got other in Melbourne, but it was of no service.'

597. To NICHOLAS TRÜBNER. 13 October.[1] Boston.
Parrish Collection.

Letter 19 has not yet been posted. 'I regret that I could not be earlier with it, but circumstances have made it impossible.'

598. To GEORGE HENRY LEWES. 1 November.
Mrs. E. S. Ouvry.

1. November 1875
(39, Montagu Square.)

My dear Lewes,

I have just completed my second journey round the world, having returned home on Saturday night. I was greeted by your volume on actors and acting & write to say how pleased I am by the book,[2] & by the compliment.[3] I have never studied the science or theory of acting as you have done,—but in almost all that you say you carry me with you. I sometimes find myself differing [? with] you as to trifles in regard to character. I have always fancied that Shakespeare intended Hamlet to be, not mad, but erratic in the brain, 'on & off'—first a little ajar, & then right again, & then again astray. In the scene you quote as displaying want of reverence it has seemed to me that the language has been intended to ape want of reverence,—to pretend to Horatio & the others that he was at ease &c &c.[4]

Your admiration of Fechter[5] I cannot understand. To me Macready[6] was a man of supreme intelligence, but with no his-

---

[1] This letter is dated, obviously in error, 13 Nov.
[2] Lewes's *On Actors and the Art of Acting.*
[3] The book is prefaced (pp. v–xii) by an 'Epistle to Anthony Trollope'.
[4] See Lewes's discussion, especially pp. 138–45.
[5] See letter No. 449, *supra.*
[6] William Charles Macready (1793–1873), the distinguished actor and stage manager. He won great renown in the part of King Lear.

trionic genius. He never moved me to tears. The greatest actors I ever saw were E Keane,[1] Rachel,[2] Mars,[3] Got,[4] Lemaitre[5]— a French lady whose name, beginning with B,[6] I forget, and M[rs] Yates,[7]—yes,—and a Frenchman whose name I also forget still alive, beginning with D,[8] and I would add Robson.[9]

I will come up next Sunday, hoping to find you.

Yours always with best love to your wife

Most affectionately

A. T.

599. To GEORGE BENTLEY. 9 November.
Montague Square. *Parrish Collection.*

Trollope wishes to consult Bentley 'about our novel'. He asks him to call at 11.30 a.m., 'if you would come and breakfast at that hour. It seems late, but I breakfast after I have done my day's work.'

600. To ? H. M. ALDEN.[10] 11 November. London.
Henry E. Huntington Library.

Trollope agrees to write an article on Australia. 'It would contain nothing as to fauna or flora as I am not at home on such matters. I should deal with the Kangaroo as a squatter and a sportsman. I should think rather of men and women and their modes of life.'[11]

[1] Edmund Kean (1787–1833), perhaps the greatest tragedian of his day.

[2] Élisa Rachel Félix (1820–58), known as Rachel, the great character actress of the Comédie Française.

[3] Anne-Françoise-Hippolyte Boutet-Monvel, Mlle Mars (1779–1847), a popular French actress. See *Nouvelle Biographie Générale*, xxxiii. 955–9.

[4] François Jules Edmond Got (1822–1901), a French actor, playwright, and diarist.

[5] Frédérick-Lemaître (1800–76), a French actor. See *Nouvelle Biographie Générale*, xxxii. 573–5.

[6] Possibly Augustine Suzanne Brohan (1807–87).

[7] Elizabeth Brunton Yates, wife of Frederick Yates, manager of the Theatre Royal. She was the mother of Trollope's colleague in the Post Office, Edmund Yates.

[8] Possibly Louis Delaunay (1826–1903).

[9] Thomas Frederick Robson (?1822–64), an actor highly skilled in burlesque and farce.

[10] On the basis of letter No. 607, *infra*, I judge that the addressee is Henry Mills Alden (1836–1919), the distinguished editor of *Harper's Magazine* for half a century, 1869–1919.

[11] The article was not written.

606. To GEORGE BENTLEY. 7 December.
Montagu Square. *Parrish Collection.*

Trollope has taken the manuscript of his new novel to Virtue's. 'I find that
I cannot change the name,—which indeed, (The American Senator) I feel
to be in itself a good name. I am sure that nobody can give a name to a novel
but the author.'

607. To H. M. ALDEN. 8 December. London.
Parrish Collection.

Trollope cannot undertake to supply illustrations for the proposed article
on Australia, and he therefore terminates the negotiations.

608. To ?[1] 27 December.
Parrish Collection.

27, December 1875.
(39, Montagu Square.)

My dear *Professor,*
I was delighted to see your name. Do come on Saturday, at
11.30, to breakfast. We will have a rare good time, talking over
the old things,—old though so very recent,—Captain Brown,
my aversion the New Zealand man, the pretty girl who went up
the mountains with me, & all the rest of it. Only a terrible misfortune has happened. I have 'swore off' smoking. But you shall
have your pipe (the old tobacco) or cigars among the books. It
will be quite a delight.

Yours always
ANTHONY TROLLOPE

[1] Possibly Charles Badham (1813–84), classical scholar, professor of
classics and logic at the University of Sydney, 1867–84. Trollope met him
in Australia (see letter No. 824, *infra*). He was described by Grote as
'the greatest of living scholars' and by Newman as 'the first Greek scholar
of the day'.

1 8 7 6

609. To Mr. Waller.[1] 10 January.
Parrish Collection.

10 January 1876.

(Athenaeum Club
Pall Mall S.W.)

My dear Waller,

I send you some books as a wedding present, to 59 M. Square. When you bring your wife home I will come and inscribe your names. You will find that I have burdened you with a great many Elizabethan plays. When you have read them all and thoroughly digested them, so as to be able to answer satisfactorily all questions as to plot, language, character, and customs, I will send you some more.

In the mean time tell your wife with my kindest regards that I hope she will be disposed to regard me with friendly eyes when she comes up to London. Yours with all good wishes, very affectionately

Anthony Trollope

610. To Charles Hall.[2] 12 January. Montagu Square.
Parrish Collection.

Trollope extends an invitation. 'Hunting or no hunting on Saturday, you will dine here Friday. We shall have a rubber. If you like to sleep for the chance of the hunting write & say so.'

611. To George Bentley. 25 February.
Montagu Square. *Parrish Collection.*

Trollope asks that the printer begin on his novel and that sheets be sent to America in order that Harper's can publish simultaneously.

[1] Possibly Samuel Edmund Waller (1850–1903), genre painter, who exhibited at the Royal Academy, 1871–1902.
[2] Charles Hall, later Sir Charles (1843–1900), was recorder of London and Privy Councillor.

612. To ? 1 March.
Estate of Carroll A. Wilson.

March 1, 1876
(39, Montagu Square.)

Gentlemen— I *hate* sitting for a photograph. I will however, look in some day when I am near you. I wont fix a day as I should have it before me, for execution,—as though I were then to be hanged

Yours truly
ANTHONY TROLLOPE

613. To RICHARD HENRY DANA, Jr. 22 March.
Massachusetts Historical Society.

22 March 1876.
(39, Montagu Square.)

My dear Mr Dana

I write a line to tell you with how very great satisfaction it was heard here that you were to come among us as Minister from the United States.[1] I see something of most sets and of both parties and I have heard no dissentient voice. It seems to have been thought a great thing that the President, in the emergency now existing, should have had recourse to a man whom all would esteem, and of whom his country may be proud in all relations.

At the present moment we do not know how the result may be. We see that the Committee of the F. R[.],[2] has reported to the Senate against the nomination; and, in English eyes, the American Senate is dishonoured by such a report from its Committee. But the Senate is not, I presume, bound by its Committee, and we may still hope to see you.

No doubt you hear from many here, and my testimony may be unnecessary. I wish, however, that you should know from as many sources as possible how anxious we in England are that you should come to us.

Very faithfully yours
ANTHONY TROLLOPE

[1] The Senate refused to confirm Grant's nomination of Dana. Dana had annoyed party leaders by his refusal to play politics, and his reputation had been damaged by slanders in a lawsuit over his edition of Wheaton's *Elements of International Law* (1866).
[2] The Foreign Relations Committee.

614. To ANNA C. STEELE. 25 March.
Parrish Collection.

25 March 1876
(39, Montague Square.)

My dear Mrs Steele,

I am made very unhappy by what you say as to your mother. I often take it as matter of reproach to myself that I never now see either you or her. If you were at Rivenhall I would hasten to go down to see you both.

I think you must be wrong in your ideas about your novel.[1] You would wish to limit Chapman to 600. That means (after free copies) a sale of 550. He now gets 15/ each for 3 vol novels. The total realised would be £412–10/— The expense of a 3 vol novel, (including paper, printing & advertisements), with some few extra publishing expenses is about £200. This does not leave enough for him to pay you a fitting price, let alone his own profit. If you only sell 600 copies, I do not think he could give you above £150, which is a very small sum. I shall be most glad to act for you if I can,—and would think nothing a trouble,—but before doing so I should have to see you. Could you come up here some morning & breakfast at 11.30—or later in the day if it suited you better,—as I feel it would.

Alas yes, Essex hunting is over for me. I will whisper something further into your ear when I see you.

Yours always
ANTHONY TROLLOPE

615. To CECILIA MEETKERKE. 10 April.
Estate of Carroll A. Wilson.

10 April 1876
(39, Montagu Square.)

My dear Mrs Meetkerke,

The date of your letter, 3 April, shocks me. But I have hoped before this to have seen John Morley who is the learned and indefatigable Editor of the Fortnightly— He however [has] been out of town, and I have not been able to catch him.

But why the Fortnightly? Of all it is the most learned,—and

----

[1] *Condoned*, 3 vols. (London, 1877).

with an Editor so indefatigable that he will weigh every word
you write down to the last pronoun. Perhaps you like to be so
weighed. All I can do however is to write to him, which I have
done.

Indeed I have nothing whatever to do with magazines. A
novel of mine is about to come out in Temple Bar, as it might
come out in any other periodical, but with the publication I have
nothing to do. I do not even know who is the Editor.[1] I simply
sell my story to the proprietors.

Remember me most kindly to Adolphus. I hope I shall see you
as you come through London.

Most sincerely yours
ANTHONY TROLLOPE

616. To ANNA C. STEELE. 14 April. London.
Mr. and Mrs. Maurice Fitzgerald.

Trollope has arranged with Chapman for the publication of a manuscript
unnamed. 'When the book is going through the press do not omit to hurry
him if hurrying seems to be necessary— An author has always to remember
that his work is not as important to the publisher as it is to him.'[2]

617. To HENRY MERIVALE TROLLOPE. 30 April.
Muriel Rose Trollope.

30 April 1876

My dear Harry,

I wish you to accept as a gift from me, given you now, the
accompanying pages which contain a memoir of my life. My
intention is that they shall be published after my death, and be
edited by you. But I leave it altogether to your discretion whether
to publish or to suppress the work;—and also to your discretion
whether any part or what part shall be omitted. But I would not
wish that anything should be added to the memoir. If you wish

[1] George Bentley performed the functions of both proprietor and editor.
[2] This is the last letter to Mrs. Steele, except possibly for one curious
undated letter published by Mrs. Bradhurst (*A Century of Letters*, pp.
262–3). If it be from Trollope, it can be dated by a reference to an article
in *The Nineteenth Century* as of 1879. But the address, the content, and the
style are so unfamiliar that I have somewhat arbitrarily decided to exclude
it from this collection. I think that Mrs. Bradhurst may have misread the
initialed signature. Letter No. 643 *infra* may, however, be addressed to
Mrs. Steele.

to say any word as from yourself, let it be done in the shape of a preface or introductory chapter.

I trust you to be careful in editing the work, as much has, I fear, been written hurriedly. Where quotations have been made references have been given in pencil, for your guidance as to correct printing,—but not for publication.

I should wish the book to be published by Fred Chapman if he is in business at the time of my death;—but of course you will do the best you can as to terms, if not with him, then with some other publisher. The volume ought to be worth some hundreds of pounds to you. You will understand that whatever are the proceeds, they are to be yours, and not to go to my estate.

Now [? Need] I say how dearly I have loved you.

Your most affectionate father,
ANTHONY TROLLOPE

The publication, if made at all, should be effected as soon as possible after my death.[1]

618. To A. H. DOOLEY.[2] 1 May.
Parrish Collection.

May 1, 1876
(39, Montagu Square.)

My dear Sir,

There is nothing I value more than greetings from your side of the water. I therefore thank you most heartily for your letter of the 6 April, and assure you that I am pleased to be told that what I have written has given pleasure to you who are so far away from me.

I did give a lecture some time last winter on the matter of 'Reading'[3]—I did not print it myself, nor do I think it was

---

[1] Henry Trollope published this letter in his preface, including the postscript, but omitting the three preceding paragraphs (from 'I trust you to be careful'). They have been restored in Mr. Sadleir's new edition for the Oxford 'World's Classics'. I did not have the full text in time for inclusion in my own edition.

[2] A. H. Dooley was a bookseller and stationer at Terre Haute, Indiana, U.S.A.

[3] On 2 Mar. 1876, at the second annual distribution of prizes to students of the Quebec Institute, Trollope lectured on 'The Art of Reading'. See *The Times*, 4 Mar. 1876, p. 11.

printed;—but I do not know. Some one had the only MS which I possessed, & what became of it I do not know.

Yours very faithfully
ANTHONY TROLLOPE

619. To MARY HOLMES. 7 May.
Parrish Collection.

May 7, 1876   (39, Montagu Square.)

My dear Miss Holmes,

I do not know how many letters of yours I have unanswered. Till I write to you, I always keep them by me,—and then they go, as do all my letters. Now I have three,—two from Chester Hill and one from Cheltenham. In the last, which is altogether musical, you tell me you have a piano, and that all your neglected forces have come back to you. I wish you could hear our Bice play & sing,—(sing especially.) I do not suppose you have heard of her. She is my brother's daughter—was born in Italy, & has lived there all her life, but is here now. Blumenthal[1] & Arthur Sullivan[2] tell me that they know nothing in private life like her voice. She affects me, as nothing else that I know in music.

I have not yet seen Annie T. though I have been to see her two or three times. My wife has seen her, and found her very fairly well. Him, (Leslie Stephen) I have seen various times. But a man recovers himself from all that so much quicker than a woman.

The Prime Minister is with me an old story—I do not even know how far it has gone. But, remember, when you read it,—if you do read it,—that though I myself am prepared to stand up for the character of the Prime Minister, and for all his surroundings, I acknowledge the story of the soi-disant hero, Lopez, and all that has to do with him, to be bad.

I send you in the Temple Bar the first number of another novel of mine The American Senator. If I can manage it, I will cause the numbers to be sent as they come out.

Yours ever faithfully
ANTHONY TROLLOPE

[1] Jacques Blumenthal (1829–1905), pianist to Queen Victoria and composer of songs which won lasting popularity. He and Trollope were close friends at the Garrick Club, frequently dining together.

[2] Sir Arthur Sullivan (1842–1900), the composer of international fame.

620. To LIZZIE ALBERT. 10 May.
Parrish Collection.

To a young lady who asks for an autograph Trollope writes: 'So slight a request so prettily asked I certainly could not refuse.'

621. To MARY HOLMES. 27 May.
Parrish Collection.

May 27, 1876.   (39, Montagu Square.)

My dear Miss Holmes,

I write a line chiefly to say that you ought to have had the Temple Bar, (five numbers,) direct from the publisher,—to whom I gave the order to pack it because he could do it better than we can. But if you have not got it, (or do not get it at the beginning of any month), do not scruple to let me know.

Daniel D.[1] has been a trying book to me. You perhaps know how I love and admire her. She is to me a very dear friend indeed. It is so, whether I have told you so or not. But I think D. D. is all wrong in art. Not only is the oil flavoured on every page, (which is a great fault)—but with the smell of the oil comes so little of the brilliance which the oil should give! She is always striving for effects which she does not produce. All you say of Gwendoline's character is true. She disgusts, and does not interest,—as a woman may even though she disgusts. But Homer was allowed to nod once or twice, & why not the author of Adam Bede and Romola?

If you have any good Christian feeling for me,—as I think you have,—you will, after what you have written to me about tobacco, be glad to hear that I have gotten down from 6 cigars a day *to one a week*,—which is about equal to the horse's allowance of a straw a day. But I, up to this, am not brought to apparent death[.]

Yours always

ANTHONY TROLLOPE

In earnest—do tell me if you do not get the Magazine.

[1] George Eliot's *Daniel Deronda* had just been published.

622. To ANNE THACKERAY. 31 May. Montagu Square.
Muriel Rose Trollope.

Trollope forwards a letter, probably from Mary Holmes.[1] 'I do not like to send on to you the enclosed from a very constant correspondent of mine without saying how glad I should be if I could see you.'

623. To GEORGE BENTLEY. 9 June. Montagu Square.
Parrish Collection.

Trollope has forwarded to Chapman Bentley's note in reference to Sampson Low's inquiry about the foreign rights in a novel.

624. To MARY HOLMES. 15 June.
Parrish Collection.

June 15, 1876   (39, Montagu Square.)

My dear Miss Holmes,

I write a line for two purposes. But first will excuse myself for writing only a line. When I have done my daily work,—which I really do daily—I have always a certain number of letters to write, which are de rigueur. Then I am tired of my pen,—often indeed sick of it; and cannot get myself to write more.

My first purpose is to say in reference to the P. M.[2] that though in former novels certain well-known political characters, such as Disraeli and Gladstone, have been taken as models for such fictitious personages as Daubeny and Gresham, it has only been as to their particular tenets. There is nothing of personal characteristic here. When that has been attempted by me,—as in all the Palliser people,—the old Duke, the new Duke and Lady Glencora, there has been no distant idea in my own mind of any living person. They are pure creations; and (as I think) the best I ever made. The Lopez part of the book has only been to me a shoe-horn for the other.

My second object is to send you a little book I wrote some

---

[1] See letter No. 624, *infra.*
[2] *The Prime Minister.*

time since about Australian life. The Harry Heathcote is my boy
Frederic,—or very much the same.

Yours always faithfully
A T

Of course I sent your letter to Miss Thackeray

If you *dont* get H. H. let me know. It will be posted together
with this[.]

625. To GEORGE BENTLEY. 19 June. Montagu Square.
Parrish Collection.

Trollope is going abroad for the summer and asks for several months'
proof in advance.

626. To GEORGE BENTLEY. 5 July. Montagu Square.
Parrish Collection.

Trollope acknowledges two more sheets from the printers and £100
from Bentley. 'I am glad you like the story as it goes on.'

627. To TOM TAYLOR. 7 July. Montagu Square.
J. H. Spencer. Not seen.

Trollope agrees to write to the Postmaster-General's office about some
signatures, apparently to a petition.

628. To ? 14 July. Montagu Square.
British Museum.

Trollope cannot participate in a proposed work on Cornwall. 'I have
nothing to do with Cornwall, and cannot therefore have the honour of
associating myself in any way with the County [*sic*]. I once placed the scene
of a very short tale somewhere on its coast;[1] but I have done the same
in reference to almost all counties and all coasts.'

---

[1] *Malachi's Cove*, the best known (but by no means the best) of Trollope's
short stories.

629. To W. P. FRITH. 10 November. *Not traced.* W. P.
Frith, *My Autobiography and Reminiscences*, 2 vols.
(New York, 1888), ii. 281–2.

39 Montagu Square
November 10, 1876.

My dear Frith,—Do you know Parson Rogers[1] of Bishopsgate—
a man who, among parsons, is about the best in these parts? He
has a giving away of prizes at his place to be effected on Tuesday, November 28, at which I have undertaken to do the speechify-
ing (which will not therefore be long). Talking to me about it
yesterday, he said that he would very much like to get some one
or two others, especially an artist, as the younkers like to see,
and be seen by, persons of whom they have heard. I said I would
ask you to come with me, and he bade me say how delighted he
would be if you would do so.

If so, you would accompany me, and we would dine with him
at six P.M. at his city parsonage in Devonshire Square. Do come
if you can. He is a very dear friend of mine.[2]

Yours always,
ANTHONY TROLLOPE

630. To KATE FIELD. 1 December.
Princeton University Library.

A forgotten engagement will prevent Trollope from keeping his appointment with Kate. He is going into the country but will call on his return.

631. To KATE FIELD. 12 December.
Boston Public Library.

(39, Montagu Square.)
My dear Kate,
Would you come and eat your dinner with us on Christmas
day at 7.30. I write because my wife is out of town— I add this
for the sake of propriety. Tom is ever so thankful for the newspapers.

Yours always
12 Dec 1876　　　　　　A. T.

[1] William Rogers (1819–96), educational and social reformer, chaplain
in ordinary to Queen Victoria, 1857; founder of schools.
[2] Frith continues, 'Trollope made a good speech, and I made a bad one.'

632. To CECILIA MEETKERKE. 14 December.
Estate of Carroll A. Wilson.

Thursday 14 Dec[r][I]
(39, Montagu Square.)

My dear M[rs] Meetkerke

Would you and Adolphus come and dine on the Tuesday. My wife, as now arranged, comes home on the morning of that day. Try whether a good tea at 5 wont enable you to get on till 7.45 for dinner. The truth is in such matters one has to do as other people around one.

What you say of it puts me in mind of the poor parson who was invited to stay a day or two with his bishop up in London. He arrived at 5 pm and they brought him tea up into his bed room. He thought it odd but took his tea humbly and went to bed. When dinner was on the table at 8 they came up to look for him and found him fast asleep.

Adolphus need not even change his trowsers if he [dis]likes all efforts in that direction.

Yours always
A. T.

633. To GEORGE BENTLEY. 16 December.
Parrish Collection.

16. December 1876
(39, Montagu Square)

My dear M[r] Bentley,

If you will read the enclosed you will see to what high (but unreal) honours it is supposed that I have risen through my temporary association with your magazine.

You will see too that the writer, of whom I never before heard, *has conceived a favourable idea of my character*, which is also pleasant.

Whether on this account or from his own merit you will entertain his application you must decide. I have referred him to yourself.

Very faithfully yours
ANTHONY TROLLOPE

[I] The year is not indicated on this letter, but in this relative period Thursday the 14th fell in 1876.

634. To MARY HOLMES. 27 December.
Parrish Collection.

Decr 27, 1876. (39, Montagu Square.)

My dear Miss Holmes,

One short line to wish you a happy Christmas and new year, and all good things. In all your letters there is ever so much that I should like to answer,—only there would be no end.

I do think that nations are as individuals are—not alike,—but to be judged by the same laws, and that there are no other laws by which to judge them. If you have been deceived ten times by either one or the other, you will on the eleventh be less ready to believe.

As to the workhouse argument, there comes the question of duty. I should not let a faineant son go to the workhouse because it wd be my duty to keep him out;—but I should cease to allow him to squander my money.

I do think the Russian better than the Turk, (infinitely better) and looking back to history I find that in spite of blots which have stained this and the other Xtian sect, the Xtian religion has carried with it humanity & softness and hatred of cruelty wherever it has gone.

Then to run away from politics as far and as fast as you do, I do not at all think that the Senator from Mickewa will be unpopular in the U. S.—rather the reverse, as he is a thoroughly honest man wishing to do good, and is not himself half so absurd as the things which he criticises.

As for parson Manleverer [*sic*],[1] and Lord R. and the odious female, you must remember that it is the part of the satirist to be heavy on the classes he satirises;—not to deal out impartial justice to the world; but to pick out the evil things. With the parson my idea was not to hold an individual up to scorn but to ridicule the modes of patronage in our church.

Lord R is what he is, merely as an appendage to the odious female,—in whose character I wished to express the depth of my

---

[1] I do not understand this reference. There is a parson Mainwaring in *The American Senator*, but no Manleverer. Mr. Robert H. Taylor tells me that the manuscript of *The American Senator* reads 'Mainwaring'.

scorn for women who run down husbands,—an offence which I
do fear is gaining ground in this country.

I will own, (in your ear)—that Larry's early schooldays at
Cheltenham with his subsequent somewhat illiterate language
were the result of a long-ago-entertained dislike of Dean Close[1]
& Cheltenham School. *But that is quite for yourself.*

Florence will write soon. I have just completed all Cicero's
works from beginning to end. He was nearer to a Christian than
any unXtian that ever lived. And in the last two months I have
read the Fairy Queen aloud.[2]

Yours ever sincerely
A. T.

635. To FREDERIC CHAPMAN. [1876.]
Pierpont Morgan Library.

Trollope cannot keep an appointment because of his duties on the Copyright Commission, which sat in Apr. 1876 and for nearly a year thereafter.
See *Parliamentary Papers*, 1876, xxiv.

1 8 7 7

636. To NORMAN MACLEOD. 23 January.
National Library of Scotland.

Jany 23, 1877
(39, Montagu Square.)

My dear Macleod,

I have left with Mr Isbester[3] [*sic*] two short articles for your
judgment. 1st a story called The Telegraph Girl. 2d an account[4]
of the young women in the London Central Telegraph Office.[5]
The cause of the two was as follows.

Some weeks since I went to see these young women at work,
and being much struck with them, my imagination went to work

---

[1] Francis Close (1797–1882), evangelical divine, rector of Cheltenham,
dean of Carlisle.

[2] Trollope's record of his reading at this period, preserved in the Trollope
family archives, shows that with his exhaustive survey of the Elizabethan
drama nearly complete he was turning his attention to non-dramatic verse.

[3] W. Isbister, founder with Alexander Strahan of *Good Words*

[4] Published in *Good Cheer*, the 1877 Christmas number of *Good Words*.

[5] Published in *Good Words*, xviii (June 1877), 377–84.

and composed a little story about one. This, when written, seemed to be to nice [*sic*], and I took it to Ludgate Hill, suggested that it might suit Good Words, and saying that there need be no hurry about it. Then Mr Isbester suggested (on hearing my description of the girls work and of the excellence of their conduct) that I should give some such description in a separate article. This I have done, and there they both are. Should you use the two the description, which is the shorter, should come the first.

I think you will be gratified at the success of this branch of female employment.[1]

Yours always
ANTHONY TROLLOPE

637. To ARTHUR LEWIS.[2] 24 January.
Bradford A. Booth.

39 Montagu Square
24, January 1877

My dear Lewis,

I am much obliged to you for the printed copy of your correspondence with 'Truth.'[3] I have been discussing the matter in various circles and at different clubs and I have heard no difference of opinion as to the low rascality of the whole thing. The first attack was very bad; but the pretense at not believing the denial was worse. But the truth is that as such periodicals can only live by being rascally, it is useless to hope that they will cease to be so. The comfort is that no such periodicals live long, and therefore we know that they are not really popular or approved.

Yours always
ANTHONY TROLLOPE

[1] This letter was published with a note by W. M. Parker in *TLS*, 26 Oct. 1940, p. 548.

[2] Arthur Lewis, a member of the firm of Lewis & Allenby, theatrical agents. He married Ellen Terry's sister Kate.

[3] The first number of the magazine *Truth* carried an article (i [4 Jan. 1877], 2–3) attacking Lewis and Allenby for maintaining a claque supporting Ellen and Marion Terry. The second number (i [11 Jan. 1877], 36–7) replied to a letter received from Lewis and repeated the charge. Then Lewis wrote two more letters, to which *Truth* responded in a third article (i [18 Jan. 1877], 67).

638. To CHARLES HALL. 29 January. Montagu Square.
Parrish Collection.

Trollope accepts an invitation. 'Wont I? That is, neither will I nor will any one else now I come to look at it; for there is no such day as that you name, Wednesday 6th of February; but if you mean Wednesday 7th of February, then I'm your man.'

639. To OCTAVIAN BLEWITT. 5 February. Montagu Square.
Royal Literary Fund. Not seen.

Trollope asks for a small grant 'for a dear old lady . . . who was formerly a schoolmistress but who for five years past has been living by writing for small periodicals—and is now I te r almost starving instead of living'.

640. To GEORGE W. SMALLEY.[1] 8 February. Montagu Square.
Donald Brien. Not seen.

Trollope invites Smalley to dine with him on the 16th and thanks him for a favour granted to Madame Blaze de Bury.

641. To KATE FIELD. 8 February.
Boston Public Library. Sadleir, *Commentary*, p. 286.

8 Feb. 1877

My dear Kate,   (39, Montagu Square.)

I read your paper[2] at once, and ought to have sent it back sooner. Had I been able to speak nicely of it you may be sure I should have done so.

It is gay and lively and in that way pleasant;—but it slaughters giants that have no existence. Who is the man of the world who exclaimed that 'a lecturing woman is a disgrace to her sex'?[3] It is like the good little books which say that Tom told a lie and broke his leg, whereas Dick spoke the truth and was at once made a lord. There is no evidence of the facts but the statement of the writer.

[1] George Washburn Smalley (1833–1916), a famous American journalist and war reporter who long headed the *New York Tribune*'s European staff.
[2] Probably a revision of her 1869 lecture, 'Woman in the Lyceum'. See *Kate Field: a Record*, p. 216.
[3] See ibid., p. 204.

All your points can be argued pro & con as to women lecturing;—but you do not, I think, catch the objections which are made;—that oratory is connected deeply with forensic, parliamentary, and pulpit pursuits for which women are unfitted because they are wanted elsewhere;—because in such pursuits a man is taken from his home, and because she is wanted at home. I am not arguing the question now. But I do not think you have hit the real objection.

Your fun is I think better than your facts;—but they are so mixed together that one cannot separate them. That Aspasia taught Socrates I doubt much. That Cornelia whipped the Gracchi I suppose to be true;—but not that she taught them eloquence. Homer's appreciation of Deborah I should think to be . . . .[1] Had Aspasia taught Socrates what would that prove, seeing that Socrates was never eloquent as far as we know.

But all this is trifling. The question is whether an Editor would publish your paper. I think not as it stands now. Were I an Editor, the first 8 pages would deter me. The remainder though it is not argumentation is good fun. I should begin less brusquely. Then if you like it I will ask Bentley if it would suit him.

I will ask the question about the Garrick pictures on Saturday week. I ought to have done it last Saturday but we were very much engaged

affectionately yours
A. T.

642. To GEORGE BENTLEY. 13 February. Montagu Square. *Parrish Collection.*

Trollope sends the address of Frances Eleanor Trollope in Rome.

643. To ? ANNA C. STEELE. 17 February. *Parrish Collection.*

17, Feb. 1877
(39, Montagu Square.)

My dear Friend,

Your little note of commendation was just a valentine,—but very pleasant. I have been, and still am very much afraid of

[1] One word illegible.

Arabella Trefoil.[1] The critics have to come, and they will tell me
that she is unwomanly, unnatural, turgid,—the creation of a
morbid imagination, striving after effect by laboured abomina-
tions. But I swear I have known the woman,—not one special
woman, not one Mary Jones or Sarah Smith,—but all the traits,
all the cleverness, all the patience, all the courage, all the self-
abnegation,—and all the failure.

How is your mother? If you would ask me I would come down
some day and see her,—and you, when the primroses are coming
out. Fancy that I should have to come to that; to pine after
primroses, and wish for the violets!

Will such a one as Arabella Trefoil be damned, and if so why?
Think of her virtues; how she works, how true she is to her
vocation, how little there is of self indulgence, or idleness. I
think that she will go to a kind of third class heaven in which she
will always be getting third class husbands.

Yours affectionately—
with much love to your mother,
A. T.

644. To OCTAVIAN BLEWITT. 17 February. Montagu Square.
Royal Literary Fund. Not seen.

Trollope asks for an address of an applicant for a grant. He has been
given money for her by Mr. Locker.

645. To GEORGE BENTLEY. 28 February.
Parrish Collection.

Feb 28, 1877
(39, Montagu Square.)

My dear Mr Bentley,
Thanks for your kind letter.

I have the American Senator printed up to Chapter 60, which
completes 12 numbers, and comprises the April number. As at
present divided there are four more parts or numbers, each
containing 5 chapters. This would carry you on to the August

[1] In *The American Senator*: a young lady in determined search for a
husband.

copy of your magazine, and I had thought that the publication of the novel two months previous to this would not have hurt your periodical. But if you wish to complete the story in your July number, the chapters must be divided as on the annexed page. I will leave you to decide on this.[1]

Thanks also for the cheque of £100, making in all £400. Did your son speak to you as to the republication of a novel by an American lady named Rebecca Harding Davis,[2] the first part of which is to come out in Lippincotts magazine of July next.

Very faithfully yours

ANTHONY TROLLOPE

American Senator—to be altered as proposed
May number to contain Chapters 61, 62, 63, 64, 65 & 66
June number to contain chapters 67, 68, 69, 70, 71, & 72 & 73
July number to contain chapters 74, 75, 76, 77, 78, 79 & 80

You will see that instead of bringing into four months what would have been extended over five, as suggested in your letter, I have had to bring into three months what would have been extended over four. This must be so as the printing is already completed up to the April number inclusive.

646. To WILLIAM ALLINGHAM.[3] 5 March.
Bradford A. Booth.

5 March 1877

(39, Montagu Square.)

My dear Mr Allingham,

My son, whose name is attached to an article on Molière[4] which I send you by the same post with this, has lately written some articles on the early French drama in Macmillan. In regard to this paper, which you will see has been printed for Macmillan,

---

[1] The novel was completed in July.

[2] Rebecca Harding Davis (1831–1910), the relentless realism of whose novels won her a wide following in a predominantly romantic age. Her *A Law unto Herself* ran in *Lippincott's* from July through December.

[3] William Allingham (1824–89), minor poet and editor of *Fraser's Magazine*, 1874–9. There are several interesting references to Trollope in *William Allingham : a Diary*, ed. H. Allingham and D. Radford (London: Macmillan, 1907), pp. 106, 180, 342.

[4] Henry Merivale Trollope, 'Molière', *Fraser's Magazine*, n.s., xv (June 1877), 743–57.

there has been some disagreement between him and the Editor as to proposed alterations. I tell you all this to explain why it is sent in its present form. I now send it to you as I think it may suit Frazer's. I took it to day to Longman who is an old friend of mine, not knowing who was now editing the magazine. He referred me to you. Now you will understand it all. I did not previously know that you were living in London. You will probably let me have a reply;— —or let him have one.

Yours always faithfully
ANTHONY TROLLOPE

647. To MR. THOMPSON. 8 March. Montagu Square. *Parrish Collection*.

Trollope accepts an invitation for Thursday, 22 March.

648. To WILLIAM ALLINGHAM. 9 March. Montagu Square. *Myers & Co*.

Trollope extends an invitation for Thursday, 15 March.

649. To [? TOM] TAYLOR. 18 March. *Parrish Collection*.

Sunday.   18, March 1877

(39, Montagu Square.)

My dear Taylor,

Will you allow me to introduce to you my old and very dear friend Kate Field. She has asked for a letter to you, and of course I give it to her with great pleasure. She has brought out, and is acting in a little piece at the St James Theatre, and she wishes to speak to you about it.[1]

Yours always faithfully
ANTHONY TROLLOPE

I saw the piece myself and liked it very much.

---

[1] This was Kate Field's own comedy *Extremes Meet*. She played under the name of Mary Keemle.

650. To THOMAS HARDY.[1] 27 March.
Berg Collection.

27 March 77. 10.PM
39, Montagu Square.

Dear Sir,

Your note of the 22 has this moment reached me. I mention this lest you should think I have been dilatory in answering you.

I sell everything thing [*sic*] out and out to my publishers, so that I may have no further bargainings. When I used to hold the cheap edition in my own hand it was my practice to sell the half-profits for such & such a time;—but it never came to much with me.

There can be no doubt that the royalty system is the best, if you can get a publisher to give you a royalty, & if you are not in want of immediate money.

It all depends on the status of the author. I have for many years been able to get good prices for my books from the magazines & from the publishers for the early and costly editions;—but after that they have been worth very little to me; —so that now, as I said before, I sell everything at once.

Yours faithfully
ANTHONY TROLLOPE

651. To CECILIA MEETKERKE. 29 March.
Estate of Carroll A. Wilson. Not seen.

29 March 1877
(39, Montagu Square.)

My dear friend

I have had your former letter beside me ever so long, and ought to have written long since. But day by day one thing

[1] Hardy tells one delightfully typical story about Trollope. In Dec. 1876 Hardy went to a conference on the Eastern Question. The speakers were Gladstone, Lord Shaftesbury, Evelyn Ashley, and the Duke of Westminster. 'Trollope outran the five or seven minutes allowed for each speech, and the Duke, who was chairman, after various soundings of the bell, and other hints that he must stop, tugged at Trollope's coat-tails in desperation. Trollope turned round, exclaimed parenthetically, "Please leave my coat alone", and went on speaking.' See Florence Emily Hardy, *The Early Life of Thomas Hardy* (New York: Macmillan, 1928), p. 148. Trollope's account book has this entry for 24 Apr. 1871: 'Meet Hardy at Chapmans.' In Dec. 1868 Meredith, reading for Chapman & Hall, had turned down *The Poor Man and The Lady*, but apparently Hardy had not lost touch with the firm.

comes after another,—sometimes over and beyond the ordinary daily pages,—and so, that which does not require to be done instantly, is put off,—always for tomorrow, but in truth so often for some further day.

I am very sorry to hear what you tell me about Adolphus, though I gather from your letter that he is now at least out of danger. You were both always young lions out of Pharaoh's lean flock, and I can easily imagine that you should require fattening.

George MacDonald[1] I just know,—or rather I don't know him. I have sat next to him at dinner, and said a word to him standing in a crowd; but that is not to know a man. He is a clever, honest, industrious, imaginative man, with a large intellect, but who has not, I think, sufficiently studied the art of expression to make him so successful a writer as he might have been. He has I believe 14 children[2] and finds the world heavy.

I don't know what is the group of conspirators, but if George MacDonald is one and I another, the group is not so bad as it might be. No. I have no photograph of myself,—except the one I append to the end of this letter, which looks very like a conspirator.

Talking of editors and articles I wish you knew how badly Harry, my son, has just been treated by a man who accepted and printed a paper of his 12 months since,—and then sent it him back because Harry rebelled against being called upon to 'rewrite it' after a second revise. There are cruelties which make one almost tempted to rush either into print or into a police court—i.e., either by abusing or by kicking the sinner. Let me have a line to say how Adolphus is and I will promise not to be so dilatory again.[3]

Affectionately yours

ANTHONY | photo-
graph | TROLLOPE

Conspirator

---

[1] George MacDonald (1824–1905), the popular Scottish poet and novelist. His best-known novels are *David Elginbrod*, *Alec Forbes*, and *Robert Falconer*.

[2] MacDonald had eleven children.

[3] This letter was kindly transcribed for me by Mr. Carroll A. Wilson, who owned the manuscript.

652. To MRS. OWEN GRANT. 4 April.
Parrish Collection.

April 4, 1877
(39, Montagu Square.)

My dear Mrs Grant,

I have forgotten neither Owen Grants wife, nor Owen Grant;
—and shall not as long as I live.

But I am not the Editor of St Pauls,—nor is the St Pauls
Magazine any longer in the land of the living. I would so willingly have done anything I could to oblige you in this matter,
and hoped that although not still an Editor myself I might have
succeeded. But it has not been within my power, and I have no
alternative but to return the story.

We are living here now and have been living here for the last
five years,—having sold our house down at Waltham Cross.

Always very faithfully yours
ANTHONY TROLLOPE

653. To GEORGE BENTLEY. 19 April. Montagu Square.
Parrish Collection.

Trollope acknowledges a cheque for £500.

654. To GEORGE BENTLEY. 9 May. Montagu Square.
Parrish Collection.

Trollope introduces his friend Madame de Peyronnet. Caroline Philip-
pine Élisabeth Bertin, Comtesse de Peyronnet, wrote a few articles and
reviews for London periodicals.

655. To OCTAVIAN BLEWITT. 18 May. Montagu
Square.
Royal Literary Fund. Not seen.

Trollope inquires at some length about recent stock sales by the Literary
Fund.

656. To JOHN EVERETT MILLAIS. 18 May. Montagu
Square. *Parrish Collection.*

Trollope accepts an invitation for 5 June.

657. To GEORGE BENTLEY. 19 May. Montagu Square.
Parrish Collection.

Trollope is leaving for South Africa and presses Bentley for a reply to his
suggestion for a novel for 1878–9. He did not again publish through
Bentley.

658. To AUSTIN DOBSON. 19 May.
G. F. C. Dobson.[1] *Austin Dobson: Some Notes,* pp. 97–8.

19 May 1877

I got your book[2] last night and read much of it with the pleasure
I always have in your poetry,—a delight in the undercurrent of
fine feeling which is supposed to be subservient to the rhythmical
prettiness[es], but which is the basis on which they are in truth
supported. *Vers de Société* are for me unalluring unless I can
sympathize with the feeling, and find a pathos even in those
which are nearest to the burlesque. It is because that touch is
never wanting in you that I always thought and still think that
you will surely be known sooner or later as a master in your art.

But I can still feel, though I have no longer the right to point
out, the passages in which a little more 'elbow grease' would
have perhaps served your purpose.

To pass to a much more important subject. Will you and M[rs]
Dobson do us the pleasure of dining with us on Monday 4 June
at 7.45 p.m.

Yours always
ANTHONY TROLLOPE

659. To JOHN BLACKWOOD. 24 May.
National Library of Scotland. Parker, p. 62.

(39, Montagu Square.)
24 May. 1877.

My dear Blackwood.

A word or two which fell from you the other day tempts me
to ask you whether you would like the novel I am now writing
for the Magazine. You could fix your own time after May 1878.[3]

---

[1] I have not seen the manuscript.
[2] *Proverbs in Porcelain* (London, 1877).
[3] *John Caldigate* was serialized in *Blackwood's Magazine,* Apr. 1878–
June 1879.

The story will be 3 full volumes,—exactly as long as N.B. and L.T. It will be written in 16 parts and that division would be best;—but might be altered should you wish it.

The name would be John Caldigates wife were it not that some such title as used by another is ringing in my ears. The scene is in England.

My price for the A. Senator, for use in the Magazine was £600. If you think that too much you can make me an offer. I have never had less.

I have already finished two volumes. As I am soon going abroad and shall probably be some time away I am anxious to make an arrangement before I start.

Yours always faithfully
ANTHONY TROLLOPE

660. To JOHN BLACKWOOD. 29 May.
National Library of Scotland.

(39, Montagu Square.)
29 May 1877

My dear Blackwood.

You will perhaps let me know your address when you return and I will see you at once. I will tell you everything about my story. I suppose you would publish it with the name that was withheld as to L.T. and N.B.

No doubt the French people one meets are all very averse to run to the street and to the Commune,—as are you and I because we have good coats which may be torn. Here, thank God, the number who have good coats or believe that they may have them, are the majority. But in France there are so many who have no coats at all and yet know how to make themselves heard. And then the Paris and town populace generally are so damnably fond of political excitement, that one cannot but fear a row.

My kind regards to the two ladies. Tell them from me that I hope they had their full fling in the Magazine.[1]

I think of starting from London on June 27th.

Yours always
ANTHONY TROLLOPE

[1] I am informed by Mr. John Blackwood, the member of the family now in the firm, that if Mrs. Blackwood and Mary ever wrote anything for the magazine, it is impossible to trace their work to-day.

661. To Donald Currie.[1] 8 June 1877.
Bradford A. Booth.

8 June 1877
(39, Montagu Square.)

My dear Mr Currie,

I was much pleased with your lecture last night, of which you will perhaps send me a copy.[2] I have a copy of that on maritime warfare which I will read as I go out.

I have not received any card as to the picnic on board your ship for tomorrow, but I find that I cannot go as I have promised myself to certain ladies for the afternoon and I do not dare to throw them over as I am going so soon.

It must [? be] the 26 June, (departing from Dartmouth on 29th). So perhaps you will kindly let your clerk arrange it and I will call some day and ask about my luggage and settle everything.

I suppose you would not come and dine tomorrow Saturday, and meet Houston[3] at 7.45? He is an old pal of mine and a wonderfully good fellow.

I hurried away last night to see President Grant, but did not meet him after all.[4]

Yours faithfully
ANTHONY TROLLOPE

662. To John Blackwood. 26 June. Athenaeum Club.
National Library of Scotland.

Trollope is leaving the manuscript of his novel with Chapman. Harry will correct the proofs.

[1] Donald Currie, later Sir Donald (1825–1909), founder of the Castle Steamship Company, M.P. for Perthshire, established a new line of communication between England and Cape Town, 1872.
[2] I have not been able to find a report of this lecture. The one on maritime warfare was privately printed (1877).
[3] Probably John Adam Houston (1812–84), a prominent London painter whom Trollope may have met through Millais.
[4] Ulysses S. Grant (1822–85), who had just completed his second term as president of the United States, was touring the country on his way from Liverpool to London. He was at Bath on 8 June.

663. To HENRY MERIVALE TROLLOPE. 2 July.
Muriel Rose Trollope. Sadleir, *Commentary*, p. 312.

Caldera[1] 2 July. 1877

Dear Harry, There are ever so many things I ought to have told you, but did not. And now I forget them all again. When the horses come up you must pay Bainbridge, getting a cheque for the bills from your mother. He is to pay Ringwood[2] 22/ a week from Friday 20 July—and he has to credit me with £20 which I sent him.

When the horses are at Pritchards you must pay him as he sends his bill,—which he does every four weeks.

I dont like any one on board, but I hate two persons. There is an old man who plays the flute all afternoon and evening. I think he and I will have to fight. And there is a beastly impudent young man with a voice like a cracked horn, who will talk to me. He is almost unsnubbable, but I think I will silence him at last, as far as conversation with me goes.

We have got through the bay of Biscay without disasters, and now the water is quite as smooth as a lake. It has not yet been very hot, but I feel the heat coming. By this time tomorrow I expect to be sweltering— I have not yet put on anything specially light as I am keeping my things for the real heat.

I fancy from all I hear and the little I see that I shall find the Cape a most uninteresting place. The people who are going there on board this ship are just the people who would go to an uninteresting Colony.

At Dartmouth I got an enormous packet from Donald Currie; but it consisted of a copy of his own lecture which I had heard. I offered it to the Captain but he had had a copy.

Mind you let me know what answer you get from Allingham.

God bless you. I hope you will have a pleasant tour, and that your biographical labours are progressing.[3]

Yours always affectionately
A. T.

[1] The S.S. *Caldera*.   [2] A family servant.
[3] See Mrs. Morgan John O'Connell, *Charles Bianconi: a Biography 1786–1875* (London, 1878). According to the writer, a daughter of Bianconi, the manuscript was 'revised by a friend'. Bianconi was the inventor of the Irish car. Trollope knew him well in his Irish days and says of him in his *History*

664. To JOHN BLACKWOOD. 21 July.
National Library of Scotland. Sadleir, *Commentary*,
p. 312; *Parker*, p. 62.

Capetown South Africa
21 July 1877

My dear Blackwood.

I write a line immediately on my arrival here to say that I
finished my novel on my way out, and that I have sent the
remainder of the MS to Chapman,—who will now have the whole
of it. It is to be called

'Mrs John Caldegate' [*sic*]

I mention this especially, as the name is not given on any one of
the parts.

As I have as yet only been on shore 12 hours I am not prepared
to give a full & comprehensive description of the country. But it
seems like a poor, niggery, yellowfaced, half-bred sort of a place,
with an ugly Dutch flavour about it. But I will tell you more
about it by and bye.

Give my kindest regard to your wife & Mary.

Yours always sincerely
ANTHONY TROLLOPE

665. To HENRY MERIVALE TROLLOPE. 23 July.
Muriel Rose Trollope.

Capetown South Africa
July 23—1877

Dearest Harry,

Here I am in South Africa. I wrote to Mamma last night & I
have just got time to send a line to you this afternoon— I have
finished the novel, & have written to say so both to Chapman &
Blackwood. I have sent the MS addressed to myself to the care of
Chapman, and have begged Chapman to put it with the other MS.

The story is to be called '*Mrs John Caldigate.*' You must
remember the name as it is not put any where on the sheets which
Chapman has. I was stupid to omit it, in making up the packet.
When I left England I had not quite settled as to the name.

of the Irish Post Office (p. 62): 'It may perhaps be said that no living man
has worked more than he has for the benefit of the sister kingdom.'

I have already become quite well acquainted with most of the people in Capetown, including all the members of Parliament, though I have not yet been here for two days— I have just heard a debate in the Assembly, in which one man Mr Paterson[1] spoke very well. I dine at the Government House this Tuesday;— though not with the Governor[2] as he has heard of the death of a sister— But still Lady Frere insisted on my coming.

Capetown is very poor as a town,—much inferior either to Melbourne or Sydney. I think I go from here to Algoa Bay[3] on Wednesday week, & hope to be back here after a tour of about four months—

I hope you are having a pleasant tour. I suppose you will be away in the Tyrol when this reaches Mamma.

Most affect. your
A. T.

How does the biography get on? I have written to Trubner to say that my first letter[4] is not to appear before 20th October as I do not want them to be back here in print before I leave. The people would abuse me for what I might say—[5]

666. To HENRY MERIVALE TROLLOPE. 3 August.
Muriel Rose Trollope.

Capetown. August 3, 1877

Dear Harry,

I have not had a letter from you and therefore have not much to say but will just write a line.

Will you pay the enclosed for me to De Roy. There were one

---

[1] John Paterson, South African M.P. for Port Elizabeth. He usually represented the merchants of the Eastern Province of the Cape Colony. On 12 May 1880 he was shipwrecked and drowned in the Atlantic. See *The Times*, 17 May 1880, p. 11.

[2] Sir Henry Bartle Edward Frere (1815–84), newly appointed governor of the Cape and first high commissioner of South Africa.

[3] Algoa Bay: a bay on the south-east coast sheltering Port Elizabeth.

[4] Trollope wrote for Trübner a series of fifteen travel letters which have not previously been bibliographically recorded. They appeared in the *Cape Times*, the *Glasgow Weekly Mail*, probably in the *Manchester Weekly Times*, and possibly in other provincial papers. I shall describe the series at length in a forthcoming article in *Nineteenth-Century Fiction*.

[5] One sentence only of this letter is published in Sadleir, *Commentary*, p. 312.

or two other things for you to pay,—a hat at Silvers in Cornhill, & I think something else.

I told you before that I had completed the MS of Mrs John Caldigate and had sent it hence to Chapman. I shall be very anxious to know whether it reached him, and of course he will not write. When you get back to London go and see and let me know.

I have begun my new book and written a chapter and a half— But at starting it is very hard to know what to write about. If it were possible such a book should be written all at once, just when the journeyings and inspections are done.

I hope you are getting on with your biography — I have no doubt you find it very dull work, but it has to be done now.

I suppose you will get this early in September, while you are at Felsenegg.[1] Or you probably may be travelling about Tyrol. I hope everything is doing well with you.

God bless you.

Always affectionately yours
ANTHONY TROLLOPE

I send a letter for Tom as you will know where he is, and will be able to get it to him.[2]

A. T.

667. To HENRY MERIVALE TROLLOPE. 9 August. *Muriel Rose Trollope.*

(Port Elizabeth Club
South Africa)

August 9, 1877

Dear Harry,

I have received the letters from Hollenthal[3] which are chiefly filled with Mungoe's [*sic*] great exploit in following the cabs down to Charing Cross. Poor Mungo. He must have been very much exercised in spirit seeing everybody running away just at the same time.

I am getting on with my work, but have not come to the heavy bone-breaking part of it. I own I look forward with dread to some

---

[1] Curhaus Felsenegg, four miles from Zug, Switzerland.
[2] One paragraph quoted in Sadleir, *Commentary*, p. 312.
[3] Höllenthal: a mountain valley in lower Austria.

of the journeys I shall have to make on post cars. Five hundred miles at a stretch,—with four five or six hours allowed at night according to the fancies of the black drivers. However other men get through and I suppose I shall. I am working hard at my book, and the letters, doing a bit peacemeal [*sic*], here and there as I get on. It is the best way with such a work, but it is troublesome and requires continued thought. I trust I shall be able to have the book out in February, if I can get the printers to be sharp.

I was out yesterday with one Captain Spoldry [? Spalding], who is on army duty here, and who is brother of the grinning partners at Virtues.

I am glad you are getting on with the biography. I am sure your mother could help you a good deal if you will let her. Do not forget the Corneille.[1]

I am staying at this club which is very comfortable;—as clean as a house can be made. Everybody is very civil, but some of the men are not quite so nice as the Club.

This place is in Algoa Bay where Diaz landed when he rounded the Cape. It was therefore the first place in S Africa visited by a European.

I suppose you will be in the Tyrol when this reaches Felsenegg. But you will get it sometime. I enclose a note for Flo.[2]

> Your most affect father
> A. T.

668. To HENRY MERIVALE TROLLOPE. 22 August. *Muriel Rose Trollope.*

> King Williamstown. British Kaffraria
> Wednesday 22. August. 1877

Dearest Harry

I have just heard that the English mail goes from here today, and have therefore half an hour for writing. I wrote to mamma the other day a letter which I think will go by the same mail as this. But I get astray about the mails. With the last lot of letters

---

[1] Henry M. Trollope, *Corneille and Racine*, in 'Foreign Classics for English Readers', ed. Mrs. Margaret Oliphant (Edinburgh, 1881).
[2] Part of paragraph two quoted in Sadleir, *Commentary*, p. 313.

which I received there was nothing from any of the family, which disgusted me. Perhaps they are astray somewhere.

I am here just in the centre of what was the scene of most of the Kaffir wars— It is now in the Cape Colony, but has been added since the wars. A little further east is the Kei river, beyond which the Kaffirs are supposed to be the owners and rulers of the land,—but by degrees we are pressing them out—

This morning about 20 Kaffir Chiefs were brought into town to talk to me. They came with an interpreter who explained the conversation backwards and forwards. Only one Chief talked, and he declared that everything was as bad as it could be; That the Kaffirs were horribly ill treated by the English;—That they were made to wear breeches instead [of] red paint, which was very cruel; and that upon the whole the English had done a great deal more harm than good. He was a dirty half-drunken savage, who wore a sixpenny watch key by way of earring in his ear. He ended by begging tobacco, and God-blessing me for giving him half a crown. The other nineteen stood by silent, and went away when he went.

I have written four of Trübner's letters and four chapters of my book. I find it very hard work to get it done as I am going along. But I must do it, or not go along. I have not as yet sent any as I do not want him to publish before the middle of October. I start for Natal on Saturday & shall send him 5 or 6 from there.

As soon as you get to London find out whether the MS of the last part of my novel duly reached Chapman, and let me know. Of course I am anxious.

I have got the Union Bank papers and find we are to have 15 per cent for our midsummer dividend. This will give you $5\frac{1}{2}$ per cent for your money,—or rather more when you consider that it comes to you income tax paid.[1]

God bless you

Yours most affectionately

A. T.

[1] The third paragraph of this letter is published in Sadleir, *Commentary*, p. 313.

669. To HENRY MERIVALE TROLLOPE. 3 September.
Muriel Rose Trollope.

Pieter Maritzburgh, 3 Sept—1877

Dear Harry.

Here I am at the extreme of my journey as far as distance is concerned. It seems odd even to me to find myself on the S.E. coast of South Africa. Africa is always queerer than the other quarters, more niggery and uncomfortable.

If you have not yet sent your Academy article to Bentley, keep it back till I am home. We will then touch it up and try the Fortnightly. It would be just a subject for Morley, if he liked the article itself.[1]

I am glad you are so far on with your carman's biography. I hope to hear of its being out in October or November. I am sure you are right about the politics. But the book is to be written to please the old man's manes, and not because the book is wanted. But of course you are to make it as readable as possible. Therefore I should say, have a political chapter, but do not let it be too long.

I am getting on with my work pretty well. I have already sent 8 letters to Trübner, telling him that the other 7 will not be sent for the next 6 or 7 weeks. I have to make my luggage as light as I can,—as every pound will cost about 15/ for carriage, on my way from here round by Pretoria and the Diamond Fields to Capetown, and therefore I have left the multiplying-writer behind me. But if he does not begin before 20th October, the day I have fixed for him, it will be all right. Perhaps you had better see him when you get to London. I shall not get my luggage till I get back to Capetown, where I must write the other 7 letters. I hope to be there about the end of October. If so I think that I may still be home by the end of the year;—and I think that I shall bring my book nearly finished with me. I am working very hard, tasking myself to write 1300 words a day,—which as I am travelling all the time is hard enough.

I suppose Popenjoy[2] will begin to come out soon after you get back;—but you must tell me all about everything.

[1] I cannot discover that the article was ever published.
[2] *Is He Popenjoy?* was serialized in *All the Year Round* from 13 Oct. 1877 to 13 July 1878.

Pray answer the enclosed civilly, saying that I am in South
Africa, (that will be profound and vague) that I am not agricul-
turally given. You will know what to say—or you live so much
in Paris perhaps the man is a friend of yours.

God bless you. I hope you are enjoying yourself.[1]

Your most affectionate father
ANTHONY TROLLOPE

670. To HENRY MERIVALE TROLLOPE. 26 September.
Pretoria, Transvaal. *Muriel Rose Trollope.*

Trollope has come to the end of his journey and is ready to begin his
return. He has bought a cart and four horses. He inquires about Henry's
forthcoming book and his own. 'I shall come back with my African book
nearly finished.'

671. To HENRY MERIVALE TROLLOPE. 7 October.
Muriel Rose Trollope.

Potchefstroom—Transvaal
7—Oct—1877

Dearest Harry,

I only yesterday got your letter of 6—August. I congratulate
you much on your progress with the Irish carman. I think the
lines you mean about rebels are in Byron's favour. When will the
book be out? Before you get this I hope. Do you mean to put your
name as Editor. If the book be good I should, and I should take
mamma's advice as to the goodness for she is never mistaken
about a book being good or bad. The electioneering chapter
must have been an awful struggle. I am glad the Jones' [?] were
at Felsenegg as he is not a bad fellow though not quite a gentleman.

I do so long to get home. South Africa is so dirty. But I shall
not do so before first week in January. Not all the books in
Xendom shall make me later than that.

I have joined myself with a young man named Farran who is
in the plough-making business and we travel as you please with
our carriage and our own four horses and our own black driver.
It is slow—35 miles a day,—but comfortable and enables me to
see the country. The public conveyances would nearly kill me.

[1] Two sentences of this letter are quoted in Sadleir, *Commentary*, p. 313.

He is very nice. But we had a great misfortune and lost one of our horses two days since with cholera. We have bought another for £23—but a miserable looking brute. When we have done we mean to sell it all. I wonder whether we shall get anything.

Love to Chapman and Mrs C. I hope to have had news sent me about the novels. Get the Chronicles from Bickers.[1] I am very anxious to know whether Blackwood will begin in January.[2]

Your most affect father

A. T.

672. To HENRY MERIVALE TROLLOPE. 9 October. *Muriel Rose Trollope.*

Mossel Bay[3]—9—October 1877

Dear Harry,

I received, with many others, at Elizabeth Bay yesterday your long letter written immediately on your return home. I am at this moment in an awful scramble, going off in 20 minutes on an expedition with a man I never saw till an hour and a half ago, in quest of grand scenery— The grandest scenery in the world to me would be Montagu Square.

I am very glad to hear that H. Merivale[4] is all right. I do not care much for the beautification of the billiard room. You tell me that Blackwood has sent for the MS of Mrs J. Caldigate: of which I am glad as I suppose he intends to begin it on January 1. You say nothing as to 'Popenjoy' and 'All the Year Round.' I suppose therefore you have not seen the sheets for correction— They had been corrected when printed in the first form— I hope he, C. D,[5] began the book sometime in October.

What was done about the £500 which was to have been paid in August by the Smyrna railway people? You were to have had shares purchased in the Bank as soon as you knew the money had

---

[1] Bickers and Son were booksellers. By the 'Chronicles' Trollope may be referring to one of the volumes in the Record Office series of *Chronicles and Memorials of Great Britain and Ireland.*

[2] Paragraph two quoted in Sadleir, *Commentary*, p. 313.

[3] Mossel Bay: a seaport resort midway between Capetown and Port Elizabeth.

[4] Herman Charles Merivale (1839–1906), nephew of John Merivale.

[5] Charles Dickens (1837–96), son of the novelist, was sub-editor of *All the Year Round.*

been paid. I dont care much about it; but should have liked to know.

I am very glad the old carman was not burned after all your trouble. I suppose he will have appeared before you get this. I shall be anxious to see what the reviews say about it.

I expect to be back in Capetown in about 10 days, and to leave that place for England about the 17 December—which, by the average of passages, would land me at Plymouth on the 8 January & bring me to London on the 9th As far as I can see such will be my programme.

I did write a scrap of a letter to your mother which I think she will get by the same mail with this. At any rate give her my love & Flo. This is written all in a muddle.

Yours most affectionately
A. T.

I sent my 10th letter to Trubner to-day—but cannot send it in duplicate[1]

673. To HENRY MERIVALE TROLLOPE. 15 October. *Muriel Rose Trollope*. Not seen.

(Government House
Griqualand
South Africa)[2]
October 15—1877

Dearest Harry

I have just received yours and your mothers letters of 27th August which had travelled to me round by the Transvaal. I have got all my letters regularly up to that date. You will not get this till the middle of November, and after that no letters should be sent to me.

I have written to this effect to the P.O. in Vere Street, and also to Cowie the newsvendor.

I shall I hope arrive in London with my book all but written, and I shall hope to have it out by the opening of Parliament. Will you see Chapman and tell him that *I shall be very anxious for Virtue to print the book*, as I shall have to go often to the printers

---

[1] Short excerpt published in Sadleir, *Commentary*, p. 314.
[2] Griqualand: a mountainous region in the Cape Province.

myself. Let him have everything settled as to the page before I come home. There will be 375 × 260 words in each volume; and there should be about 375 pages in a volume and 260 words on a page. He can have it cast accordingly. If you will look to this specially I shall be able to go to Virtues with a part of the MS the day after I arrive.

I am very glad that you write so hopefully about the 'Car man.' I shall be very interested to see the book.

I will not describe to you this most detestable place because I must write about it, and you must read what I write. I have been handling diamonds till I am sick of them. But the great hole out of which they come is certainly the most marvellous place I have ever seen.

We have had such adventures with our cart and horse!—but sold them yesterday by auction for £100. All that however will be in the book. But I shall not put in the book that I had to get the Governor to send the Inspector of Police to the auctioneer before I could get my money.

It was very nice your liking the Joncs's.

Always most affectionately
Your father
A. T.

What a lounge for you that you will not have to answer this.

The sun is here 94 in the shade—148 in the sun.

I wonder whether my MS of the novel reached Chapman—[1]

674. To HENRY MERIVALE TROLLOPE. 18 October.
Muriel Rose Trollope.

Kimberley.
18—October—1877

Dearest Harry,

Buy for me, *so that I may have it on my arrival*, the Colonial Office list of 1877. You can get it at Harrison 59 Pall Mall. If he cannot sell it (I am almost sure he can) call on the Hon. R. Meade at the Colonial Office, and ask him for it in my name— saying you cannot buy it. He is Assistant Under Secretary and is a friend of mine— (Cosmopolitan).

[1] Paragraphs five and six published in Sadleir, *Commentary*, p. 314; paragraph three published in Sadleir, *Bibliography*, p. 160.

I also want the Blue book about the Transvaal. (I think number C 1748) published early in 1877—*before* the annexation. I have the continuation treating of the annexation. Meade will probably give you this for me, or put you in the way of getting it.

As I am writing special about this, I say nothing else and send no messages.

Heat here—96—shade
              100—sun
Supposed heat in Infernal Regions
              94—shade (?)
              150—full brimstone—
                                      God bless you
                                      Always your most affectionate father
                                      AN TROLLOPE[1]

675. TO HENRY MERIVALE TROLLOPE. 23 October.
Muriel Rose Trollope.

Boshof—Orange Free State
23 October 1877

Dearest Harry,

I write to night partly for the sake of sending you the enclosed absurd advertisement, and partly because I want something to do in this quiet little Dutch town where I have to pass the night waiting for the coach on the road from the Diamond Fields to Bloemfontein. At home we have hardly a conception how quiet such a place can be. And yet there are two large squares in it, and two hotels— Perhaps there are 30 houses. The country all round is flat and at present without a blade of grass. You can imagine nothing uglier. I am very glad to get away from Kimberley. The heat was knocking me up. It is hot here also, but the change has refreshed me.

My first letter for Trubner was published I suppose on Saturday last, 20th Oct. He has 7 more, which will take him on to December 9th— In order to be sure of reaching him on time for December 16th I must write one (and probably also another for Decr 23) on my coach down to Capetown before I reach my proper writing apparatus.

[1] Excerpt published in Sadleir, *Commentary*, p. 314, misdated 8 Oct.

The first of these will go by the same post as this direct to Trubner;—but there can be no copy as I have not the multiplying process with me. Will you go and see whether he has got it all right, and explain this to him, and tell him that there will probably be two without copies. I shall get to Bloemfontein tomorrow, Thursday, and will write the letter for him Wednesday & Thursday & post it with this for the mail from that place on Friday. He will then get the letter about the end of November,—by the same post as this. I may be so hurried at Bloemfontein as not to be able to get another letter written. If so, give my best & dearest love to mamma and explain this to her. My best love to Florence.

Yours most affectionately
A. T.

676. To HENRY MERIVALE TROLLOPE. 24 October. Bloemfontein. *Muriel Rose Trollope.*

Trollope acknowledges receipt of several letters. He discusses Henry's book and is 'glad to hear ... that the Cicero is at last to appear!'[1] He adds, 'Since this morning I have seen the President of the Orange Free State[2] who seems to be a good sort of old gentleman, very quiet with a good sort of old wife,—very quiet too. Everything here is very quiet.

I have bought
a coat
waistcoat
trowsers
3 pair of socks
     and
a hat
all ready made'[3]

---

[1] Trollope's *Life of Cicero* was not published until late in 1880.

[2] John Henry Brand, later Sir John (1823–88), president of the Orange Free State, 1863–88.

[3] Mr. Sadleir's arrangement of the list of items purchased into a caricature of Trollope's figure (*Commentary*, p. 314) is highly ingenious but I think not justified by the text.

677. To HENRY MERIVALE TROLLOPE. 19 November.
Muriel Rose Trollope.

Rathfelden—Wynburg
near Capetown—19—Nov. 1877

My dear Harry—

Thanks for yours of 11—and 18—October which I got on reaching this place yesterday. I shall be very anxious to see the art in the Edinburgh, which is probably by Reeve.[1] He at least loves an occasion to descend to such puerilities from his high critical pedistal.

No doubt many a literary artist so conceals his art that readers do not know that there is much art. But they like the books and read them,—not knowing why. You are quite right as to Moliere and Macaulay. I would not have you bracket your third example with such names to other ears than mine lest you be laughed at.

Chapman is an old fox, as he always was. He takes credit for paying the £400,—for which I had his bill, so that he could not help paying. I never let such payments soften my rigour for a moment in reference to the £200 a quarter. I dare say he will have paid it before you get this.

I am glad the Cassaba money came up right. To get money out of Turkey at all seems to be wonderful. The £17–10 was some remnant of interest. I suppose you will have bought for me 12 bank shares.

I have *not* got the Daily News you sent[2]— You say it was all up with Cleopatras needle.[3] I suppose you mean all down. I am sorry for it. Yes—the Turks seem to have had it hot enough in Armenia. I feel sure that the sooner they are licked the better it will be for humanity in general.[4]

---

[1] 'Mr. Anthony Trollope's Novels', *Edinburgh Review*, cxlvi (Oct. 1877), 455–88. The article on the whole is very laudatory. Reeve begins, 'We have little hesitation in asserting that the present generation owes a larger debt of gratitude to Mr. Trollope than to any other writer of fiction, living or lately dead.'

[2] There is nothing on Trollope from 23 Sept. through 10 Nov., and it is of course impossible to say what clipping Henry Trollope thought might interest his father.

[3] In 1878 Ismael Pasha sent a 68½-foot red granite obelisk to England as a gift from Egypt. It stands on the Embankment near Waterloo Bridge and is known as Cleopatra's needle.

[4] In the Russo-Turkish War of 1877–8 the Russians defeated Muktar

I suppose your carman will be out by the time this reaches you. I shall be very anxious to see it. Get me a copy. I hope you will have put your name—'Edited by H. M. T.'

Get on with the Corneille as soon as you can, so as to get it out one of the early ones. I am sure you should not be too elaborate.

I don't see at all why Morley should not take the article on the F. A.[1] But we will see.

You do not say whether Blackwood has printed any of Mrs John Caldigate. I hope it is to come out on Jany 1.[2]

Write me a letter addressed P.O. Funchal Madeira. I shall get it on my way home, & it will cheer me.

I send to-day letter N° 11 to Trubner, and I have done 2/3 of my book. I never worked harder.

I hope the horses are all right

Most affectionately yours
A. T.

678. To HENRY MERIVALE TROLLOPE. 20 November. *Muriel Rose Trollope.*

Capetown 20. Nov. 1877

Dear Harry—

I have got further letters from you and mamma just as the post is going. I have written to that crack-brained lady about Lady Anna. My story was pure fiction. I never made use of stories from private life. But I think she is mad.

All right about the bank shares. One must do something with one's money.

And about Dickens bill for £200.

I hope Chapman has paid the £200 he owes.

I dont suppose your words are really shorter than mine;—but that you have not as yet quite got into the way of writing for lengths. The book should have been 350 pages. But one cant do all these mechanic tricks at once—

Pasha and, capturing three large fortresses, overran nearly all the districts inhabited by Armenians. The armistice came on 31 Jan. 1878. See Lord Eversley, *The Turkish Empire* (New York: Dodd, Mead, 1923), pp. 326–9.

[1] The French Academy. See letter No. *669, supra.*

[2] The first number of *John Caldigate* was published in *Blackwood's* in Apr. 1878.

I dont care much for Alice Rhodes or Cleopatra's needle as it is late and I am very tired—

I do care for the French assembly and hope MacMahon[1] will be forced to resign. There will be threats on a [? the] govt.

Tell mamma I have got hers of the 19th— But I wrote to her this morning.

What does Dalan's card mean.

Yours always affect
A. T.

1878

679. To JOHN BLACKWOOD. 9 January.
National Library of Scotland. Parker, p. 62.

(Montagu Square 39.)
9. January 1878

My dear Blackwood.

I have got back alive—and well; and as I have survived the passing of various nights in a Boer's best bed, I think I may say that I am qualified to undergo any hardship. What about a novel? In writing to Henry you suggested some suggestions—what are they? I am a reasonable man and up to anything short of rewriting the second volume, which poor William Longman once proposed that I should do.

When is the first number to appear?

Yours always faithfully
ANTHONY TROLLOPE

680. To [? CECILIA MEETKERKE]. 25 January.
Robert H. Taylor.

25 Jany, 1878.
(39, Montagu Square.)

My dear Friend,

Your letter has caught me in the middle of a violent fit of influenza, so that I wish myself back in South Africa.

---

[1] Marie Edmé de MacMahon (1808–93), president of France, 1873–9. He was forced to resign in 1879 after a term of office made tempestuous by struggles with Gambetta.

I am very hard at work on my book, writing it, altering it, correcting the press, and revising it all at once.

I should so much like to see you. Which will be best [,] for you to come here, or for me to go to you?

You must have something to do in London. I have nothing to do in Hertfordshire, now that hunting is over for me.

We can put you up for a couple of nights or so,—you, but unfortunately not a maid, but my wifes maid can do what you want. And I would get a publisher to meet you. Would not this be best? I fear, however,—I fear no publisher will put out the volume without a guarantee. —But you shall see the man of books face to face if you will come.

If you wont, which I shall think nasty, I will go to you.

Yours affectionately
A. T.

Love to Adolphus & my younger cousin.

681. To JOHN BLACKWOOD. 29 January.
National Library of Scotland.

(39, Montagu Square.)
29 Jan. 1878

My dear Blackwood.

Not having had an answer to my last letter[1] I am led to think that I have subjected you to an unpleasant alternative—that you do not want on your own account to do what I proposed, and that you do not like to disoblige me by refusing. I, on my hand, do not think that I ought to subject you to any annoyance in the matter, and I therefore write to say that I will assent to your proposal, (to begin in June or July 78 and end in Sept or October 79), if that is best for you. Let me have a line that I may know. I do not like to think that I am in any way a trouble in your mind.

Yours always
ANTHONY TROLLOPE

682. To JOHN MURRAY. 13 February. Montagu Square.
Parrish Collection.

Trollope cannot accept an invitation for the 19th.

[1] Since a long letter from Blackwood dated 11 Jan. is among Trollope's papers (Bodleian), one suspects that Trollope's 'last letter' has been lost.

683. To CHARLES DICKENS, Jun. 21 February.
Montagu Square. *Parrish Collection.*

Trollope is concerned about the termination of *Is He Popenjoy?* 'The end of June will do;—but I should be sorry to see the story end later.[1] My feeling was that I, as author, should not be injured because I had given good measure.'

684. To FRED POPE. 2 March. Montague Square.
Parrish Collection.

Trollope is engaged and cannot be present at the meeting regarding the Marylebone Burial Ground. Fred Pope was the proprietor of a public house in Old Street, Shoreditch. See *Post Office London Directory, 1872,* p. 471.

685. To WILLIAM BLACKWOOD.[2] 6 March.
National Library of Scotland. Parker, p. 62.

(39, Montagu Square.)
6 March 1878

Dear Blackwood.

Thanks for your letter and the revise. *But a revise to me is of no use unless I can have with it the first corrected proof.* Could you send me that? And will you please have sent to me with the proofs the MS, which I always want for reference and like to keep.

I thought your uncle looked as though he *had been* very ill, much thinner than his wont, especially in the face. But he was evidently so much on the mend that he was as gay and full of life as ever. I have no doubt his trip to Italy will be of great service to him. But I suppose he has in truth been ill.

Alas—alas—my hunting is over. I have given away my breeches, boots,—and horses.

The abnegations forced upon us by life should be accepted frankly. I have not therefore waited to draw the cup to the last drop.

Yours always faithfully
ANTHONY TROLLOPE

1 The novel did not conclude in *All the Year Round* until 13 July 1878.
2 William Blackwood (1836–1912), a nephew of John Blackwood. He entered the firm in 1857 and became a partner in 1862 after the death in 1861 of his father, Major William Blackwood.

686. To FREDERIC CHAPMAN. 6 March.
Montagu Square. *Pierpont Morgan Library*.

Trollope proposes that George Smith be given the profit from the sale of *Framley Parsonage* in the proposed eight-volume 'Chronicles of Barsetshire' edition in order that the novel, of which Smith held the copyright, might be included in the series.

687. To GEORGE SMITH. 7 March. Montagu Square.
Sir John Murray.

Trollope offers Smith one-fifth of the profit from the sale of the proposed Barsetshire series.

688. To TOM TAYLOR. 7 March. Montagu Square.
Mrs. Arthur Helps.

Trollope asks for a subscription to 'put Thackerays bust into marble' for the Garrick Club. The bust was executed by Joseph Durham (1814–77), a sculptor who excelled in figures of boy athletes. His Thackeray is not considered a good representation. Professor Gordon Ray dates it as of 1864.

689. To ? 11 March. Montagu Square.
Parrish Collection.

Millais having spoken to some sculptor unknown about the bust of Thackeray, Trollope arranges to call for a discussion.

690. To GEORGE SMITH. 22 March. Montagu Square.
Sir John Murray.

Trollope sends Smith a copy of his agreement with Chapman for 'The Chronicles of Barset'.

691. To GEORGE W. SMALLEY. 23 March.
Parrish Collection.

March 23, 1878
(39, Montagu Square.)

My dear Smalley,
 I can not tell you how much gratified I was by your review[1] in the Tribune on my South African Book. It was by far the pleasantest that I have read.

[1] Smalley's long and favourable review appeared in the *Tribune*, 4 Mar. 1878, p. 6.

And it was the more agreeable because I am sure you would not be led by any feeling of friendship to speak of any book otherwise than you thought.

Very faithfully

ANTHONY TROLLOPE

692. To WILLIAM BLACKWOOD. 26 March. Montagu Square. *National Library of Scotland.*

Trollope is amenable to any proposal the Blackwoods make. He would like to have sheets in advance as he is going abroad in July. He will be glad to have a second copy of the magazine to send to Fred in Australia. 'I am very glad to have so good an account of your uncle.'

693. To WILLIAM BLACKWOOD. 9 April. Montagu Square. *National Library of Scotland.*

Trollope returns corrected the second part of *John Caldigate.* 'My wife got a letter from Rome this morning saying that the "Blackwoods had not yet turned up".'

694. To KATE FIELD. 11 April.
Boston Public Library. More Books, ii (July 1927), 134.[1]

11 April 1878

(39, Montagu Square.)

Dear Kate

No;—I dont care two pence for the Shakespeare Memorial or Mr Flower. If there be any one who does not want more memorials than have been already given, it is Shakespeare! Mr Flower is a worthy old gent,—who wants to go down to posterity hanging on to some distant rag of the hindermost garment of the bard of Avon; but I dont want or care to assist his views. £1000 and a site!! Surely he can hang on to a rag without costing me five guineas! And there seems to be a lot of money. All Stratford-on-Avon seems to run over with £100's. What would be my 5 guineas?

In truth it is all leather and purnella [*sic*] to me. I have not many guineas to spare, but when I have I find so many mouths

---

[1] See Zoltán Haraszti, 'Kate Field and the Trollope Brothers'. *More Books* is the bulletin of the Boston Public Library.

into which it can go;—mouths that want it, whereas neither Shakespeare nor Flower want anything.

Yours affect.

AN TROLLOPE

Nor dont you turn around and be cross with me, and pitch my little mite of assistance to yourself at my teeth, as if I were bad at the core! For yourself there would be other mites if they were wanted.

695. To JOHN [? TILLEY]. 12 April.
Muriel Rose Trollope.

12—April 1878

(39, Montagu Square.)

My dear John,

It is so hard to answer Beauforts[1] letter without seeming to be overbearing and unfriendly.

The poets of the day are legion. The manuscripts which lie in the hands of publishers and Editors of Magazines are tens of thousands. I do not say a word against the Miltonic, Homeric, Virgilian, Petrarchan merits of his poet,—or poetess; nor can I, as of course I have not seen a line. But, as he writes of his friend, all the other thousands write of theirs. In the midst of all this who is to hold out a helping hand?

Now and again from amidst the million some one, selected by some sort of competitive examination, comes up, and, lo, a poet is there. Beaufort's poet has as good a chance as any one else. But the struggler has to know that he or she must struggle amongst 10,000, and must look to 9,999 chances of absolute failure. In the teeth of this what hope can one hold out, or what advice can one give? No doubt great numbers of poems find their way up to all the Magazines, and all the papers and many of the Reviews. Now and again one makes it's way in and then,— with a very much rarer now and again, one comes forth at last as a name recognized and well known! But the competitor must go through all but hopeless struggle, and must send his poem up to the Editors,—or to some Editor, not much matter what.

Yours always

ANTHONY TROLLOPE

[1] See letter No. 38, *supra.*

696. To Nicholas Trübner. 12 April.

Montagu Square. *Not traced.* Edmund Gosse, *English Literature: an Illustrated Record,* 4 vols. (New York: Macmillan, 1935), iv. 321.

Trollope thanks Trübner for a book about 'ostriches. The book is a good book; but then so very few people can [? know] about ostriches! I feel that the sale of such a book must be small.'

697. To John Tilley. 18 April.
Mrs. Arthur Tilley.

18 April 78
My dear John   (39, Montagu Square.)

It is impossible to have such a letter from you and not to answer it;—and it would be unsatisfactory not to write before I see you, which I shall do probably before I go out of town next week.

In some respects you are different from other men. As far as I can tell, your health is as strong as that of a man of forty. As far as outward appearance goes you have about reached your prime. If there were no question of a pension,—if it were the case that you would be paid if you did work and not paid if you did not work,—it would not occur to you now to go, more than it would have occurred to you twenty years ago! If so, why not continue the work simply because a man who works for his bread is so much nobler than he who takes his bread for nothing?

You of course know more of yourself than others see. There may be inner fatigue; there may be a creeping on of the weariness of old age,—though your outside gives the lie to it. If the work go against the grain with you, that may be reason for leaving it. But if it be easy with you I do not think the mere fact of your age should induce you to leave it;—nor the fact that your pay would come to you though the work were abandoned.

You say of me;—that I would not choose to write novels unless I were paid. Most certainly I would;—much rather than not write them at all.

The two points to be looked at are, your happiness,— (provided that the happiness of others dependent on you is indifferent in the matter,—) and your duty. What future employment do you propose for yourself? In some respects you have limited yourself more clearly than many men. You cannot stand in a club window; you cannot play cards; you cannot farm. Books must be your resource. I hardly know whether you can be happy four hours at a spell with a book. I do know that such happiness comes only from practice, and that the habit will not be acquired late in life.

As to duty I am convinced that you ought to go if you believe it to be better for the service that you should do so;—or to remain for the same reason. I do not think that the money should be counted as any thing. That is no source of trouble. The Post Office has been so beneficent to you that you owe it everything. If it be that weariness tends to make your work unserviceable, I think you should go. If there be no such conviction, I think that for your own sake you should remain another term.[1]

Your happiness is so much to me that I cannot but write about it much in earnest.   Yours always

ANTHONY TROLLOPE

698. To [? WILLIAM] BLACKWOOD. 28 April.
Montagu Square. *National Library of Scotland.*

Trollope thanks Blackwood for his note about Sampson Low. 'I hate the Mammon doings so utterly that I wash my hands of them altogether, and leave everything in the hands of Chapman.'

699. To WILLIAM BLACKWOOD. 3 May.
Montagu Square. *National Library of Scotland.*

Trollope thanks Blackwood for his cheque. 'Your proposition as to the money is very liberal indeed. I heard from my brother as to your uncle. He had not been altogether well. I think he was complaining of some soreness on the chest.'

700. To ? MR. HAYTER. 6 May. Montagu Square.
Parrish Collection.

Trollope accepts an invitation. The name of the addressee is almost illegible, but I judge it to be that of Henry Heylyn Hayter, government statistician and authority on the state of Victoria in Australia.

[1] Tilley served two more years, retiring on full pay of £2,000 on 16 Apr. 1880.

701. To WILLIAM BLACKWOOD. 16 June. Montagu Square. *National Library of Scotland.*

Trollope goes to Iceland next week and will also be away through August and September.

702. To JOHN BURNS.[1] 12 July. *Parrish Collection.*

12 July, 1878
(39, Montagu Square.)

My dear Burns,

Many thanks for your note,—also for McKenzie's book;[2]—also the presentation copy of the memorial of your grandfather. The one shall be preserved carefully;—the other returned as carefully. When I opened that parcel I said,—'surely James Burns[3] has recommended packing up in earnest.'

Tell Lena that as I have no stern parent to repress my feelings, I send her my love,—which I think I may do to the daughter, seeing that I certainly love the father.

But I want to know whether she has guessed the riddle.

I also have been shattered, moderately;—but I am coming to.

We certainly had a great success. My wife is flaunting about with those little buttons you gave me.

Yours always
ANTHONY TROLLOPE

703. To FREDERIC OUVRY. 16 July. Montagu Square. *Parrish Collection.*

Trollope makes an appointment to audit the accounts of the Literary Fund, of which he was for many years the treasurer.

[1] John Burns, later Sir John and Lord Inverclyde (1829–1901), was chairman of the Cunard Steamship Co.
[2] Sir George Steuart Mackenzie (1780–1848), mineralogist specializing in Iceland; joint author of *Travels in Iceland* (1811).
[3] James Cleland Burns, a brother of John Burns.

704. To WILLIAM BLACKWOOD. 17 July.
National Library of Scotland.

(39, Montagu Square.)

My dear Blackwood.   17 July. 1878

I have been so knocked about since I came home from Iceland, that I have omitted to answer your last letter as I should have done.

I have returned the revise of the last number of J. C., for press, being the 6th. My brother who is here asked me just now who was the author of J. C.,—which he was then reading! He was much surprised when I told him.[1]

I am very glad indeed to hear so good an account of your uncle. I saw him one day in London when he was very far from well. But he picked up afterwards wonderfully. Give him my kind regards.

Before I started I promised to write a paper on Iceland for the Fortnightly.[2] It is not a good subject, being too hacknied. I have however done it.[3]

Yours always
ANTHONY TROLLOPE

705. To WILLIAM BLACKWOOD. 23 July.
Montagu Square. *National Library of Scotland.*

Trollope is leaving for Felsenegg, Switzerland.

706. To ?[4] 24 July.
Capt. F. L. Pleadwell.

(39, Montagu Square.)

Dear Sir,   July 24, 1878

I have to write to you a letter of apology which I hardly know how to make both apologetic and intelligible. Did I not receive a letter from you as to the republication in your columns of a novel of mine? Surely I did! But having carried it in my pocket till I should meet a certain publisher whom, with myself, it

---

[1] Blackwood's pencilled comment: 'Is not this good?'
[2] 'Iceland', the *Fortnightly Review*, n.s., xxiv (Aug. 1878), 175–90.
[3] Paragraph 2 published in *Parker*, p. 63.
[4] Possibly to John Dicks. See letter No. 708, *infra*.

would concern, I have lost it, and forgot the name it bore! I am indifferent as to your thinking me careless, if you will not think me uncourteous.

If the answer should be made to you, I have to say that for this year and for my work of next year, 1879, my engagements are all made, so that I have no power to sell further rights to my work than I have sold. Should you like to make any proposition as to the year beyond that, (1880)—if any of us be then living,— I should be very glad to listen to it.

But my chief object at the present moment is to avoid being uncivil.

Yours faithfully
ANTHONY TROLLOPE

707. To GEORGE ELIOT. 13 August.
    Parrish Collection.

Felsenegg, Zug, Switzerland
13 August 1878.

Dear friend,

Your kindest letter has at length found me here.

After seeing you last, there came to me an invitation to join a party in a trip to Iceland, and to Iceland I went. How I fared in Iceland and was driven to talk Latin to my guide,—in which accomplishment I was barely his inferior,—you may see in the Fortnightly. After my return I came off after my wife, first to the Black Forest and then on here, having been in London only so long as was necessary to finish some literary work which I had on hand. I mention this to say how it has come to pass that I have lost the pleasure of going to Witley.[1]

My brother is at Margate, whither I, by this post, send him your letter. It is his purpose to remain in England till the last week in August. I imagine that he will be delighted to go to you, if his engagements allow him. I grieve to say that his engagements have, since he has been in England, been chiefly dependent on doctors. He too has had gout and has been made the subject of not only various, but most varying prescriptions. The last was

[1] Witley: a village near Godalming in Surrey where the Leweses were living. An excerpt from this letter is published in Sadleir, *Commentary*, p. 318. The Leweses entertained the Tom Trollopes later in the month. See J. W. Cross, *George Eliot's Life as Related in Her Letters and Journals*, 3 vols. (New York: Harper, 1903), p. 240.

an anathema against smoking, to which, when I left England, he had bowed his neck with lamblike submission after a devotion of half a century to the weed. He no doubt will write to you.

Here we are on the top of a mountain, where I write for four hours a day, walk for four hours, eat for two, and sleep out the balance satisfactorily. I am beginning to think that the more a man can sleep the better for him. I can take a nap of nine hours each night without moving, in these latitudes.

Give my kind love to Lewes. Tell him that I have come here with a MS translation of the Odyssey in my portmanteau, which I have to read and advise the translator as to publishing.[1] It is just the job which he would like. Seeing that we have two really good versions of the poem in English, I should have thought that an aspirant might have gone elsewhere for a task.

Yours always most sincerely
ANTHONY TROLLOPE

708. To JOHN DICKS.[2] 14 August.
Parrish Collection.

Felsenegg. Zug. Switzerland

August 14, 1878
(39, Montagu Square.)

Dear Sir,

Your note of August 9th. has followed me here; but not the copy of your annual number, so that I am in ignorance of the length you would require for a story.

My price *for the copyright* would be £2 per MS page of 260 words;—so that you can calculate the cost. Retaining the copyright I should charge less;—but I cannot say how much less till I knew the proposed length. The longer the story the more valuable would be the copyright to me.[3]

I shall be here for another fortnight.

Yours faithfully

John Dicks Esq   ANTHONY TROLLOPE

[1] Trollope was probably reading for Blackwood a translation by Sir Charles Du Cane (published 1880).

[2] John Thomas Dicks (1818–81), proprietor of *Reynolds' Newspaper*, *Bow Bells*, &c. He had one of the largest printing and publishing houses in England.

[3] The story was probably 'Catherine Carmichael', published in the Christmas number of the *Masonic Magazine*, 1878.

709. To? 15 August.
Yale University Library.

Felsenegg—Zug. Switzerland
August 15—1878
(39, Montagu Square.)

Dear Sir,

Your note of 8th August has followed me here. I will keep it so that when I return home I may send you a photograph of mine if I shall find myself to possess one. I do not like photographs, and dislike my own worse than all others. But if I can find one you shall have it.

My Mothers books are so numerous, as also, alas, are my own, that I can hardly supply you with a list. I have written about 40 novels— She, I think, wrote over 30— And yet she was over 50 when her first work was published. If there be any of mine which you wish to see I would lend them to you when I get home— Hers I never allow to go out of the house, as I should be unable to replace them—

Yours faithfully
A N T H O N Y T R O L L O P E

I have nothing to guide me in addressing you but the written name. You may be M^r—M^rs or Miss,—or may go by any other title!

710. To JOHN BURNS. 20 August. Felsenegg.
The Hon. Mrs. Corfield. Sadleir's transcript.

Trollope returns proof of *How the 'Mastiffs' Went to Iceland.* 'I have only to ask that in using my name there may be no addition as to "Author of" such or such words [*sic*]. I never have it put on my own books. . . . Ryder's[1] name has been written by me in error instead of Farquhar's.[2] Of course I have corrected it. Fancy poor little Ryder filling Farquhar's breeches!'

711. To JOHN BURNS. 25 August. Felsenegg.
The Hon. Mrs. Corfield. Sadleir's transcript.

Trollope writes about emendations in the text. 'I have told them to put out the pigs and dogs, in compliance with Mrs. B. Where I got the informa-

---

[1] Alfred Phillips Ryder, later Sir Alfred (1820–88), commander-in-chief in China, 1874–7; admiral, 1877; admiral of the fleet, 1885.

[2] Arthur Farquhar, later Sir Arthur (1815–1908), commander-in-chief on the Pacific coast, 1869–73.

tion I cannot guess, but I think from McDiarmid's little book,—James Burns has it.' I do not know to what book Trollope refers unless it be to John MacDiarmid, *St. Kilda and Its Inhabitants* (Edinburgh, 1877).

712. To JOHN BLACKWOOD. 7 September.
Parrish Collection.

Höllenthal. Freiburg

My dear Blackwood.　　　　Duchy of Baden. 7, Sept. 1878

I was delighted to receive your letter of the 2nd, forwarded on from Felsenegg. I will answer you about the novel in a day or two, when I return back the proof corrected; but I do not like to lose a post in saying how happy we are, my wife, Florence and myself, in having so good account of your health. Give my best love to your wife and tell her that I do not in the least doubt that she is quite right as to the saunter round the wood with a cigar of a damp night!! I fear, indeed, that you are kittle cattle to drive; and that now that you are once more master of your own legs and your own health, you may not be so obedient as when things were less agreeable with you. But, in truth, we are *very glad* to hear of your convalescence and trust that you may not do anything to delay it through strong headed over-virility—

I am very sorry to hear that Collins is suffering from his throat. I suppose he has left you, otherwise remember me to him most kindly. I shall probably hear from him and write to him when I get back to England. He is a man whom I greatly like as a companion and esteem as a man—

We remain here probably for another month, and then go home— Now we have beautiful weather;—most lovely. In Switzerland we had continued rain. But I have been on my legs among the hills every day for 4 hours, and have every day done 4 hours of writing. I then sleep 8 hours without stirring. The other 8 are divided between reading and eating,—with a preponderance to the latter. It is a healthy innocent, inexpensive life. The wines are very light,—so much so as to make the water almost preferable. I take great pride in my abstinence, and console myself with thinking of the play I will make with the first bottle of claret when I get home!

We send all our joint loves and are in real truth delighted to hear so good an account of yourself. You say that £200 is due.

Send it, whenever you please, to my account at the Union Bank of London, Prince's Street, Mansion House, London. Your payments are all premature.

I will, as I have said, answer your letter further about the tale.

Yours most faithfully
ANTHONY TROLLOPE

713. To JOHN BLACKWOOD. 12 September.
National Library of Scotland.

My dear Blackwood.   Höllenthal   September 12, 1878

A few days since I wrote, and the day afterward I returned the proof of N° 9 corrected. Will you kindly ask them to send the MS to me to Montagu Square. I always keep the MS. I have that of the previous parts.

I now write a line chiefly in answer to your suggestion, as to some possible alteration in the way in which Caldigate repays a sum of money to the rascals. When I get further proofs, and as I get them, I will endeavour to do something, *if I find anything feasible*; but I am bound to say that I have never found myself able to effect changes in the plot of a story. Small as the links are, one little thing hangs on another to such an extent that any change sets the whole narrative wrong. There are so many infinitesimal allusions to what is past, that the whole should be re-written or it will be faulty. I may be able to alter expressions so as to produce some changed effect on the reader's mind; but I doubt I cannot alter the incident. It seemed to me that such a payment, made under two influences,—put [*sic*] the sense that honour demanded a repayment, and secondly the hope that such repayment might be effectual in stopping the trouble,—was not more unnatural than conduct which we often see in the world. I may probably have been wrong. I shall think I have been if you say so. But I fear I cannot twist it otherwise. Nevertheless when I have the matter before me I will see what can be done.[1]

Yours always,
with our kindest love
ANTHONY TROLLOPE

[1] See 'Restitution', *John Caldigate*, ii, chap. viii. It does not seem likely that any extensive revision was made.

714. To M I S S B R A C K E N B U R Y. 3 October.
   Parrish Collection.

In the letter that follows Trollope writes of the death of Mary Holmes.

3, October 1878
(39, Montagu Square.)

My dear Miss Brackenbury

   My neice has given me your letters telling her of your aunts death. I do not know whether you knew the story of my friendship,—or rather of my correspondence, with her. For the last 14 years I have been in the habit of hearing from her at great length, and of writing to her, I fear, with much less frequency. But she knew that I am a busy man with little spare time at my command, whereas her hours were more at her own command. She wrote to me at first, simply because another correspondent had died, and she chose me to supply his place. The former correspondent was William Thackeray.

   I found her letters to be full of piety, good sense, and and [*sic*] of most excellent literary criticism. She never spared me when,— as was very often the case,—she thought I had strayed either from truth to nature or from good sense in my writing. But when she was pleased by what I did, she spoke her praise very openly. I may truly say that I attended more to her censure than her eulogy—

   She was an honest, religious, and a high minded lady, and I feel that her death has robbed me of a friend.

Yours very faithfully
A N T H O N Y T R O L L O P E

715. To W I L L I A M B L A C K W O O D. 9 October.
   National Library of Scotland.

   John Caldigate was written for serialization in 16 numbers, but Chapman plans to republish in June, when only 15 numbers will have appeared. 'Can you tell me what are your uncle's intentions?' (Blackwood managed to publish the novel in 15 numbers.)

716. To JOHN BLACKWOOD. 11 October. Montagu
Square. *National Library of Scotland.* Excerpts in
Sadleir, *Commentary*, p. 316; *Parker*, p. 63.

This longish letter, chiefly about plans for the arrangement of chapters in
the serial publication of *John Caldigate*, begins: 'I am very sorry to hear
about William B. Pray tell him so from me. I suppose it will not much
interfere with his hunting as you say the fracture is not bad. To a hunting
man a broken leg out of season is nothing. Many a man would think it simply
a beneficent arrangement of Providence so to break all his limbs about the
middle of April as to have them again fit for the saddle on 1st November.'
Trollope thought that John Blackwood wanted several chapters of *John
Caldigate* condensed. After raising some objections he finally gives in: 'Tell
me what reduction you require,—or how many pages you can allow. Then
I will make the reduction accordingly,—but with an aching heart!'[1]

717. To JOHN BLACKWOOD. 15 October.
Montagu Square. *National Library of Scotland.*

Trollope gives instructions for dividing the last six parts of *John Caldigate*
into five.

718. To JOHN BLACKWOOD. 19 October. Montagu
Square. *National Library of Scotland.*

On behalf of his brother, Trollope asks if 'a life of Victor Emanuel would
have a chance of becoming a popular book in England?' Tom 'doubts
whether English readers would care for the subject. My idea is that the
popularity of a book depends more on its treatment than its subject.' (Blackwood was apparently not enthusiastic, for the book was never written.)

719. To BEATRICE TROLLOPE. 20 October.
The Hon. Mrs. James Cecil.

Sunday morning, 20 Oct 1878

Dear Bice,   (39, Montagu Square.)

I have much considered what you said to me. There are four
ways in which you might proceed. I could write to your father.
You could speak to him. You could get Fanny to speak to him.
Or you could write to him. Were you to ask me to do so I should
write,—but it would make him *very* angry. This might not
practically hurt me, but would be very prejudicial to your

[1] Blackwood's end-note: 'Trollope had misunderstood & I have written
to him explaining that I intended the parts to be lengthened.'

happiness, for a time. I would do so if you asked me, but I think it would cause too great a disruption to your own life!

You say of yourself that you would break down if you were to attempt to speak to him. I can easily believe it. It would be a most difficult task, and I doubt whether you possess the necessary self-composure and hardness. Fanny would do it best, as having the greatest influence over him. But you best know how far you would choose to trust such a task to her. She is true to him as gold; but I am not sure that she can sympathise with an opposing interest. I think you must either write to him, or continue in silence to bear what you feel to be a hardship. If you write, you should, I think, do it in this way—

'Dear Papa,

I hope you will not be angry with me if I write to you about my money matters and tell you just what I think. I do feel that I am straightened in some things in which I ought to be more comfortable. Would you mind reconsidering the amount allowed to me. Of course if there were real need I would give up everything to you, but, as things are, could I not be allowed to be more comfortable? What I would ask is to have £150 or £140 and to pay out of it all my journeys and expenses of that kind. As it is I am sometimes so hard pressed as to be hardly able to pay for such expenses as washing bills and the like. Dear papa, pray do not be angry but think of all this for me.'

Should you write such a letter you must be prepared to be asked whether you had consulted me. If you are so asked, you must tell the truth. He will not probably accede to your request at once; but the letter would, I think, lead,—after much heartburning,—to some yielding on his part. You had better see me again before you send it.

A. T.

720. To CHARLES HALL. 26 October.
Parrish Collection.

Oct 26, 1878
My dear Hall,   (39, Montagu Square.)

I saw your father[1] the other day & told him I was going to give you a lift in your profession. I want an opinion.

[1] Sir Charles Hall (1814–83), barrister, authority on real property law, vice-chancellor, 1873.

If A leave to B by will an estate X, and also leave to C a sum of £1,000, will C be able to get out of X [? B] his legacy, if on A's death there be no other property beside or beyond the estate X?[1]

Yours always

ANTHONY TROLLOPE

Where are you and what are you doing? Have you shares in the Glasgow Bank?[2]

721. To? 13 November. Montagu Square.
Parrish Collection.

Trollope will call on his correspondent the day after the architects' dinner. 'I shall be most delighted to meet Mr Dunkley [*sic*] who is quite a publisher after my own heart. A member of the late Govt assured me the other day that if I wished to be considered a Liberal I was bound to know his article in the XIX Century by heart.' Henry Dunckley (1823–96), editor of the *Manchester Examiner and Times*, 1855–89, was a frequent contributor to periodicals under the pseudonym of 'Verax'. He was an authority on constitutional and political questions. The article to which Trollope refers is 'The Progress of Personal Rule', iv (Nov. 1878), 785–808.

722. To MRS. LINNAEUS BANKS.[3] 16 November.
Harvard College Library.

16, November 1878
(39, Montagu Square.)

My dear Madam.

Your note with the enclosed Circular reached me at Manchester, at the house of my friend the Postmaster. This will explain the two addresses given on the Circular, and the 10/- enclosed—

Singularly enough on the day before I got your letter your name was mentioned as follows,—and I trust you will not think that I behaved otherwise than with proper sympathy and in a true spirit of literary friendship in what I ventured to do.

At a semi-public dinner,—there were speakers but no re-

---

[1] 26 Oct. 1878 was the day Trollope began *Cousin Henry*. The inquiry relates to the situation which develops shortly after the story opens.

[2] For an account of the failure of the Bank of the City of Glasgow, see *The Times*, 2 Oct. 1878, p. 5.

[3] Isabella Varley Banks (1821–97), known generally as Mrs. Linnaeus Banks, was a prolific miscellaneous writer, and the author of the well-known novel *The Manchester Man* (1876).

406

porters,—the Mayor of Manchester in speaking of his feelings regarding the city said how powerfully he had been moved by a tale called 'The Manchester Man' and written by Mrs Banks, and he declared in very strong language his admiration for the genius displayed. At the time the remembrance of what had come to my knowledge a few days before at the Literary Fund Committee meeting, and the entire sympathy expressed by the gentlemen there in reference to your misfortunes, was full in my mind; and when the dinner was over I spoke to the mayor, making no reference of course to your application, but telling how far your reward in literary life had fallen short of your deserts. He then asked whether I thought that he might be allowed to contribute something to your relief, and I said that I would convey to you whatever he might wish to say. On the following morning I received the enclosed, which you will perhaps acknowledge to him.

Had you heard the language in which he spoke of your book that would at any rate have given you unmixed pleasure.

very faithfully yours
A N T H O N Y   T R O L L O P E

723. To A L E X A N D E R   I R E L A N D.[1] 29 November.
Yale University Library.

29, Nov 1878
(39, Montagu Square.)

My dear Mr Ireland

I will supply you with a novel written by myself in 24 chapters, of the length described by me to you, for publication in your weekly Examiner newspaper, for the sum of £150, if used in your newspaper only or £200 if divided between you and another newspaper.

The novel will be called Cousin Henry and shall be with you before the end of the year. It is to be published by you in the months of February and March next;[2]—but is to appear only in your own newspaper or in any other newspaper with which

---

[1] Alexander Ireland (1810–94), publisher and business manager of *The Manchester Examiner*, 1846–86.
[2] *Cousin Henry* appeared in the *Manchester Weekly Times* and the *North British Weekly Mail* from 8 Mar. to 24 May 1879.

you may agree. It must be understood however that the publication in the other newspaper must be contemporaneous.

Yours faithfully

ANTHONY TROLLOPE

724. TO ALEXANDER IRELAND. 2 December.
*Buffalo Public Library. Descriptive Catalogue of the
Gluck Collection of Manuscripts and Autographs in the
Buffalo Public Library* (Buffalo, 1899), pp. 115–16.

2 December 1878

(39, Montagu Square.)

My dear Mr Ireland,

I shall have finished my story in about a week. I find that there arise in it various legal points,—not legal questions with which I should not dabble,—but matters of phraseology and form. I suppose it would be out of the question for you to have it printed at once in slips, so as to enable me to get a barrister to read it? I could not ask a friend to do this in MS. I have had this done before, but I can understand that it would be out of the question to do it when the type are so constantly required as in a newspaper establishment. It is however as well to ask the question.

Yours always faithfully

ANTHONY TROLLOPE

725. TO ALEXANDER IRELAND. 10 December.
Parrish Collection.

10 Decr 1878

(39, Montagu Square.)

My dear Mr Ireland

I have finished my story and will send you the MS as soon as I have read it through.

If you have not yet advertised it you may choose out of the following three names—

Cousin Henry,
Getting at a secret,
Uncle Indefer's Will

The second is exactly apposite. My wife says that it sounds clap trap. The other two are quite appropriate.

Will you kindly send me the slips *in duplicate*, both for the first correction and for the revise.

Yours faithfully
ANTHONY TROLLOPE

I am writing a short memoir on poor George H. Lewes for the Fortnightly, whom we buried last week. He was one of my dearest friends.[1]

726. To CHARLES LEE LEWES. 11 December.
University of Leeds Library.

11. Dec. 1878.
(39, Montagu Square.)

My dear Lewes,

Your father in his preface to the Aristotle[2] calls his work the 'final portion' of a much greater enterprise which he indicates as a sketch of 'The Embryology of Science'.

Had he any idea of carrying out the same purpose in the 'Problems of Life and Mind'?

Yours always,
ANTHONY TROLLOPE

1879

727. To CHARLES BERTHOUD.[3] 8 January.
Muriel Rose Trollope.

8 January 1879

Dear Sir,

In reference to your letter of 28 December as to the translation of the 'Warden' into French for publication in Switzerland,

---

[1] 'George H. Lewes', *The Fortnightly Review*, n.s., xxv (1 Jan. 1879), 15–24.

[2] Lewes's *Aristotle* appeared in 1864; his *Problems of Life and Mind* was a posthumous publication (1879).

[3] Charles Berthoud, who translated *The Warden* into French, lived at Gingins, Canton de Vaud, Switzerland. He published *Études et biographies* (Neuchâtel, 1894) and *François d'Assise*, translated from the German of Dr. Karl Hase (1864).

I do not remember what passed between us. I do not however in the least doubt that the permission was given.

I think, however, that you were not justified in changing the title of the book.[1] In granting permission to translate I gave permission to you to publish with my name a French version of my book, and not of another.

It will not be in my power to extend the permission to any other book of mine.[2]

I am dear Sir,
Your faithful servant,
ANTHONY TROLLOPE

728. To FREDERIC CHAPMAN. 15 January. Montagu Square. *Parrish Collection*.

Trollope thinks he had better see Barnard.[3] If not, he suggests 'the novels in which Lady Glencora is brought out'.

729. JOHN MORLEY to ANTHONY TROLLOPE. 27 January. *Bodleian Library*.

When Trollope agreed to do the sketch of Thackeray for the English Men of Letters series, he received the following letter from John Morley, the general editor.

Brighton.
Jan. 27. 79

My dear Trollope,

I am delighted that it is to be, and particularly as we have such friendly assent from Stephen and his sister-in-law.[4] But I confess to a touch of disappointment that the world is never to have a full life of him, and a selection from his letters, which must have been full of flavour. I don't know how far you will

---

[1] In a letter to Trollope (written in French) preserved in the family files, Berthoud says that he changed the title to *Legs de John Hiram* because *Gardien* presented difficulties. He understands, he adds, that there are two other books, forming a trilogy, and he asks to be permitted to translate them.

[2] My text is Trollope's copy of his letter, written in the hand of Florence Bland.

[3] Apparently about illustrations for some projected reprint. Frederick Barnard (1846–96), an artist, had just finished the many cuts for Chapman & Hall's 'Household Edition' of the works of Charles Dickens. There are no recorded illustrations of Trollope novels by Barnard.

[4] Leslie Stephen and Annie Thackeray Ritchie. To her Trollope sent an elaborate questionnaire which with her replies is now among Trollope's papers (Bodleian).

feel free to tell his story, but I hope you will give us as much as ever you can in the personal vein, by way of background to the critical and descriptive.

The end of March will do perfectly well. In fact I shall hardly be ready before. So I will book you for *Mar.* 31, w^h is exactly 9 weeks from to-day.

It is to be not less than 180 pp., nor more than 200; and perhaps I ought to write down on paper what I mentioned to you, that the fee is to be 200£ (say two hundred pounds—as they put so mysteriously in legal documents—why, I wonder?) [.]

Macmillan is quite as well pleased as I am at your accession to our band.

I return Stephen's letter. When the day comes, I will tell you the printers to whom copy is to be sent.

Yours always,
JOHN MORLEY.

730. To CECILIA MEETKERKE. January. 'Anthony Trollope', *Blackwood's Magazine*, cxxxiii (February 1883), 319.

*   *   *

You sent me 'Balzac,' you say, and a Christmas card,—no doubt meaning them to be incentives to me to do what you were not at the moment minded to do yourself. The Christmas cards, I own, pass by me not unobserved, but with that small amount of attention which is always vouchsafed to one in a crowd; but when I am written to, I answer like a man, at an interval of a week or so. But in truth, I am growing so old that, though I still do my daily work, I am forced to put off the lighter tasks from day to day: to-morrow will do—and to-morrow! I do not feel like that in the cheery morning; but when I have been cudgelling my overwrought brain for some three or four hours in quest of words, then I fade down, and begin to think it will be nice to go to the club, and have tea, and play whist, and put off my letters till the evening: then there is something else, and the letter is not written.[1]

*   *   *

[1] I am able to identify the addressee of this letter through the kindness of Mr. John Blackwood of Edinburgh.

731. To BRET HARTE. 2 February. Montagu Square.
Estate of Carroll A. Wilson.

Having heard from Smalley that Harte is in town, Trollope invites him to
dine at the Garrick Club. (Apparently Harte could not accept, for on 1 July
Trollope still had not met him. See letter No. 751, *infra.* But he certainly
met him at the Royal Academy dinner of 1 May 1880, where Harte responded
to the toast of Literature. See George R. Stewart, Jr., *Bret Harte: Argonaut
and Exile* (Boston: Houghton Mifflin, 1931), p. 266.)

732. To JOHN BLACKWOOD. 6 February.
National Library of Scotland.

Trollope discusses *John Caldigate.*

(39, Montagu Square.)
February 6, 1879

My dear Blackwood

Thanks for the cheque for £100. Touching my 'legalities'
I had an infinite amount of 'bar' advice, having consulted quite
a crowd of lawyers, including judges, ex attorney friends, and
the like. But I do not say that I put any question specially as to
the admissability of evidence from the woman claiming to be the
wife. If I have done wrong I shall hear of it when the book comes
out in 3 volumes. I too felt for old Shand when he found himself
bound by hospitality to offer the dangerous comfort.

As to amendments in the telling of the story as between Caldigate and Hester, I tried my hand at it and failed. The task of
interpolating new work on a tale is to me so hopeless that I feel
that I am sure to destroy the old by the new. My new wine is
sure to burst the old bottles. Such as it comes at first it must
remain. There was a touch of downright love in the depicting
of Bagwax. Was I not a Bagwax myself?

Yes;—I have got the Thackeray in hand and a terrible job
I find it. There is absolutely nothing to say,—except washed out
criticism. But it had to be done, and no one would do it so
lovingly.

Are your Ancient Classics finished? You ought to have a
Quintillian. I am reading him and am halfway through. It would
be much nicer to write about old Latin schoolmasters than
modern novels.

My kind regards to your wife. I am sorry to hear your nephew is so robbed of his hunting.

Yours always
ANTHONY TROLLOPE

733. To [? WILLIAM HOWARD] RUSSELL. 20 February. *Parrish Collection.*

Trollope consults one of Thackeray's Garrick Club friends for anecdotes and first-hand information.

Feb 20.

Dear Russell   (39, Montagu Square.)

Do not trouble yourself to make any MS. My biographical chapter will be finished today. I did not like to do it without letting you know, and some dozen others, so that if there were any little trifle to say, it might be said. An incident here or there I have got. What passed between us at the Club was probably more valuable than any letter.

Yours always
ANTHONY TROLLOPE

A man,—genus literary—writes me a letter addressing it to Arthur Trollope, which of course I did not notice. Then he sent me a long apology in which he remarks that he has been led away by the doubtfulness of my signature!

734. To OCTAVIAN BLEWITT. 24 February. *Royal Literary Fund.* Not seen.

The Minutes of the General Committee meeting of the Royal Literary Fund held on 12 February show that Trollope moved 'That no letter shall be read to the committee . . . except by the Secretary, and that any letter so read shall be left in the hands of the Secretary'.

24th. February 1879

My dear Mr Blewitt,   (39, Montagu Square.)

I think that I had better not attend the committee on Wednesday next, but will trouble you to read this letter to them.

I feel very strongly the kindness shown to me by those who at our last meeting suggested that a concession might be made to me in the matter I had brought forward—not because I was

413

right, but simply because I wished it. This was the more flattering as it was done simply with the view of inducing me to keep
my seat. But I altogether deprecate this, feeling that my services
are not worthy any surrender of opinion such as that. Our
President[1] was kind enough to say that, as regards himself, he
would for the future abstain from that mode of communication
with the Committee to which I had objected. This would no
doubt do all that I required. But I cannot bear that he should
be hampered in doing his work after his own fashion by what he
may think to be a foolish craze on my part. By remaining on the
Committee on such terms, I should do more harm than good.
If I carry him along with me—and other Gentlemen who form
the Committee, then I should be rejoiced to remain.

I will attempt to explain my purpose which I fear I have
hitherto failed to do in my endeavour to avoid personal offence.
At our Board the influence of our President has ever been,
and I hope always will be, very great. It is too great to be
delegated to another. We have no right to expect that it shall
always be exercised by him in person. It may well be that it
should suit him and us to record our opinion in writing. But
we cannot endure a second President. Such would become the
case should it be customary with us to receive at Board one of
ourselves, carrying, as it were, the President in his pocket.

In the resolution which I proposed I endeavoured to avoid
personality, but in so doing I have been vague. One of our
number remarked that though I had shown strong feeling in
the matter, I had given no reason. I felt this to be so true that
I have now been compelled to give my reasons, though it has
troubled me to do so. But I think that my resolution, as it is
worded, stands on good grounds. At all Committees with which
I have been conversant it has been the custom that documents
required to be read should be read by the Secretary. Gentlemen,
if they will look back upon the practice as they have met it, will,
I think, remember that it is so. Such a practice has certainly
prevailed at our Board. The Secretary, when reading such documents, is himself colourless, having no vote; and such should,
I think, be the position of him who is to make known the opinion
of another.

[1] The Earl of Derby.

I am aware that when we discussed the matter at our last meeting the Committee was altogether against me. Though I think it right now to explain myself:—being perhaps more able to do so in writing than by speech,—I am far from supposing that I shall persuade Gentlemen to agree with me. I only hope to be able to make them acknowledge that, with my strong convictions on the subject, it is better that the committee should be relieved from the presence of a member who would be at discord with them. I am closely attached to the Literary Fund and most willing to act on its behalf to the best of my energies;— but a member thoroughly discordant must be rather injurious than beneficial. I think, moreover, that a man can sometimes accomplish by dying that which he cannot do by living. If by my dissolution I can achieve any such victory—which may not be impossible—I shall, I think, have made the sacrifice to good purpose.

yours faithfully

Oct. Blewitt Esq.   ANTHONY TROLLOPE

---

735. TO OCTAVIAN BLEWITT. 26 February.
Royal Literary Fund. Not seen.

At the meeting of the General Committee of the Royal Literary Fund on 26 February, Trollope absent, Dr. Richardson[1] moved a resolution in substantial accordance with Trollope's. It was adopted.

Feb. 26 1879
(39, Montagu Square.)

My dear Mr Blewitt,

I forget the words of D^r. Richardson's resolution. I did not quite understand that it was to be moved in lieu of my own. It does not much matter if, as I suppose, the point is carried that all letters are to be read by the Secretary. But I should like to see the words if it will not give you too much trouble to send them. What became of the resolution which I proposed?

yours faithfully
ANTHONY TROLLOPE

[1] Benjamin Ward Richardson, later Sir Benjamin (1828–96), physician, president of the Medical Society of London, 1868, editor of the *Journal of Public Health and Sanitary Review*, registrar of the Royal Literary Fund.

736. To OCTAVIAN BLEWITT. 27 February. Montagu Square.
Royal Literary Fund. Not seen.

Trollope approves D^r. Richardson's resolution. 'It will prevent the evil of which I complained quite as well as my own. But why the committee should have objected to mine and then have agreed to his I cannot understand.' Trollope attended the Annual General Meeting on 12 March and was re-elected Treasurer.

737. To W. J. FITZPATRICK.[1] 24 March. *Not traced.*
W. J. Fitzpatrick, *The Life of Charles Lever*, 2 vols. (London, 1879), ii. 269–70.

March 24, 1879

*   *   *

Charles Lever was an intimate friend of mine whom I very dearly loved, but I do not know that I can tell you any details that will serve the purpose of your book.

Of all the clever men I have known, his wit was the readiest. In conversation he was the quickest goer and the best stager [stayer?] I ever knew, never failing even in ill health, never showing sign of weariness after any labour. But all that is simply my feeling of the man. I had many letters from him, as he wrote for a Magazine which I edited, but I never kept one. Though he lived always in Italy, with short intervals in London, he never dropped his Irish manner or his Irish tongue. In literature it was peculiar to him to have altogether changed his manner and tone, from the time of 'Harry Lorrequer' to that of 'Tony Butler,' and to have been quite at home and quite successful in each. He became attached to the Conservative party; but yet I doubt whether he had any strong political feeling. His was a kind friendly nature, prone to cakes and ale, and resolved to make the best of life when, as you no doubt know, things were often very sad with him.

*   *   *

738. To WILLIAM BLACKWOOD. 3 April. Montagu Square. *National Library of Scotland.*

Blackwood has not kept an appointment. 'I hope you did not expect a letter. I understood I was not to write if the appointment suited.'

[1] William John Fitzpatrick (1830–95), historian and biographer of Irish scenes and personalities.

739. TO ALEXANDER IRELAND. 3 April.
Parrish Collection.

3 April 1879
(39, Montagu Square.)

My dear Mr Ireland

May I ask you to ask your printers to let me have my own way about my own paragraphs. They have an idea as to the arrangement of dialogue opposed to my idea. I will not contest the question with them as [to] which is right. But I am exasperated. It is my duty to write as I think best, and theirs to print as I write.

I should not trouble you but that they persevere after former special requests made to them. The intelligence of printers and their sedulous care is beyond all praise. I have met none superior to yours. They read my bad writing, and no doubt often correct my bad spelling. But they should not alter my forms of expression, because they do not, and cannot, know my purpose.

Very faithfully yours
ANTHONY TROLLOPE

We are here all elated by the effect of the last debate.[1]

740. TO ADRIAN H. JOLINE.[2] 2 April. *Not traced.*
Adrian H. Joline, *Meditations of an Autograph Collector*
(New York: Harper & Bros., 1902), p. 224.

4 April 1879
(39, Montagu Square.)

Dear Sir,

The remarks you quote were made by me. You say that it would be dangerous to interfere with the 'family arrangement.' I think it is impossible to do so to any great extent. You cannot, by Act of Congress or Parliament make the woman's arm as

---

[1] On 1 Apr. debate was concluded on the conduct of Trollope's friend Sir Bartle Frere in the South African campaign against Cetywayo. Frere was accused of disobedience in permitting General Thesiger, outnumbered ten to one, to cross the Tugela, a manœuvre that ended catastrophically at Isandhlwana on 22 Jan. 1879. The attacks on Frere were largely political.

[2] Adrian Hoffman Joline (1850–1912), lawyer, collector of autographs and rare books, author of four books on the pleasures of bibliophilism.

strong as the man's or deprive her of her position as the bearer
of children. We may trouble ourselves much by debating a
question which superior power has settled for us, but we cannot
alter the law. To avoid, or lessen that trouble, it is I think
expedient to explain and make manifest to all, the facts as they
have been settled for us by that superior power,—not as doubting what may be the result. The necessity of the supremacy of
man is as certain to me as the eternity of the soul. There are
other matters on which one fights as on subjects which are in
doubt,—universal suffrage, ballot, public education, and the like
—but not, as I think, on these two.[1]

Yours faithfully

ANTHONY TROLLOPE

741. To HENRY PHILLIPS.[2] 5 April.
Historical Society of Pennsylvania.

April 5—1879

(39, Montagu Square.)

Dear Sir.

I have to thank you very heartily for the present you sent me
last year of your translations from Spanish and German Poems.[3]
I had not observed the printed notice in the volume or I should
have written to you when the volume reached me.

As I do not know the originals I can only speak of the versification and speak of the poems in the form you have given them,
both of which evidently possess very high merit.

faithfully yours

ANTHONY TROLLOPE

Henry Phillips Esq

[1] In the light of Trollope's reputation to-day one of Joline's comments is
most interesting: 'I have a bookish friend who actually prides himself on the
possession of a complete set of first editions of Anthony Trollope! It cost
him a good deal of time and toil, and I know not how many golden shekels.
But why not E. P. Roe, or T. S. Arthur, or William Gilmore Simms? I
should as soon think of accumulating first editions of the Congressional
Record' (pp. 74–5). Joline actually had a *very* high opinion of Trollope, but
the books brought nothing on the open market.

[2] Henry Phillips (1838–95) of Philadelphia, Penna.

[3] *Poems Translated from the Spanish and German*, privately printed
(Philadelphia, 1878). Only 100 copies were printed.

742. To JOHN BLACKWOOD. 5 April.
National Library of Scotland.

(39, Montagu Square.)
5 April 1879.

My dear Blackwood,

Your nephew was speaking to me the other day about N.B. &
L.T. I can quite understand that you should wish to get back
something for the copyrights, and that nothing should be to be
had [*sic*] without the name.

I suppose there would be no sale in the tales now with the
names in their present form? If any such step were practicable I
would authorize the use of the name for this purpose for £50
each. But I suppose this is out of the question.

What would Smith give you for them? If you would name a
lump sum it might be worth my while to buy them from you,
and you would be as willing, probably, to sell to me as to them.

If our arrangement can be made in either of these ways, then
you may do as W. B. suggested.[1]

We go to Lowick[2] on Monday for three weeks.

Yours always
ANTHONY TROLLOPE

743. To W. LUCAS COLLINS. [? April.]
Not traced. Sadleir, *Commentary*, p. 393.

*   *   *

That I, who have belittled so many clergymen, should ever
come to live in a parsonage! There will be a heaping of hot coals!
You may be sure that I will endeavour to behave myself accordingly, so that no scandal shall fall upon the parish. If the bishop
should come that way, I will treat him as well as e'er a parson in
the diocese. Shall I be required to preach, as belonging to the
Rectory? I shall be quite disposed to give every one my blessing. . . . Ought I to affect dark garments? Say the word, and I
will supply myself with a high waistcoat. Will it be right to be

---

[1] Blackwood bound up both *Nina Balatka* and *Linda Tressel* (the four
volumes in two) and sold each novel for 3*s*. 6*d*.
[2] Residence of W. Lucas Collins. See letter No. 743, *infra.*

quite genial with the curate, or ought I to patronise a little? If there be dissenters, shall I frown on them, or smile blandly? If a tithe pig be brought, shall I eat him? If they take to address me as 'The Rural Anthony,' will it be all right?[1]

*   *   *

744. To Miss Reddie.[2] 10 April.
Not traced. Sadleir, *Commentary*, pp. 317–18.

Lowick,
Thrapstone.
April 10, 1879.

My dear Miss Reddie,

I am very much obliged to you for sending me Thora's letter, —the divine Thora.[3] I now return it. You ought to send it to Wilson—[4] Whether it would be a comfort who could say, because she makes no mention of him! Do you remember when she gave Wilson the bit of grass to eat?

If you write ask her whether the young guide, I forget his name, got a little Caesar which I promised to him and sent to him by post.

Give my regards to your grandfather and all the . . .[5] folk who remember me.

Yours always,
very sincerely
ANTHONY TROLLOPE

Tell Thora that I shall look forward anxiously to her book of travels in which she is to mention me.[6]

---

[1] *Dr. Wortle's School* was begun at Lowick on 8 Apr. 1879.

[2] Miss Reddie of Wemyss Bay, one of the party on the voyage to Iceland.

[3] Thora Pjetursson, daughter of the Bishop of Iceland, spoke English and helped to entertain the party.

[4] Captain Wilson Dennistoun of the Royal Navy had been attracted to Thora.

[5] Mr. Sadleir's copy is defective at this point.

[6] In a letter to Miss Reddie from Reykjavik Thora had threatened to retaliate for Trollope's account of her by writing not only a book of travels but a 'special book' about him.

745. To FREDERIC CHAPMAN. 26 April. Lowick.
Pierpont Morgan Library.

Trollope asks for 'Morleys book on Diderot'.[1] He adds, 'I shall come back to town next week, on Wednesday, almost without a shilling, and you must give me a cheque for £200, at once.'

746. To MRS. HANSARD. 29 April. Lowick.
Parrish Collection.

The Trollopes 'have been vacationing down here,—snowed up for the most part, so much that we could hardly get across the road to church'. Trollope and Florence Bland will call. 'As I gather now, we are not to make an appearance till Sunday 11 May, on which day, if all goes well, we will pursue our oriental travels, and come in upon you dying for tea at about 4—'

747. To WILLIAM BLACKWOOD. 26 May.
National Library of Scotland.

(39, Montagu Square.)

My dear Blackwood   26 May 1879

Thanks for your cheque £100, making a total sum of £600 paid for use of John Caldigate in Maga.

I was sorry to hear from Langford a bad account of your uncle,—and am the more so now as it seems from your letter to have been very severe. I trust that he is getting over it. Give him my very kindest remembrances. I still hope we shall see him before long.

I shall be very anxious to see George Eliots book.[2] I called on her one day last week—just as she was about to leave town to Witley and sat with her for an hour. I found her cheerful, but she said nothing about her own book. She never does.

I have just had a letter from Collins who says that the warm weather is agreeing with him. He will be home about the middle of June, unless called sooner by a chance, which is, I hope, now improbable,—the death of S. Sackville.[3] He was very bad, but is I think better.

Yours always faithfully

ANTHONY TROLLOPE

[1] John Morley, *Diderot and the Encyclopaedists*, 2 vols. (London, 1878).
[2] *Impressions of Theophrastus Such* (1879).
[3] Sackville George Stopford Sackville (1840–1926), M.P. for North Northants., 1867–80.

748. To ALEXANDER IRELAND. 28 May. Montagu Square. *Parrish Collection.*

Trollope writes at length about *Cousin Henry* and about his intention to serialize another novel, which he offers to Ireland for his paper.[1] 'I wish you would come up & see us here and have a little politics and discuss the novel too.'

749. To ? 3 June. Montagu Square. *Parrish Collection.*

Trollope tells a correspondent that he wrote nothing on the Civil Service in the *Fortnightly*, that it must be his lecture to which reference was made. 'Since that time I have risen above or fallen below the file of Secretaries.'

750. To JOHN BLACKWOOD. June [dated in another hand]. *Parrish Collection.*

Trollope welcomes the Blackwoods back to town and invites them to call.

751. To GEORGE W. SMALLEY. 1 July. Montagu Square. *Parrish Collection.*

Trollope particularly wants to meet Bret Harte, but unfortunately he has a dinner party at home on the 14th.

752. To JOHN BLACKWOOD. 16 July. Montagu Square. *Parrish Collection.*

Trollope has two novels to offer: one, written at Lowick, is the length of *Nina Balatka*; the other is the length of *John Caldigate*. He hopes Blackwood will choose the longer.[2] He leaves town on 6 August.

753. To DR. RIDDING.[3] 22 July. Montagu Square. *Parrish Collection.*

Trollope presents a set of 'The Chronicles of Barsetshire' to Winchester College.

[1] Trollope may have had *Ayala's Angel* in mind, but no further novels were serialized with Ireland.

[2] Trollope refers to *Dr. Wortle's School* and *Ayala's Angel*. Blackwood chose *Dr. Wortle's School*, the shorter, and it was serialized from May to December 1880.)

[3] George Ridding (1828–1904) was headmaster of Winchester, 1866–84; called the 'second founder'. Trollope was a pupil at Winchester, 1827–30.

754. To JOHN BLACKWOOD. 8 August.
   Parrish Collection.

Gerardmer Vosges,[1] August 8—1879
address (39, Montagu Square.)
My dear Blackwood,
   I am afraid you must be unwell, or you would probably have answered a letter I wrote to you some weeks since in consequence of a message I had received from Collins. It was, indeed, about two months ago, and had reference to a new novel. Do not trouble yourself about it, but consider rather that though I shall receive no answer I shall consider my letter as answered.
   Write to me a line simply to tell me how you are, and what you are doing, or intending to do, this summer. When last I saw Joe Langford before leaving London he gave a somewhat better account of you.
   My wife went off nearly a month since. I left London on 1st. August and caught her here;—a most detestable place to my thinking, as are all these places in France. One has to get into Switzerland or South Germany before one finds a pleasant country or a pleasant people. We go on, first to the Canton Zug and then to the Black Forest. I purpose being back in London about October 1st.
   If you are too feckless to write, get Mrs Blackwood to write a line to my wife.
   With kindest regards to her and Mary I am
                         Yours always faithfully
                         ANTHONY TROLLOPE

755. To HENRY MERIVALE TROLLOPE. 29 August.
   Muriel Rose Trollope.

Felsenegg. 29 August 1879
(39, Montagu Square.)
Dear Harry,
   We were very glad to hear something of you, by your letter to your mother,—though it was very little except that you had spent most of your time drinking vermouthe at Chambery. Let me know something of your doings at Hollenthal, where we shall be on September 2.
   I went down to Baden to see your uncle, & shall do so again

───────────
   [1] In central France near the Swiss border.

on my way to Freiburg. He has suffered dreadfully from sciatica; and though the pain is I think diminished, he has been so pulled down, as still to be in a very sad condition. When next I write I will tell you what I think of him.

We have altered our plans about Florence so as to relieve you from the task of taking her down to Cranorth [?]. We will all go home by the usual route via Luxembourg, & then she will return to Jersey from Southampton. It will be much cheaper, and less troublesome to all concerned.

Do not, however, make this an excuse for coming later to us. I shall hope to see you in the first days of October, so as to stay into the new year. I am sure it will be better for you to make a tolerably long stay in London.

Have you heard from Mrs Oliphant? I have been disappointed in not having a word from Blackwood. I fear that he must be very far from well.

Try to bring at any rate a portion of that archaeological work with you to England in translation.

Jones succeeded in buying for me two of those ground rents in Montagu Square for £840— They will give us 7½ per cent for 24 years.

God bless you
Most affectionately yours
ANTHY TROLLOPE

756. To FREDERIC CHAPMAN. 30 August.
  Pierpont Morgan Library.

Felesnegg.   August 30, 1879
Address. Hollsteig.   (39, Montagu Square.)
   Freiburg
     Baden—

Dear Chapman.

I send back to you the first 6 sheets of Atherton Wylde[1] corrected, and I now send a letter which I will beg you to

---

[1] 'Atherton Wylde' was Frances Ellen Colenso, daughter of Bishop Colenso. The manuscript which Trollope read was *My Chief and I; or, Six Months in Natal after the Langalibalele Outbreak* (London, 1880). See letter No 759, *infra*.

direct on to Col. Durnford.[1] I do not know his address, which you have got.

The book is clever and will probably sell,—but it is shamefully personal. In England it would I think subject the writer,—or publisher as the book is anonymous, to an action for libel. What may be the case in the Colony in this respect, I do not know. I cannot but think that were I the author's father and were living in the Colony I should be most unwilling that such a book should be published.

I do not like not to tell you all this.

Yours always faithfully
ANTHONY TROLLOPE—

I have told almost the same to Col. Durnford.

757. To HENRY MERIVALE TROLLOPE. 7 September.
Muriel Rose Trollope.

Höllenthal 7, Sept. 1879
(39, Montagu Square.)

My dear Harry, I have just got your letter with the quotations from Milton, for which I am much obliged. It was long since I wanted the passage for something I was writing— I hope I got it right, but I altogether forget. I think it ought to be 'God' and not 'Lord'— But that was Milton's affair.

I am glad you heard from M[rs] Oliphant, though I think that she has been what I call indifferent in the matter. You however, exceeded the time suggested to you, and cannot turn upon her,— as yet. You must wait a few months, and then if you do not hear, write to her again. Poor Blackwood I fear must be ill, because I do not hear from him.

My brother has got up to the Rigi Staffel[2] whither he had been ordered, having had a very troublesome & painful journey. We have yet to see what effect the place may have on him. He has suffered damnably.

Get the scientific MS if you can for work here in England.

We are all very well, & your mother has been doing wonders

---

[1] Lt.-Col. Edward Durnford, husband of 'Atherton Wylde'. His father, Col. Anthony William Durnford, was killed in South Africa 22 Apr. 1879.

[2] Rigi Staffel: a group of mountains above the Lake of Lucerne.

in walking,—ten miles one day—about three hours 5 days a week. In London she cant walk a mile.

Be as early as you can in October.

Your affectionate father
ANTH TROLLOPE

758. To HENRY MERIVALE TROLLOPE. 18 September.
Muriel Rose Trollope.

Holsteig—
18 Sept. 1879

Dear Harry,

Thanks for the Moratin—[1] It was the only one of the three I really cared for. Do not take any trouble as to the Prevost[2] and Mingault.[3] I supposed that if you found them they would be very cheap.

What did that 'pleasant' fellow Young say about Caldigate? You can tell me however when we meet—

As to the Devils aptitude for thinking I do not see why you should deprive him of it. I do not see how he was to contrive the worlds damnation without much thinking.

Middleton,[4] the American is here— He is rather a bore. But I have a certain liking for him.

Your uncle has gone down to Lucerne. He can hardly say or tell whether he is really better, for he has again had recourse to morphine.

Yours always aff.
ANTHONY TROLLOPE

[1] Leandro Fernández de Moratín (1760–1828), Spanish playwright after the fashion of Molière.

[2] Antoine François Prévost d'Exiles (1697–1763), a French abbé best known for his novel *L'Histoire du Chevalier des Grieux et de Manon Lescaut.*

[3] I am uncertain of the reading here, and I cannot identify the writer referred to.

[4] Possibly, though not at all certainly, Nathaniel Russell Middleton (1810–90), president of the College of Charleston.

759. To FREDERIC CHAPMAN. 18 September.
   Pierpont Morgan Library.

Holsteig Baden
                                    (39, Montagu Square.)
      Sept 18—1879
My dear Chapman,
      Thanks for the cheque.
      I do not think that the catching of Cetywayo[1] will make any
difference with the book,[2]—with which however I am not pleased
as I go on with it.
      I have sent back the last sheets I have, except a few pages,
which I have been forced to keep as I must put in the heading of a
chapter, which I cannot do till I see how the chapter goes. I suppose however the thing will keep back now till the authoress
arrives.
      You need not fear about libel here. My feeling has been as
to what would be said and thought and felt in the Colony.
      I hope your bones are all right again. We shall be home on
October first.
                              Yours always
                                    ANTHONY TROLLOPE

760. To FRANCES ELEANOR TROLLOPE. [September]
   Not traced. What I Remember, p. 486.

                    *   *   *

      For you, I cannot tell you the admiration I have for you. Your
affection and care and assiduity were to be expected. I knew you
well enough to take them as a matter of course from you to him.
But your mental and physical capacity, your power of sustaining
him by your own cheerfulness, and supporting him by your own
attention, are marvellous. When I consider all the circumstances,
I hardly know how to reconcile so much love with so much self-
control.
                    *   *   *

      [1] Cetywayo (*c.* 1836–84), king of Zululand, defeated the British at
Isandhlwana. He was captured and exiled, but later reinstated.
      [2] By 'Atherton Wylde'. See letter No. 756, *supra.*

761. To BEATRICE TROLLOPE. 3 October.
The Hon. Mrs. James Cecil.

3 October 1879

My dear Bice,

I am very glad to hear your news and I wish you joy with all my heart. I suppose your Charlie Wortley[1] is the son of the late Recorder of London. If so I have more than once met his mother at her mothers, Lady Wenlock. I suppose it is he whom you now call your Charlie Wortley. I hope I may very soon make his acquaintance. Pray tell him that we shall be delighted to see him, —but especially at 8 o'clock. When do you come up to town & when do you go to Italy, for I suppose your matrimonial engagements will not be so sudden as to prevent your return.

When I last saw your father he was suffering dreadfully. The sciatica had got such a hold of him that he could not shake it off— That was at Baden. Since that he has progressed rapidly. But still I long to hear that he has passed over his long journey, if not comfortably, at any rate without great pain.

Goodbye, dearest B. I wish you joy again and again with all my heart.

Your aff. uncle
ANTHY TROLLOPE

762. To JOHN BLACKWOOD. 15 October.
National Library of Scotland.

(39, Montagu Square.)
October 15, 1879.

My dear Blackwood,

Touching the Lowick story Chapman is to have it for publication (or republication) next winter, i e, in October, November, or more probably December 1880. He has just published one, 'Cousin Henry,' of the same length, and tells me that he has done very well with it. He has now succeeded with two, two years running.

Will you have it for the Blackwood? You may choose your time from now till December 1880. The story is intended to run

---

[1] Charles Beilby Stuart-Wortley (1851–1926), *cr.* Lord Stuart of Wortley, 1916. See letter No. 833, *infra.*

through 8 months, but might be otherwise divided if it suited you. I told you as to the price suggested—£200—only £200 to you, sir, for the use of it.

How are you, and your wife? Where are you, and your wife? Collins comes up to town the end of the month. Do you want to know the truth about the Critics? If so, come to Nottingham and hear me lecture.[1]

Yours always faithfully
ANTHONY TROLLOPE

We got home the first day of this week.

763. To WILLIAM BLACKWOOD. 28 October.
National Library of Scotland.

My dear William Blackwood   Birmingham 28 Oct. 1879

I have been glad to gather from your letter of the 24th that your uncle is better than he has been. When I last wrote to him I had heard nothing of the last attack or I should not have troubled him.

Touching the 'Bowick School'[2] I understand that the arrangement is made. It is to be printed in the Magazine so as to be completed by December 1, 1880 and is not to be republished by Chapman before that time. Price for use £200. Shall I send the MS. to Joe Langford? Not having heard, and not thinking it probable that your uncle would like to republish, I made my arrangement with Chapman. But I have no objection to your using my name with the 'Nina Balatka' and 'Linda Tressel' if it will be of any service. Let me know if you do.

All right about the little article on whist which I return corrected. *Only pray keep the secret.* Enquiries have been made of me as to the authorship.[3]

---

[1] Trollope lectured at Nottingham on 23 Oct. 1879 not on 'Critics' but on 'The Zulus and Zululand'. See the *Nottingham and Midland Counties Daily Express*, 24 Oct. 1879. The manuscript of this unpublished lecture is owned by Miss Muriel Trollope. An account of it will appear in a forthcoming issue of *Nineteenth-Century Fiction*.

[2] The first title, later discarded, for *Dr. Wortle's School.*

[3] This is Trollope's little *jeu d'esprit* 'Whist at Our Club', *Blackwood's*, cxxi (May 1877), 597–604. Reprinted in *Tales from Blackwood*, n.s., xii. 102–22. It was not published in book form until Feb. 1881.

Give my kindest regards to your uncle. I hope to hear that he is getting better.

Very faithfully yours
ANTHONY TROLLOPE

764. To W. ISBISTER. 6 November.
Parrish Collection.

Trollope sends some verses from his cousin, Cecilia Meetkerke, for *Good Words* or *Good Cheer*. The verses do not appear in *Good Words*, and I have not been able to find a copy of *Good Cheer* for 1879.

765. To R. S. OLDHAM. 19 November.
Muriel Rose Trollope.

19 November 1879
(39, Montagu Square.)

My dear Oldham,

If I wrote the book as you propose for the SPCK,[1] I would charge £250 for the copyright. It should be of about the length of the volume I put into your hands. The society should have the option of rejecting it, after it had been read by some reader on their behalf. And I would agree to place the MS in your hands by the last day of February. As regards the price, it would be just half what I am now receiving from my publishers for such work. The privilege of rejection I offer because it is incumbent on the Society to put forth nothing but that of which it approves. It is altogether contrary to my usual habit. Indeed I have not accorded such a privilege to any publisher for more than 20 years.

Now I will, as best I may, explain my reasons,—or what may rather be your reasons,—against such an arrangement, should it in other respects be acceptable. You said words to the effect that if I did this work for the Society I should have in a measure have [*sic*] made myself one with the Society. I cannot agree to that. I hold opinions on some subjects which I do not doubt are opposed to those taught by the Society. Creeping doubts have become common among members of the Church of England, clergy as well as laity, which 30 or 40 years since, would, if declared, have been received by churchmen with scorn. I am inclined to welcome such doubts rather than to repudiate them,

[1] The Society for the Propagation of Christian Knowledge. Negotiations between Trollope and the Society soon collapsed by mutual consent.

(not being a clergyman) and to think, whether I share them or not, that they are doing good. Such being the condition of my mind, I am unwilling to become one of you to the extent indicated by you; or to acknowledge by writing a book for the Society, that, however near our boats may be, I am altogether in the same boat with the Society.

It will now be for you to judge how far the Society should avail itself of my services.

Yours affectionately

A. T.

766. To GEORGINA HOGARTH.[1] 17 December. Montagu Square. *Parrish Collection.*

Trollope says thank-you for an edition of Dickens's letters. 'I have read the two volumes of letters with great delight, and most heartily congratulate you and your niece on your success in bringing them out.'[2]

767. To ? 17 December. Montagu Square. *Parrish Collection.*

Trollope cannot tell a correspondent where he could find a copy of *The West Indies and the Spanish Main.*

768. To MARY CHRISTIE. 18 December. Montagu Square. *Parrish Collection.*

Trollope is not surprised that Mary has not heard from Strahan. He invites her to come to breakfast.

1880

769. To MAX SCHLESINGER. 3 January. Montagu Square. *Parrish Collection.*

Trollope returns a volume borrowed for reference.[3] 'Mommsen[4] does not use the word Triumvirate.'

[1] Georgina Hogarth, sister of Dickens's wife, remained with Dickens as his housekeeper when the Dickenses separated.

[2] *The Letters of Charles Dickens,* ed. Georgina Hogarth and Mamie Dickens, 3 vols. (London, 1880–2). Trollope must have been presented with the first two volumes before publication.

[3] Trollope was studying for his *Life of Cicero.*

[4] Theodor Mommsen (1817–1903), the famous German historian. Trollope refers to his *Roman History* (1854–6).

770. To TOM TAYLOR. 11 January. Montagu Square.
J. H. Spencer. Not seen.

Trollope acknowledges receipt of a correction, apparently to the second edition of the *Thackeray*. He adds, 'I should have cared nothing for the article in the Pall Mall as a simple criticism. I have been too long at it to be much moved by what the folk say of me, good or bad, but these new circumstances may thus connect it with Annie, which makes me unhappy.'[1]

771. To WILLIAM BLACKWOOD. 11 February.
National Library of Scotland.

(39, Montagu Square.)
Feb. 11, 1880.

My dear Blackwood,

I think you will find the club a pleasant lounge when you are in town.[2] A man with so many calls up to London as must come in your way now could hardly be comfortable without belonging to a first rate club.

As to the novel, you talk of beginning it in May or June. Of course it is open to you to commence it in either of those months so it is finished in December, but as it was written with the intention of being seen through eight numbers May would be the best.[3] In writing a story in numbers a novelist divides his points of interest, so as to make each section a whole. It will often happen that his divisions should be recast to suit circumstances. But this cannot be done without a certain amount of detriment to the telling of the story.

I hope that Mrs Oliphant and Harry will hit off their difficulty.[4] I cannot but think that she has in some respect over-acted her part of editor, having assumed an imperiousness which would have been very foreign to Collins or to your uncle.[5] Her first

---

[1] See the severe review in the *Pall Mall* of 18 Oct. 1879, p. 12, where Trollope is criticized for inadequacies as critic and scholar. The reviewer adds, 'It must be a source of satisfaction to Thackeray's children to be assured on Mr. Trollope's authority that "the comfortable income"—the precise figure is stated—which he left behind *was* "earned honestly, with the full approval of the world around him".'

[2] Blackwood had just been elected to the Garrick Club.

[3] *Dr. Wortle's School* began in May 1880.

[4] The difficulty arose over Henry Trollope's editing of the *Corneille and Racine* volume in Mrs. Oliphant's 'Foreign Classics for English Readers' series. It was published by Blackwood in 1881.

[5] John Blackwood had died a few months before.

allegation was that Harry had not sufficiently admired his author, complaining of him that he had not written 'con amore'. Racine and Corneille have never been accepted altogether with enthusiasm by English readers,—nor will they ever be. Nevertheless their undoubted pre-eminence as French tragedians makes it important that they should be included in your series. Had she required nothing but praise instead of criticism, she should have said so beforehand.

She then requires poetical translation of extracts, not at all knowing how often the attempts have failed always. She kindly offers to do it herself;—but look at the attempts in the Moliere! Relieved from the superintendence of such an older critic as your uncle, she is I think a little without a guide.

Yours always faithfully
ANTHONY TROLLOPE

772. To WILLIAM BLACKWOOD. 8 April.
National Library of Scotland.

(39, Montagu Square.)
April 8, 1880.

My dear Blackwood,

I am very glad that you should like the beginning of the story. I think I have managed the question as to the marriage so as to give no offence.

You will find 24 chapters. The novel is divided into eight parts. And there is are [*sic*] three chapters for each part. I return the three first, separated from the others. Please send me sheets in duplicate as they are printed. But you may print so well that revises will not be needed, unless in cases in which I ask for them specially.

Say anything you like about Gladstone, not touching his personal character. Say that he is rash, unstatesmanlike, dangerous, foolish,—the last man in England to rule the country. But don't say that he [is] insincere or unpatriotic. Then I shall either agree with you,—or disagree as men must do about politics.

Goodbye
Yours always most faithfully
ANTHONY TROLLOPE

773. To HENRY MERIVALE TROLLOPE. 13 April.
Montagu Square. *Muriel Rose Trollope.*

Trollope has forwarded some manuscript to Mrs. Oliphant. 'I have no news,—except that your mother and I are thinking of leaving London and going into the country. Do not mention it at present. I mean for good & all.'

774. To WILLIAM BLACKWOOD. 13 April.
Montagu Square. *National Library of Scotland.*

Trollope discusses the breaks in his novel for the serialization, and adds: 'I had heard before that the Scotch clachans were likely to go against Disraeli;—in fact that a great effort would be made to carry . . .[1] part of the country. But the change in Lancashire and Yorkshire startles me;—not that they should be minded to vote as they have done, but that they should have voted so differently from what they did before.'[2]

775. To WILLIAM BLACKWOOD. 17 April.
Montagu Square. *National Library of Scotland.*

Trollope encloses something that will explain everything. 'It does not now matter much, as I think you have come to a right decision. But I beg your pardon for the confusion I have occasioned you.'

776. To HENRY MERIVALE TROLLOPE. 24 April.
Muriel Rose Trollope.

24 April 1880
aetat 65.

(39, Montagu Square.)

Dear Harry.

Thanks for the book of Renan and his Xtianity.[3] I have read them as far as I seemed to want them. I have not time for merely promiscuous reading. I am getting old and I prefer going to bed. But for the earlier portion of them I was gratified. Renan is very well informed; but he seems too much intent on teaching the world.

---

[1] Proper name illegible.
[2] The Conservatives, in power since 1874, were routed in 1880.
[3] Ernest Renan (1832–92), French theologian famed for his *Origines du Christianisme: Vie de Jésus* (1863), *Les Apôtres* (1866), *St. Paul* (1869), *L'Antéchrist* (1873), *Les Évangiles* (1877), *L'Église Chrétienne* (1879), *Marc-Aurèle* (1881).

The Bojesman or Bosjasman seems to have been a Dutch word for Bushman. I should translate it Bushman if the word applies to South Africa. They are a race of savages much smaller and more savage than the Hottentot, & still exist.

The 'curee' in regard to a fox hunt I should translate 'the kill', making it in that way. But it would not do in regard to a hunt in which the huntsmen do not desire to kill,—as is the case with men staghunting. Zolas meaning is that as the hounds eat the fox, so do the functionaires eat their pickings.[1] John Tilley has come in for his share of the Tory curee.

Gladstone is Prime Minister and Ch. of the Exchequer,—after the old established fashion. What Lord Hartington[2] is to be we do not yet know, but I should suppose it the War Office. Vernon Harcourt[3] Home. Forster[4] Colonial. Lord Northbrook[5] India. Granville[6] F. O. of course. Lord Selborne[7] says he will not be Chancellor in a Cabinet including Dilke;[8]—but he did not say it to me!!

Yours always affectionately
ANTHONY TROLLOPE

777. To JOSEPH LANGFORD. 27 April. Montagu Square. *Parrish Collection.*

Trollope thinks the W. Lucas Collinses have gone to Brighton, but he sends their London address.

[1] Henry Trollope must have been engaged in translating Zola's *La Curée* (1871).

[2] Spencer Compton Cavendish, Marquess of Hartington and (1891) eighth Duke of Devonshire (1835–1908), secretary of state for India, 1880–2.

[3] Sir William George Granville Venables Vernon Harcourt (1827–1904), home secretary, 1880.

[4] William Edward Forster (1818–86) did not go to the colonial office, but was appointed chief secretary for Ireland, 1880–2.

[5] Thomas George Baring, first Earl of Northbrook (1826–1904), became first lord of the admiralty.

[6] Granville George Leveson-Gower, second Earl Granville (1815–91), minister of foreign affairs, 1880–5.

[7] Sir Roundell Palmer, first Earl of Selborne (1812–95), lord chancellor, 1880–5.

[8] Sir Charles Wentworth Dilke (1843–1911) was the leader of the radical section of Gladstone's government. He had made himself unpopular among all moderate liberals by his efforts to extend the franchise to agricultural labourers. He was appointed under-secretary to the foreign office, 1880–2.

778. To WILLIAM BLACKWOOD. 1 May.
Montagu Square. *National Library of Scotland.*

Trollope acknowledges a cheque and a copy of the *St. James's.*[1]

779. To HENRY MERIVALE TROLLOPE. 9 May.
Muriel Rose Trollope.

9 May 1880.

Dear Harry.   (39, Montagu Square.)

I think we are becoming fixed in our intention of settling ourselves at Harting near Petersfield in Sussex. We shall move I think some time in July. As soon as ever we are settled I shall expect you to come over and put up the books for me. Oh the books—and oh the wine! I am beginning to tremble at the undertaking.

I write now to ask what are [we] to do with your books? It will hardly serve your purposes to take them down into Sussex. There are still here about 700 volumes. Shall I go and ask for room for them at Chapmans? Though I fear that the Chapmans would or might object. Or shall I ask John Tilley, or Charles Trollope;[2]—or what else?

Yours always affectionately
A. T.

780. To HENRY MERIVALE TROLLOPE. 21 May.
Muriel Rose Trollope.

21 May 1880.

My dear Harry,   (39, Montagu Square.)

Your Dyce[3] shall be sent to you at once. If you want any other book or books sent with it, speak now or for ever after hold your tongue. When the books have once been stored at Taylors[4] you must have all or none. I could put half a dozen light books in

---

[1] I find nothing relevant in either the *St. James's Gazette* or the *St. James's Magazine.*

[2] Sir Charles Trollope (1808–88), brigadier-general in the Crimea, 1855; general, 1877. See M. N. Trollope, *A Memoir of the Family of Trollope* (London, 1897), pp. 68–9. Sir Charles was a member of another branch of the family. See letter No. 237, *supra.*

[3] Alexander Dyce (1798–1869), a scholar who published editions of many of the Elizabethan dramatists.

[4] Probably 'Charles Taylor, the depository, Southwark'—a large warehouse. See the *Post Office London Directory 1882*, p. 2508.

with the Shakespeare without a damage. I will take them down and have them packed at Chapmans.

When your author,—the Sociology,[1]—quotes English authors, I should put the simple name, 'Lubbock',[2] and drop the 'L'homme prehistorique.' You must either get the page in an English edition, or probably he will be contented that you should drop the page altogether. It will not do to put in the French paging. If he is a decent fellow he will help you in all this. Of course you cannot be expected to buy the English books.

What you say of Madame Guyon[3] and Madame de Stael[4] is quite true, and shows the unfitness of such a woman as M^rs O to edit such a work.

I can assure you that old . . .[5] has not been to me; but if he comes I will tell him that he is in good hands.

Do not make your summer engagements without coming to us. We shall expect you for August. Shall that be fixed?

Yours always affectionately
ANTHONY TROLLOPE

781. To HENRY MERIVALE TROLLOPE. 26 May.
Muriel Rose Trollope.

26 May. 1880.
(39, Montagu Square.)

Dear Harry   I have sent off the Shakespeare,—by 'petite vitesse', and have enclosed with them only a book which has come from —— with a bill.

I think the phrase for Bas Empire, to be 'later' or 'lower' Empire.

I have found the word under 'Empire' in Spicer's Dict. It is 'Lower Empire'.

---

[1] C. Letourneau, *Sociology based upon Ethnology*, trans. by H. M. Trollope in 'The Library of Contemporary Science' (London, 1881).

[2] Sir John Lubbock (1834–1913), first baron Avebury, 1900; author of *Prehistoric Times* (1865).

[3] Jeanne Marie Guyon (1648–1717), a French mystic who was persecuted because of the alleged heretical character of the Quietist doctrine which accompanied her methods of charity. She collected a devoted band of disciples.

[4] Anne Louise Germaine de Staël (1766–1817), French critic and novelist whose *salon* in Paris was the most distinguished of her day. She wielded a tremendous influence over men and manners.

[5] The proper name here is illegible.

I have lost your letter and cannot remember whether there is anything further in it to be answered.

I have done my Cicero,—but have not read it, which now remains for me to do.

Yours affectionately
ANTY TROLLOPE

782. To ?[1] 27 May.
Parrish Collection.

27 May 1880
(39, Montagu Square.)

My dear Friend,

What does a dangerous speculation mean? If I said it were not dangerous, and the bill came in for £12–12/ with little as diminution for sale, what would you think of my common sense? There is, of course, danger. People will not buy poetry unless it becomes peculiarly recommended. How many books of poetry by unknown authors have you ever purchased? And if not you, why others? It may do. There may come the turn in the tide of your affairs, the wished for moment of success, and then you would be so amply repaid. But it is only a chance. Put by your £12 before you spend it, and then venture as though expecting the loss. Then anything that comes will be so pleasant a surprise.

We are all going down into the country, permanently, for ever and ever,—and we start on July 6th!!! I forgot whether our purpose had been made up and declared before you left London.

Very affectionately
ANTHONY TROLLOPE

our address will be
South Harting
Petersfield.

783. To HENRY MERIVALE TROLLOPE. 3 June.
Muriel Rose Trollope.

June 3. 1880
(39, Montagu Square.)

My dear Harry.

I am glad that you got your Shakespeare;—but I think the money paid for the carriage was very dear.

—— may be a vile Jew,—I have known other booksellers to

<hr>

[1] Possibly to Lady Wood.

be so. There are so many tricks going in trade now that one does not know how to be on his guard against them.

Aurora Leigh[1] is certainly a very fine poem, but did not please me when I last read it as when I first encountered it 20 years ago. It seemed to be less real, and more forced.

Your books will soon be packed up now,—and then farewell to them for ever!!! I have put the Dukes Children among your novels.

Could you not come to us early in August? You could finish your translation while with us.

I have done my Cicero, and am endeavouring to come to terms for the publication.

I hope you will find me all among the proofs.

Yours affectionately
ANTHY TROLLOPE

784. To HENRY MERIVALE TROLLOPE. 14 June.
Muriel Rose Trollope.

14 June 1880
(39, Montagu Square.)

Dear Harry.

I have put the 20 volumes together and they shall go down to Harting.

As to the others, they will not incommode us. You make up your mind as to what you would wish. It may be that you should be a good deal at Harting. And when I die it will be convenient to have them altogether. But you will have to pay for taking them down;—and if they are stored in London, you will have to pay for storing them. You must judge for yourself. If you let me know by the end of the month you will be in time.

Yours affectionately
ANTHY TROLLOPE

785. To HENRY MERIVALE TROLLOPE. 14 June.[2]

14 June 1880
(39, Montagu Square.)

Dear Harry,

The correction of the errors will be a great trouble, as every word of it must be verified,—quotations I mean, & such like. It will be very tedious.

[1] Mrs. Browning's poem.
[2] Either this letter or the preceding is misdated by Trollope.

Be very careful in reading over your volume on Sociology in regard to style;—so as to soften as far as may be possible all awkwardness of phrase. You have done it very fast, and will so have done it best. But you owe to it that care. Can not that be done at Harting?

Touching your books here,—mamma seems to think that you had better allow us to take them down to Harting. I do not think so, but will do so if you wish it. They will have to be brought up again. At Taylors you will be able to get them when you want them, but can only get them altogether. You must decide whether we shall store them,—or take them with us.

I think Ringwood has brightened up with the calm of going into the country. He has informed me that his London pals make him drink—and he does not want to drink. When he does drink he does not become drunk, but is exactly like an owl. He is very keen about going down to the country.

Fancy ten acts of Corneille at one sitting! Where [? were] you like an owl when it was over?

Yours always
A. T.

786. To HENRY MERIVALE TROLLOPE. 18 June. Montagu Square. *Muriel Rose Trollope.*

Trollope advises Henry on problems of translation in connexion with the book on sociology. 'In the general text I think I would soften down the broad assertions as much as possible,—so as to give to the narration as thorough a tone of cold philosophy as possible.'

787. To GEORGE BENTLEY. 18 June. Montagu Square. *Parrish Collection.*

Trollope asks £400 for a three-volume novel to be run in *Temple Bar* and republished in May 1882. The novel was probably *Marion Fay*. Bentley did not take it. It finally appeared in the *Graphic*, 3 Dec. 1881 to 3 June 1882. Trollope did, however, get his price.

788. To HENRY MERIVALE TROLLOPE. 23 June. Montagu Square. *Muriel Rose Trollope.*

Chapman would like Harry's book on sociology shortened, and he suggests £60 as a reasonable fee for the translation.

789. To HENRY MERIVALE TROLLOPE. 24 June.
Montagu Square. *Muriel Rose Trollope.*

Dickens & Evans are pressing for the manuscript of the 'Sociology', but Trollope cautions Harry not to send up slovenly work.

790. To HENRY MERIVALE TROLLOPE. 27 June.
Muriel Rose Trollope.

Sunday 27 June 1880
(39, Montagu Square.)

Dear Harry,

I would,—as you propose, leave out the majority of the footnotes, merely retaining those which are essential to the reading of the text.

If I were you I would at once send over the first half to Chapman,—*if you are contented with the translation.* I mean that you must judge whether the translation requires to be read again. If it do not, then send it.

Yours always
A. T.

Let me know when you get a proof of the Racine. You ought to have it now.

In one week more we start from here. It makes me melancholy;—though I believe I shall be happier there than I am here. I dislike dinner parties and all going out. I do wish you were coming to be with us during next month, but I will put up with looking forward to your coming. Every day in August I shall think we are hardly used that does not see you.

I do firmly expect that we shall have 15 p cent from the Union Bank this half year. The shares have gone steadily up and are now at 39.

791. To WILLIAM BLACKWOOD. 3 July.
Montagu Square. *National Library of Scotland.*

Trollope returns proof of *Dr. Wortle's School.*

792. To SAMPSON LOW. 3 July. Montagu Square.
Not traced.[1]

Trollope accepts from Low, on behalf of Harper's, £100 for the early sheets of the *Life of Cicero.*

[1] My text is Trollope's copy of this letter (Bodleian).

793. To HENRY MERIVALE TROLLOPE. 8 July.
Muriel Rose Trollope.

July 8—1880
Petersfield.

Dearest Harry,

Here we are on our journey down to Harting. Indeed we have been hard at work at Harting all day and have retired here for our mutton chop at night.

Yes; the Union Bank is going to pay us 15 / p cent, and the shares have gone up to 40–½. They are very nearly at the price at which you bought them. But what is that to the Standard Bank of S Africa? I bought a year ago at £37–10/– and they are now at £52—£14–10, netted on each share!

As to your MS—Chapman told me that it had reached him.

I should not much regard what that Frenchman has said about his book. If anything requires to be left out, or to be suppressed in language (softened down) I would not be deterred from doing it by his threats. He cannot assert the claim at law to be translated verbally. He has no such law, to force you into publishing his indecencies. Do it as well as you can & as literally; but do not allow yourself to be driven into publishing what you feel to be indecencies.

The cheque for £13-odd was the amount due to you for interest on the advance payment for your shares. You were bound to pay the first call on a certain sum, and the remainder in 3 months. You paid all at once, & they had to pay you interest on the money

Yours faithfully & affect.
ANTY TROLLOPE

794. To HENRY MERIVALE TROLLOPE. 23 July.
Muriel Rose Trollope.

Dear Harry,   Harting Petersfield—23 July 1880

I do not know how long it is since I heard from you. You will say that it is as long since you heard from me, but I am not sure that you will be right. We are in our new house, but not half settled yet. You may imagine what a trouble the library has been. At present though the bulk of the books are placed; and are placed on their old shelves and with their own numbers, still that which is not the bulk, but which forms a numerous portion, is all in confusion so that sometimes I am almost helpless. I cannot describe to you the room. It is very much larger than the library in London, but still will not hold as many books. It is two shelves lower, and let a room be ever so long or broad you can only put books on the outside, round the walls. Now in London there was much wall space every mil of which was utilized. So it is here,—but still there is not room for so many books. Nevertheless I hope to get them in order before you come, merely leaving for you the small task of preparing the alterations in the catalogue. I find that I must have another catalogue printed.[1] That however shall not be touched till you come.

If however I am in confusion with my books, I have got my wine into fine order, and have had iron bins put up in the cellar.

We have the two horses, and a brougham, and a pony carriage. The pony is a nice little beast but rather old.

We like the neighbors as far as we have seen them as yet. But we are looking forward to your coming with great impatience.

I do not know that Chapman has put your sociology book into the hands of the printers, but I shall hear no doubt next Tuesday. We are still in such confusion that I do not know how he can carry on at all. Sir Herbert Sandford[2] has gone to Australia to do the work for the Melbourne Exhibition, and Mr Harding has become our Chairman.

Write soon and tell me all the news—

Yours most affectionately

ANTHY TROLLOPE

I am writing a series of papers for the Pall Mall Gazette about tradesmen (or rather about trades) in London. The tailor, butcher, chemist, &.[3]
I think I would delay writing to Mrs Oliphant or Blackwood till you come to England

[1] There is a copy of Trollope's library catalogue, prepared in 1874, in the Victoria and Albert Museum. I have never seen a later catalogue.

[2] Sir Herbert Sandford (1826–92), a director of Chapman & Hall.

[3] 'London Tradesmen', eleven articles, appeared at irregular intervals in the *Pall Mall Gazette* from 10 July to 7 Sept. 1880.

795. To HENRY MERIVALE TROLLOPE. 30 July.
Harting. *Muriel Rose Trollope.*

Trollope has received the first sheets of Harry's 'Sociology'. He urges Harry to come down. 'Your mother has got your room [? ready] for you. It is small, but very pretty, looking on to the garden.'

796. To R. P. HARDING. 13 August.
Not traced.[1]

13. August. 1880

My dear Mr Harding.

Chapman showed me last Tuesday the statement of the account for the Dukes Children, my last novel— Mr Whinney[2] came in, and that you had to be gone prevented my speaking to you about it. The Company loses £120 by the venture. I cannot allow that. It is the first account I have ever seen of one of my own books. The bargain was made as far back as June 1878.

I will repay to the Company the amount lost, viz £120, if you think that fair, and will take some opportunity of speaking to you about the transaction.

A T.

797. To JOHN MORLEY. 24 August. Harting.
Parrish Collection.

Trollope sends copy for the *London Tradesmen.*

798. To ? 23 September. Harting.
Parrish Collection.

Trollope addresses 'Mr. Warden' and is glad to accept his invitation for 13 October. 'I write a line separately to the Sub-warden and Bursar.' The place addressed, written at the foot of the letter, is scored through, but letter No. 800, *infra*, makes it clear that New College, Oxford, is referred to. New College records indicate that the Gaudy was held on 13 October. In 1874 Trollope had declined a similar invitation because of illness. See letter No. 566, *supra.*

799. To WILLIAM BLACKWOOD. 8 October. Harting.
National Library of Scotland.

Trollope thanks Blackwood for the cheque and hopes the story will be a success. He has not seen or heard of George Eliot.

[1] I print from Trollope's copy (Bodleian).
[2] Mr. Whinney was a partner of Harding, Whinney & Co., accountants.

800. To WILLIAM BLACKWOOD. 16 October.
St. George's Square. *National Library of Scotland.*

Trollope is late with the proof because he has been down to Oxford.

801. To GEORGE W. SMALLEY. 17 October. Athenaeum Club.
John W. Watling. Not seen.

Trollope asks Smalley to dine with him at the Garrick Club. 'A man has given me a haunch of venison, there will be nothing else to eat.'

802. To A. ELLIS. 22 October. St. George's Square.
Parrish Collection.

Trollope begs off writing a story. 'The work of the construction of a story is very heavy and compels me to refuse your offer.' Arthur Ellis (1850–94) was city editor of the *Daily News*, 1880–94, editor of the *Statist,* 1878–80.

803. To A. ELLIS. 31 October. Harting.
Parrish Collection.

Trollope refuses another offer. 'I am accustomed to write Christmas stories for magazines, but not to do other literary work.'

804. To HENRY MERIVALE TROLLOPE. 21 December.
Muriel Rose Trollope. Not seen. Excerpt in Sadleir,
Commentary, p. 319.

> 21, December 1880
> (39, Montagu Square.)
> [Harting.]

Dear Harry

I ought to have written to you before, but one day has passed after another and I have not done as I ought.

I miss you most painfully. But I had expected that. I only hope that you may come back with the summer. This is the longest day of the winter and I shall begin now to look for the lengthening days. Ah, me! How I used to look for the shortening days, when I was hunting, and had the first of November as a golden day before me for which my soul could long. I have now to look for the time when the green things in the garden may begin to shew themselves. But the expectation of green things in another garden prevents me from being sad.

I finished on Thursday the novel I was writing, and on Friday I began another. Nothing really frightens me but the idea of enforced idleness. As long as I can write books, even though they be not published, I think that I can be happy.

I am anxious to hear of your book coming out,—that about Racine & Corneille. As to the other, that may take its time. And I am very anxious to know that you are at work on the Dickens French book. So plan it that it shall not last beyond 30 June. It is not worth giving more time to it,—at such a price. I think the price sufficient,—but not sufficient for a studious work.

I am going up to-day to a meeting, and we have to take some immediate steps as to moving the stock.

Yours always affectionately
ANTHONY TROLLOPE

805. To CHARLES LEE LEWES. 24 December.
Mrs. E. S. Ouvry.

The following letter relates to the death of George Eliot.

24 December 1880
(Harting,
Petersfield.)

My dear Lewes.

Your letter has shocked me more than I can say. I had no idea that she was ill. Nor indeed, as you say, had any one. I had only been saying on the very morning that she died[1] that I would go and see her, whether she was in the town or country.

I did love her very dearly. That I admired her was a matter of course. But my affection for her was thorough and the wound, though not such as yours or poor Cross's,[2] is severe.

When will she [? be] buried.[3] I would fain be present if it be possible.

---

[1] 22 Dec. 1880.
[2] John Walter Cross (1840–1924), who had married George Eliot just seven months before.
[3] She was buried beside George Henry Lewes on 29 Dec. *The Times* for 30 Dec. does not list Trollope as among those present at the funeral.

Remember me most kindly to Cross. He of course knows that I have been living in the country for the last 7 months.

Yours always most sincerely

ANTHONY TROLLOPE

806. To WILLIAM BLACKWOOD. [? 1880] Harting.
National Library of Scotland.

Trollope returns proof of *Dr. Wortle* and asks for duplicates hereafter.

807. To ALFRED AUSTIN. [? 1880]
Not traced. Austin, p. 113.

*   *   *

Yes, we have changed our mode of life altogether. We have got a little cottage here, just big enough (or nearly so) to hold my books, with five acres and a cow and a dog and a cock and a hen. I have got seventeen years' lease, and therefore I hope to lay my bones here. Nevertheless I am as busy as would be one thirty years younger, in cutting out dead boughs, and putting up a paling here and a little gate there. We go to church and mean to be very good, and have maids to wait on us. The reason for all this I will explain when I see you, although, as far as I see at present there is no good reason other than that we were tired of London.

*   *   *

1 8 8 1

808. To HENRY MERIVALE TROLLOPE. 4 January.
Athenaeum Club. *Muriel Rose Trollope.*

Trollope has a proposal to make at the Chapman & Hall board meeting. He has been down to see W. Lucas Collins and is beginning to hear some people talk of his *Cicero.*

809. To FREDERIC CHAPMAN. 7 January. Harting.
Carl Pforzheimer.

Trollope jockeys for a favourable date for the Chapman & Hall meeting.

810. To HENRY MERIVALE TROLLOPE. 9 January.
Muriel Rose Trollope.

January 9, 1881
(Harting,
Petersfield.)

My dear Harry.

I have just got the Union Bank letter. 15 per cent. It gives you £9–5–0—annual income in the half year;—for which you paid only £26–17. Therefore, bar[r]ing the inferiority of the security, you have certainly done well. But the security is I think ample. The shares have gone up 20/– since your purchase. They now touch 44/– which is the outside price I ever gave

I sent you to-day a criticism in St James as to Cicero.[1] It is intended to be good natured; but the critic had not read the book. Why should he? It is simply his object to write something readable.

I read that review in the Temps. I know nothing about it, but it seems to me that the other fellow, Wolf, must have written to give Sarcey[2] something to write about. Were the two French plays so dull?

I find that I shall receive £87–3–9 for you on your Union shares this time.

Yours always affectionately
A. T.

You saw I suppose that the South African shares had a great fall. They came at one moment to 50— They have now re-covered, up to 53. The distress in the Transvaal was the cause. I do not agree with you that we were wrong;—nor do I think that you would say so if you knew the whole question. What were we to do? When the Dutch would not defend themselves against the blacks? Let 300,000 niggers overrun and massacre 30,000 white men,—and we with 20000 on hand, for them to attack next?[3]

---

[1] This is the *St. James's Gazette*, founded in 1880 by Frederick Green-wood (1830–1909) when the *Pall Mall Gazette* changed hands and changed sides in politics. I have not been able to trace the review.

[2] Francisque Sarcey (1828–99), dramatic critic of *Le Temps*, 1867–99. He became well known for his 'imaginary conversations'.

[3] In 1877 the South African Republic (Dutch), suffering from long civil strife and turmoil with the natives, capitulated to Great Britain. After further bloody uprisings in 1881 local autonomy was granted, though the British continued to direct external affairs.

811. To HENRY MERIVALE TROLLOPE. 14 January.
Muriel Rose Trollope.

14 January, 1881
(Harting,
Petersfield.)

Dear Harry

As you get the Daily News I do not send the copy which came for you and which contains the report of the Union Bank. It gives little or no information to outsiders— But it promises some amelioration in affairs—which means I think an increase in dividend. You have had (or will have) for the last half year about 5 3/4 per cent on all your money invested in it, which, as being free of income tax, means fully 6 per cent. That for the winter half year is not bad.

I send an article on the Cicero from the World.[1] The writer probably knows nothing about the book or the subject; but it is good natured. There is an article also in the Pall Mall,[2] written by a man who does know what he is talking about. He praises the book very highly, but falls foul of the scholarship. I do not profess to be a scholar,—but simply one who has read enough of Latin literature, (and have sufficiently understood it,) to be able to tell my story. I send the paper; but, though I like the review, I cannot for the life of me, find out that I have been wrong in the translation to which he refers either from the Pro Lege Manilia or from Lucan. The latter is in truth untranslateable so as to be intelligible,—but in the paraphrase I have given there is no absence of a knowledge of the Latin language,—though I admit an absence of knowledge of the finer rules. You need not send back either.

I think we[3] shall succeed in taking the house in Henrietta Street.

Yours always
ANTHONY TROLLOPE

[1] See the issue for 12 Jan. 1881, p. 19.
[2] xxxiii (10 Jan. 1881), 123–4. The *Pro Lege Manilia* passage is found in Trollope's *Cicero*, i, Appendix D, p. 345; the Lucan passage is from Appendix E, p. 347. My colleague Professor Arthur Patch McKinlay has examined Trollope's translation and agrees with the *Pall Mall* critic in the first instance, but supports Trollope's free translation of the second.
[3] Chapman & Hall.

812. To KATE FIELD. 17 January. *Boston Public Library.*
Sadleir, *Commentary*, pp. 341–2.

(Harting,

Jany 17, 1881   Petersfield.)

Dear Kate.

I hardly know how to answer your letter because though I was
very intimate with George Eliot, she never spoke to me of her
life before I knew her, nor, as far as I am aware, did she to her
other friends.[1] Nor did he. He was a friendly affectionate man,—
but very reticent, especially as to those matters which concerned her.

I do not know where G. E. and Lewes became acquainted.
I think it was in the pages of Blackwood, if the word can be
applied to a magazine. I think I may say that the two were
acquainted some time before Adam Bede came out. I knew them,
being together, shortly *after* the publication of Adam Bede. But
my impression, though I feel sure of it for my own purposes,
cannot be taken as a positive assertion. Then you may say that
she had lived down evil tongues before Lewes' death. She was
asked to dine with Queen Victoria's daughter, (Crown Princess
of Prussia,) when the Princess was in England. I mention this
because the English Royal family are awfully particular as to
whom they see and do not see. That at any rate is true, because
I saw her there.

But in truth she was one whose private life should be left in
privacy,—as may be said of all who have achieved fame by
literary merits.

Affectionately yours

ANTH TROLLOPE

813. To HENRY MERIVALE TROLLOPE. 20 January.
Muriel Rose Trollope.

Jany 20—1881. Harting

Dear Harry. I write on this scrap, in order to be able also to
send the enclosed for 2½—, if by good nature of the Post Office
it may be possible.

[1] Kate Field had written a sketch of George Eliot for the *New York
Tribune* (23 Dec. 1880) and was probably contemplating something more
ambitious. There is no record, however, of a further article.

Here we are altogether snowed up. Florence went to London on Tuesday and was dragged down in the brougham under difficulty, and had to pay 10/ for the only cab at the Vauxhall. But she did go. Miss Matherstone[1] in trying to go was stuck for 5 hours in the snow and had to come back with four cart horses. Twice I have intended to go to London; but have received telegrams telling me not to attempt it.

Dalton[2] writes to me asking me to pay your dividend on the Madras stock,—as though you had received it, and saying *that you had promised to pay it to him*. What passed between you? I do not remember that you saw him except in my presence, when he told us that you could lose the Madras income; 'but,' said I, 'he will get the Bank interest.' But I have written to him to explain, and have written also to [the] Bank to ask whether the Madras dividend was paid to my credit.

Yours always aff.
A. T.

814. To DR. SMITH.[3] 21 January.
Berg Collection.

Harting,
Petersfield.

My dear Dr Smith,

I send enclosed my suggestions as to the Literary Fund Report. You will no doubt send it on to Mr Locker with your reminder. My feeling is that we sing our own praises too loudly, and that we seem to claim support by the high-sounding titles of those who have supported us. Some I think shun us because of our assumed grandeur.

Yours very faithfully
ANTHONY TROLLOPE

[1] I have not been able to identify this person.
[2] Probably Benjamin Neale Dalton, stockbroker. See *Post Office London Directory 1872*, p. 804.
[3] Probably William Smith, later Sir William (1813–93), the editor of classical texts and compiler of dictionaries of Greek and Roman antiquity. He was a member of the committee of the Literary Fund.

815. To HENRY MERIVALE TROLLOPE. 24 January.
Muriel Rose Trollope.

24 Jany 1881
Dear Harry.   (39, Montagu Square.)

Mamma and I have just settled that you are a pig. You promised to get cards and got none. Here we are snowed up in a most exigent manner. I went to day up to the top of the white hill, but to get there was a wonderful undertaking. To get down was worse. There were 3 or 4 feet of snow and a white mist blinding every thing. When will it go away? We have had a week and not a grain has moved as yet. It is very melancholy.

I go up to town tomorrow,—if I can get there. I was not there last week. Florence has been there, having got up last Monday before the storm was over,—and had to pay 10/ for a cab. She will not come home till Friday next.

I sent you two reviews on Dᵣ Wortle in the Pall Mall[1] & Saturday.[2] Do not return them. There is a word in the Saturday shewing that they mean to be very heavy on the Cicero. I wonder whether you observed it.

Blackwood ought to send you your money. I suppose the book is not yet out. Will you be able to give Chapman the book about Mad Neckar[3] by March? He expects it,—or says so. Are you doing much with Dickens' job this weather. You will be able at any rate to describe Paris in the snow.

Sarcey's criticisms,—or rather critical peices, —are to my taste very heavy. I do not think that such lucubrations would be widely read in London.

God bless you
Affectionately yours
A. T.

I am glad to see that paper about Genests[4] work. Perhaps it may turn out to be valuable some day. Let us agree to sell it and to have a joint lark with the money,—a regular fricasseed chicken at Peters with the &s.

[1] xxxiii (10 Jan. 1881), 11–12.
[2] xi (Jan. 1881), 121–2.
[3] Viscount d'Haussonville, *The Salon of Madame Necker*, translated from the French (London, 1882).
[4] John Genest (1764–1839), author of *Some Account of the English Stage from the Restoration in 1660 to 1830* (1832).

816. To HENRY MERIVALE TROLLOPE. 23 February.
Athenaeum Club. *Muriel Rose Trollope.*

Trollope asks Harry to come to the Chapman & Hall meeting on 5 March and stay with them. 'Chapman told me that he meant to have the Raffael done in part by his wife!!'[1]

817. To HENRY MERIVALE TROLLOPE. 27 February.
Harting. *Muriel Rose Trollope.*

Trollope gives Harry further and more explicit instructions about the coming week-end.

818. To WILLIAM BLACKWOOD. 28 February.
Harting. *National Library of Scotland.*

Trollope wonders whether or not Blackwood would be interested in looking at *The Fixed Period.* Serialized in *Blackwood's* October 1881 through March 1882.)

819. To MR. FISHER. 2 March. Harting.
Parrish Collection.

Trollope asks that no further sheets be sent until his return. Mr. Fisher was probably manager of J. B. Nichols & Sons, printers, who were doing *Ayala's Angel* for Chapman & Hall.

820. To WILLIAM BLACKWOOD. 5 March.
Athenaeum Club. *National Library of Scotland.*

Trollope leaves within the hour for two months in Rome. He will forward his manuscript when he returns.

821. To HENRY MERIVALE TROLLOPE. 24 April.
Florence. *Muriel Rose Trollope.*

Trollope arranges for Harry to meet the family in Paris. 'God send we may get through safe for I am getting heartily sick of the continual battle with railway porters, and almost expect to succumb on our way home.'

[1] *The Life, Works, and Times of Raphael*, translated from the French of E. Muntz, new ed. by [? W.] Armstrong (London: Chapman & Hall, 1881–7).

822. To HENRY MERIVALE TROLLOPE.
[? April, 1881.] Florence. *Muriel Rose Trollope*.

Trollope asks Harry to 'procure me in Paris about 4 Havannah cigars. Bring them in your pocket to the station,—the best you can get. I shall have then smoked my last, and have done pretty well with what I took.'

823. To WILLIAM BLACKWOOD.
7 May (misdated 7 April). Athenaeum Club.
National Library of Scotland.

Trollope sends *The Fixed Period*. He is just back from Italy, where (in Florence) he met Mrs. Oliphant.

824. To MISS BADHAM.[1] 9 May.
Parrish Collection.

May 9, 1881   (Harting,
                                                       Petersfield.)

My dear Miss Badham,

I have been travelling on the continent and have just returned from Rome;—hence my delay in answering your letter.

They say that historical novels do not at present pay. They mean that the taste of readers is against them;—which is true unless the historical novel be specially good. A new Ivanhoe would be acceptable, But accuracy in a novel is by no means the thing needed. Is Ivanhoe accurate? I doubt whether Scott prepared himself by reading many memoirs of John's reign. But he had the peculiar gift which made an historical novel palatable to readers.

I do not think that I would choose Australia as a scene for a first novel, because readers do not care for a narrow sphere of life. But, again, if the Australian novel be good, men will read it,—as they did those of Henry Kingsley.[2]

The fact I take it is that the thing itself must be Good of its

---

[1] Probably the daughter of Professor Charles Badham of the University of Sydney. See letter No. 608, *supra*.

[2] Henry Kingsley (1830–76), brother of Charles Kingsley. His two best-known Australian novels are *Geoffry Hamlyn* (1859) and *The Hillyars and the Burtons* (1865).

kind; and that it is not within the power of every clever person to write a good novel,—though it may be quite within the compas of a person not clever.

But my dear Miss Badham, the opinions of fathers and mothers and brothers *and sisters are worthless*. You may have the knack;— but fathers and mothers will certainly think that you have it. The cruel, hard-hearted, indifferent public must be the judge and you must fight your way before the judgment seat as best you may. And you will only injure your chance by teaching yourself to think that you, specially, are cruelly used.

You cannot hope to get into a magazine with a first venture. I am very intimately connected with the firm, or rather Company, of Chapman & Hall,—of which Mr Chapman is the manager and I am one of the Directors. If you like to send your MS to that house I will take care that it is read by their reader, at any rate with friendly eyes. The address should be

> Fred. Chapman Esqr
> Chapman & Hall
> Henrietta Street
> Covent Garden

and you should mention my name in the note. I do not know how I can do anything more for you.

My kind regards to your father & mother.

Yours with true sincerity and very heartily

ANTHONY TROLLOPE

825. To GEORGE SMITH. 13 May.
Mrs. Reginald Smith.

> May 13, 1881
> (Harting,
> Petersfield.)

My dear Smith,

The enclosed, having reached me to day, has given rise to many recollections of the past. Who has written the 'Roman Penny a liner'? Not I. Leslie Stephen must have been greatly in error.[1] But I would it could have been so! It was 22 years since,

[1] The reference is probably to something in the *Pall Mall* which I have not been able to trace.

or nearly, when I received the first proof for correction. And then, since that, there have been recollections so tender! Think of all the names that crowd upon me. And all the cheques!!! Alas,— that they can never be repeated!

Yours always
ANTHONY TROLLOPE

826. TO MR. MERIVALE.[1] 12 June.
Parrish Collection.

12 June 1881   (Harting,
                                                        Petersfield.)

My dear Merivale

Looking back I find that I got from Longmans after the first year for a novel called The Warden, £9–8–8. It was a short novel but considered to be a great success. In the next year I got £10–15/–. This was on half profits. For my next novel, being not contented, I demanded £100 down. I then wanted an advance, but Longmans would not give it. Therefore I left them, and have not traded on the half profits system since. All was honest with the Longmans. But they did not lay themselves out to make money for me,—but to ensure security for themselves.

I regard the system as very valuable as a mode of enabling young authors to come before the public so as to take a subsequent advantage of any success they may achieve. But as a mode of making money it is almost always ineffective. It will be for you to judge of your own position, and of what hopes you may have,—or what powers,— of securing a sum down. You may reply to Blackwood that you will accede to the terms on the payment of a certain sum down, on the score of your half profits, —£100 as I did, or any other greater sum you may name.

Chapman & Hall's Limited,—of which Company I am a Director,—might consider your proposition. But we are at the present moment anything but liberal.

Yours always
ANTHONY TROLLOPE

[1] Probably Herman Charles Merivale (1839–1906), playwright and novelist, nephew of Trollope's friend John Merivale.

827. To CHARLES MACKAY.[1] 19 June.
Parrish Collection.

19, June 1881
(Harting,
Petersfield.)

Dear Sir,

I had not heard of the Critic[2] or Daily News[3] or Truth;[4]— nor if a word be said against me in any newspaper, do I think much of it. I fancy that we authors owe more to critics than any injustice we receive from them. I am sure that if any critic wanted to spite us, he could better do it by holding his tongue than by speaking evil of us.

very faithfully yours

C. Mackay Esq ANTHONY TROLLOPE

828. To HENRY MERIVALE TROLLOPE. 9 July.
Harting. *Muriel Rose Trollope.*

Trollope sends Harry a report on the Union Bank dividend.

829. To ARTHUR LOCKER. 13 July.
Not traced. Sadleir, *Commentary*, p. 320.

The following letter is full of the difficulties encountered in the serial publication of *Marion Fay.*

(Harting,
Petersfield.)

13 July 1881.

My dear Sir,

It is quite out of the question. I will call between 12 and 1 on Thursday and explain this.

Your letter would appear to me to be most unreasonable, but then you and M[r]. Heaton[5] must misunderstand each other.

[1] Charles Mackay (1814–89), a prominent journalist, editor of the *Glasgow Argus* and the *Illustrated London News*, special correspondent of *The Times* in New York.

[2] See R. H. Stoddard, 'The Trollopes', *The Critic*, i (16 July 1881), 193. Mackay must have seen this article in manuscript or in proof.

[3] A review of the *Life of Cicero* appeared in the *Daily News*, 16 May 1881, p. 4.

[4] I have not been able to see a copy of *Truth* for this date.

[5] I cannot identify this man further than that he was probably one of the sons of John Heaton, a prominent printer and bookseller of Leeds.

I say in one of my letters to him, in which he had written about the American Reprint: 'I must beg it to be understood that the book will be published here in May 1882 whether completed in America or not.' I name, in a further letter, May 1st, but have not as far as I am aware ever named May 15th. But that is not of much moment.

You have had the book for months on your hands and have printed nearly all. The book is a regular 3 volume novel, *exactly* of the same length as my other 3 vol. novels. You have the advantage of the greater length than you expected. You have had more than a year to find out how to work it. June is altogether a bad month, June 24th is quite impossible. It seems to me that you ask me to rectify your mistake by asking me to abandon my own interests.[1]

But I will call on Thursday.

Yours faithfully
ANTHONY TROLLOPE

You complain of the chapters. They are nearly all of the same length. No writer ever made work come easier to the editor of a Periodical than do I.

830. To WILLIAM POLE.[2] 18 July.
Parrish Collection.

July 18, 1881 (Harting, Petersfield.)

My dear Pole

I send you up by book Post a life of Robin Hood,[3] and a beautiful picture of Maid Marian dancing a Morris dance. He

---

[1] Locker had said that *Marion Fay* was too long, that he could publish only two chapters a week, and that the novel would therefore not be completed until 32 weeks after 3 Oct., at which date he was bound to begin under the American and Australian contracts. The serial would not be finished until 8 July, so that book publication by 15 May was out of the question. Owing to a stipulation by Harper's, book publication should take place a fortnight before completion; *i.e.* 24 June.

[2] William Pole (1814–1900), a distinguished civil engineer, university professor, and musician; an authority on whist and an acquaintance of Trollope's at the Athenaeum Club.

[3] Probably J. B. March, *The Life and Adventures of Robin Hood* (London, 1864).

was Robert Fitzooth, and he was Earl of Huntington. She was Marian—daughter of Lord Fitzwalter, but became proverbial as a Morris dancer under the name of Marian, Marrian, or Mariana & others.

But you will find all about it in the book.

Yours always
A. T.

Make them read it all at home, as you have a Marian of your own.

831. To HENRY MERIVALE TROLLOPE. 19 July. Harting. *Muriel Rose Trollope*.

A social and business note. 'I do my task day by day; but when that is done, the energy is gone from me, and I am up to nothing . . . I heard from John Tilley about you—. I asked how you were and he said "very thin". I asked what you did, and he only allowed that you "grew thin". Edith said the same. Do not altogether vanish.'

832. To HERMAN CHARLES MERIVALE. 23 July. Harting. *Parrish Collection*.

Trollope advises Merivale to send his manuscript to Chapman and to ask for £100 in advance of the half profits. Merivale's three-decker novel *Faucit of Balliol* was published by Chapman & Hall in 1882.

833. To HENRY MERIVALE TROLLOPE. 25 July. Harting. *Muriel Rose Trollope*.

Trollope urges Henry to come to Harting, discussing the best time in view of their summer engagements. He adds, 'Do you know that Bice is very ill.[1] Fever after her confinement. The child, a girl, is well. I will keep this letter open till the morning, so that I may send you any news I may have by first post.'

[1] Beatrice Trollope Stuart-Wortley died the following day. Her daughter is the Hon. Mrs. James Cecil. In 1886 Charles Stuart-Wortley married a daughter of Sir John Everett Millais.

834. To Lady Pollock. 14 August.
Parrish Collection.

August 14, 1881　　　　　　　　　　　　　　　(Harting,
　　　　　　　　　　　　　　　　　　　　　　　　　　Petersfield.)

My dear Lady Pollock,
　　My brothers address is at present

　　　　　　　　367 via Nazionale
　　　　　　　　　　Roma.

He is somewhere in the neighbourhood of Vienna, but has
directed me to write to his home in Rome. I waited to get a reply
from him before answering you, as I have had to write to him
myself. Poor Bice's child is living, but is a delicate little girl. Is
it to be wished that the poor motherless little baby should live?
I left Charley Wortley down at Wortley when I went to the
funeral. He was well; but complained bitterly that the world was
all desolate to him.

　　I doubt whether you quite understand the antecedents of
Bice's life. The fault was that she had been too much spoilt in
every thing,—allowed to have her own way and to make a
society for herself. This she did with the best of people. But it
was her fault, rather than her fathers,—certainly rather than her
stepmothers, that she was not happy at home. Everything was
done for her that could be done;—but there were not carriages
nor parties. I say this in justice to my brothers wife, who has
been very very good. The fault was my brothers in allowing her
to have her own way, till her own way ceased to please her.
Poor Bice! But her year of marriage was certainly a year of
happiness

　　　　　　　　　　　　Most affectionately yours
　　　　　　　　　　　　　Anthony Trollope

835. To Alexander Ireland. 29 August. Harting.
Not traced. Maggs Catalogue 337 (Whitsun 1915).

'Can you kindly send me "The Crown and the Cabinet"[1] by "Verax".
I have the reply of "Verax", but I find that the C. & C. has been lost.'

[1] *The Crown and the Cabinet: Five Letters on the Biography of the Prince
Consort* (London, 1878). 'Verax' was Henry Dunckley (1823–96).

836. To ? August.
Not traced. Sadleir, *Commentary*, p. 268.

To a correspondent who asked him to write one more chronicle of Barset, Trollope wrote: 'I am nearly seventy years of age and cannot hope to do what you propose. Though I still go on writing, the new characters are much less troublesome than old ones, and can be done without the infinite labour of reading back again and again my old works.' Trollope did, however, return to Barchester for his novelette 'The Two Heroines of Plumplington', published in *Good Cheer* 1882, the Christmas supplement of *Good Words*.

837. To HENRY MERIVALE TROLLOPE. 2 September.
Muriel Rose Trollope.

2 Sept 1881   (Harting,
Petersfield.)

Dear Harry.

I send a clip out of the Times with an article about Bayeux which you may like to see. I took it up to London but forgot to give it you. I think you are right about the plans of towns. They are expensive, and though sometimes useful are not essential for such a book. You should have at least one good map of the district. That is essential.[1]

I spent a very dull evening and lost 7/6. It would have been nearly as dull had I won the money.

God speed you on your work. If it be successful it may be the beginning of a great affair. I know you will not shun trouble; but it will require thought in the management. I am sure you should give as much of the present autumn to it as is practicable.

I find here a sheet from Clay & Son[2] and send it on.

Yours affectionately
ANTHONY TROLLOPE

838. To HENRY MERIVALE TROLLOPE. 9 September.
Harting. *Muriel Rose Trollope.*

Trollope gives Harry a message from Isbister about format and urges him to pursue his work relentlessly.

[1] Henry Trollope was engaged in writing a descriptive guide-book to Normandy. It is not possible to-day to trace all his ephemeral journalistic enterprises, most of which were published anonymously.

[2] Probably Frederick Clay, printer. See letter No. 522, *supra*.

839. To William Blackwood. 9 September. Harting. *National Library of Scotland.*

Trollope returns corrected the first number of *The Fixed Period.* 'As I go on I will endeavour to put out all the profanities. Would you have the MS sent to me now—& always. I often cannot make out a word & I do not remember what I said. But what I did say was the best thing.'

840. To Henry Merivale Trollope. 21 September. Harting. *Muriel Rose Trollope.*

A letter devoted chiefly to advice on business dealings with Isbister. 'I should not dream of returning money to Isbister. You have not charged yourself as yet with the cost of the journey from London to Normandy. . . . You will find him a fairly honest fellow but dilatory and vague. At least that is my reading of his character.'

841. To Henry Merivale Trollope. 25 September. Harting. *Muriel Rose Trollope.*

Trollope good-humouredly berates Harry for his negligence in keeping the family posted on his shifting address.

842. To Henry Merivale Trollope. 29 September. Harting. *Muriel Rose Trollope.*

Trollope has discussed with Isbister details of Harry's book. All his letters have not arrived. 'Would you like me to send you 10 bushels of apples!!'

843. To William Blackwood. 30 September. Harting. *National Library of Scotland.*

Trollope thanks Blackwood for his cheque on account of *The Fixed Period.* 'I sincerely trust that it may answer.'

844. To Henry Merivale Trollope. 5 October. Harting. *Muriel Rose Trollope.*

Trollope discusses Harry's writing and travelling plans. 'I think myself that Isbister is a fair dealing man; but that he understands very little of his trade. He knows the paper and printing part of it. But is altogether astray as to whether a book will or will not pay.'

845. To William Blackwood. 13 October. Athenaeum Club. *National Library of Scotland.*

Trollope returns the second part of *The Fixed Period* corrected. 'I am very glad that you should like it.'

846. To HENRY MERIVALE TROLLOPE. 24 October.
Harting. *Muriel Rose Trollope.*

Trollope has received a letter from Harry 'written from "Fleas." I can make out no other name. But you had before told me to write to Falaise, where I addressed a letter which is I suppose there now.'

847. To HENRY MERIVALE TROLLOPE. 26 October.
Harting. *Muriel Rose Trollope.*

Trollope discusses Harry's working schedule. 'Your fault always is in being somewhat too long a time,—not thinking quite enough of the days as they run by; and in being a little too timid as to the work as you do it. In this work on which you are now employed you should remember that the time is hardly your own, and that you are bound to make each day go as far as you can. I do not doubt but that you will have done the work well.'

848. To HENRY MERIVALE TROLLOPE. 15 November.
Muriel Rose Trollope.

Caperthorne—Cheshire
15—Nov 1881

Dear Harry.

Baldachino is simply 'canopy,'—which may be of wood or drapery. The head of a four-post bed would be the baldachino,— or the sounding board of a pulpit. I would use the Italian word, as from certain notable pictures it has become well known in English. There is a famous Madonna of Raphael's called the 'Baldachino,' in the Pitti palace.

Thanks for the list of the Bibliotheque Nationale. It may be endless as it comprises all languages of literary excellence.

I am down at Davenports[1] for a few days. Eating and drinking;—all eating and drinking! But as I dislike eating or drinking more than is usual, the time runs heavy.

But alas it has come to that, that all times run more or less heavy with me, unless when I am asleep.

God bless you
Yours always affect
A. T.

[1] Possibly Ellen Heseltine Davenport, sister of Rose Trollope, or Bromley Davenport, of the Cosmopolitan Club (see *Autobiography*, chap. ix).

849. To HENRY MERIVALE TROLLOPE. 23 November.
Muriel Rose Trollope.

23. November 1881
(Athenaeum Club)

Dear Harry,

I dont think I will have your Molière or your Horace at the price. People with money are such fools that men put on prices simply to tempt them by the money to be paid.

Chapman expects your goods when they will arrive.

The Secretary tells me here that you will come up on the second ballot after Parliament meets,—viz in February. What a twitter I shall be in, and how I shall tear my hair if they blackball you.

I think I would make an appointment with Dr Clip of Petersfield & go on thence to have my beard cut.

You are speaking of a very short time here. Do you really mean to return on the 3 or 4 of January after arriving here on 23 December?

Joe Langford is to be here on 30th December and Tedder the Athenaeum librarian.[1]

Yours always
A. T.

850. To WILLIAM BLACKWOOD. [? November, 1881.]
Capesthorne, Cheshire. *National Library of Scotland.*

Trollope sends the proof of the third part of *The Fixed Period*. He mentions Blackwood's recent bereavement: 'I had not known your mother, but believe me I have been very sorry to hear of your grief.'

851. To ARTHUR TILLEY. 5 December.
Not traced. Sadleir's transcript.

5 December 1881
(Harting,
Petersfield.)

My dear Arthur,

Who is your friend, and why does he suspect that you desire to go into the Church? Dont. Nothing cripples a man more certainly.

[1] Henry Richard Tedder (1850–1924), an uncle of the present Lord Tedder. His portrait hangs in the Front Hall of the Athenaeum.

'Barchester Towers' was written before you were born.[1] Of course I forget every word of it! But I dont. There is not a passage in it I do not remember. I always have to pretend to forget when people talk to me about my own old books. It looks modest;—and to do the other things looks the reverse. But the writer never forgets. And when after 30 years he is told by some one that he has been pathetic, or witty, or even funny, he always feels like lending a five-pound note to that fellow.

Whenever am I to see any of you again?

Yours affectionately
ANTH TROLLOPE

852. TO HENRY MERIVALE TROLLOPE. 8 December. Harting. *Muriel Rose Trollope.*

Trollope writes Harry a brief dissertation on the etymology of the word 'gargoyle'.

1 8 8 2

853. TO HENRY MERIVALE TROLLOPE. 4 January. *Muriel Rose Trollope.*

(Harting,
Petersfield.)

January 4. 1882

My dear Harry

I wish you to consider the wine lying in the two further binns as your own. They are the upper and lower binns on the right hand side as you enter. They contain Leoville, in the lower, and Beycheville in the upper binn. As you will be my executor I write this note to justify you in claiming them.

There are at present 24 dozen in each, the numbers being as they were first brought from Paris. The Leoville cost 72/ a dozen and the Beycheville 54/. It is 1874 wine and will not be fit for use until 1884 at the earliest.

Should I take a few bottles for use I hope you will pardon the intrusion.

Yours
ANTHY TROLLOPE

H. M. Trollope Esq

[1] Not quite true. Arthur Tilley was born in 1851, and *Barchester Towers* was not begun until 1855.

854. To Henry Merivale Trollope. 15 January.
Muriel Rose Trollope.

(Harting,
15 January 1882   Petersfield.)

My dear Harry,

When Davis sends his bill I will pay it, deducting 15 per centage,—whatever the bill may be. This I will do whether the bill arrive before or after the golden 21st of the month.

I think you have done well with Isbister;—only that he has thrown in a spice of the Jew at last, in the matter of the 13 to the dozen.[1] But you will at any rate get your £100 for expenses. And if you should get nothing more, there will be something to have done Normandy free of expense.

I pity you your Sunday work. Molière is very well. But two long plays early in the day, is a large order!

I send you Cross'[2] letter which return. I shall of course pay him £5.5/. But he is a Jew;—and he must know that I think him so. I hear that all persons are abusing him for his prices, but that no one dares to tell him of it.

I went to another doctor in London, a young man, one Dr Murrell.[3] He pretends to know especially the inns [*sic*] and outs of Angina pectoris. He says that I have not a symtom [*sic*] of A. P. and that Cross is an old idiot. I am disposed to believe him. Therefore I am going at once to walk up all the pikes in the country.

God bless you
Yours affectionately
Anthy Trollope

---

[1] In certain circumstances a bookseller who ordered twelve copies was given an extra copy free. Isbister probably refused to pay a royalty on the free copy.

[2] Since in 1882 there were in London three physicians named Cross, it is impossible to identify this man more closely.

[3] William Murrell of Portland Place. See *Post Office London Directory 1882.*

855. To Henry Merivale Trollope. 21 January.
Muriel Rose Trollope.

(Harting,

21—Jany. 1882   Petersfield.)

Dear Harry.

Your Union Bank shares are now paid and, after paying various little bills and your January money, I have £120 of yours in hand.

I understand Cross's letter very well. He intends to make the best of his situation;—and to stick to charges which he knows we shall not dispute.

What Dr Murrell says is mainly true;—but then what Dr Cross said about me was also mainly true. I do not believe that I have any symptom of Angina pectoris, but I have got to be old, and nearly worn out by another disease.[1]

David did deduct 15/, but I do not understand it. He made the bill to be paid exactly £7, and that I have paid.

Barney has turned up again as fresh as paint. We wrote to the Protestant parson, and he says he saw him walking about Banagher every day,—only just a little the worse for wear.

Langford never heard a word about Normandy or Brittany from me;—nor did any man except that wretch Evans. I was very glad you got your engagement from Isbister;—because of the second £50.

John Merivale says that he will have an action against you for recovery of that claret. I held it on trust for my friends, and had no right to make it over secretly to a son. He said a great deal about your going to him when you were back in London.

Yours most affectionately

A. T.

---

[1] Trollope suffered from a bad hernia. See letter No. 919, *infra.*

856. To Henry Merivale Trollope. 23 January.
Muriel Rose Trollope.

23 Jany 1882
(Harting,
Petersfield.)

Dear Harry

I send the £5. As you say the Athenaeum will not break you. It may break me without breaking you. But that is only a joke. I shall be obligated to pay that money,—on your account.

Yes; Browning is a stodger. In Milton there are many true things. In Tennyson there are some. In Browning there are a few. His phraseology is as you say sometimes fearful.

I have not yet walked up the South Gardens. But last Sunday I did walk to the Station and back again. I will not do it again just at present. I discredit much the French ministry;—not Gambetta[1] personally, though I know nothing about him. But I do doubt the people he has around him.

I have not been in London for a fortnight. But I shall be there this week,—and the next and the next, for your sake.

Yours ever affect
Anthony Trollope

857. To Alfred Austin. 23 January.
Parrish Collection.

(Harting,
Petersfield.)

23, January 1882

My dear Austin,

You say I promised to send you a list of the Committee of the *Garrick*. Was it not of the Athenaeum? Either way I will do it, and shall be up in London next week. Only send me a line to the Athenaeum saying which list it is you require. However I feel sure it was the Athenaeum, though you wrote the Garrick.

I have been well,—off and on. That is I have been in the doctors hands and have had dreadful things threatened me,— angina pectoris and God knows what. But I do not believe them.

---

[1] Léon Gambetta (1838–82), the French statesman and orator who shaped the constitution of the Third Republic and was an unpopular prime minister, 1881–2.

Tom and Fanny write in very good spirits. They are coming here about July 1st—for a month. He writes as though a life indefinitely prolonged had allurements. Do you know Tennysons 'Two Voices'? Each voice speaks falsely. The small voice counsels death for wrong reasons; and the other, life by arguments equally fallacious. See if it be not so. There is nothing to fear in death,— if you be wise. There is so much to fear in life, whether you be wise or foolish. That should have been the line of the argument.

I have seen your wifes name as collector for the Irish fund. What does she mean to do with the money? She cannot walk into a gentleman's house and offer him a £10 note. Of course her money will go to a common fund. But what will the common fund do with it? The fact is all charity is wrong,—and only to be excused by the comfort it gives to the giver. Tell her with my love that them is my opinions. But I learned the other day that she is a stiff-necked young woman.

I shall be in town this week at the Athenaeum on Thursday & Friday, and the next week Wednesday Thursday and Friday.

Yours affectionately
ANTHONY TROLLOPE

858. TO HENRY MERIVALE TROLLOPE. 28 January.
Muriel Rose Trollope.

28 Jany, 1882
(Athenaeum Club)

My dear Harry.

You are all in a turmoil now in Paris. What does Gambetta intend to do? Retire into private life and come out again in a year or two? I cannot believe that. Or does he intend to show by the intensity of his opposition, that no one can be minister without him.

Do not get into a mess with telling too much of the truth respecting the 'Temps', and remember that Mad de Montalk's[1] stories are worth nothing. She thinks that she knows a great deal, but she does know nothing.

You misunderstand me about the Athenaeum; though I do not remember what I said. I blundered no doubt and then what

---

[1] It is possible that Mrs. Trollope's translator of 1835 was still alive.

I write is illegible. But you would be more comfortable paying for the club, for the very reason you give. However it will be paid instantly for you, if you get in.

Chapman agrees with what you say about the books.

Yours very affectionately

ANTY TROLLOPE

859. TO WILLIAM BLACKWOOD. 28 January.
National Library of Scotland.

28 January 1882

My dear Blackwood,

I think you should print the Fixed Period from your own pages, and let me have them to give a final revise. I have observed no blunders in the Maga.

I had originally made a mistake about the gun, imagining that the weight should be the weight of the shot and not of the gun. But I think it is all right as it has been published.

It is very hard to make a story not too short and not too long. I am far from saying that I have hit the medium correctly. But I fear it cannot be altered now.

What do you think of Longman bringing out Mrs Oliphants novel[1] at 12/6 for 3 volumes? Answer this question.

Yours always

ANTHONY TROLLOPE

860. TO MRS. ALFRED AUSTIN. 30 January.
Parrish Collection.

(Harting,
Petersfield.)

January 30, 1882

My dear Mrs Austin

I cannot argue with you,—specially at this distance. But I am not wrong-headed, at least I think not. Nor, as I believe, hard hearted. But I am sceptical. I believe rather in forcing people to do their duty than in doing it for them. Indeed as to giving money I doubt whether both be not damned,—he who gives it and he who takes it. And of money so collected only a part reaches the hands of those for whom it is intended.

[1] *In Trust* (1882).

470

But having said so much to anger you, I send my mite. I have spent all the morning reading your cases, one after another. They are very piteous. But how are you to know the truth. Who compiles them and gets them together? To whose hands is the redistribution entrusted?

But I send my mite believing altogether in your goodness

Yours always sincerely

ANTHONY TROLLOPE

M.O. for £1— enclosed

861. To HENRY MERIVALE TROLLOPE. 2 February. *Muriel Rose Trollope.*

2 February 1882

(Athenaeum Club)

My dear Harry,

My own impression is that the Scrutin de liste[1] had better go to sleep for the present.

I think that Gambetta has perhaps been hardly used in having been made to think that he was every thing. But he went to work too much as though he was everything to have my full sympathy. I think he has wanted to have all Paris and all France in his pocket.

Triptych is the word as τρεις for three does not contain the requisites for a γ.

I have finished my Palmerston,—yesterday, & will send it to the publisher in a fortnight. It will require careful reading.

Yours always

A. T.

862. To M. COOKSON.[2] 7 February. Harting. *Parrish Collection.*

Trollope enlists the interest of Mr. Cookson, who will remember Henry Trollope as a law pupil, in his son's candidature at the Athenaeum Club.

[1] Vote by list. See a discussion in *The Times*, 26 January 1882, p. 10.
[2] Montague Hughes Cookson, barrister of Lincoln's Inn. See *Post Office London Directory 1882.*

863. To HENRY MERIVALE TROLLOPE. 11 February.
Athenaeum Club. *Muriel Rose Trollope.*

Trollope has called on Lord Arthur Russell and engaged his support for Harry's candidature. Arthur John Edward Russell (1825–92), brother of Odo William Leopold Russell, was given the style of a duke's son, 1872. His house was a meeting-place for literary and political society.

864. To A. ARTHUR READE.[1] 11 February.
Not traced. A. Arthur Reade, *Study and Stimulants* (Manchester and London, 1883), p. 141.

February 11, 1882.

*   *   *

I have been a smoker nearly all my life. Five years ago, I found it certainly was hurting me, causing my hand to shake and producing somnolence. I gave it up for two years. A doctor told me I had smoked too much (three large cigars daily). Two years since, I took it up again, and now smoke three small cigars (very small), and, so far as I can tell, without any effect.

*   *   *

865. To ROSE TROLLOPE. [? February.]
Muriel Rose Trollope.

(Athenaeum Club)
Dearest Love.

They tell me that Harry is safe. Though in truth a man is never safe; but in truth a great many more have written their names on his card.

I shall be down to breakfast on Tuesday, so save the pony for me. If it is fine Flo can come.

Ever your own
A T.

I dined at Smith's last night and met Annie Thackeray, & we smiled at each other, and we had a thorough good talk. I am very glad because my memory of her father was wounded by the feeling of a quarrel.

[1] Alfred Arthur Reade (1851–?) was the author of *Literary Success, How to Write English,* and other journalistic pamphlets in the literature of self-help.

866. To HENRY MERIVALE TROLLOPE. 13 February.
Muriel Rose Trollope.

(Athenaeum Club)
(13 February 1882)

Dear Harry

You have been elected by 204 votes to 4— I have not heard of so overpowering a majority. They tell me here that they do not know of anything like it. However you are now a member of the Athenaeum.

God bless you
Your own father
A. T.

867. To HENRY MERIVALE TROLLOPE. 16 February.
Muriel Rose Trollope.

(Harting,
Petersfield.)

16—Feb—1882.

Dear Harry.

It was a jolly triumph. I was awfully nervous. But when the balloting began the Secretary came to me and told me that you would certainly get in. Knowing the club so well I suppose he understands all the whisperings. I remained there—as did Millais. And we did the best we could. Nevertheless up to the end I was in a funk. When the bulletins came over at six oclock I retired into the card room as it was necessary I should remain somewhere to hear the news. At a quarter to 7 a dozen men backed by the Secretary came to me and told me the result. Somebody said that they had never remembered so large a majority. One blackball in 10 excludes,—but one in 50 would not have kept you out. I congratulate you with all my heart. I wrote immediately after the ballot, but it was too late for the post.

I dont expect you will ever condescend to look into the Garrick again. Palgrave Simpson[1] assured me, three times over, that he knew you very intimately at the Garrick. It's a great comfort to think that when it has been done once it has been done for ever.

There is a bundle of papers here which the Secretary has sent

[1] John Palgrave Simpson (1807–87), dramatist and novelist.

down for you, which can be kept for your arrival. The only one that means anything is a demand for £31–10– Entrance

and £8– 8– Subscription

£39–18

which is £10–10 more than I had thought. But it shall be paid at once.

Yours most affectionately
A. T.

You first joined the Garrick,—then in a months time the Athenaeum, and then, in another month, were born.[1]

868. To HENRY MERIVALE TROLLOPE. 19 February. *Muriel Rose Trollope.*

19 Feb. 1882
(Harting,
Petersfield.)

My dear Harry

I have read Zola's case, but I cannot tell whether Zola be wrong or right. He knew that there was a lawyer named Duverdy and he made his lawyer an objectionable beast.[2] If I wished to shew spite against Sir Henry James[3] and put a man into one of my books as a thieving advocate under that name I doubt whether I should not be libellous.

I can get you the portmanteau if you wish it, or I can send George Hitchen[4] the cheque for the money. Tell me what you will. He would buy the article cheaper and better. But if you wish me to do it, you must repeat the particulars.

I think that you should buy a scarlet uniform and a white feather and spurs, to go into the Athenaeum. There should be some little ceremonious observance of that sort. But if you feel yourself too 'umble for that I will take you to that dragon the porter and when we have passed him we will go and have a

---

[1] Mr. Sadleir has suggested to me that this cryptic postscript means that Trollope had entered Harry for these clubs before he was born. But since Trollope himself was not a member of either club in 1846, he could scarcely have been in a position to enter his son's name.

[2] Denis-Charles Duverdy (1829–98), lawyer and journalist.

[3] Henry James, Lord James of Hereford (1828–1911), lawyer and statesman, M.P. 1869–95, solicitor-general, attorney-general.

[4] Not listed in the *Post Office London Directory 1880*.

modest mutton chop together. After the porter there are no dragons.

As to your coming back I certainly would not advise you to come for the club. Any day will do for that. If you can manage the Normandy without a visit to London I would advise you to do so. Only in that case you must be careful to draw Isbister for the £50 before you start. I think you should write to him at once if you can name the day.

I am thinking of taking a run over to Ireland in reference to a book I am thinking of writing.[1] But as I should take Florence I could not go unless I could have you here with your mother. Would you not be able to be here in May, for a fortnight, between Normandy & Brittany.

Yours always affectionately
ANTHY TROLLOPE

I have not mentioned this to your mother as yet.

869. To WILLIAM BLACKWOOD. 24 February.
Harting. *National Library of Scotland.*

Trollope is indignant because he has received proofs marked 'Gone to Press'. 'But I have not seen one of them until they reached me today! It is of no use my correcting the sheets if they have gone to press.'

870. To HENRY MERIVALE TROLLOPE. 27 February.
Muriel Rose Trollope.

27—Feb 1882   (Harting,
                                                    Petersfield.)

My dear Harry.

I do think that Zola is badly treated now,—but he has brought it all on himself. He made Duverdy, who seems to be known as an advocate, abominable and odious. But certainly it would trouble me if they desired to put out every Palliser from all my novels before they could be sold.

I fear Northampton will re-elect Bradlaugh.[2] And then what

---

[1] *The Landleaguers.*

[2] Charles Bradlaugh (1833–91), free-thought advocate and politician; proprietor of the *National Reformer* from 1862. He was excluded from parliament five times, but always re-elected. In 1886 he was permitted to affirm instead of swearing on the Bible, and he then took his seat.

good will have been done? Such men should never be made
martyrs. The intention of the country is that a mans position as
Member of Parliament shall not depend on his religion. It is a
good intention; but cannot be brought about without injury, if
so base a creature be converted into a hero.

I would not wait long in Paris to correct the proof. I would let
Dickens know on what day I should have to leave Paris and beg
him to send the sheets as quickly as possible. They can let you
have them a day or two after they get them. I would then allow
myself a week after the day I had fixed.

Have not we what dictionaries you will want for the writing
of the Normandy book? At any rate you will have the Athenaeum
if you come up for a few days, and Tedder to help you. Do you
intend to have the book out by beginning of June?

I am still thinking of the Irish plan;—but I am almost afraid
of myself, whether travelling would not be too much for me.

Yours affectionately
A N T H O N Y   T R O L L O P E

871. To William Blackwood. 2 March. Harting.
National Library of Scotland.

Trollope thanks Blackwood for his cheque, hopes the book will be a success, and invites him to breakfast.

872. To Rose Trollope. 11 March. Athenaeum Club.
Muriel Rose Trollope.

Trollope will be home for breakfast on Tuesday. 'It seems that I have been
living in London for the last 10 years, and yet I have dined here but once.
The Trollopes, the Pollocks, John Reiss and now John Tilley have or are
going to feed me.'

873. To Henry Merivale Trollope. 21 March.
Muriel Rose Trollope.

21—March 1882   (Harting,
Petersfield.)

Dear Harry,

I send £5 as desired. I wish it were going to a better purpose
than the dentist. I suppose you will be off now to Normandy as

soon as you have got Isbisters money. I hope he will pay you, (and I think he will) for he has just induced me to renew a bill of his for £150, which is exactly the same as borrowing the money. I have his counter bill in my drawer. This is like Chapman.

I think Scherer[1] in his criticism on Alceste has shewn not only want of critical ability, but absolute stupidity. I think the character on the whole to be the best of Molière.

I have just finished the 12th and last volume of French history.[2] There are fine episodes; but there are enormous longueurs. At last it becomes very tedious.

Yours affectionately

ANTHONY TROLLOPE

874. To ROSE TROLLOPE. 23 March. Athenaeum Club.
Muriel Rose Trollope.

Trollope instructs Rose to keep a box which will come for him from the chemist's. 'I have, alas, been the whole day among the doctors.'

875. To HENRY MERIVALE TROLLOPE. 28 March.
Muriel Rose Trollope.

28 March—1882.   (Harting,

Dear Harry.   Petersfield.)

I am very sorry to hear about your knee. It will be a monstrous bore for you, with so much on your hands to do at the present moment.

It will affect me, as to your return in May. I want to start for Ireland on 15 May; and as Florence is to go with me, and as I do not wish to leave mamma alone, I was very anxious that you should be here. And I want to take you into the club. That any one can do—or for the matter of that you can walk in without any one taking you. Or I might find you in London when I came back in June. On what day do you think you will be able to be here if all goes well with you?

---

[1] Edmond Scherer (1815–89), a French critic who exercised considerable influence in forming nineteenth-century taste and who won the praise of Arnold, Saintsbury, *et al.*

[2] I do not find a 12-volume history in either French or English, but Trollope must have been reading from Henri Martin, Michelet, or Guizot.

Have you observed how the Standard Bank shares have gone up? To day I got the biennial circular explaining the mystery by an extra 5/ per share bonus. This will give me £16–5/ on 65 shares,—or £32–10 per annum if the extra bonus be continued. May the Bank live for ever

Yours always affect
A. T.

876. To CHARLES STUART-WORTLEY. 29 March. Harting. *The Hon. Mrs. James Cecil.*

Trollope sends an invitation to dine at the Garrick. 'I have been to Mandeville Place and made two or three attempts to find you, but of course in vain. I have been there in the day time, and in the day time you have been in your Chambers or at the house.'

877. To [? GEORGE] BENTLEY. 30 March. Harting. *Robert H. Taylor. Taylor,* p. 88.

Trollope offers Bentley his next novel. 'I am going over to Ireland and shall bring out a novel as to the condition of the country,—which you will agree with me is lamentable enough.' This letter is in another hand, presumably that of Florence Bland. It is addressed to *Richard* Bentley, but it is clear that *George* Bentley, editor of *Temple Bar,* is meant.

878. To HENRY MERIVALE TROLLOPE. 30 March. *Muriel Rose Trollope.*

30 March 1882   (Harting,

Dear Harry,   Petersfield.)

Of course you can draw the April money. I dont quite understand the question. Do you want any more besides Isbisters?

I am glad you are getting over your trouble so well. I suppose when you get Macmillan's cheque you will send it to me. I shall be very glad to know that you have got the money.

Scherer must be very odd if he cannot do better than let his ill humour off by hard criticisms on Molière. Molière will not be the worse for it. There is a comfort in that.

I have now a proposition to make to you. I fear it is necessary that I should live a portion at least of my time in London. I suffer from asthma, and the air here is [? not][1] too good for me. I am

[1] The manuscript *may* be correct. Asthmatics are often most comfortable in rainy weather.

only beginning to find it out. Can not we have three rooms
(to ourselves)
between us, and some kind of servant for us. A small flat would
be the thing if it is not too dear.

Yours ever affectionately

A. T.

When do you think that you will be able to be with your mother?

879. To HENRY MERIVALE TROLLOPE. 18 April.
Muriel Rose Trollope.

Dear Harry

I opened this imagining it to be on the Company's business.

I had heard that they had declared that they would pay for the
book, when it was published.

If they say so in their answer I think you should tell them that
an author bringing a work to be published is to be treated differently from one who is employed to do a certain task. The
proof that it is so consists in the fact that they have to pay you
for your work whether they publish it or not. But the original
author has only to be paid if his work be published. You have
done your work,—as ordered.

Yours affectionately

A. T.

18 April 1882

Have you heard from Isbister?

880. To ADMIRAL [? RYDER]. 11 May.
Athenaeum Club. *Parrish Collection.*

Trollope cannot accept a dinner invitation for 19 May because he will be
in Ireland. 'I trust I may come back then, so as to be able to call in Montagu
Square and tell you my adventures.'

881. To ROSE TROLLOPE. 16 May. Rugby.[1]
Muriel Rose Trollope.

Trollope and Flo arrived here last night and will press on this morning.
His only adventure thus far has been that of losing and recovering his purse.

[1] Rugby: a hunting centre in the nineteenth century and seat of Rugby
School, 30 miles east of Birmingham.

882. To ROSE TROLLOPE. 18 May. Dublin.
Muriel Rose Trollope.

Trollope goes on to Cork in the morning 'in order to find Judge O'Hagan[1] and Mr Vernon[2] both of whom I am anxious to see. . . . I have done nothing but talk since I have been here, till I am very tired of it.'

883. To ROSE TROLLOPE. 20 May.
Muriel Rose Trollope.

Cork

20 May 1882   (Harting,
                                                Petersfield.)
Dearest Love

I am getting on pretty well, breakfasted with the Land Law Judge this morning, dine with Mr. Munn[3] today, & with the Judge tomorrow—Sunday. On Monday I go to Dunmanway to visit the Court there, and come back here and on Tuesday I go to Limerick. I suppose we go to Lord Emlys.[4] But I have written to him to say that I have a lady with me. I think he knows it, but I am not sure.

It is astonishing how one loses here all sense of rows and riots & how soon one begins to feel that the world is going on the same as ever. Do you remember how we heard from the Times at Clonmel, that at the bakers shops at Clonmel . . . .[5]

884. To ROSE TROLLOPE. 23 May.
Muriel Rose Trollope.

Limerick. 23. May 1882
Dearest Love.

I have got your letter written on Sunday, and believe if I send this to the London hotel it will reach you. In the first place we are

[1] John O'Hagan (1822–90), judicial commissioner under the Land Law of 1881, justice of the high court of justice, 1881–90.
[2] John Edward Vernon (1816–87), director of the Bank of Ireland, one of the three land commissioners, 1881–7.
[3] Possibly, but not at all certainly, Alfred Moore Munn, attorney of Dublin and Londonderry. See *Thom's Irish Almanac and Official Directory* (Dublin, 1878), p. 880.
[4] William Monsell (1812–94), Baron Emly, 1874; M.P. for Limerick, 1847–74, Postmaster-General, 1871–3.
[5] Remainder of letter missing.

both of us safe hitherto. I do not think that there is any danger that we shall be hurt. We are now, (in an hour) going out for a drive with Clifford Lloyd,[1] and I wont send this off till we have got back,—so that you may know we are over that danger.

You can hardly bring yourself to understand the state of the country here, for among the men, who are well-informed & thoroughly loyal, there are so many opinions. My own idea is that we ought to see the Parnell[2] set put down. We should try it out with them and see whether we cannot conquer them. I do not doubt but that we could, them and the American host at their back.

I am very glad that you have enjoyed yourself. Harry evidently spends most of his time writing letters at the Athenaeum.

You were nearly in grief with the plunging cab horse. Luckily it deferred its last plunge till you were out.

I was much obliged for the Observer. There was an excellent article in it, probably by Dicey, against Gladstone.

Florence will have told you how kind the Morrisons [?] were to us just the same as ever,—only he somewhat more stupid.

> God bless you
> Your own
> A. T.

885. To ROSE TROLLOPE. 26 May.
Muriel Rose Trollope.

(Gurteen-Le Poer,
  Kilsheelan.)   26 May 1882

Dearest Love

We are at the house 4 miles from Clonmel at which you may remember that a dreadful tragedy occurred while we were living here. It seems odd that after so many years I should have come here. We are just going to drive up to the slate quarries, where

---

[1] Charles Dalton Clifford Lloyd (1844–91), resident magistrate for co. Down, 1874–81; restored order in co. Longford, 1881; special resident magistrate at Kilmallock, co. Limerick, May 1881—Sept. 1883; arrested Father Eugene Sheehy and other land-leaguers, 1881.

[2] Charles Stewart Parnell (1846–91), a political leader who aimed at securing legislative independence for Ireland; was jailed in Oct 1881 for incendiary speeches; released 2 May 1882.

I remember going, you and I and the two Sankeys,[1] nearly 40 years ago!! The present Mrs Le Poer, (it used to be called Power)[2] is Lord Emlys daughter. He is here now. Her husband is a Count. But why a Count I do not know.[3] They are very gracious and civil. Tomorrow we go back to Limerick and then to Galway.

You had better address to Galway up to Monday inclusive morning and evening. After that to General Post Office Dublin, till you get different instructions.

I am quite well as regards asthma, *except that I cannot stoop.* I sleep without any reference to it,—well or bad from other causes. I do take Murrell's medicines, and no doubt with good effects. But I know nothing of them. When I get back I shall see whether the asthma returns at Harting.

How are you? I still long to hear how you found the place looking. Love to Harry. I will write to him tomorrow.

God bless you.

Your own A T

886. To HENRY MERIVALE TROLLOPE. 1 June. Recess.[4] *Muriel Rose Trollope.*

Trollope asks Harry to persuade Charles Dickens to send a bill at a month for his novel.[5] 'It is necessary to keep him up to his prices as to dates.'

887. To ROSE TROLLOPE. 1 June. Recess. *Muriel Rose Trollope.*

Trollope has been hard at work at Cork, Limerick, &c. 'Now I am taking a holyday;—but still am in the midst of Irish difficulties and Irish rebels. I do not think I can get home till the 14 or 15. . . . How is the garden, and the cocks & hens, & especially the asparagus bed.'

[1] See letter No. 135, *supra.*
[2] Edmond James de Poher de la Poer, of Gurteen Le Poer, High Sheriff of co. Waterford, 1879. The family name was changed from Power in 1863. See *Burke's Landed Gentry of Ireland* (London: Harrison, 1904), p. 495.
[3] A Count of the Holy Roman Empire—a Papal dignity.
[4] Recess: a village in co. Galway, west-central Ireland.
[5] *Mr. Scarborough's Family* was serialized in *All the Year Round* from 28 May 1882 to 16 June 1883.

888. To Rose Trollope. 4 June.
   Muriel Rose Trollope.

Westport[1]
   4—June 1882

Dearest Love—

Read the enclosed and tell me when I come home what I ought to say in answer to it. Do not take the trouble to write. It is a simple request for £20 a year.

Do you remember that the Master of Gurteen, one Mr Power, shot himself while we were living at Clonmel. He was the father of our host of the other day, who was then an infant.

I am glad to hear so good an account of Ringwood. But it was hard that Harry should have seen him turn into the pot house when he went back from the station.

I will give up being Surveyors clerk as you dont seem to like it, but in that case must take to being guide at Killarney.

How has your dinner party gone off with Mary Davies?[2] I am very glad that she came back again. It will be too late to send her my love, although she is at Harting at this moment. I cannot as yet say anything more definite as to our return than in my last. The uncertainty depends on my being or not being able to see certain persons. I think we shall be home either Tuesday 13, or Wednesday 14th. I may have to leave Florence for another night in London.

God bless you
Ever your own
Anth Trollope

Tell Harry I will write to him by next post.

888. To John Dicks. 14 June.
   Parrish Collection.

(Athenaeum Club)
14. June, 1882.

Dear Sir

I called at your office yesterday in reference to your letter to me which had followed me to Ireland but which was not accom-

[1] Westport: a sea-coast town in co. Mayo, north-west Ireland.
[2] From early days in Ireland Mary Davies and Rose Trollope were life-long friends.

panied by the copy of Mr Sala's Tales. I was not therefore able to make any answer to your application and did not know what might be the length of the work required. I understand you to desire to have the possession of the copyright of the stories in question for your own unrestricted purposes.

I would write for you the ten stories, making in their complete form a length equal to that of Mr Sala's, for seven hundred pounds.

I could supply these at the rate of one per month, which I understand would suit you; and it would be convenient that the money should be paid for each story as the manuscript is delivered.

Yours faithfully

Address   A N T H O N Y   T R O L L O P E

Harting

Petersfield

890. To J O H N D I C K S. 18 June.
    Parrish Collection.

(Harting,
Petersfield.)
18, June, 1882.

My dear Sir

Our two letters crossed. Yours of the 13th having followed me down here. Of such stories as you propose the copyright would be of no value to me. I should not, indeed, attempt to use them.

I observe, as I ought to have done before writing my last letter, that you require the tales once a fortnight, and not once a month, as I had suggested. I fear I could not manage this, as I could not give up all my time for three or four months. I would undertake to have them completed at regular intervals of six months.

Yours faithfully

A N T H O N Y   T R O L L O P E[1]

John Dicks Esqre

[1] Only the complimentary close and the signature are in Trollope's hand.

891. To HENRY MERIVALE TROLLOPE. 9 July.
Muriel Rose Trollope.

9 July 1882

Dear Harry,

Hurrah. Those liberal gentlemen in Rivers Street have given us a bonus of 3/9 a share, making your sum up to £101–5/, and mine to £102–5/— I only hope they will keep up their good humour through the winter. But this is too much to expect.

What are you doing and where are you? You are not fried yet;—at least we are not but are wet through.

God bless you
Yours affectionately
A. T.

892. To HENRY MERIVALE TROLLOPE. 13 July.
Muriel Rose Trollope.

July 13, 1882
(Harting,
Petersfield.)

Dear Harry,

What a muddle about these unfortunate books! I hope you are not waiting in Paris for them all this time! But mamma did her best, and could not send them quicker. You should try to look after your things. I am very stupid in such matters. But then I am old. You are young enough to remember things.

We have at last walked into those Egyptians, and have shewn what an ass that man Arabi[1] has been. But is it not dreadful that it has needed so many lives and so much money to have shewn this?

Your affectionate father
ANTHY TROLLOPE

893. To HENRY MERIVALE TROLLOPE. 31 July.
Harting. *Muriel Rose Trollope.*

After a discussion of bills, bank shares, and dividends, Trollope writes: 'I can't understand why you went to Tours, but I suppose it is all right. You will be glad to have seen the

---

[1] Ahmed Arabi, leader of the Egyptian nationalist revolt of 1881–2.

Cathedral. It is second class among French Cathedrals. Why did you change the whole £50? I hope it is not all spent. But it is your own affair.

'We shall do very well in Egypt I think, if the Turks do not go there. I think they will not for three or four months as they have no money. It would be well that we should do it ourselves.

'No;—by "broken furniture" I meant not fortifications, but the burning and looting of all the houses in Alexandria. The bill for every thing will be sent to us. I do not say we shall pay it.

'There will be an autumn Session this year,—unless the present one be continued till near Christmas. Gladstone means to pass his bill for parliamentary conduct.

'We expect Tom and Fanny tomorrow, and I will keep this letter till they have come.

'Your uncle and Fanny have arrived quite safe. He is looking very well.

'Touching lodgings I have seen none. I think I must wait for you before I go and look after them. I still think that I must take lodgings somewhere. But I must first go to Ireland. I suppose we shall start about 14 August. Then Tom will have gone away. He dislikes to stay longer.

Yours ever most affect
A. T.'

894. To HENRY MERIVALE TROLLOPE. 9 August.
Muriel Rose Trollope.

Augt 9, 1882   (Harting,
                                                    Petersfield.)
Dear Harry.

I have just got your letter. Mamma is already in Germany. Tom & Fanny left us this morning. We ie. I & Flo, start for Ireland tomorrow. Ringwood is to be left in a most melancholy state. He is to have no wages, but to be left in the house and the maids are to give him his food. But he is to have no beer. He begged piteously to have a shilling to be allowed to walk up and down the village with. But I refused. We shall see what will become of it.

I thought that I did write once to you one letter at Limoges.

Indeed I know I did. You tell me to write to Figeac.[1] This I do; but it will be a long time before you get the letter. I never did hear of Figeac before. The Department of Lot I have heard; and have always thought that it was remarkable for a pillar of salt. Tulle I suppose is dedicated to thin dresses.

We start on Friday 11th and expect to be home on 11 September (ie in London) My present trouble is chiefly about my lodgings. I have done nothing. I have put up with Harting for the last fortnight so as to [be] here when Tom & Fanny were with me. But the asthma has been very badly [*sic*] lately. I think I will wait until you come and look for them— I suppose you will be back at any rate early in October. *I certainly cannot live here all the winter.*

What are you doing with your work? Are you filling note books? And are you all alone,—which I should think a bore?

My ideas as to Egypt are that we *are doing the best*. If the Turks will only stay away, I think things will go right. I wish I could say as much for Ireland.

God bless you
Your affectionate father
ANTY TROLLOPE

895. TO ROSE TROLLOPE. 14 August.
Muriel Rose Trollope.

(Harting,
Petersfield.)

Glendalough[2]
August 14, 1882

Dearest Love.

You are at the delightful old Herne.[3] We are here at this beastly place. It is chiefly beastly because a man has come and got our rooms,—though we had bespoken them! Consequently we have to go away or stay till Thursday. The rest of the house is abominable. It is very well that you did not come here. There would have been a kettle of fish! I grumble fearfully. The beggars I think would have brought you to an untimely end. However the brook still warbles just beneath our windows. The cooking is

---

[1] Figeac: a town in southern France about 125 miles east of Bordeaux.
[2] Glendalough: a town in co. Wicklow just south of Dublin.
[3] Herne Bay: in Kent, eight miles north-east of Canterbury.

wretched,—with good tea and coffee. But the sauces! Everything is done with melted butter, and the melted butter is all varnish paste,—which you could paper a room with. However I am trying to get some work done.

Mrs Frisby had full instructions about all our letters—yours, & Toms and mine. Consequently I have had one, *intended for Tom.*

I dare say you have had a letter from Harry and have sent it on. So that I can write to him. Not that I have anything to say. But I have no one else to write to.

What do they say about Egypt in your parts? It seems to me that everybody is getting more or less angry. But that they are all angry because we have done so well. I am half reconciled to Gladstone; but nothing can reconcile me to a man who has behaved so badly about Ireland.

Remember me very kindly to the Vardys. I do hope you like your old quarters. With my best love, always your own

A. T.

896. To Rose Trollope. 16 August.
Muriel Rose Trollope.

Glendalough

August 16, 1882   (Harting,

Dearest Love,   Petersfield.)

I got your letter today of the 12th and am glad to find that you are getting on so well. Though you say little about the people you are with I know that you like them from the tone of your letter.

I am sorry to say that I have had a bad attack of the asthma.— so bad that I must go away from this. I suppose it is too far up ammong [*sic*] the mountains. But this morning from 4 till 7 I was very bad. Tomorrow we will go to a place called The Wooden Bridge[1]—at what they call 'The Meeting of the Waters.' At any rate it is not among the hills. If that will not do I will go to Kingstown[2] or Bray. In the meantime you had better address here. God bless you. I leave the other side for Florence. Ever your own

A. T.

---

[1] Wooden Bridge: a village in co. Wicklow. See Tom Moore's 'The Meeting of the Waters'.

[2] Kingstown and Bray are both suburbs to the south of Dublin.

897. To Rose Trollope. 18 August.
Muriel Rose Trollope.

(Harting,
Petersfield.)

August 18 1882.
Wooden Bridge.

Dearest Love,

Alas, alas;—I got a terrible attack of asthma the third night we were at Glendalough. It comes in the morning and absolutely forces me to sit upright in bed. Then I get a cup of tea and it is gone. This place is very nice & pretty, and we shall remain here for a while; but I can fancy that we shall get tired of it. However you must address here till I give you another address.

I want to know how you get on with your friends, old and new; —though, for the matter of that, Vardy is an older friend even than the Fairs [?].

Tom seems to have gone up to London for two days, and to have culminated in a halo of glory. He dined with Mulford [?] at his club, and met Escott.[1] The great man was all smiles, as was also the less great man who is to be the new Editor of the Fortnightly. Fanny is to write for it.

Have you heard from Harry? I have not. Send me his latest address if you have nothing else to send. Florence is well,—as also am I, barring the asthma. I hope that you are well and enjoying yourself.

I do not like to write to you by any hand but my own; but I fear you will not read it.

Ever your own
A. T.

We dined with such jolly people named Booth.[2] He is a gin maker and a friend of Lord Monks [*sic*],[3] and gave us the best dinner that I ever ate. Address—Wooden Bridge, Avoca, Co Wicklow

[1] Thomas Hay Sweet Escott (*c.* 1850–1924) succeeded John Morley as editor of the *Fortnightly* and became Trollope's first biographer.
[2] Sir Charles Booth (1812–96).
[3] Sir Charles Stanley Monck (1819–94), first Baron Monck of Bally-trammon, Lord of the Treasury, Governor-General of Canada; member of the commission to carry out the provisions of the new Irish Land Acts, 1882–4.

898. To Rose Trollope. 21 August.
Muriel Rose Trollope.

It will be observed that during these last few months and weeks Trollope's letters become more repetitive and confused. And the hand becomes almost illegible.

Wooden Bridge
Dearest Love—   August 21—1882

I have just got your letter of the 17— I have kept you hitherto informed of all our movements, such as they have been. Flo told you how we dined with certain rich people of the name of Booth. Our only adventure is that we are going to stay a night at Lord Monck's next Wednesday. I did tell you that I had been obliged to move down here by the asthma, having had a terrible attack at Glendalough.

You say that you will be at the Hollenths [*sic*] till the 26th You will get this letter before that. I will then write so that you shall receive my letter at Lucerne on the 29th You say you will want money when you get home. Therefore I send £10— You will find that I had arranged with Willis [?] for board wages for 4 weeks—

Do not stay a Sunday in London. It will be 29 August and would kill you with dullness. Either stay the day at Folkestone or Dover. It would be be [*sic*] new and would be better than London. Or get out of London by the early train. In that case bribe them at the club to make sure of an early club [? train]. Is there not another train would take you down to Guildford? And would it not be better? Nothing could be so deadly dull as Sunday in London— There is a train to Guildford at 10.15, & another at 2—

God bless you dearest. Ever your own
A. T.

899. To Rose Trollope. 28 August.
Muriel Rose Trollope.

28 August 1882
(Harting,
Dearest Love,   Petersfield.)

I have just got your letter acknowledging the cheque for £10. But in a former letter you said something about £5. Am I to send you a cheque for £5—also to Harting? You are to get home to Harting by the 6th. But I fear you will have it very hard the Monday, Tuesday and Wednesday. We intend to get to London the Monday following, and to spend Monday in town, so as to see the last of Tom and Fanny. Then, unless we change our plans, we shall come home on the Tuesday to breakfast.

We have been staying the last two days with Lord and Lady Carysfort.[1] They live two or three miles from here. They are both nice and she very. Singularly enough I knew something of her people, the Heathcotes, and I knew his elder brother who killed himself by a fall from the box of a coach. I used to know him when hunting down in the Fitzwilliam country. He has spent an enormous sum of money here. They were quite clever.

We go from here to Kingstown, where we shall stay for a week. This place does suit me in respect to asthma; but I do not get altogether free from it. I had it bad at Lord Monck's. Do you think I could get a small Aetna[2] so as to boil water and make a cup of tea in 15 minutes. Nothing seems to do me so much good as a cup of hot tea. Taking them all together I think the Vardys have done well,—at any rate better than M[rs] C. Remember me to them.

God bless you
Your own A. T.

Address.   Royal Marine Hotel
            Kingstown, Ireland

900. To W. Bennett.[3] 28 August.
H. W. L. Dana.

Trollope is happy to have his name added to the Committee for Longfellow's bust and to contribute five pounds for the purpose.[4]

---

[1] Sir William Proby, fifth Earl of Carysfort (1836–1909), of co. Wicklow, Ireland.
[2] An etna was an alcohol lamp for heating liquids.
[3] Probably William Cox Bennett (1820–95), miscellaneous writer.
[4] Trollope was one of 26 on the original 'steering' committee. He actually contributed five guineas, and of 450 subscribers to the Memorial only ten gave a larger sum. There are a number of references to Trollope in Longfellow's journal.

901. To CHATTO & WINDUS. 15 September.
Not traced.[1]

Trollope rejects an offer of £1,200 for reprint rights for *Marion Fay* and *Mr. Scarborough's Family* and book rights for *The Landleaguers*. 'Your offer of bills at *four months* date from the day of publication is not attractive. It amounts to a deduction of ten pounds for each work.'

902. To HENRY MERIVALE TROLLOPE. 24 September.
Harting. *Muriel Rose Trollope.*

Trollope has arranged to occupy the first and second floors at Mrs. Garlant's hotel in Suffolk Street.

903. To ROSE TROLLOPE. 3 October. London.
Muriel Rose Trollope.

Trollope is coming down to Harting for the week-end. He must see Dr. Murrell again on Tuesday. He wants the first six chapters of his new novel, and he discusses business matters briefly.

904. To ROSE TROLLOPE. 5 October. London.
Muriel Rose Trollope.

Trollope makes plans for 26 October. 'Of course we will go to the Mansion House. It will be an outing as Mrs F says. Mind you carry a bottle of claret in your pocket and if you could take one of your fowls it would be a good thing.'

905. To ROSE TROLLOPE. 10 October.
Muriel Rose Trollope.

Oct 10, 1882
Suffolk Street

Dearest Love,—

I got the *dunn* at last; and . . .[2] it.

I have finished with Chatto: as to the two novels, selling them, for £600 apiece, at *3* months date. I have also sold Marion Fay to them for £600, subject to Chapman who has got the offer of it. But I am to see him tomorrow. This is at one months date. I can settle that tomorrow. I have paid £1.11.6

[1] I quote from Florence Bland's copy of this letter among Trollope's business papers (Bodleian).
[2] One word illegible.

for you for theatre tickets. I suppose I am to put down £1.10 for yourself and Mrs Raker.

I have written to Florence about the doctor. There is nothing really to say,—except that I am to see him again next week.

Harry is going to give me a dinner to day at the Garrick with *M Bramston*.[1] Tomorrow we both dine at Goods. But he has warned me that the wine is *beastly*. I think I will be taken ill and carried away in the middle.

God bless you
Your own
A T.

When you come up to dine with the Lord Mayor wont you borrow Harry's bed room? He can go down to Harting,—or the Devil for that matter.

906. To Rose Trollope. 11 October.
  Muriel Rose Trollope.

11 Oct. 1882.

(Harting,
Petersfield.)

Dearest Love

I will bring 4 lb of coffee, and some fish. Those young women have made themselves awfully troublesome. They have set themselves to work to do so,—and have succeeded. I suppose it to have originated with Eliza but one cannot tell.

The reason for turning Harry out and taking his room would be that you would see what sort of place I live in and would get your breakfast here with me. But we will talk about it. If you like to get off the Lord Mayor, come up some other day to the theatre. But we will talk about it.

Your own
A. T.

Best love to Flo. I hope she is still getting better.

[1] The Bramstons listed in the *Post Office London Directory 1882* were all tradesmen not likely to be members of the Garrick or even guests there.

907. To Rose Trollope. 24 October.
Muriel Rose Trollope.

               (Harting,
Tuesday night,   Petersfield.)
 24. Oct. 1882

Dearest Love,

 I wrote to Fred yesterday. I start tomorrow to Somersetshire, and regret as I always do, that I have promised to go. But still I think it is better to go about. I had a bad night on Monday, rather. That is I got up and took some chloral, but last night was better & I took none.

 I cannot get home till 6 'clock on Saturday as I must settle about some rooms I have seen. I am vacillating between Halfmoon Street and Victoria Street, the first furnished, & the second not so.

 I have seen Hambly [*sic*][1] who has come back infinitely disgusted with Wolseley.[2] There is to be a terrible row in the house about it.

             God bless you
              Your own
               A. T.

908. To Lord Emly. 27 October.
Commander Monsell. Not seen.

 This is probably Trollope's last letter. On 3 November, one week later, he suffered the stroke which ultimately proved fatal.

            (Athenaeum Club)
              Oct 27 1882

My dear Emly

 Your letter has travelled about after me and has found me at last.

 I am infinitely obliged to Cardinal Newman for his kindness in regard to my asthma. I have ventured to write to tell him so. In regard to his specific, though it shall have full loyal attention

---

[1] Sir Edward Bruce Hamley (1824–93), lieutenant-general (later general), fought under Wolseley in Egypt.

[2] Garnet Joseph Wolseley, Viscount Wolseley (1833–1913), adjutant-general (later field-marshal). In 1882 he was sent out to Egypt to put down Arabi Pasha's rebellion, in which he was very quickly successful.

from me, I fear that it will do but little for me; not because it is inoperative, but because I am not in want of it. I find all fumigatory receipts to be of no avail, because I have not fallen into the period which they affect. Great spasmodic want of breath is the evil which affects me, and which at night sometimes becomes very hard to bear. I am indeed obliged to sit upright so as to catch my breath or to remedy the disease by taking chloral. But my throat is never so affected as to be touched by any kind of smoking. As before said, however, I will try saltpetre in the form recommended by the Cardinal and you no doubt will hear the result. I can hardly tell you the amount of pleasure which I have received from the Cardinal's opinions of my novels.

Very faithfully yours
ANTHONY TROLLOPE

Letters of Uncertain Date

909. To LADY AMBERLEY. Garlants Hotel.
Parrish Collection.

Trollope is sorry he was not in town last Tuesday and inquires about Lady Amberley's dinner hour. The address suggests the autumn of 1882 when Trollope was living in London, but the hand is earlier.

910. To ALFRED AUSTIN. Garrick Club.
Parrish Collection.

Trollope has arranged for Chapman to 'give up all the books for £75, and also any (if he has any) copyright on the two novels [Austin's] Won by a Head and Lord of All'.

911. To ALFRED AUSTIN.
Austin, p. 129.

*   *   *

I observe when people of my age are spoken of, they are described as effete and moribund, just burning down the last half inch of the candle in the socket. I feel as though I should still like to make a 'flare up' with my half inch. In spirit I could trundle a hoop about the streets, and could fall in love with a young woman just as readily as ever; as she doesn't want me, I don't—but I could.[1]

*   *   *

912. To ALFRED AUSTIN.
Austin, p. 131.

*   *   *

We are all so very smooth in our usual intercourse that any urgency takes the guise of violence. I own I like a good contradictory conversation in which for the moment the usual subserviency of coat and trousers to bodies [? bodices], skirts, and petticoats, may be—well—not forgotten—but for the moment put to one side.

*   *   *

913. To ALFRED AUSTIN.
Austin, pp. 131–2.

[On a highly eulogistic article on his own personal and literary merits, from the pen of a partial writer:] 'I don't like such notices, particularly when they are written by friends. I would much rather be left to the mercies of the real critics. Sydney Smith used to say, speaking of practical jokes, that it was impossible to say how much melted butter a gentleman would bear to have poured into his dress-coat pocket; I dislike it almost as much when it is poured down my back.'

*   *   *

914. To MISS DAVIES.[1]
Parrish Collection.

Mr. Trollope presents his compliments to Miss Davies and thinks that if she chose to be severe about his novel, it would

---

[1] A reference in the article would seem to date this letter about 1876.
[2] Probably Emily Davies (1830–1921), the active feminist and educator. See Barbara Stephen, *Emily Davies and Girton College* (London: Constable, 1927). Trollope met her at Emily Faithfull's in 1861–2, where their views on woman's place in life must have clashed. In her *The Higher Education of*

have been much more noble on her part to have signed her name than to have written anonymously. Miss Davies no doubt knows a great deal more about love than Mr. Trollope can pretend to do, but Mr. Trollope thinks it very odd Miss Davies should quarrel with a man for being in love with two ladies at once, when,—as Mr. Trollope very well knows,—Miss Davies has been in love at the same time with at any rate five gentlemen.

915. To MRS. DUNCAN. Clarendon.
Parrish Collection.

Trollope is sorry to have missed Mrs. Duncan but hopes to be more successful another time. 'Many thanks for your offer as to Mrs Stewarts ball, but I will not accept it as I am a bad hand at balls. I do not even know what men do at them who are over 40.'

916. To KATE FIELD. Montagu Square.
Boston Public Library.

Trollope is trying to arrange introductions for Kate. 'I hear that Mr. Tilley is not in town. If you like it I will take you and see some other pundit.'

917. To JAMES T. FIELDS.
Harvard College Library.

Writing about the piracy of *North America* [see letter No. 180, *supra*], Trollope attacks Lippincott's weak excuse for his dilatoriness. 'It amounted to an admission that he allowed the grass to grow under his feet while he had the sheets,—and while Harper who had no such advantage was hard at work.
'Of course I suffer much; but I should not begrudge that in the least if I could bring about any better state of things.'[1]

Woman (London: Strahan, 1866) she quotes Trollope scornfully as saying, 'We like our women to be timid.' She had also undoubtedly read chapter xviii ('The Rights of Women') in *North America*. It must have made her furious. It is quite possible that Trollope's lecture, 'The Higher Education of Women' (1867–8), was intended as a reply to her book. At any rate, they certainly did not agree. Where Miss Davies's review was published I cannot discover, but it may well have shown more ill-nature than critical spirit. It is possible, however, that in this third-person note Trollope intended to be jocular. Incidentally, Miss Davies became editor of the *Victoria Magazine* in 1864 and published one of Thomas Adolphus Trollope's best novels, *Lindisfarne Chase.*
[1] This letter exists only as a fragment copied by Annie Fields.

918. To James T. Fields. [? Boston.][1]
Berg Collection.

Through Mr. Fields Trollope is sending a gift to a woman acquaintance. 'The box contains books *written by myself* and *published in England*—nothing else. I am just off to Concord.'

919. To E. A. Freeman.[2] Harting
Parrish Collection.

11 Suffolk Street,[3]   (Harting,
Pall Mall.   Petersfield.)

My dear Freeman.

With a great deal of perseverance I have made out that Wednesday 25 October will suit you for me to come. Is it so? And to go some day so as to get home the same week.

But my big dinner here, at the Garrick, comes off on the 1st of November, which it appears will not suit you. But it is odd if we cant name some day for a little dinner which will suit you, and which will be pleasanter. I can, with due time, walk up anything,—only I cant sleep, walking or not walking. I cant write, as you see, because my hand is paralysed. I cant sit easily because of a huge truss I wear, and now has come this damnable asthma! But still I am very good to look at; and as I am not afraid to die, I am as happy as other people.

What I believe about Frank, I can only tell you, not write. But I will tell you.
                    Yours always
                    ANTHONY TROLLOPE

920. To Admiral Sir Anthony Hoskins. Harting.
Maggs Catalogue 628 (Summer 1936).

Trollope asks for the address of Admiral Ryder and concludes, 'How is a person to bear in mind all the Vice Admirals of the white and the Rear-Admirals of the red.' Sir Anthony Hiley Hoskins (1828–1901) was lord commissioner of the admiralty, 1880; admiral and senior naval lord of the admiralty, 1891.

[1] Therefore written in 1861–2 or 1868.

[2] Edward Augustus Freeman (1823–92), the distinguished historian, a regular contributor to the *Saturday Review*, 1855–78, regius professor of modern history at Oxford, 1884–92. In 1869 he and Trollope had engaged in a famous dispute over the cruelty of field sports. See Sadleir, *Commentary*, pp. 256–9.

[3] The place suggests that the letter was written in 1882, in which year 25 October fell on a Wednesday.

921. To Cecilia Meetkerke.[1] 'Anthony Trollope',
Blackwood's Magazine, cxxxiii (February 1883), 318.

My dear Friend,—The verses which are very pretty, I have sent
on, withdrawing your note and substituting one from myself.
They may not improbably print them and publish them; I do not
think they will pay for them. But A. T. will neither in one case
nor the other have done either good or harm in the matter. If
you don't believe in one's own honest ground, what should you
believe in? As for favour, you should not condescend to accept it;
but there is not much favour in it—though perhaps a little. The
owner of the magazine wants to make money, and would sooner
have the worst verses a man could put together with Tennyson's
name to them, than the most charming poetry from you, because
Tennyson's work would sell the periodical. But for you, as for
me formerly, there is nothing but honest ground that will do any
good, and no good coming from anything else is worth having.

Your most affectionate friend
and mentor
A. T.

922. To Cecilia Meetkerke.
Blackwood's, cxxxiii (February 1883), 317.

On being consulted as to the advisability of an author joining with an
actor in bringing out a play, Trollope wrote: 'Pray, pray do not be tempted
to pay money to have your play brought out! It is working the wrong way,
and nothing is to be got from it—neither fame nor profit. If the theatres will
not take your plays, put up with it—bear your burden of disappointment as
so many have to do. Labour on, if you have perseverance and think that
there may be a chance of success; but do not be tempted to an attempt to buy
for money that which should come in quite a different fashion.'

923. To Cecilia Meetkerke. Autumn 1882.[2]
Blackwood's, cxxxiii (February 1883), 319.

When his correspondent had reproached him for some imaginary neglect,
in the words 'a worm will turn', Trollope answered: 'A woman will turn,—

[1] The identification of the correspondent was kindly made for me by Mr.
John Blackwood from the files of *Blackwood's Magazine*.
[2] Mrs. Meetkerke described the letter as 'probably the last he ever wrote
with his own hand'.

so will a worm, or a fox, or a politician, but, like the politician, has often
no honest ground for turning: the truth is, a woman delights to have the
opportunity of turning, so that she may make herself out to be injured.'

924. To Lady Pollock.
Parrish Collection.

Sunday
(39, Montagu Square.)

My dear Lady Pollock,

I have read your article with great pleasure. It has the fault,
which is common to all good magazine papers,—the reverse of
which is common to all that are bad. It is necessarily too short
for its subject, and is therefore, by constraint, contracted at the
end. I agree with you in your criticism as to most of our Americans,—not quite as to all,—noticeably not as to E Poe and Mrs.
B. Stowe. To the former I give credit for more power than you
allow. The latter to me is falsely sensational and therefore
abominable. Washington Irving, Longfellow, & especially Haw-
thorne you have hit with exactness. Emerson is more of an
Essayist than a poet, and I am not quite sure that I go with you
altogether 'in re Bee'.[1] Bryant, I am ashamed to say, I do not
know.

In your strictures on literature generally I only partly coincide
with you. As to the money-making side of the question, I think
that the argument is the same for lawyers, painters, poets, and
tailors. The best price will get the best article. You talk of 'the
pay becoming the first object of the writer'. In so speaking of any
man earning his bread we should be careful to analyse the word
'first'. In an ordinary way we may say of us all that our first
object is to provide for our wives, children, and ourselves. Il faut
vivre. But with those of us who are highminded there is an
over-riding object, one more first even than the first,—that of
doing our duty; which comprehends such excellence in his work
as the workman may attain, though it be attained at the expense
of profit. As the best lawyers have made the most money,—so
have the best painters. Titian & Reubens were the Eldon[2] and

[1] A reference to Emerson's 'The Humble-bee'?
[2] John Scott, first Earl of Eldon (1751–1838), lord chief justice of common pleas, lord chancellor.

Sugden[1] of their art. Shakespeare did his work for money, quite unconscious of its abnormal excellence. Macaulay & Carlyle have been very careful to write for money, & Tennyson is as careful to do so as any one. What is needed in writing, as in other work, is honesty;—honesty to see that the work given is as good as can be sent out. If that be present, Professors of Literature will not hurt their profession by seeking those awards which are dear to the whole human race. But I speak, as did the fox who had lost its tail.

As to the other, greater question—which is however wrapped up. . . .[2]

925. To James Pycroft.[3]
Escott, pp. 114–15.

Trollope discusses Mrs. Proudie.

*   *   *

Before you put her down as a freak of fancy, let me ask you one question. Review the spiritual lords and their better halves such as you have known, and tell me whether it is the bishop or the bishop's wife who always takes the lead in magnifying the episcopal office? If you and I live long enough, we shall see an indefinite extension of the movement that has already created new sees in Manchester and Ripon. In the larger and elder sees there will be a cry that the diocesan work is too heavy for one man; then will come the demand for the revival of suffragan bishops. You now speak about the higher and lower order of the clergy; you will then have a superior and inferior class of prelates. If at some great country-house gathering there happen to be a full-grown wearer of the mitre and his episcopal assistant, you may expect to hear the hostess debating whether the suffragan should have his seat at the dinner-table when the guests sit down, or whether his chief might not prefer that he should come in afterwards with the children and the governess to dessert. He, good easy man, may take it all meekly enough, but

[1] Edward Burtenshaw Sugden, Baron St. Leonards (1781–1875), lord chancellor, an infallible oracle of the law.

[2] The rest of this letter is unfortunately missing.

[3] James Pycroft (1813–95), clergyman and author, published *Oxford Memories* and wrote widely on cricket.

not so his lady. When the suffragans are multiplied, human nature will undergo some great revolution if the suffraganesses do not contain a good many who are as fussy, as officious, as domineering, and ill-bred as my chatelaine of the Barchester palace.

*   *   *

926. To GEORGE SMITH. Waltham.
Not traced. Sadleir's transcript.

Trollope sends an article for the *Pall Mall* on the Post Office. 'Why attack the P.O. What does your writer really know against it? Let him give me instances and I will see them properly noticed. I hope you will publish the letter I send you. Surely unjust and sweeping attacks made, without cause, must be bad.' I have not been able to find Trollope's article.

927. To WILLIAM FOLLETT SYNGE. Garlant's Hotel.[1]
Dr. Eric Millar.

Synge had asked Trollope to engage rooms for himself and party, but Trollope writes that 'it is almost impossible to decide for another man what may suit him—specially so if ladies be concerned'. He therefore asks Synge to 'come down & look yourself'.

928. To ARTHUR TILLEY. Montagu Square. Monday 4 July. *Not traced.* Sadleir's transcript.

Trollope asks Arthur to dine with him. 'There will be sundry other learned pundits and pundettas (if that be the feminine gender).' Trollope must have misdated this letter. 4 July fell on Monday in 1870, but not again until 1881. Trollope lived in Montagu Square between these dates, but not at either one.

929. To CHARLES STUART-WORTLEY. Harting.
The Hon. Mrs. James Cecil.

Trollope extends a cordial dinner invitation. 'To tell the truth I cannot without difficulty climb up to your rooms. Since I saw you last I have become asthmatic,—which is a great misfortune. I fear the place does not agree with me.'

[1] Therefore probably written in 1882.

930. To CHARLES STUART-WORTLEY. Harting.
The Hon. Mrs. James Cecil.

Trollope tries to arrange for another dinner, mentioning his activities at all three of his clubs. 'But I am generally to be heard of at the Athenaeum.' Both this letter and the preceding were, of course, written in 1881-2.

931. To LORD ? Waltham Cross.
Parrish Collection.

Trollope is happy to accept an invitation and is much obliged by the correspondent's kindness 'with reference to Mr A Irvine' (possibly Alexander Irvine (1793-1873), botanist and friend of John Stuart Mill).

ADDENDUM

351a. To CHARLES KENT.[1] 18 October.
Henry E. Huntington Library.

(Waltham House,
Waltham Cross.)
October 18th 1867.

Sir,

I shall be most happy to be one of the Stewards at the dinner proposed to be given to Mr Dickens on Saturday November 2— & will certainly make one of the party on that occasion.[2]

Your faithful Servant

ANTHONY TROLLOPE

[1] William Charles Mark Kent (1823–1902), editor and proprietor of *The Sun*, 1853–71, and long a close friend of Dickens.
[2] Kent made all the arrangements on this notable occasion, which he subsequently described fully in *The Charles Dickens Dinner* (1867). Trollope not only appeared to honour Dickens on the eve of the latter's departure for the United States but made one of the principal speeches, responding to the toast to Literature. His remarks, not previously noticed by his biographers, are reported verbatim in Kent's pamphlet

INDEX

This Index includes references to all persons mentioned in the text and selected references to persons mentioned in the footnotes. Biographical notes identifying correspondents and other persons named occur (with only a few exceptions) at the point of the first reference. Except in a few instances the only place-names recorded are those from which Trollope wrote letters when away from his home. The many towns and cities which he visited in his Irish travelling are not entered separately but appear under 'Ireland'. Under Trollope's name will be found a selected list of general topics discussed in the letters. References to individual books will be found under the separate titles.

INDEX

Morley, John, 190–2, 284, 350–1, 379, 387, 421.
Letter to: 444.
Morning Post, The, 85.
Mortray Station (Australia), 288, 340–2.
Mossel Bay (S. Africa), 381.
Mr. Scarborough's Family, 482.
'Mrs. General Talboys', xxiii, 75, 77–9.
Mudie, Charles Edward, 83.
Munn, Alfred Moore, 480.
Murray, John (the elder), 9.
Letter to: 3.
Murray, John (the younger).
Letters to: 200, 389.
Murray, Sir John, 80, 91.
Murrell, Dr. William, 466, 482.
My Chief and I ('Atherton Wylde'), 425.
Myers & Co., 250.

Naples, 336.
Napoleon Bonaparte, 10, 260.
Napoleon III, 206.
'National Gallery, Our', 91.
National Review, The, 43.
Neale, Sarah, 146.
Nevill, Julia Lever.
Letter to: 341.
Newman, John Henry, Cardinal, 494–5.
New York, 95, 215, 224, 297.
Niagara, 220.
Nicholson, Edward Williams Byron.
Letter to: 254.
Nicolson, Harold, xx.
Nina Balatka, 180–2, 187–9, 193, 282–3, 371, 419, 422, 429.
Noble Jilt, The, 227.
North America, 94, 109, 117, 130, 497.
Northbrook, Lord, 435.
'Northern States, On the Present Condition of the', 129, 145.
Norton, Charles Eliot.
Letter to: 96.
Norwich, 80, 115.
Not Wiseley But Too Well (Rhoda Broughton), 221.

'O'Conors of Castle Conor, The', 49.
Odyssey (Homer), 399.

Oecumenical Council, 253.
Old and New, 315.
Old Mortality (Scott), 342.
Oldham, Richard Samuel.
Letters to: 203, 253, 430.
Oliphant, Laurence, 77.
Oliphant, Margaret, 424–5, 432–4, 454, 470.
Oliver Twist (Dickens), 78.
Omnium, Jacob, *see* Matthew James Higgins.
Once a Week, 228, 235, 269.
Orley Farm, 69, 75, 109, 183–4.
'Our National Gallery', 91.
Ouvry, Frederic, 287.
Letter to: 396.

Palfrey, John G., 97.
Pall Mall Gazette, 161–4, 169, 185, 198, 432, 449, 452.
Paris, 39, 190, 453.
Paris and the Parisians in 1835 (Frances Trollope), 1, 2.
Parker, Mrs. Theodore, 216, 219, 225.
Parkes, Henry.
Letter to: 295.
Parkhurst, R., 69.
Parnell, Charles Stewart, 481.
Parrish, Morris L., vii, xxiii.
Partington, Mary Anne, 9.
Paterson, John, 375.
Paton, Joseph Noël, 81–2.
Peel, Sir Robert, 294.
Pender, Sir John, 319.
Pennell, Cholmondeley.
Letter to: 180.
Peregrine Pickle (Smollett), 233.
Petrarch, 393.
Peyronnet, Comtesse de, 369.
Philadelphia, 97.
Phillips, Henry.
Letter to: 418.
Phillips, Wendell, 101.
Phineas Finn, 194, 235.
Phineas Redux, 84, 297.
Pietermaritzburg (S. Africa), 379.
Pitt, William, 10.
Plutarch, 260.
Pjetursson, Thora, 420.
Poe, Edgar Allan, 104, 500.
Pole, William.
Letter to: 458.

514

PRINTED IN
GREAT BRITAIN
AT THE
UNIVERSITY PRESS
OXFORD
BY
CHARLES BATEY
PRINTER
TO THE
UNIVERSITY